Art Nouveau and Art Deco Lighting

Alastair Duncan

ART NOUVEAU AND ART DECO LIGHTING

171 illustrations
36 in colour

Thames and Hudson

Pro Francis; *sine qua minima*

Filmset by Keyspools Ltd, Golborne, Lancs.

Text printed in Great Britain by Camelot Press, Southampton, Hants.

Monochrome illustrations printed in Great Britain in Finetone Screenless Offs[illegible] by United Printing Services, London.

Colour illustrations printed in Great Britain by Balding and Mansell Ltd, Wisbech, Cambs.

Contents

ACKNOWLEDGMENTS for help in the compilation of this book are as geographically widespread as they are numerous.

In Belgium, very special gratitude to Mr Weynans and to Mr Meurrens, of Brussels. Also, to Mr and Mrs Roland Gillion Crowet, Mr L. Wittamer-De Camps, and Father J.-G. Watelet, also of Brussels; and in Liège, to Dr Joseph Philippe, Conservateur at the Musée du Verre, and Mr Defèchereux.

In the United Kingdom, to Mr Roger Billcliffe of the University Art Collection, Glasgow; Mrs Bury and Miss Campbell of the Metalwork Department at the Victoria and Albert Museum; Miss Nicola Redway of Sotheby Belgravia; Miss Rachel Russell of Christie's; Mr and Mrs Robin Evans of Richmond, Surrey; Mr William O'Dea; Mr Bowers of the Science Museum; Mr Robin Symes; and Mr Christopher Morcombe.

In France, in Paris, to Mlle Yvonne Brunhammer, Conservatrice at the Musée des Arts Décoratifs, for her guidance; Mme Marie de Beyrie; Mr Robert Walker; Mme Daly Roux; Mr Jean René Delaye; Mr Christian Sapet; Mr and Mrs Patrick Bidermann; and Christine Coville of Réalités. *A special thanks, in addition, to Mr Felix Marcilhac for his supply of photographs and to Mr Jean-Pierre Camard both for his help and for his article on 1900 lighting in the March 1973 issue of* Réalités *which provided the inspiration for this book. In Arcueil, to Mr Eric Philippe, and in Nancy, to Mlle T. Charpentier, Conservatrice at the Musée de l'Ecole de Nancy.*

In the United States, in New York, to Mrs Lillian Nassau; Miss Barbara Deisroth of Sotheby Parke Bernet; Mr and Mrs Lloyd Macklowe; Mr Neil Isman; Mrs Minna Rosenblatt; the Jordan-Volpe Gallery; Mrs Marilyn Bordes of the Metropolitan Museum of Art; and to David Robinson at Christie's for his photography. In Connecticut, to Professor Robert Koch; in Virginia, to Mr and Mrs Sydney Lewis and Frederick Brandt, the curator of the Lewis collection; Mr Paul Doros of the Chrysler Museum in Norfolk; and to Mr Pinkney Near of the Virginia Museum of Fine Arts; in Pennsylvania, to Mr Christian Revi, editor of 'The Spinning Wheel'; in California, to Mr Vern Halcomb of Corinthian Studios; in Florida to Mr Eugene Gluck; and in Louisiana to Mr Howerton.

Very sincere thanks, also, to the staff of the six libraries in which I did research: the Musée des Arts Décoratifs and the Bibliothèque National, in Paris; the Victoria and Albert and the British Library, in London; and the Central Library and Lincoln Arts Center Library, in New York.

My thanks, finally, to Kate O'Connell and Sue Murphy for typing the manuscript, and to the following for providing me with food and shelter while on my travels: Charles and Marie Ducamps, Richard MacRae, Vincent and Anne Mai, and Mary Anne Ballard. Much appreciated.

1

A Survey of Lighting Techniques

I An unsigned blown glass and bronze peacock table-lamp; French, *c.*1900. The shade has enamelled peacock feather 'eyes'.

II, III Gallé. A signed pair of mould-blown double overlay rhododendron table-lamps.

IV Tiffany. A hydrangea table-lamp.

V Tiffany. Four very rare 'turtle-back' candlesticks. The bases are composed of pieces of iridescent turtle-back tiles. Two of the candle-nozzles have glass jewels set into a reticulated bronze mount.

VI Tiffany. A spider web table-lamp with leaded glass shade on a bronze and mosaic glass base designed as flowering narcissi.

VII Tiffany. A dragonfly table-lamp on a rare matching bronze and mosaic glass base.

VIII Tiffany. A ball lamp with autumn leaf design. The pendant butterflies are also by Tiffany.

IX Tiffany. A unique table-lamp. The Favrile glass shade rests on a ceramic base by Clement Massier. Tiffany's association with Massier stemmed from his business dealings with Samuel Bing in Paris.

X Daum. The poppy, symbol of sleep, provided the theme of this night-light by the Daum brothers.

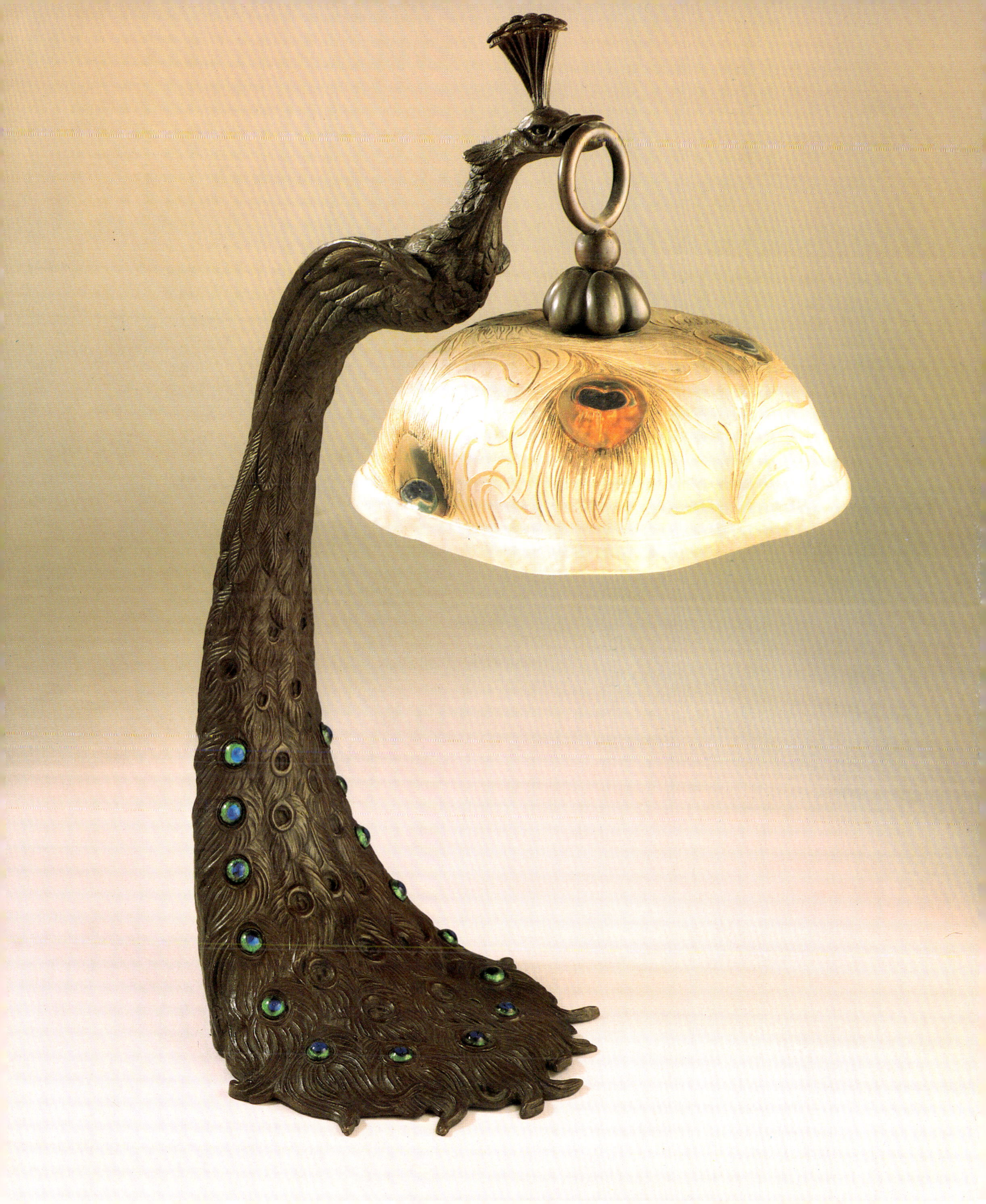

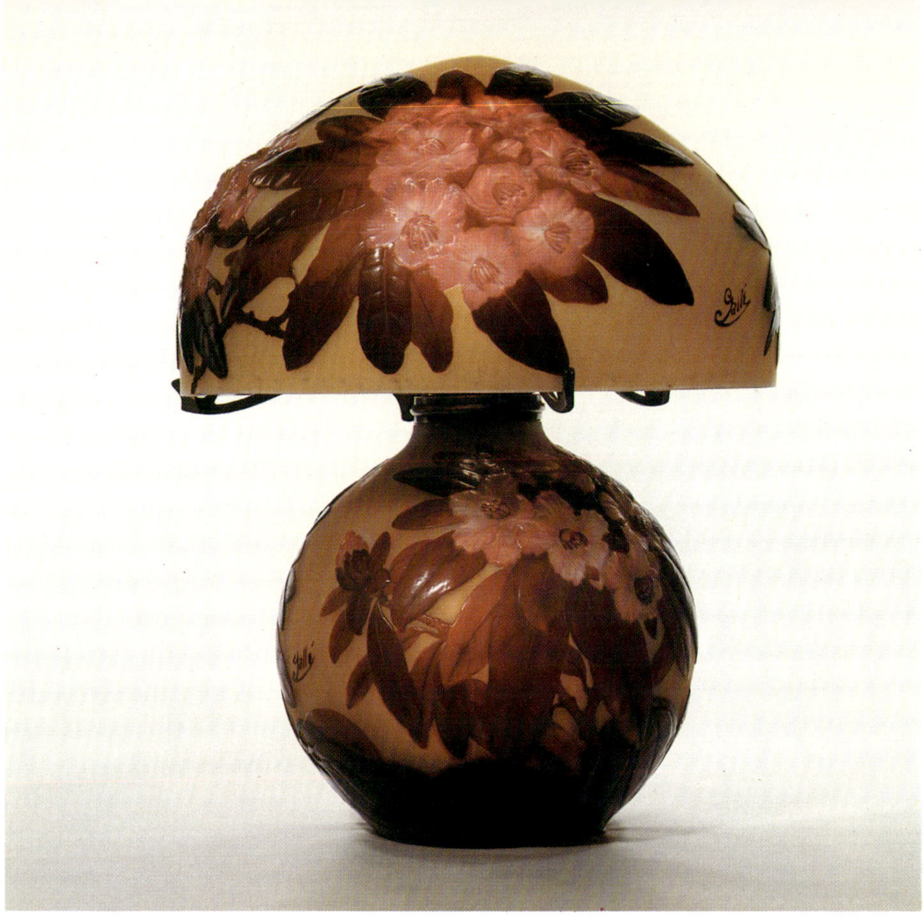

II

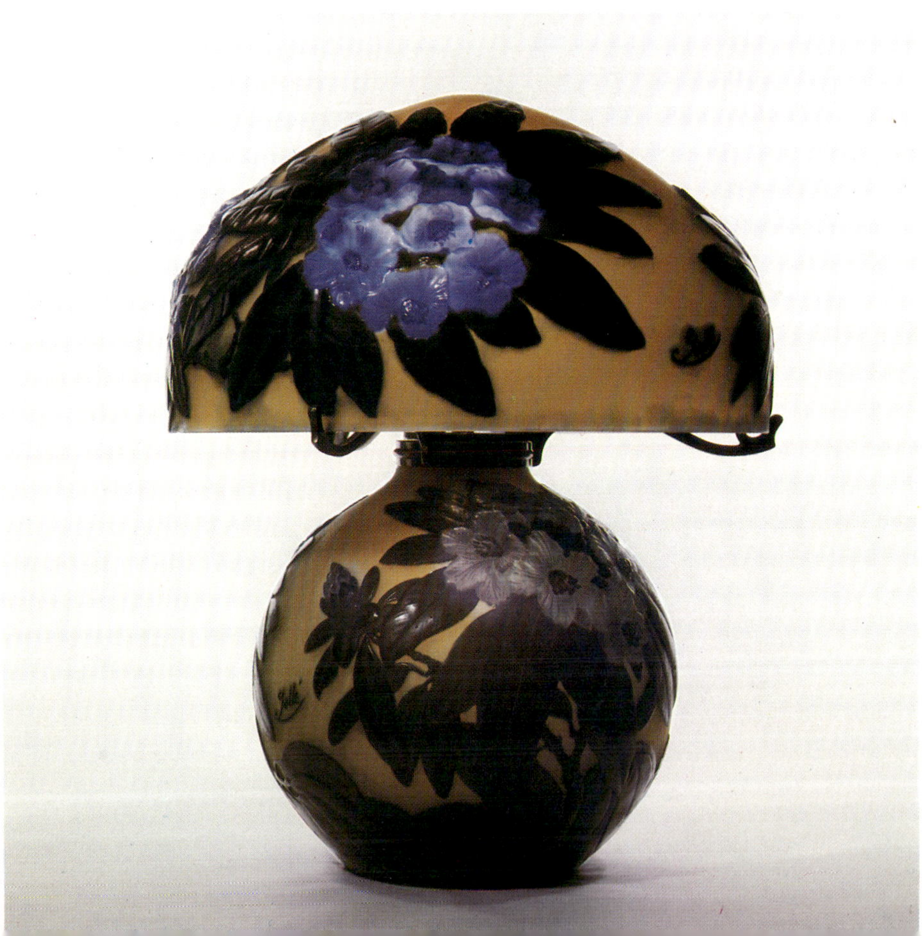

III

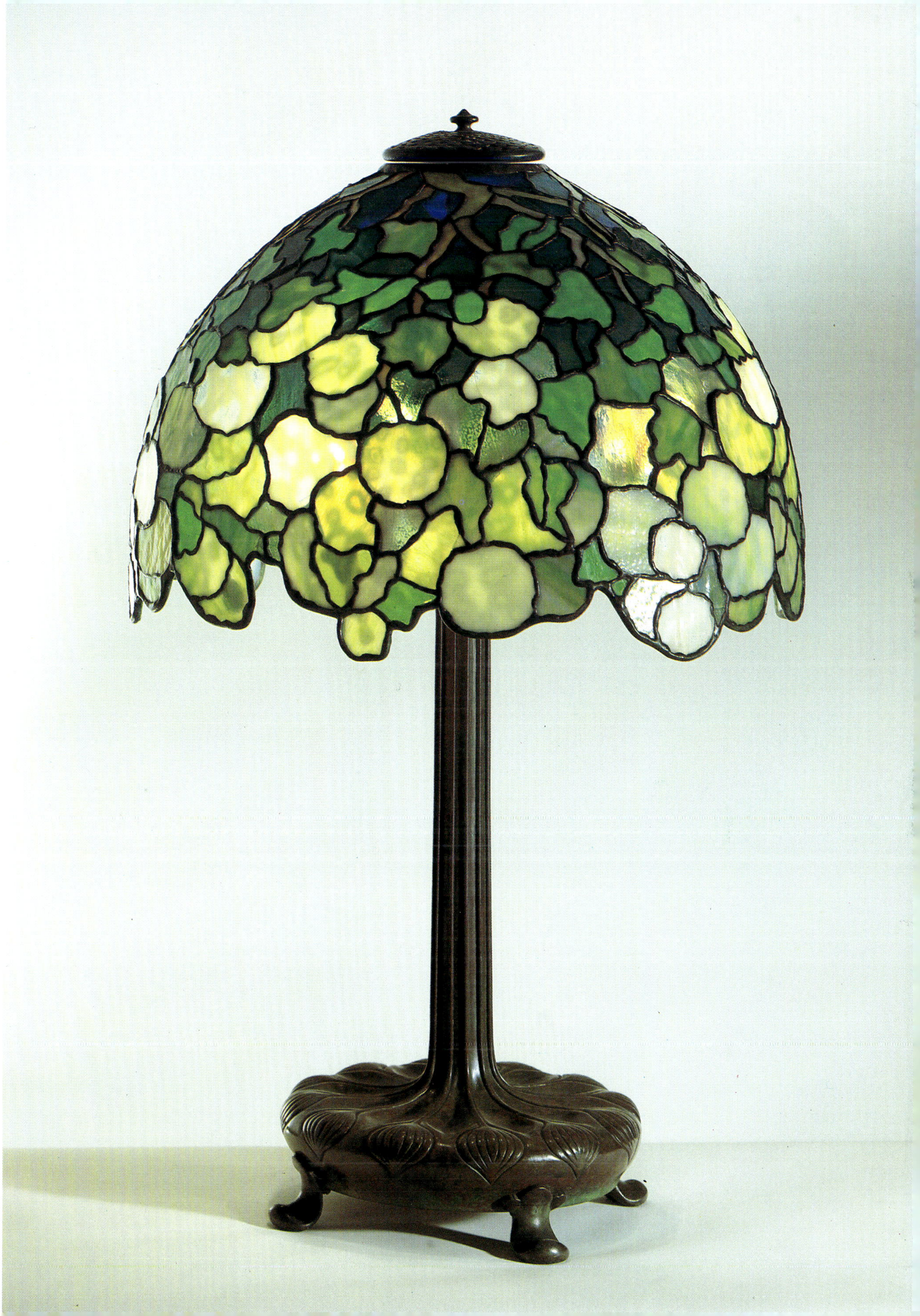

IV

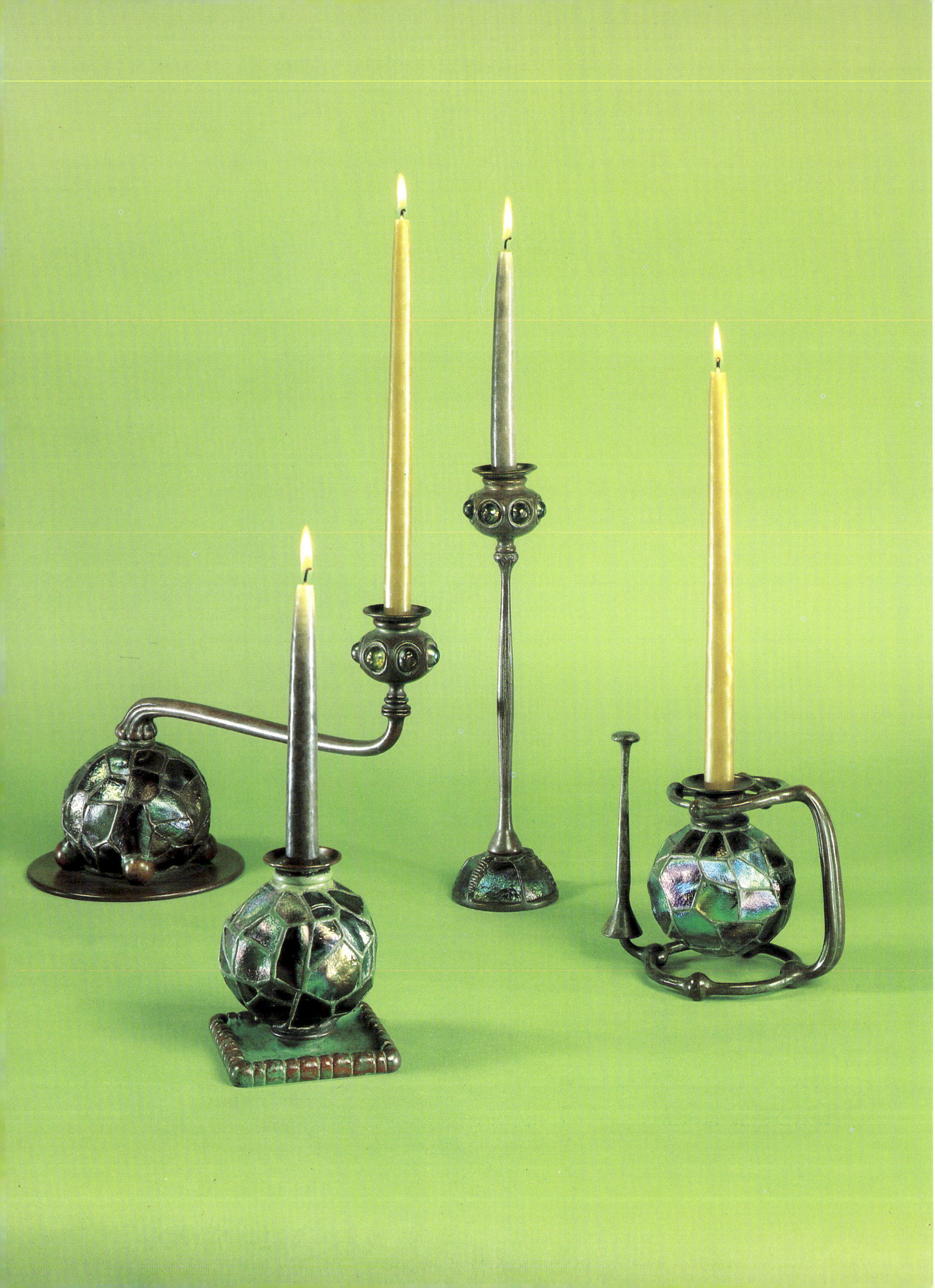

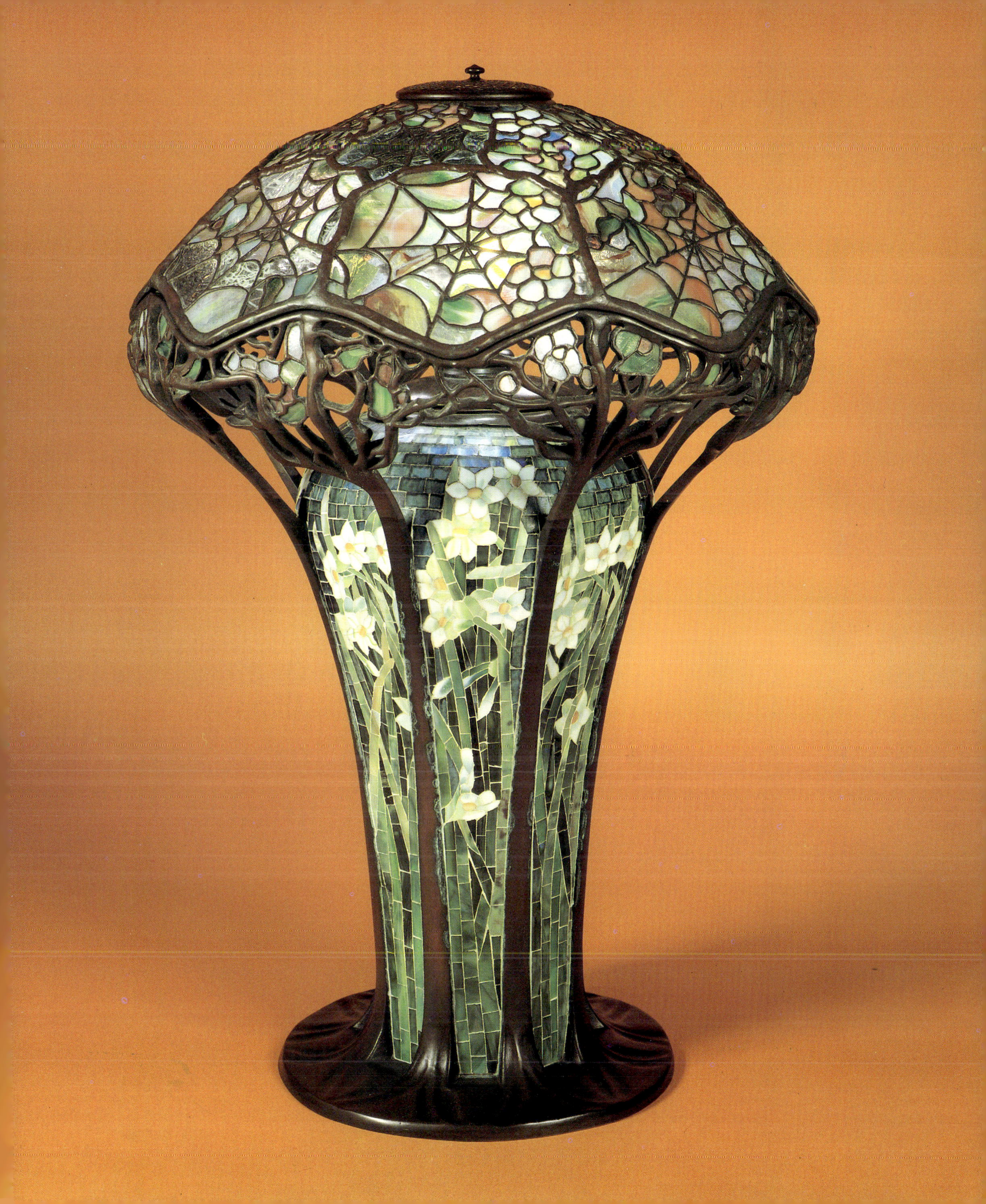

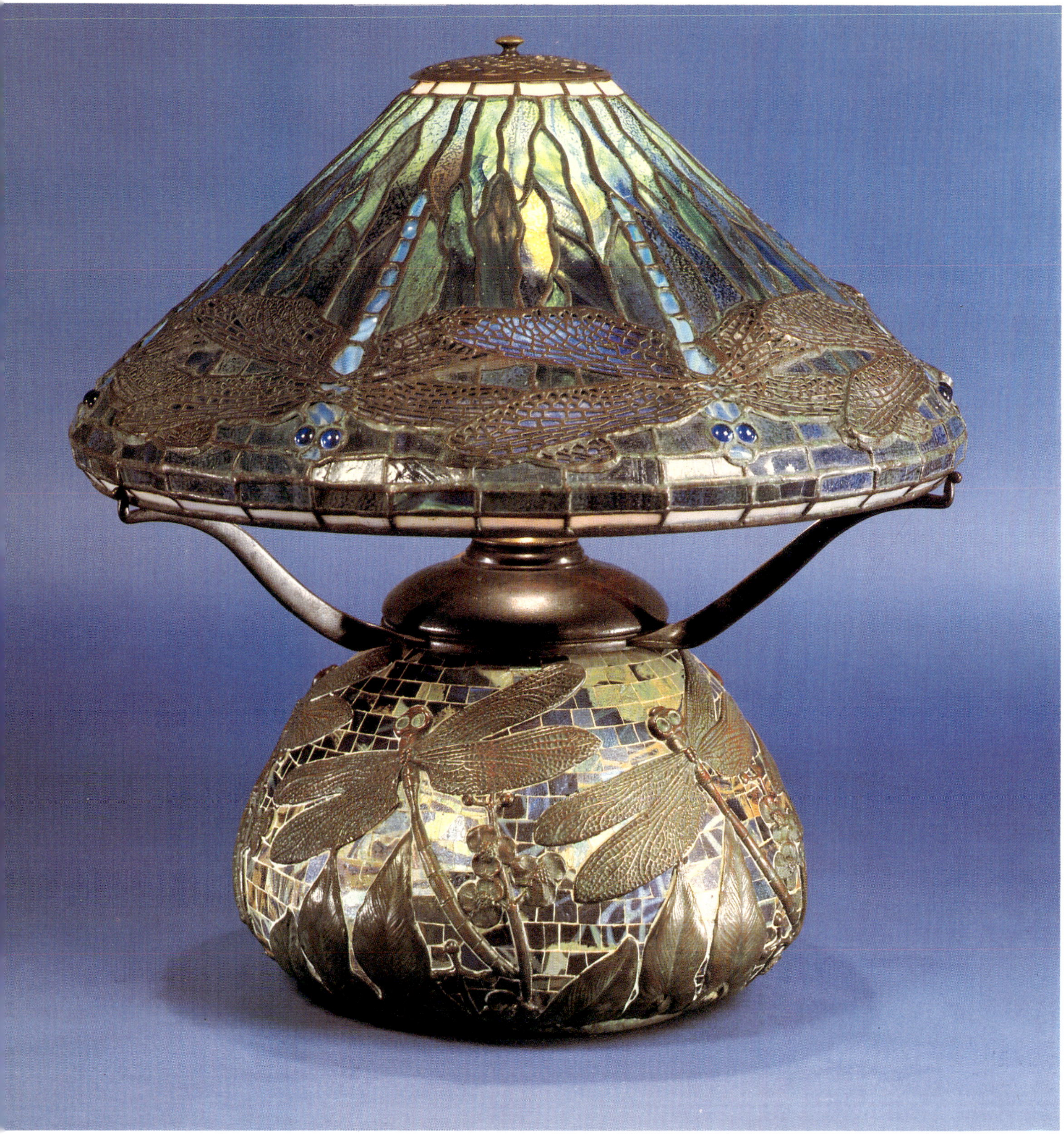

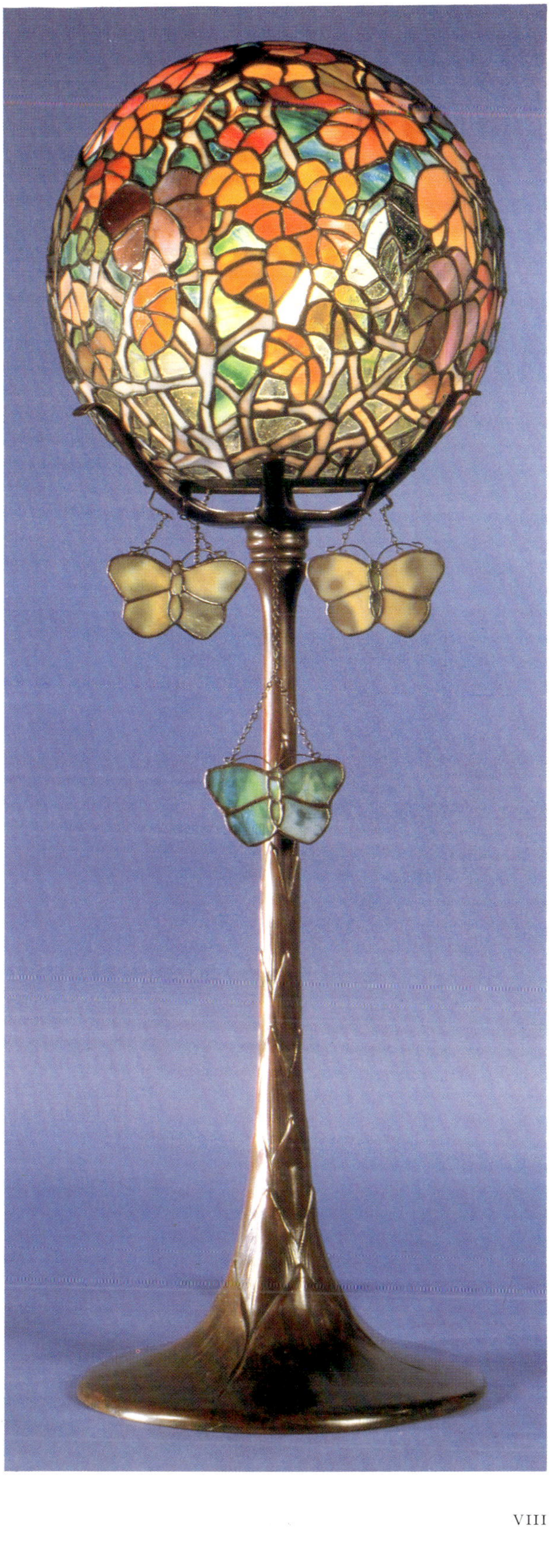

VIII

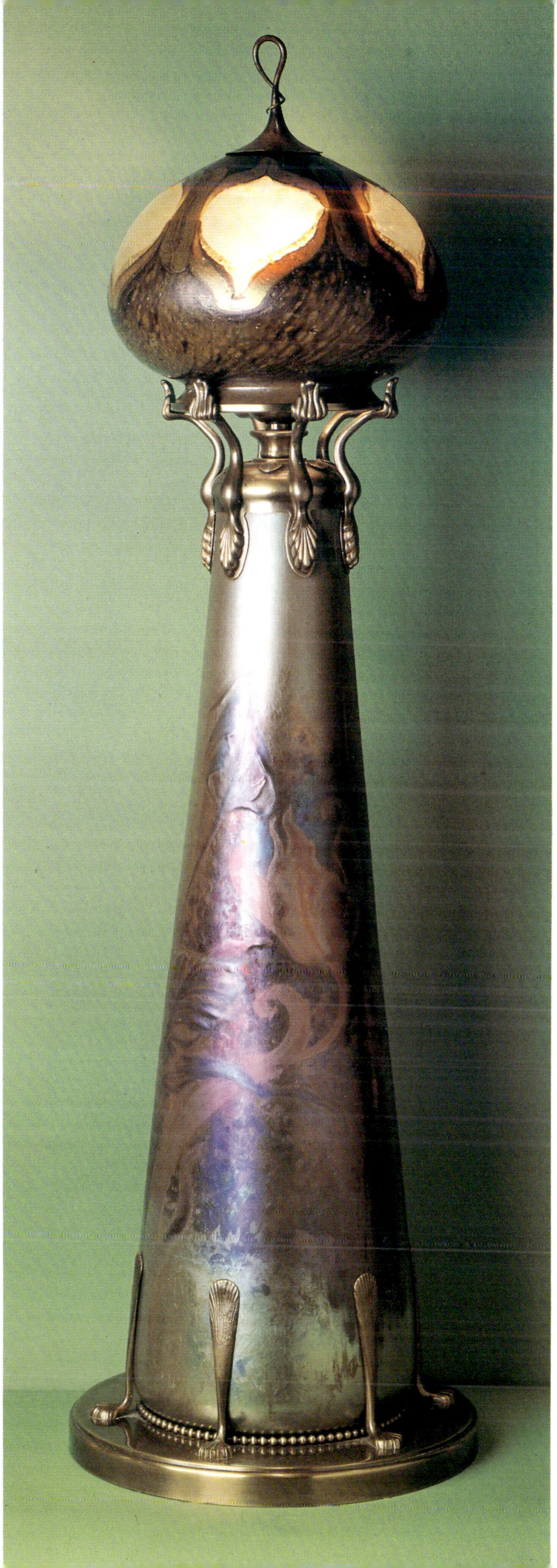

IX

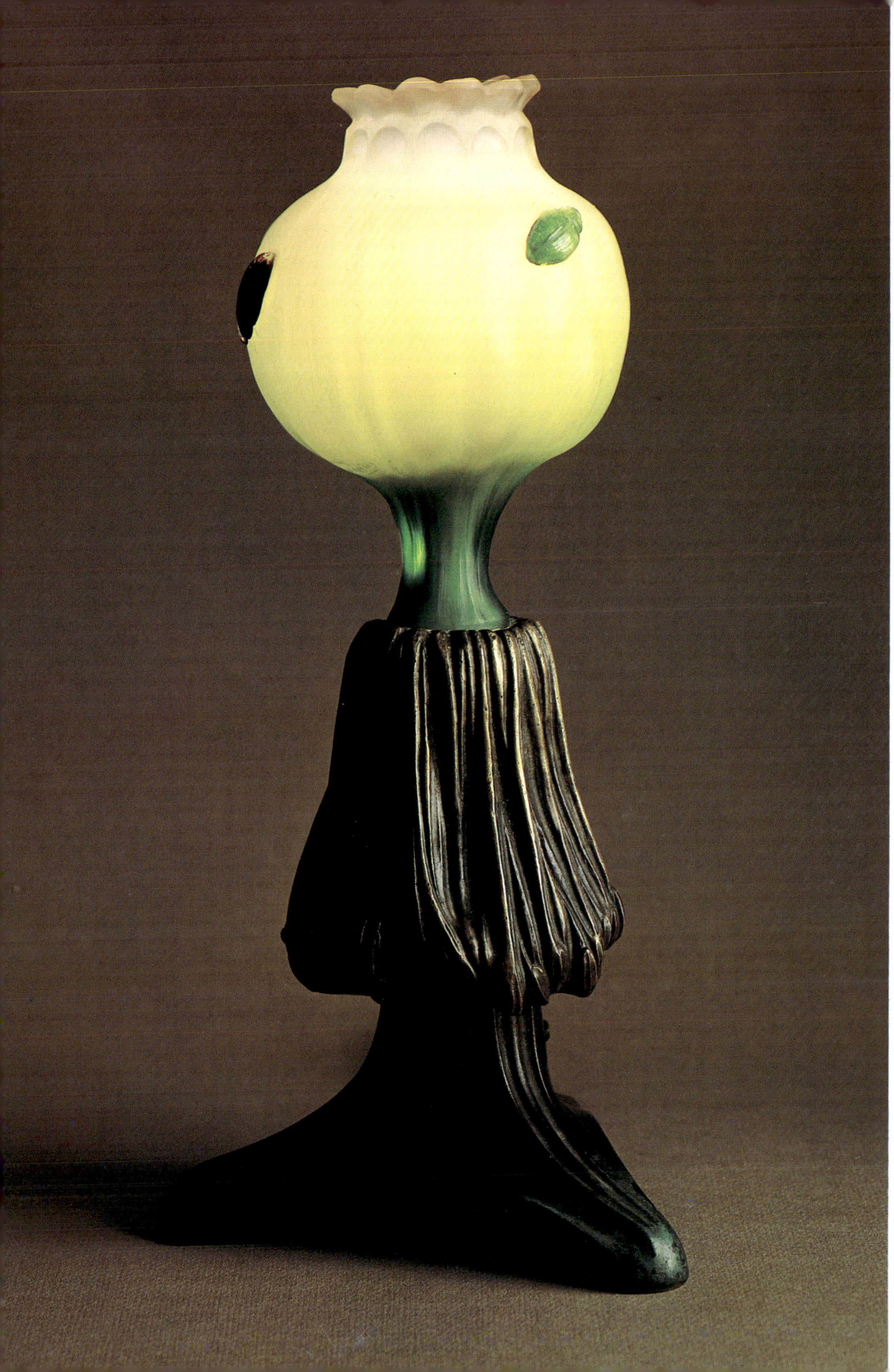

X

A survey of lighting techniques up to, and including, the 1900 and 1925 eras

Strange as it may seem to younger readers, light has not always been a mere switch away. Nowadays the use of such appliances as fluorescent tubing, dimmer switches, and 'strobe' lighting – not to mention the standard household bulb – is so commonplace that one can be forgiven for taking its magic and immediacy for granted. Yet less than seventy-five years ago the electric light was still a curiosity, and one whose future was by no means assured.

The road from Prometheus to the first neolithic flint miners in Sussex, and then through the 'Dark Ages', past fabled Aladdin and his djinn, finally to Edison, was a long and arduous one, on which more time was spent on stops and detours than on progress.

CANDLES

By the late nineteenth century the candle had improved considerably since Shakespeare had written in *Cymbeline*,

> *Base and illustrous as the smoky light*
> *That's fed with stinking tallow.*

In 1820, for example, a Frenchman named Cambacères discovered that plaiting, instead of twisting, the cotton wick resulted in a snuffless candle.* Between 1842 and 1845 John Tuck and Brian Palmer marketed a candle-moulding machine that made the manual operation – still basically the same as that which had been illustrated in Diderot's *Encyclopédie* of 1765–72 – finally obsolete.

* Snuffing entailed cutting off the carbonized part of the wick with 'snuffers' to prevent it from bending over into the molten tallow at the top of the candle. This, in turn, resulted in 'guttering': rivulets of molten tallow would overspill and flow down the candle.

But if the candle was approaching a stage of perfect efficiency, it appeared, by comparison with its lighting competitors, increasingly rudimentary and antiquated. Its major disadvantages were that it constituted a fire hazard (gusts of wind blew curtains and bedding into the naked flame) and that, as it burned, the position of the source of light changed. Candle guards were introduced to offset the former problem, and adjustable rachet holders the latter, but the candle's survival – at least in the salon *soirées* of those who purchased the decorative candlesticks shown in this book – was based on *non*-functional considerations. Its gentle, flickering light was (and, of course, still is) romantic and intimate, seductive and discreet.

OIL

The early oil lamp's great advantage was its simplicity of operation. A single spurred wheel was the only mechanism necessary to control the fuel supply. This it did by lifting the oil by capillary action on to the wick.

Yet there were continual refinements. In 1781 John Miles invented the 'bird fountain feed', which kept the oil at the same effective level in the reservoir. This ensured a more even flow to the flame and thus the elimination of the two extremes of oil starvation and oil excess – both of which resulted in a smoky, inconsistent light.

It was in the next year, however, that the first truly revolutionary improvement in lamp design occurred. A Swiss, Ami Argand, bent the traditional flat wick into the form of a circle and allowed air to get to the inside of the flame along a central tube. This resulted in up to a twelve-fold increase in the light obtainable from a single wick; and when Argand later added a flint glass chimney – to regulate aeration – the candle was permanently relegated to the oil lamp's commercial penumbra.

The next major advance occurred eighty years later, in 1860, when Colonel Edwin L. Drake discovered the Pennsylvania oil wells. Bituminous shale and coal were refined to produce paraffin (or kerosene), and whereas this had been available in limited amounts in Europe ten years earlier, this new source was so prolific that world markets were quickly flooded. And when, in 1865, Stephen Hinks introduced his duplex burner, consisting of two parallel flat wicks about $\frac{1}{8}''$ apart, which gave a still brighter flame, it seemed that the paraffin lamp was the perfect illuminant. The American Hitchcock lamp, marketed soon afterwards, boasted of a steady light that 'has not the appearance of a conflagration nor a moonlight'.

By the 1890s the oil lamp's advantages were, in fact, considerable. It was reliable, clean, and nearly odourless and smokeless; its flat wick was easily trimmed; its flame emitted a pleasant light; and it was cheaper than other fuels. Against this had to be weighed its need for continual attention and, therefore, easy accessibility for daily filling. For lamp designers, though, its main disadvantages were aesthetic. An oil lamp's components dictated its shape, thereby considerably limiting experimentation in interesting new forms. The reservoir was a bulky encumbrance that had to be incorporated somehow into the design. The chimney, although transparent, likewise predetermined to a large extent the final shape. And the strictly vertical flame meant that an oil lamp could not even be positioned at an angle, let alone be inverted. It remained, therefore, largely an undisguisably functional object from which the designers of the '80s and '90s deliberately shied away.

GAS

The knowledge that gas would constitute a viable form of combustion lighting goes back to a time long before its actual application: the cost of establishing the necessary gas-works and runs of piping proved to be a prohibiting factor until the early 1800s. Then, at the very moment of its inception as a general household illuminant, it suffered an almost fatal blow in public credibility through the chicanery of its first entrepreneur: a German named F. A. Winsor. Winsor founded his National Light & Heat Company in London in 1804, and advertised the new lighting medium as 'more congenial to the lungs than oxygen' and 'absolutely non-explosive'. No figures remain of the numbers of those asphyxiated, or summarily blown up, but Winsor nevertheless raised the capital required for his company by offering 20,000 shares of £50 nominal value, of which £5 had to be paid on application (the balance was to be paid out of an estimated profit of £570 per share per annum!). No more than eighty years after the South Sea Bubble, the citizens of London were again duped by promises of something which they desired, but could not understand.

Gas survived, but for some time remained very much less than an ideal form of lighting. Supplies of gas existed only in larger towns, and even then were limited. Moreover, the brass burner quickly corroded, thereby impairing the intensity and constancy of the flame. The imperfections of gas lighting were, in fact, declaimed almost as persistently as its potential virtues had formerly been extolled, and journals published cartoons showing people searching for their gas lights with a candle! Gladstone was to state in Parliament that 'Decision by majorities is as much an expedient as lighting by gas.'

Yet there was slow progress, and the London *Sunday Times* of 23 April 1854 contained this report: 'Filthy tallow candles and stinking oil lamps have been rendered obsolete by the introduction of gas.' It was only in 1858, however, when William Sugg introduced his burner with a steatite orifice, that the future of domestic gas lighting began to look really promising. The burner's steatite top neither corroded nor allowed as much heat as previously to escape from the flame. Sugg's revised Christiana model, in 1874, contained a governor that increased the output of light (from the same volume of gas) by more than 50 per cent.

The advantages of gas over its competitors were soon manifest. It was clean; it was easy to use (no time had to be expended on filling and trimming oil lamps or snuffing candles, to say nothing of the constant trouble of these operations and the spots of oil and grease that accompanied them); it was smokeless; and, although it was more expensive than other fuels, a large part of this cost could be apportioned – because of the heat emitted by a gas flame – to one's heating bill.

One could reasonably have expected that the commercialization of the incandescent filament bulb, from the early 1880s, would have put paid to gas's recent rapid advancement, but electricity suffered its own teething troubles, and at the time when it began to assert itself, gas not only drew abreast, but actually forged ahead. That this occurred was due to Count Auer von Welsbach's invention in 1893 of the incandescent gas mantle, a device which, when fitted to existing burners, produced a brilliant white light. Householders could therefore postpone the huge financial outlay that conversion to electricity would entail (if, that is, they could even consider such costs: the great majority of the populace could not). Not only were the gas mains and pipes already in operation, but gas cost less than the early electric bulb. It was not until 1913, in fact, that electricity's advantages began to justify conversion for the average home-owner.

Welsbach's incandescent mantle provided fierce competition for electricity for many years, and it is still preferred for street lighting in many towns throughout Europe.

For designers of Art Nouveau lighting, however, gas created problems. The need for a pipe to supply the gas meant that the lamp or chandelier had to be in a fixed position; the pipe itself needed to be disguised; a naked gas flame required the same chimney or globe protective covering as did all combustion fuels; the mantle had to be vertically positioned; and, finally, the stopcock, which regulated the supply of gas, had to be readily accessible. Such factors contributed to a bulkiness which, although less intrusive than the fuel reservoir of an oil lamp, still predetermined form.

ELECTRICITY

Electricity's potential as a form of illumination had been known long before it practical implementation. As early as 1808 Sir Humphry Davy had demonstrated his carbon arc-lamp at the Royal Institute in London. Light was obtained by placing two pencils of carbon in an electrical circuit, at a set distance apart, so that when the current was switched on, an arc of light jumped across the gap between the pencils to complete the circuit. The problems inherent in Davy's arc-lamp were those manifest in the subsequent experiments by Jean Foucault and Edward Staite: first, that no satisfactory regulator had been devised which would maintain the pencils the same distance apart as they burnt away (which they did rapidly) during combustion; secondly, that only one arc-lamp could be used at a time because of limitations in the generators that ran such circuits; and thirdly, and most important from a domestic standpoint, that the arc light was far too brilliant for any purpose other than that of illuminating large areas. Although the Russian Paul Jablochkov's subsequent invention of his 'candle', in 1876, went some way towards eliminating these problems, the arc-lamp's fundamental shortcoming remained: it could not be broken down into a series of less harsh sources. The arc-lamp was found to be indivisible. In the late 1870s, the question was, 'Who can divide the electric light?' Effort was concentrated on an alternative potential means of illumination, which had been pursued in parallel with that of the arc-lamp from mid-century: the incandescent filament bulb.

The theory behind the incandescent filament bulb had been demonstrated by Edward Staite in a lamp that he first exhibited in the Sunderland Atheneum in 1845. If one took a glass bulb, pierced with two platinum wires which supported between them a carbon filament, and then passed an electric current through this system, the filament would become heated to such an intensity that it would incandesce, i.e., glow.

The theory, however, had to wait several years for the practice to catch up. It was essential, for the operation to be successful, that the bulb be hermetically sealed. If the filament were not in a vacuum it would react with the residual air in the bulb and become carbonized. This, in turn, resulted in the gradual disintegration of the filament and a subsequent blackening of the inside of the bulb (due to the carbon particles being transported mechanically by the air to re-form on the glass).

It was only when the German Hermann Sprengel invented his mercury vacuum pump in 1865 that sufficiently high vacua for the bulbs could be achieved. As is so often the case, it required one invention to generate another.

The further problem remained of which material, and in what shape and thickness, would best serve the filament's needs of durability and incandescence; and to this several inventors now turned with increased zeal. The end was in sight, and platinum, parchmentalized paper, and carbonized bamboo were interchanged as the race quickened and narrowed.

Who, then, was the first to snatch up anew the spark of Prometheus? History affords the honour to Thomas Alva Edison, in 1879. Yet chronologically he was not the first, and neither, really, was the Englishman Sir Joseph Swan, whose model had come out a year earlier, and with whom Edison was subsequently involved in an acrimonious exchange concerning patents and precedence. As William O'Dea, ex-curator of the Illumination Department at the Science Museum, London, wrote: 'Swan was first, but not the first. Edison did better, but not for long. Both got together and went ahead more successfully for having done so. Comparisons were never more odious. Let us settle for the fact that two great men at first impacted and then allied themelves. And let us never forget that had it not been for the vacuum pump of Sprengel . . . neither Swan nor Edison could have been successful at that time.'*

Previously there had been the experiments of William Sawyer, Sir Hiram Maxim, and several others, yet Edison's model was deemed to be the first – and this is the key to it – *practical* model. The others had flickered and glowed briefly, and then expired. Edison's lamp was the first to have definite commercial possibilities. Francis Jehl, a member of Edison's staff and later his biographer, described the historic event: 'The lamp held out heroically that night [20 October] and the following morning until, between one and two o'clock in the afternoon of Thursday, October 21st, 1879, it had reached forty hours of life!' Swan's lamp had managed roughly two hours. This

* *Lighting*; a Science Museum illustrated booklet, W. T. O'Dea, HMSO, 1967, book 2.

certainly was an impractical amount of time, but so too, commercially, was a lamp that lasted for only forty hours. History has passed Swan by, although he was no doubt entitled to bask in some of the public glow that Edison's bulb afforded him.

The personal conflict between Edison and Swan resolved itself on a commercial level with the formation in 1883, in England, of the Edison & Swan United Electric Co., Ltd. So quickly did competition materialize that they found it expedient to combine forces to thwart this threat, against which they used litigation on numerous occasions to shield their patents.

For lamp designers at the turn of the century, the advent of the electric bulb provided the opportunity for which they had so long waited. Gone were all the design restrictions caused by combustion lighting. There remained only two drawbacks, both of which were soon to be remedied and neither of which influenced design considerations. First, the electric bulb was thought to be too bright. The bulb itself was a great novelty in the beginning, and so little attempt was made to conceal it. Secondly, it provided a short-lived pleasure. As René Dulong wrote in an *Art et Décoration* article as late as January 1902: 'In electric lamps, the incandescent bulb lasts about 400 hours and then must be replaced. Here, then, is an object of little durability and consequently of little value.'

As electricity slowly asserted itself over the other forms of domestic lighting, the previous competition between fuels switched, by the Art Déco era, to that between manufacturers of electric bulbs. Mazda, Philips, Opalux and Gal, for example, each tried to be both brighter and less dazzling than the others. There were other illuminants – osmium (1897), tantalum (1905), tungsten (1909), neon (1922), mercury (1932) and fluorescent tubular lamps (1940) – but these were generally for specialized, usually commercial, placement, and thus complemented, rather than challenged, the ascendency of the electric bulb.

2

Art Nouveau Lighting

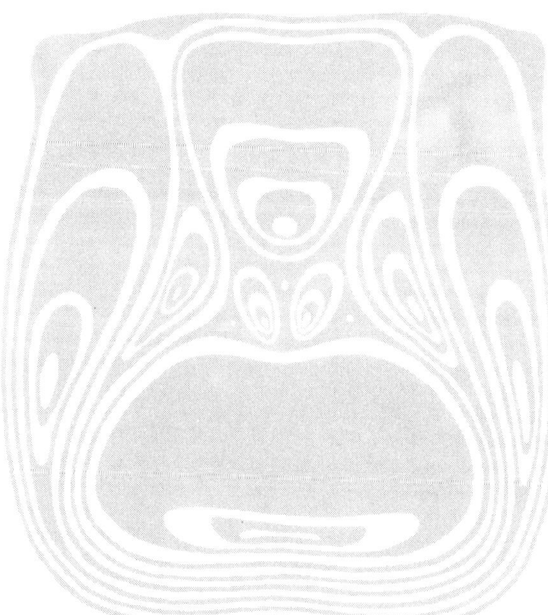

Art Nouveau lighting

That era in the decorative arts now known as 'Art Nouveau' provided, on the one hand, and coincided with, on the other, the two ingredients that were to make it the single most creative period in the annals of domestic lighting. This was due, first, to the philosophy within the decorative arts that was to spawn the 'New Art' movement: tired of, and exasperated by, the dull pretensions of revivalism that had been the norm throughout most of the 1800s, *fin-de-siècle* designers decided, once and for all, to slough off such artistic bankruptcy. No more Neoclassicism, Renaissance, Baroque, Rococo, Empire, Louis XV, Directory, or whatever. The *ancien régime*, if only in the applied arts, was, as Edmond de Goncourt wrote, to be 'tumbrilled and guillotined'. The term 'Art Nouveau' became, therefore, the international battlecry of common dissent, allied to the attempted dissolution of the then hierarchy of major and minor arts, of artist and craftsman.

For these modernists, the new broom swept clean. That hotchpotch of interior design and ornamentation known euphemistically as 'eclecticism' was 'out'; 'in' were totally integrated interiors, and such was the preoccupation with harmony – from a building's façade to the colour and shape of its furnishings, to the very key escutcheons on its doors – that everything had to be *en suite*. Even architects of the stature of Gaudí, Horta, Van de Velde, and Guimard found themselves designing objects which would normally be construed as being well beyond the boundaries of their profession: hairpins, jewellery, *jardinières*, and bibelots.

It was this craving in the new aesthetic for unity which became the major constant of Art Nouveau in all its manifestations and which led so many more turn-of-the-century 'creators' – architects, artists, artisans and interior decorators – to design light fixtures than would be normal in any one period. *Everybody*, in fact, seems at some stage to have designed a table-lamp, chandelier, candlestick, or wall-bracket. The reasons for this are to be found not only in the philosophy of integrated design, but also in the fact that lighting constituted, in effect, the lowest common denominator of such a pursuit of congruity: whereas certain furnishings suited to the design requirements of a particular room were not similarly suited to those of others, all rooms required a means of illumination. No other feature of interior design, such as chairs or cabinets, was as fundamental or as indispensable to every room as was its lighting.

Another contributing factor was the coincidence of the birth and first wobbly steps of the infant electricity. Between the need for Art Nouveau exponents to provide light fixtures, and the discovery that the incandescent filament bulb, so newly commercialized, would as magically liberate them from all the design constraints imposed by combustion lighting as it would magically glow, lay the preoccupation with lighting between 1895 and 1905. Not only *bona fide* designers, but sculptors, glass artists, ceramicists and metal workers joined in the pursuit of the new discovery.

Interpretation of its best application varied accordingly – the Belgian Philippe Wolfers, for example, used it to heighten the jewellery-like effects of the *plique-à-jour* enamel 'eyes' in a bronze peacock, while the French sculptor, Emmanuel Frémiet, employed it as a decorative fillip for a humorous baboon group – leading a critic to write in a derogatory article in *Mobilier et Décoration* in 1927 that so disparate were the approaches to home illumination in lighting's embryonic years (*c.* 1895) that its main feature was its *non*-functionalism, and he was largely right. The incandescence that Louis Tiffany obtained in his Favrile shades was due to the light rays being intercepted and trapped by the opalescent glass in order to highlight the latter's innate luminosity. Whereas the effect was incomparable from an aesthetic standpoint, only those rays that escaped downwards were of any practical use. The stark functionalism of the German Richard Riemerschmid's chandeliers, which consisted of a series of naked bulbs hanging from reticulated wires, was the exception, not the norm. By and large, Art Nouveau lamps generated more heat than light.

Light fixtures around 1900 were made of numerous materials, of which one – bronze – deserves special mention. Art Nouveau provided opportunities for sculptors and designers to execute objects which, both in size and in subject-matter, they would normally have considered 'beneath' their *métier*. This occurred largely because foundries, on discovering that an expanding bourgeoisie allowed more and more of their buying capacity for home ornamentation, started to run serial bronzes to meet this demand. Large foundries such as Susse *frères*, Siot-Décauville, E. Colin, Louchet, Valsuani and Barbedienne in Paris, therefore, either negotiated copyrights with prominent sculptors to reproduce various of their works in metal, or commissioned them to create maquettes of specific objects. Sculpture was thus 'adapted' into garniture mantel sets, ashtrays, épergnes, inkwells, lamps, etc., so that prominent sculptors such as Raoul Larche, Maurice Bouval, and Villé Vallgren could depend, if they wished, less on the commissions from one-of-a-kind orders than on the royalties from the mass-reproduction of their works in bronze, pewter, ormolu and spelter. It is understandable that, at a time when Rodin was being hailed as the new Phidias, many of his contemporaries felt the need *not* to compete and therefore reduced the scale of their sculpture. The result, as far as lighting is concerned, was a bonanza; not only did more sculptors apply themselves to the medium than would normally have done so, but many more lamps have consequently survived the ravages of time and collectors' caprice.

For the motifs for their light fixtures, most Art Nouveau designers resorted to the same range of themes that they applied to other aspects of their interior decoration. The lamps of Emile Gallé and Daum *frères*, for example, employ the same botanical and entomological motifs so prevalent throughout the decorative arts of the Nancy School; Mackintosh's lamps show the austere and architectonic interplay of verticals and horizontals so characteristic of his Glaswegian buildings; the Parisian designers followed that city's predilection for the whiplash curve and *fin-de-siècle* 'Woman' in her many guises; and Horta's fixtures echo the almost narcissistic delight of the openwork wrought-iron balustrades of his Maison de Peuple. All the period's most readily recognizable themes – and clichés – were used: entrelac and scrollwork designs were transformed into metalwork wall-bracket supports; the insect world of the praying mantis, the cicada, and the stagbeetle swarmed and crawled across cameo lampshades; even the peacock was cunningly transformed into table lamps. The three most common themes, however, were the flower, 'Woman' and – that combination of the two – the *femme-fleur*. These warrant special mention.

The most frequently used motif for light fixtures was the flower. The floral aesthetic of 1900 and the incandescent filament bulb formed the most natural and immediate of artistic liaisons. Sap-conducting stems were transformed into the metal conduits for the wires for the electric bouquets; corollas became the glass shades that shielded the viewer from the light's glare; calyxes became the wax-pans for candlesticks; the fluted corona in such plants as the jonquil formed candle nozzles; whorls of leaves or petals acted as the reflectors for a centrally positioned bulb, or cluster of bulbs. The advent of electricity also made it possible to simulate the angle at which a flower naturally hangs – usually downwards; the design no longer had to allow for a vertical flame.

Specific flowers were either copied or stylized. The entire botanical gamut became, in fact, a limitless wellspring of inspiration for artists and designers. Phantom species likewise blossomed; e.g., unrecognized heliotropes whose energy-giving light came from within. But identity did not really matter; the only criterion was that the flower should enhance, and be enhanced by, the electric light. Among the most popular of the flowers used was the convolvulus family; an electric bulb seemed almost to belong in its trumpet-shaped flowers. Others favoured were the orchid, poppy, cyclamen, and sprays of honesty, while the Nancy School had a partiality for the cow parsley, an umbel of its native Lorraine.

The other major theme to dominate lamps, as in the case of all Art Nouveau *objets* and graphics, was 'Woman'. Freed from the real-life metal and whalebone harnesses into which fashion had locked them, and freed also from their equally stifling bourgeois respectability so aptly portrayed in the novels of Stendhal, Balzac and Flaubert, *fin-de-siècle* women – at least, as depicted by Art Nouveau designers – threw caution, clothes and corsets to the winds. They became the most instantly recognizable theme of the Art Nouveau movement. Interpreted as nymphs, naiads, or undines, who were variously nubile, fleshy, melancholic, ethereal, Rubensesque, or somnambulistic, these young maidens were the most obvious means for personifying electricity. Moulded as a caryatid supporting a lamp shade, or brandishing a torch to herald in the virginal new century, or, again, simply as a statuette clasping some object that was wired for electricity, the female form was ubiquitous. Their hair coiffed in stylized vermicelli tresses à la Mucha, these women-figures were mainly naked, although some, where modesty prevailed, were dressed in *décolleté* V-neck robes.

The public, however, soon tired of these bronze and pewter sirens, and the critics likewise voiced their disapproval, in a lighting context, of the random way the bulbs were positioned on and around the woman's person. No less an accomplished exponent of sculptural lighting than Léo Laporte-Blairsy, for example, incurred the displeasure of the critic Maurice Hamel in a *Revue des Arts Décoratifs* article (1901): 'These figures with their tormented and crushed draperies do not seem to me to be really naked, and their proportions are disconcerting. And then the strange idea of adapting an electric bulb as a woman's stomach . . .'

So popular were the flora and woman themes that they were frequently combined into the hybrid known as *femme-fleur*. Mythological Daphne was born again, not only to be transformed into a laurel, but into all manner of botanical delights and in such numbers that Robert de Montesquiou, the prominent Parisian aesthete, wrote in his poem *Blumenmädchen* of the predilection of so many Art Nouveau designers for woman and flowers in association: 'Fleur-femme, femme-fleur, laquelle est le plus l'autre?' It was, in fact, an artistic symbiosis that easily lapsed into vulgarization, as the critics were quick to remind numerous offenders. One wrote in an article for *L'Art* (1902) of 'a poor little female body in the middle of roses which are, in fact, actually electric lamps, so that the unfortunate girl appears to be on the point of being devoured by the flames.'

Initial attempts to adapt existing lamp designs to the opportunities afforded by electricity were not considered successful. The critics felt that the designers, suddenly freed from all the constraints which combustion lighting had imposed, would immediately swamp the market with new models. At first, however, few were forthcoming, and by the late 1890s the decorative arts reviews, alarmed at the lack of response, took up the challenge. Among these, one of the first was Eugène Grasset who, as a member of the jury that organized the monthly design contests in *Art et Décoration*, laid down the conditions for an electric lamp competition in the magazine's April 1898 issue. Stipulating at length what he required – a two-bulb table- or desk-lamp on a cast copper base, bulbs sheathed in shades to shield the glare, etc. – he offered a first prize of 75 francs. The jury, however, found that the entries had all, to varying degrees, misunderstood the aesthetic aims of the competition and no first prize was awarded. Grasset did not conceal his disappointment, and professing gloomily that the fixtures submitted seemed no less banal than those that already existed for gas, wrote: 'It is regrettable and even a little astounding that this programme was not better attempted, for it is one of those that takes most advantage of modern construction techniques.'

More competitions followed. In 1898 again *Art et Décoration* ran a contest for an electric *suspension* for a dining-room, and in 1904 another for a table-lamp. *L'Art Décoratif pour Tous* (a supplement of *L'Art Décoratif* which was published briefly between 1902 and 1904) ran various competitions for gas, oil, and electric lights in wrought iron and semi-precious metals (*orfèvrerie*); while *L'Art Décoratif* in 1906 invited its readers to submit designs for an antechamber lantern. To back these up, the reviews published numerous articles on lighting, the most important of which appeared in the January 1902 edition of *L'Art Décoratif*.

Even *The Studio* (London) belatedly joined in the campaign to exorcise all ill-conceived designs: its critic in the 1906 Year Book began his review of recent English fixtures as follows: 'Now, strange as it may be to have to state so self-evident a proposition, the primary function of all lighting apparatus is to give light . . .'

Despite all the censure – and it became eminently fashionable to find fault with contemporary lamp designs – one cannot but feel, in retrospect, that things were not *quite* so bad as the critics made them appear. Even a cursory glance through these pages will show the creativity and sheer exhilaration that was often applied in domestic illumination.

The year 1900 was both the birth of the new century and the coming-of-age of electricity, and the spectacular setting of the Paris International Exposition was a fitting celebration of both events. If the 1889 Exposition had shown electricity to be in its adolescence, the organizers of the electricity section in the 1900 affair were determined to prove that by then it had reached adulthood; that if it had previously been eclipsed commercially by gas, it would now, and for all time, outshine its competitors. And what more impressive way to promote its cause than to link it inextricably to the new century, which was to disassociate itself completely from the foibles of the previous one.

For the five million visitors who flocked to the 1900 International Exposition, the Palace of Electricity resembled something out of a fairy tale. The Palace itself, by the architect Jean Renard, had a curious part-Hindu, part-Basque façade that was crowned by a 30-foot-high group by the sculptor Auguste Alméras of two winged monsters bearing a goddess up into space. The lines of the building were picked out by thousands of coloured electric bulbs, and vast galleries inside housed both the latest achievements of industrial technology that were powered by electricity, and sections on electric bulbs and lamps.

In front of the Palace was the greatest wonder of all: a magical fountain of water and light called the Château d'Eau. Victor Champier, in a 1900 article in the *Revue des Arts Décoratifs*, wrote that

> the Château d'Eau . . . furnishes the incomparable spectacle that one expects of it. When, in the evening, the gushing fountains cascade from basin to basin, the polychromatic water sparkles and streams, lighting with magical glows the group of statues which appear as living stalactites – guardians of the symbolic and monumental tabernacle where they glitter like the eyes of the night: petrified constellations illuminated by the torrential waters.

Electricity's cause could not have had better window-dressing, and the wide range of models of modern electric lamps inside the Palace and in various other displays throughout the grounds reinforced this first impression. Some of the models were discussed in an illustrated two-part article by Gustave Soulier in *Art et Décoration.* Drawing first on the analogy of changing from a horse-drawn to a horseless carriage – in which the designers of automobiles presumed, erroneously, that they must place the engine where the animal had been – Soulier stressed that a new system demanded new forms. The shape of electric lamps was not governed by the fuel requirements of combustion lighting. This, of course, was hardly news to lamp designers – they had been subjected to similar admonishments by the critics throughout the 1890s – but what followed must surely have been unanticipated: Soulier felt that the lamps shown at the exposition were, for the average viewer conditioned to the heaviness of gas and oil fixtures, 'strangely light and stripped'. They had, therefore, overstepped their brief: the public would feel that it was not getting its money's worth, visually or literally.

The designers, foremost among whom was Jean-Auguste Dampt, could not have helped feeling betrayed, especially by Soulier's summing-up: most of the exhibits were 'deplorable', showing an overall lack of science and taste.

Yet the 1900 exposition represented, all in all, the single most successful event up to that time in the electric light's campaign to win over the average householder. The exposition was also the scene of the highpoint in the career of the American dancer, Loïe Fuller, who, more than anybody else, was to pioneer and to utilize the aesthetic possibilities of the new Electricity. Born in Fullersburg, Illinois, in 1862, Loïe's birth had something of the messianic about it: she was delivered in midwinter in a hotel bar room that had been especially converted into a makeshift maternity ward for this purpose. A colourful and varied early career followed: at the age of six weeks she appeared in a dance hall play in what was billed as 'a minor sleeping role'. Bit-parts in music-hall burlesques followed, and later she appeared in vaudeville and in a series of small-town repertory productions, even touring with Buffalo Bill in 1883. In none of these experiences could one foresee her subsequent emergence as a popular rival of the period's great tragedienne, Sarah Bernhardt, ten years later in Paris, by which time she had fortuitously stumbled on the effect that was to determine her future dance routine and to immortalize her as 'Loïe Fuller: Apotheosis of Light'. While rehearsing for a play, she tried on a voluminous silk skirt; standing in front of a mirror, she noticed that the sunlight, which was falling through the yellow blinds of the window behind her, illuminated the gauzy material, and as the silk billowed, it seemed like light itself. In her autobiography, *Fifteen Years of a Dancer's Life*, Loïe Fuller described what happened on stage:

> My robe was so long that I was continually stepping upon it, and mechanically I held it up with both hands and raised my arms aloft, all the while that I continued to flit around the stage like a winged spirit.
>
> There was a sudden exclamation from the house: 'It's a butterfly! A butterfly!'
>
> I turned on my steps, running from one end of the stage to the other, and a second exclamation followed: 'It's an orchid!'

This was the origin of Loïe Fuller's Skirt Dance, later to be termed 'The Serpentine Dance', and its success paved the way for a European tour.

At the Folies-Bergère, her various illuminated dances led to an immediate and spectacular success; one which spurred her on, in turn, to ever greater experimentation in the interplay of coloured lights. The following account in the London *Sketch* bears witness to the impact on the audience:

> The orgie of colour was so wonderful as to leave objection mute. Light came from every side. La Loïe danced upon glass, from which the vivid splendour of the headlights was reflected, while from the wings, stage and orchestra, wonderful luminous streams seemed to flow toward her. With the rhythm of the music the colours changed, and where white ruled before, there was a kaleidoscopic vision. Violet, orange, purple and mauve movements succeeded in rapid succession until a rich deep red dominated the dancer, and she became for one brief moment, a living rose, with palpitating heart and flying leaves. Then the hues of the rainbow came from all sides, and ranged themselves upon the ever-moving draperies. Every fold had its tint and scheme of colour intensified by the surrounding darkness until the eye could scarcely bear to look. Just as the strain was becoming intolerable, the colours disappeared, there was a white flash of appalling brilliancy, and La Loïe faded under diaphanous drapery.

It was the phenomenon of 'becoming light', as Isadora Duncan described Loïe's act, that made her the inspiration for the legions of artists and sculptors who endeavoured to convey the magic of her performances on paper or in metal.

The most appropriate of the numerous small sculptures of Loïe Fuller were, of course, those that incorporated hidden lighting. Of these, the one- and two-bulb table-lamps by Raoul Larche are the best known, although Clara Pfeifer, a compatriot of Loïe's, also designed and executed a most charming table-lamp which she exhibited at the 1901 Salon of the Société des Artistes français.

The intrigue that Loïe Fuller's ethereal image conjured up in turn-of-the-century Paris has been revived in recent years, and objects depicting the 'Architect of Light', as she called herself, are now highly prized, and correspondingly priced. In this respect collectors should bear in mind that not all Art Nouveau sculptures of a dancer – even those incorporating electric bulbs – are of her. Examples of misattributions in sales catalogues abound: most notably in the cases of the *jeu de l'écharpe* gilt-bronze table-lamps by Agathon Léonard and Léo Laporte-Blairsy's Grecian figurine. These are of dancers and contain bulbs, but none of them is of Loïe Fuller. The subject of misattributions brings up that of anonymity. In all categories of Art Nouveau there are numerous light fixtures that are unsigned. The Austrian firm of Loetz, for example, seems to have made it a policy not to sign a large percentage of their glassware. Thus, even when one is 'certain' that an object is by Loetz, one can only classify it as 'attributed to' or 'in the genre of'. Fortunately for art historians, few major designers subscribed to this perverse pride of anonymity, but there are still innumerable chandeliers, wall-brackets and table-lamps in circulation that have neither the artist's signature nor, in bronzes, a founder's stamp.

XI Gallé. 'Les Coprins', Gallé's famous mushroom table-lamp. Only three models exist; the original was commissioned as part of the décor of a dining-room designed as a forest.

XII Larche. A gilt-bronze table-lamp called 'La Libellule' (dragonfly).

XIII Truffier. This gilt-bronze wall-bracket with malachite, amethyst and emerald pendant scarab earrings was designed by Adolphe Truffier and executed by the founder Barbedienne. It was exhibited at the Société des Artistes français in 1901. Truffier designed several similar light fixtures for the annual Salons at the turn of the century, and was awarded First Prize in the sculpture section in the 1900 competition organized by the French Bronze Manufacturers Society.

XIV Rombaux/Hoosemans. A pair of three-branched candelabra, each with an ivory maiden among scrolling silver foliage.

XV, XVI Majorelle. A gilt-bronze Magnolia wall-bracket and matching table-lamp with Daum glass shades. The flowers, by opening to various degrees, emit different amounts of light.

XVII Laporte-Blairsy. 'Chrysanthemum' table-lamp.

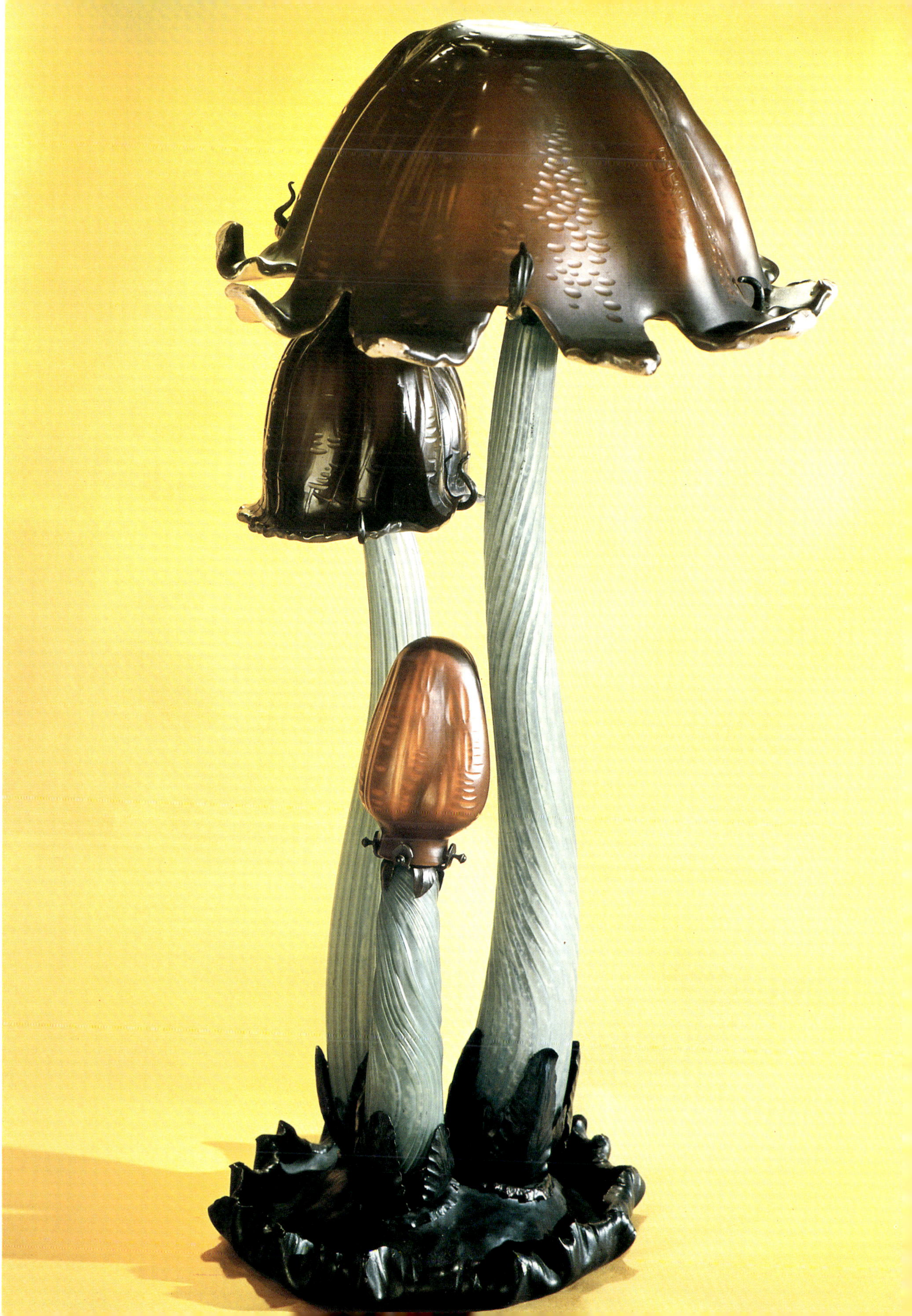

XI

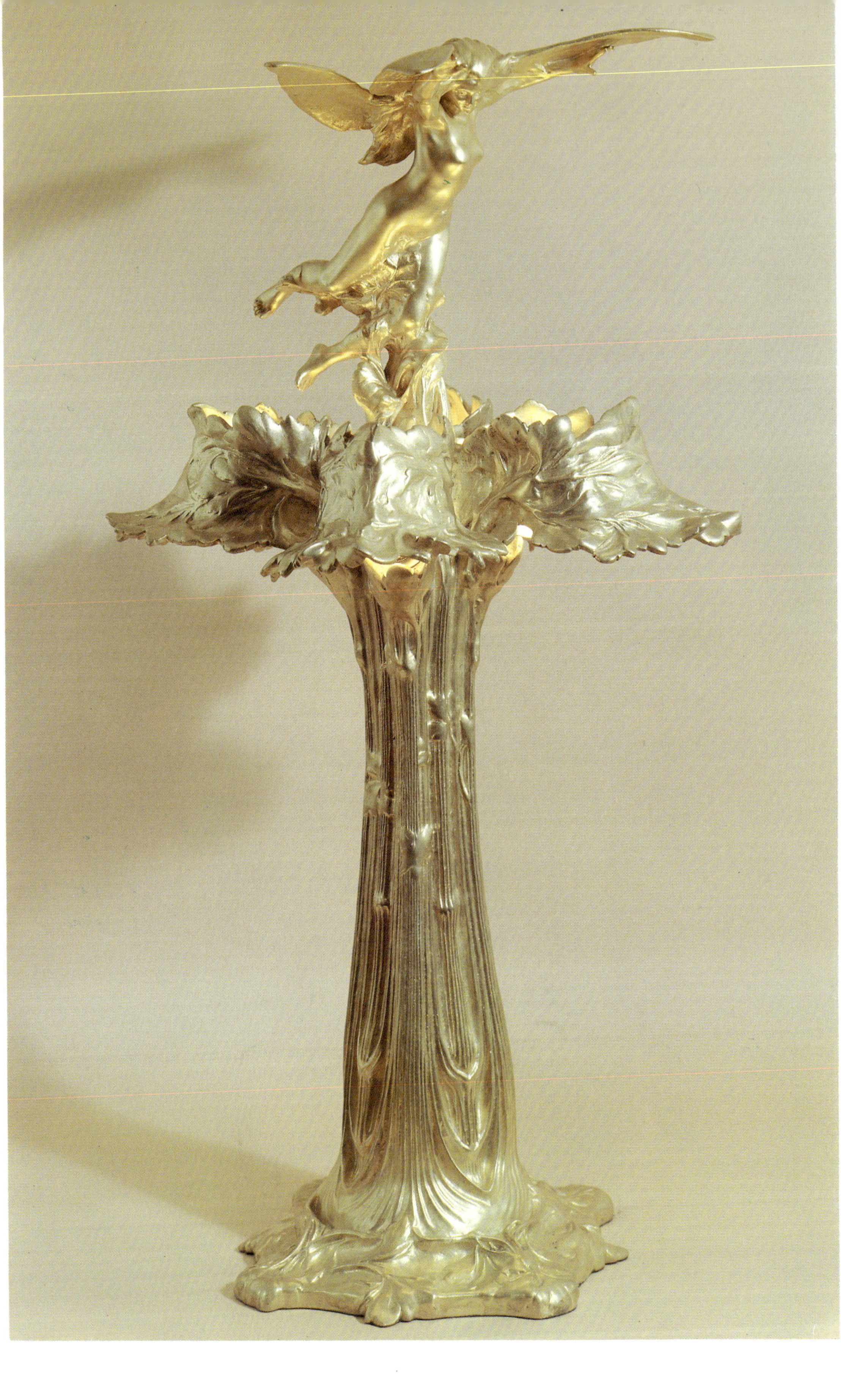

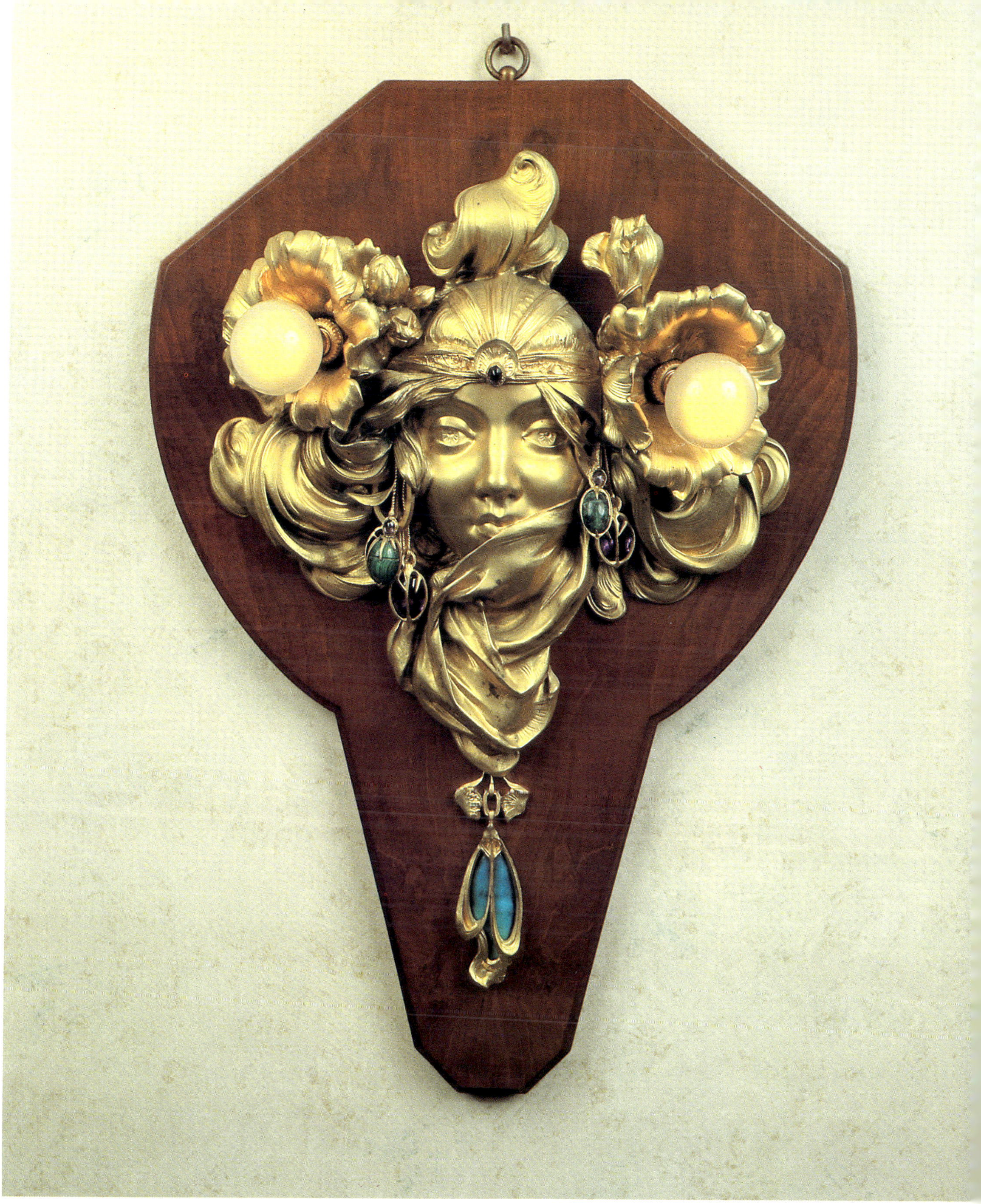

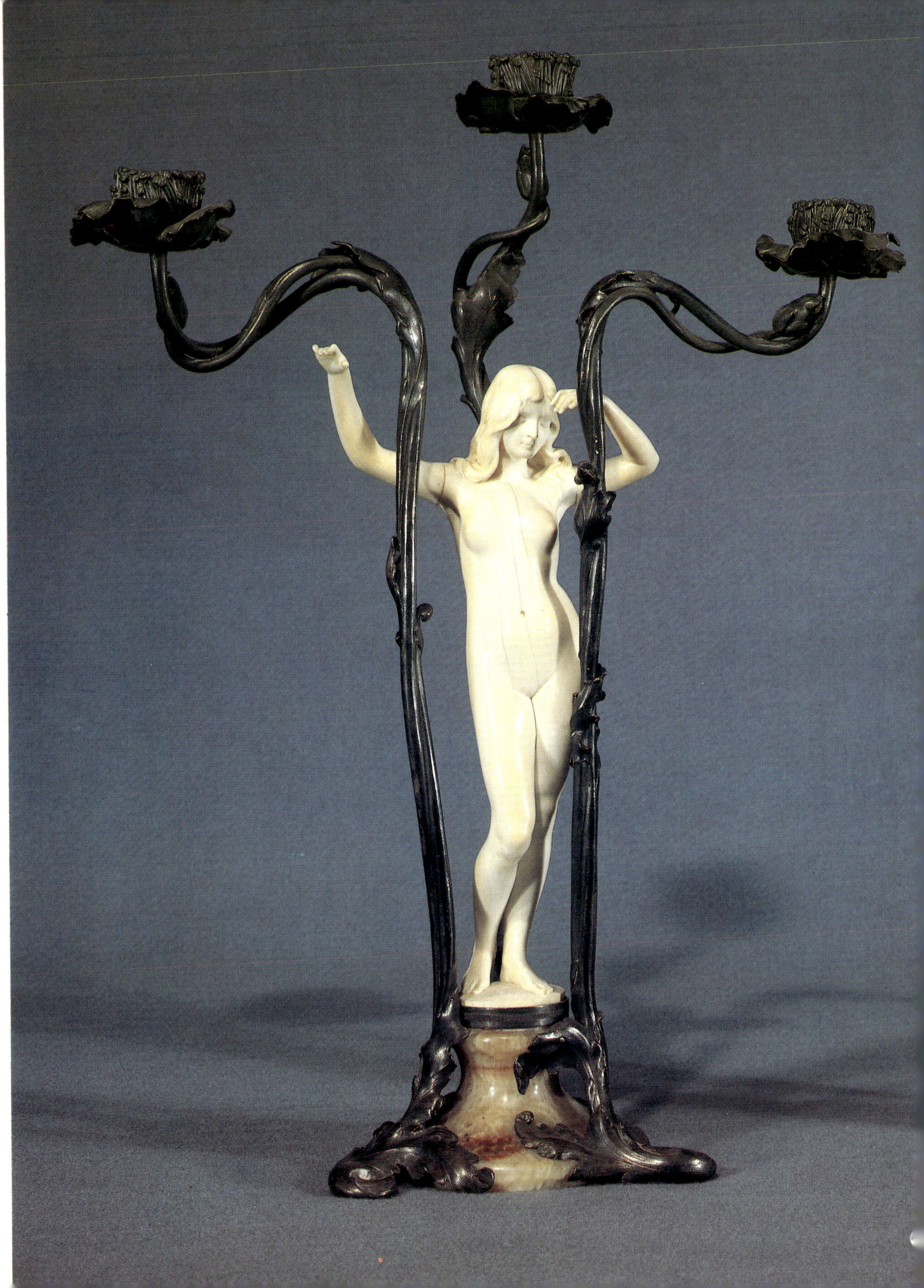

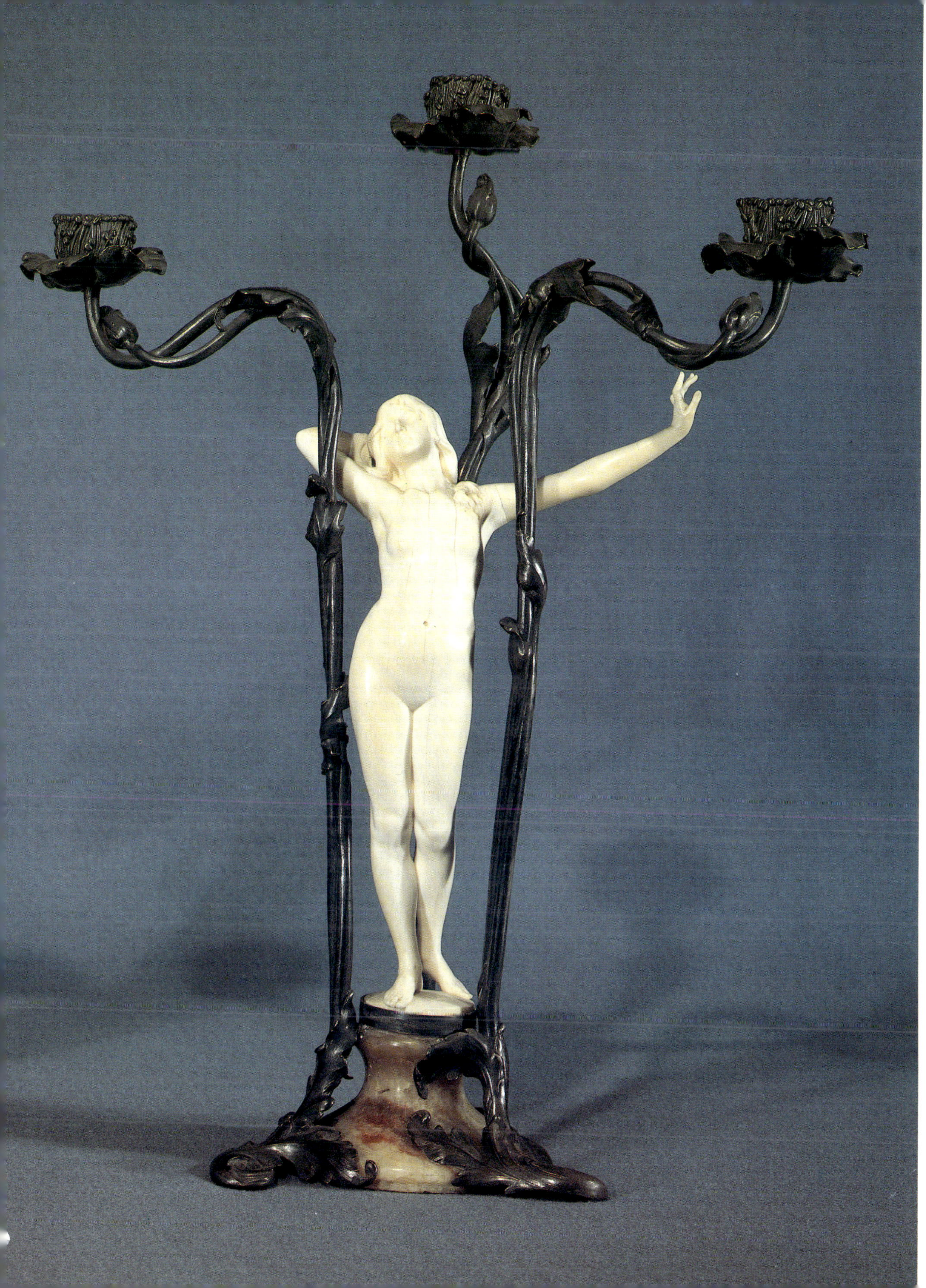

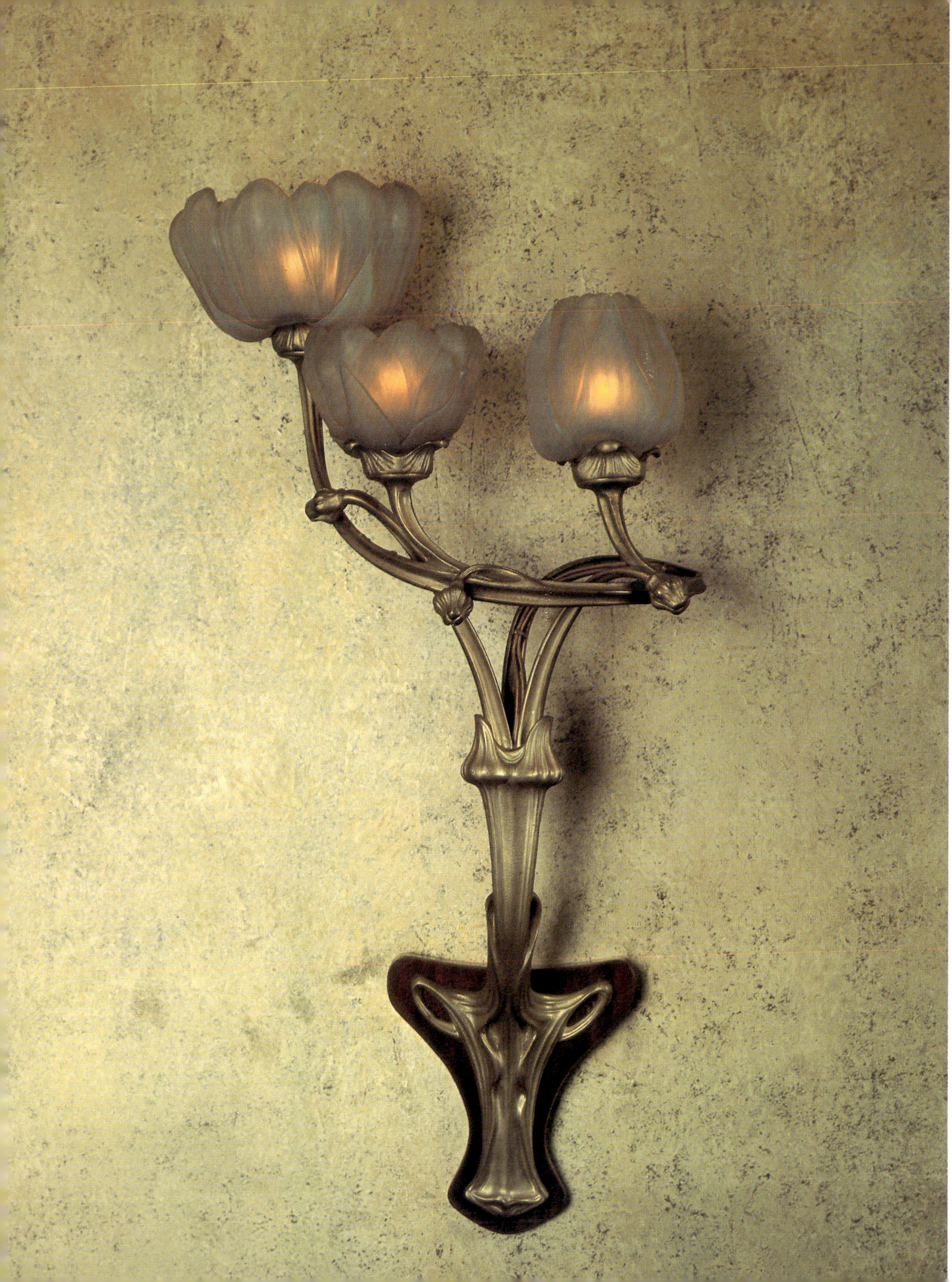

XV

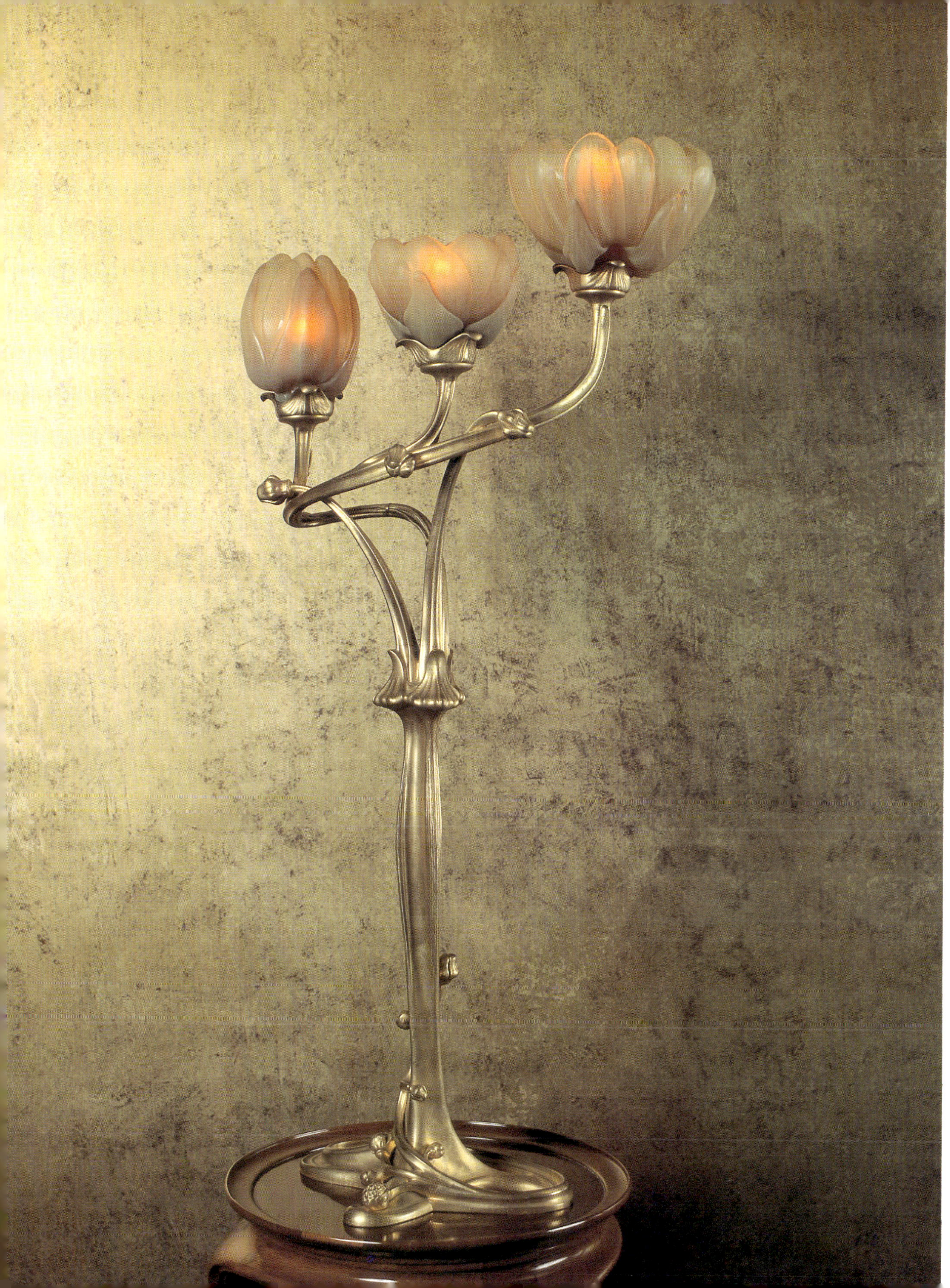

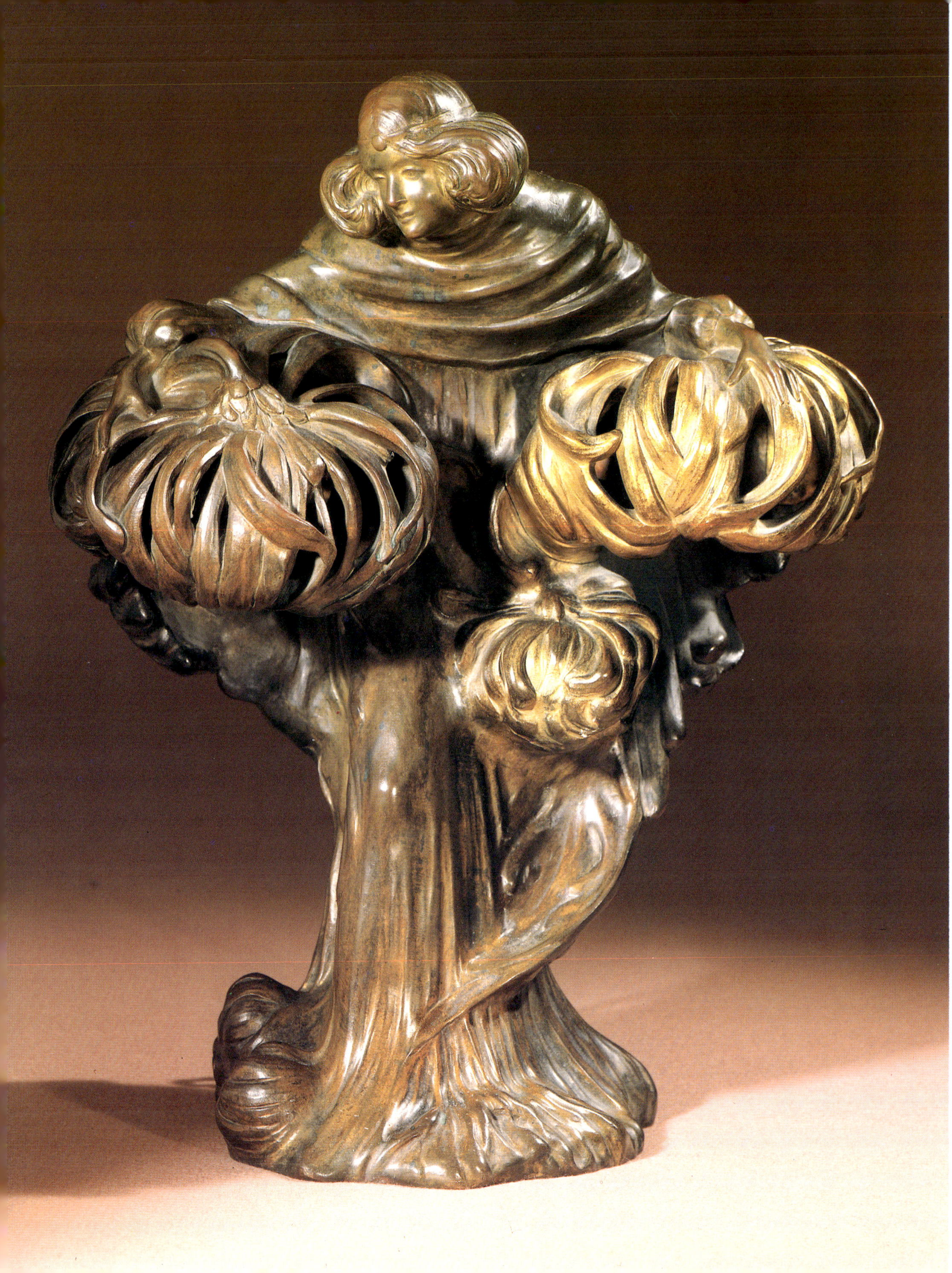

XVII

3

The Art Nouveau Designers

The following section contains an alphabetical breakdown, by country, of those Art Nouveau exponents who applied themselves to various forms of light fixtures. So many artists designed lamps around 1900 that the question 'Who made Art Nouveau lamps?' is perhaps more quickly answered by asking 'Who did *not*?' The ultimate choice of whom to include in this book has been a subjective one, reached by analysis of all accessible information and then by determination of each artist's respective merits in terms of the aesthetics and the range and quantity of his or her work in the field of lighting. For this reason I have decided to omit a Spanish section. *Aficionados* of Antoní Gaudí and his fellow Catalan Lluis Domenéch y Montaner may feel let down, but in neither instance could I discover examples of their work in lighting that I considered to be representative of their architectural genius. Another Barcelonan who designed forms of illumination was Antonio Bofill, a sculptor who settled in Paris and exhibited his bronzes through the Société des Artistes français between 1894 and 1921; but only one example of his work in lighting – a *femme-fleur* table-lamp – appears to have survived.

The Art Nouveau designers

UNITED STATES OF AMERICA

Whether of unusual design or not, most American Art Nouveau lamps were composed of the same basic two materials which distinguished the light fixtures of Tiffany and his compatriots from those of their transatlantic counterparts. These were opalescent glass (called, significantly, by the French *verre américain coloré)* and copper foil. Both remain almost solely an American phenomenon, the former usually being manufactured in sheet form and of sufficient opacity to conceal the light source (this for aesthetic reasons), the latter a less bulky and more malleable means of housing the pieces of glass than by the traditional H-framed lead 'calme'.*

It is important initially to stress Tiffany's influence. In no other country was any single person to dominate the realm of lighting to such a disproportionate degree: the word 'Tiffany' has become, for the general public, a generic term that defines all turn-of-the-century American lampshades. Needless to say, this is a backhanded compliment to Tiffany, but one which underlines his monolithic influence in this sphere of the decorative arts.

It is equally important, however, to stress that there *were* others, and that their work, had they not had the misfortune to be overshadowed by a man of such extraordinary stature, would now be compared favourably with some of the best of their European contemporaries. Duffner & Kimberly and Handel, for example, executed certain lamps whose designs and workmanship would in no way have embarrassed Tiffany Studios (although the glass would have done so). Of those US lighting exponents not covered in the following pages, mention should be made of the following (the best reference book on the subject is A. C. Revi's definitive work entitled *American Art Nouveau Glass*: see Bibliography):

*For those readers who wish to learn how American-styled glass lampshades are made, may I recommend my own book on the subject: *The Technique of Leaded Glass*, London and New York 1975.

Bradley & Hubbard, a New York-based firm that specialized in bent-panelled lamps with metal filigree overlays; Bigelow & Kennard, a Boston firm that made neat leaded-glass shades often supported by Grueby pottery bases; Pairpoint, whose lamps are important and collectable, but which, I feel, were not quite 'Art Nouveau'; Fulper's pottery lamps; and the Fostoria Glass Speciality Co., in Ohio, that made blown art-glass lampshades.

Beyond these there were a host of commercial imitators who manufactured leaded-glass or bent-panelled shades: for example, the Carl V. Helmschmied Manufacturing Co. and the U.S. Art Bent Glass Co., both in Connecticut; Williamson and Co., the Moran and Hasting Manufacturing Co., and the H. J. Peters Co., all of Chicago; and the Albert Sechrist Manufacturing Co., of Denver.

Such lamps can still be found in great numbers throughout the US and Canada, but the best non-Tiffany lighting may be seen in Neil Isman's Madison Avenue shop and among the antique shops on Atlantic Avenue, Brooklyn.

DUFFNER & KIMBERLY

The firm of Duffner & Kimberly is first listed in the 1906 edition of Trow's Business Directory of Greater New York under the heading of 'Gas and Electric Light Fixture Makers'. Located at 11 W. 32nd Street, Manhattan, the firm was listed in each consecutive year until 1911, after which only the name of the Kimberly Co., at the new address of 317 E. 38th Street, appeared.

The partnership between Mr Duffner and Mr Kimberly existed, therefore, for at least six years, during which time leaded glass table- and floor-lamps, chandeliers, and wall-brackets were produced, in addition to a range of electric candle sconces and chandeliers in which each bulb was housed in a small blown shade. Sales catalogues of the firm made available to me by the Chrysler Museum in Norfolk, Va., do not mention that the firm manufactured its own glass, so presumably both the sheet and blown varieties were purchased commercially.

Whether, as is frequently speculated, both Duffner and Kimberly worked at the Tiffany Studios before 1906 is uncertain. Professor Robert Koch wrote, in an article in *Antiques Guide to New York* (Vol. 1, no. 2, 1971), that Mrs Kimberly had confirmed that her late husband had at one time worked for Tiffany, but no evidence appears to exist on Duffner's earlier experience. Certainly the workmanship of the leading on their lampshades is comparable to that of Tiffany, although their designs are distinctly more formal.

The firm's output was relatively small, a fact which is no help today when one attempts to identify works of which a high proportion were neither signed on the shades nor on the bronze or brass bases. One characteristic of some of the Duffner & Kimberly table-lamps, however, which can help as a means of identification, is a special circular locking mechanism whereby the shade is secured on to the top of the base.

The sales catalogues list a wide range of prices from $20 for simple, panelled leaded shades up to expensive $500 models. The calibre of workmanship in the leading and the careful juxtaposition of colours in the glass justify the high prices that these lamps are once again bringing.

Following the dissolution of the firm in 1911, Kimberly continued on his own and introduced into his range of light fixtures a series of 'Ancient Texture Lamps': twelve different models of early English, Jacobean, and Chinese influence. These, in English antique glass, were painted with scenes depicting heraldry, the crusades, and the signing of the 'Magna Charta' (*sic*).

The prices of Duffner & Kimberley leaded glass lampshades have risen sharply in recent years. In 1977, two table-lamps, both of floral design and 24 inches in diameter, were sold on Madison Avenue for $3,675 (£2,150) each.*

HANDEL, PHILIP

Following the foundation in 1885 of a glass-decorating company in Meriden, Connecticut, by Adolph Eyden and Philip Handel, the latter bought out his partner in 1893 and changed the name of the firm to Handel & Company. The name was changed, again, in 1903, to The Handel Company, Inc., which lasted until its dissolution in 1941.

Although manufacturing a general range of domestic glassware – for example, vases, *tazzas*, and tobacco jars – the firm concentrated mainly on lampshade production, the designs and decoration of which were undertaken by Handel's ever-expanding studio of artists and craftsmen. No fixture was too big or too small, from large ceiling- and floor-lamps to painted opal night lights, all of which were housed in mounts manufactured in the firm's own metalwork department.

Nobody, except perhaps Gallé, was to incorporate a more diverse range of techniques into his manufacture of glass lamps at the turn of the century than did The Handel Company, a fact all the more remarkable since it does not appear that the firm made a great deal – if, in fact, any – of its own glass. Sheets of machine-rolled glass and moulded glass blanks were purchased commercially and then 'finished'. This entailed, in the first instance, cutting the sheets into the individual pieces of which the floral or geometric lampshades were composed and, in the second, decorating the blank with, for example, reverse-painted designs. Other techniques were enamelling, etching, filigreed metal overlays, and the application of a 'chipped' frosted finish to the outside surface of the shade.

Of all Tiffany's American lamp-making contemporaries, Handel is today the most collectable, since nearly all his work was signed and the volume of his production was large.

Handel's lamps fall roughly into two categories: those that are of leaded (*i.e.*, unpainted) glass, and those that are painted. In the former category his use of

* When actual sales figures are being quoted, the price is given in the currency of the country where the sale took place, with the dollar or sterling equivalent at that time. In the case of estimated values, currency rates as of the first quarter of 1978 are used.

commercial glass and his stylized, rather 'Arts and Crafts' flower designs, suffer when viewed alongside the unique glass and exact floral reproductions of Tiffany. Handel might have done better to specialize in his painted and 'chipped' shades, techniques nowadays immediately identifiable as his when one searches through the multitude of non-Tiffany, 1900 glass lamps found in antique shops.

Of Tiffany's competitors, Handel's lamps consistently bring the highest prices. A good, signed Handel floor- or table-lamp now costs between $3,500 (£1,800) and $5,250 (£2,750). A reverse-painted 'Bird of Paradise' table-lamp brought $9,100 (£5,200) at Miami Beach in 1976.

QUEZAL

The brilliant iridescent plumage of the Quetzal bird from Central America provided the inspiration for the name of the Quezal Art Glass and Decorating Company, formed in Brooklyn in February 1901, by Martin Bach and Thomas Johnson. Both ex-employees of the Tiffany Studios in Corona – the former as a batch mixer and the latter as a gaffer – they took a thorough working knowledge of Tiffany's glass-making with them, as can be seen from their subsequent plagiarization of his art glass.

The firm produced a wide range of glass tableware – bud-vases and compotes, bowls, sherbets, wine glasses, and even an iridescent vase that was a shameless copy of Tiffany's 'Jack in the Pulpit' – but concentrated on its output of lampshades. These, in sizes normally of up to six inches in length, were blown (*i.e.*, non-leaded) into a variety of lily, trumpet, and everted bowl shapes to house a single bulb. Easily mistakable (not all Quezal shades were signed) for a similar range of small shades by Tiffany, Lustre Art, and Steuben, those by Quezal nevertheless show excellent quality of workmanship, both in their lustre finish and in their motifs: for example, gold hooked feather, orange zipper, ogee, and pulled leaf patterns.

The main criticism against them is summed up by A. C. Revi in his *American Art Nouveau Glass*:

> Some very beautiful Art Nouveau glass was made at the Quezal factory. It should be noted, however, that Quezal never introduced anything new in design or technique, but seemed content to copy the colors and decorating techniques initiated at the Tiffany glassworks.

The firm, which experienced a series of financial setbacks between 1905 and 1918, closed in 1925.

STEUBEN

Incorporated in 1903 at Corning, New York, the Steuben Glass Works took its name from the county in which it was located. Set up initially to manufacture the glass blanks and crystal ware for the glass-cutting company of T. G. Hawkes & Co., the firm got off to a promising start with the appointment of the Englishman Frederick Carder as its Art Director.

It was Carder who extended the Steuben production to encompass all aspects of domestic glassware – from vases, goblets, and millefiori paperweights to candlesticks and lampshades – while providing the creative genius behind all aspects of its art glass.

Like Quezal, Steuben manufactured a range of hand-blown light fixtures, although the latter's emphasis on lighting, as a percentage of its total output, was not as pronounced as that of Quezal. Small table-lamps, branched chandeliers consisting of several single-bulb shades, and candlesticks were made in various of Carder's finishing techniques: for example, gold and blue Aurene, Ivrene, marvered Cintra, and *verre de soie*. Perennial favourites were the lustred Aurene shades, often decorated with etched or engraved designs or with applied 'optic' patterns, and the Ivrene ones with their nacreous iridescence and soft luminosity.

Preferred motifs included the feather, guilloche, and trailing lily pad.

Steuben Art Nouveau lampshades and candlesticks tend to be less expensive than similar items by, for example, Quezal and the Fostoria Glass Speciality Co. In 1975 two pairs of Steuben gold Aurene single-bulb shades sold in New York for $420 (£210) per pair.

TIFFANY, LOUIS COMFORT

At the turn of the century, Louis Comfort Tiffany was responsible for the production of a range of *objets d'art* which, in their design and technical virtuosity, rivalled anything the world had seen since the *quattrocento*. Tiffany did not bring *either* the munificence of the Medici *or* the creative genius of Raphael to his lifework, he brought *both*: the former by his birthright (as a son of the eminent and prosperous New York silversmith, Charles L. Tiffany) and the latter by a felicitous blend of genes, ambition and boundless energy.

Tiffany concentrated on the art of lighting (as against the science of lighting – an Art Déco pursuit), for which he found the contemporary commercial glass that he first purchased from Louis Heidt and other Brooklyn glasshouses to be totally inadequate. From this began his own research to create in glass those effects – for example, iridescence, mottling and incandescence – which he desired. This odyssey was punctuated along its way by the discovery of such varieties as his Cypriote, fractured, and lava glasses. It is for his Favrile shades that Tiffany is best known. These can be divided into two general categories: those of floral and those of geometric design. The former includes a great part of the botanical kingdom: for example, the peony, wistaria, poinsettia, rambling rose, and woodbine. The latter, often incorporating turtleback tiles or glass jewels as a decorative fillip, rely on fundamentally sound geometry allied to the inimitable qualities of translucency in the glass. The individual pieces, in their lattice of soldered copper foil, resemble *cloisonné* enamel when seen by reflected light (*i.e.*, when the light is off) and *plique-à-jour* when seen by transmitted light. It is interesting also to note the distinction between Tiffany's interpretation of a floral motif for a lamp and those of, say, Gallé or the Daums. The School of Nancy portrayed the chosen flower in a series of vignettes around the lampshade and on its baluster base. Tiffany, on the contrary, designed the lamp as a complete organism, the shade becoming the incandescent blooms and the bronze base the plant's stem and roots.

Despite a vast and moneyed American clientèle that included the Vanderbilts, Havemeyers, Mellons, and the White House (under President Chester Arthur), Tiffany was not, surprisingly, an international celebrity. A 1901 *L'Art Décoratif* article, for example, paid muted tribute to the 'Art de Yankee', and he is only now, in the auction room, being afforded the acclaim his work so richly deserves.

The prices of Tiffany's light fixtures continue to rise at a meteoric pace. In 1977 prices ranged from $1,400 (£800) for a three-light lily table-lamp to over $100,000 for a unique magnolia standard floor-lamp. I have seen three Tiffany lamps priced at $100,000 (£60,000) and up. For one of the more commonplace lamps, such as a 24-inch clematis, 22-inch dragonfly, or 20-inch poppy, the price in New York can be upwards of $22,750 (£12,000). There is also a firm market for Tiffany's bronze bases (*i.e.*, bases without accompanying shades): these fetch anything from $500 (£265) to $10,000 (£5,300).

BELGIUM

Brussels, crucible of avant-gardism (*Les Vingt* was founded as early as 1884), was the fountainhead of both Belgium's and Europe's *Le Modern Style*. To the realm of lighting its Art Nouveau exponents were to apply the same abundant talent and enthusiasm that they did to other media, while drawing on as wide a range of themes – though in the case of Serrurier-Bovy, Horta, and Van de Velde, slightly more stylized – as their French neighbours.

DUBOIS, FERNAND

After settling in Brussels in 1877, and subsequent tutelage under the sculptors Constantin Meunier and Charles van der Stappen, Fernand Dubois took up a professorship in the city's professional School of Applied Art, which was inaugurated in 1894. Working in bronze, pewter and enamels, he produced a wide range of ornaments, such as jewellery, medallions, plaques, bas-reliefs, fans, and candelabra for the Salons of La Libre Esthétique. His 'marriage casket' in ivory and silver-bronze, displayed in the Congo Palace at the 1879 Tervueren chryselephantine sculpture exposition, was highly praised by the most eminent Belgian art critic of the time, Octave Maus. In lighting, Dubois is known principally for his five-branched candelabrum (see illustration no. 15), of which one pair is on display at the Horta Museum in Brussels. This – in the tangled exuberance of its arboreal sinuosities – was to represent the apogee of legitimate Art Nouveau; thereafter such hyperbole of design overspilled into vulgarity.

Very little of Dubois' work, other than several pairs of the illustrated silvered bronze candelabra, has survived.

DUBOIS, PAUL

Paul Dubois, compatriot and colleague of Constantin Meunier and Victor Rousseau as creator of monumental sculpture (see, for example, his bust of the Count of Mérode in the Place des Martyrs in Brussels), was also to design and execute *objets d'art*, such as vases, beltclasps, candelabra, plaquettes, jugs, and paperweights, examples of which were frequently displayed at the expositions of *Les Vingt* and, subsequently, at the Salons of La Libre Esthétique. His works generated the praise of *The Studio*'s critic, who wrote in an 1898 article, 'Of all the Belgian sculptors who, in addition to their monumental work, have taken up applied art, the most successful is unquestionably M. Paul Dubois, of Brussels. His candelabra, salt-cellars, bon-bon boxes, etc., are at once artistic in appearance and well adapted for everyday use, two qualities not often found in combination. Moreover, accustomed as he is to studying the beauties of bronze, and all its possibilities in the way of oxidation, M. Dubois has sought and found all sorts of effects obtainable in pewter.'

Among his productions was a series of florally-inspired candelabra, remarkable in their fidelity to nature. A jonquil candelabrum in patinated bronze has upturned flowers, the corollas of which act as the nozzles for the candles, and the adjoining petals as wax-pans. In another, the same theme is adapted to the iris; in a third, to the magnolia.

Dubois does not appear to have applied himself to the advent of the incandescent filament bulb for domestic lighting, though *The Studio* makes reference in 1898 to two 'electric poles' – one by Dubois and the other by J. Lagae – that were commissioned by the Brussels botanical gardens.

A pair of iris candelabra, in bronze, by Paul Dubois were sold in Paris in 1975 for FF2,400 ($480).

HORTA, VICTOR

Victor Horta's contribution to the field of domestic lighting is in line with his philosophy of 'a return to a total harmony between architecture, fixtures, and fittings'. An architect, Horta applied himself to designing not only the building itself, but its entire contents down to such components as the chandeliers and even to the very doorhandles and key escutcheons. Inspired by the Gothic revivalist Viollet-le-Duc's ideas on structure as an architectural expression in itself, Horta broke with his classicist master, Alphonse Balat, in 1892, declaring that to copy is dishonest. Freed in this way from historicism, Horta quickly developed his own unique style in which the skeletal framework of his buildings – the iron pillars, balustrades, window frames, etc. – remained visible, and in this emphasis on their structure he created a link between them and their interior furnishings.

The decorative idiom that these iron supports expressed was to become known as the 'Horta line': biomorphic, serpentine, voluptuous, light as air. They twist and writhe in Gaudiesque manner, and it was from the ends and joints of these that his chandeliers and wall-brackets often protruded – not as separate entities, but simply as extensions of the whole, each as a harmonious *pars pro toto*. (It is for this reason that Horta's lighting fixtures, like those of Serrurier-Bovy, can appear so exaggerated when viewed on their own and so incongruous in a non-Horta ensemble.)

Each Horta light fixture was designed specifically for the interior in which it was to be placed: for example, the Hôtel Aubecq, the Château de la Hulpe, the Maison de Peuple, and his houses for Messrs Tassel, Frison, Solvay, Baron van Eetvelde, and the one that he designed for himself in the rue Américaine. In the latter, now the Horta Museum, and in the Hôtel Solvay can be seen a marvellous range of chandeliers and clusters of lights that sprout in profusion from his chimney-pieces, stairwell banisters, and cornices. The bulbs are frequently housed individually in small, clear, flower-form shades, giving an overall effect, when lit, of electrical bouquets or blossoms. Horta also designed several conventional standard floor- and table-lamps for his interiors. Of these, often in gilt-bronze, few remain.

It is unlikely that any Horta light fixtures will appear on the Art Nouveau market; most of them are still in their original settings in buildings which have had preservation orders placed on them by the Belgian Government.

ROMBAUX/HOOSEMANS

Rombaux/Hoosemans or Hoosemans/Rombaux? Either, depending on whether one considers Rombaux's ivory figurines or Hoosemans' silver foliage to be the more important. But such an assessment may be invidious, as it was only in the union of their respective talents and materials that their delightful range of candelabra and table-lamps took form.

Egide Rombaux, son of the sculptor Félix Rombaux and student of Charles van der Stappen and Joseph Lambeaux, was one of the more eminent of the Belgian School at the turn of the century. Sculptor and medallist, he principally did ivory groups (such as his 'Venusberg', displayed at the 1897 chryselephantine Tervuren exposition, and his 'Daughter of Satan', now at the Musée Royale des Beaux-Arts in Brussels), portrait busts (for example, that of Paul Janson) and statues, while his light fixtures fell into the category of *petites oeuvres*.

Franz Hoosemans, likewise from Brussels, was the silversmith who fashioned the plant-form supports that enveloped Rombaux's sculpted and polished ivory maidens and which culminated in either flower-form candle-nozzles or bulb holders.

Although executed with charm and grace, the young woman/flora theme is disappointingly repetitious.

There are very few Rombaux/Hoosemans candelabra left on the Art Nouveau market. I know of only one pair and two individual pieces outside of the ones in Berlin and Hamburg museums. One of the individual pieces was on sale for £2,000 ($4,000) in 1975 in London.

SERRURIER-BOVY, GUSTAVE

The Liégeois Serrurier-Bovy was the third of Belgium's trinity of Art Nouveau architectural decorators (along with Horta and Van de Velde) to design a wide range of furnishings for his interiors. Initially a devotee of William Morris and the English Arts and Crafts movement, Serrurier-Bovy shows this influence in the motifs of his textiles, wallpapers, pianos, clocks, window garnitures, and his much-acclaimed suite of collapsible birchwood 'Silex' furniture. As a result of his philosophy of a total ensemble in which each element had a role to play, his contribution to the field of lighting was substantial, and although most of the archives on his work have disappeared, sufficient information – both textual and illustrative – remains to show his extension of the Serrurier style into this sphere.

In a 1902 article in *Art et Décoration* on metal furnishings, Serrurier-Bovy's friend and associate René Dulong used examples of the designer's electric, gas, and oil lamps and chandeliers to illustrate his own tenets on the determination of a fixture's shape by its fuel and function. The photographs show twisting wrought-iron and copper supports that house – almost incidentally – the light sockets, gas mantles, and oil reservoirs. Sometimes the light source is left uncovered, often its rays are reflected by, or transmitted through, *verre américain coloré* or cloth shades. Everywhere there is a spidery lightness, almost an ethereality, which on occasion becomes a trifle overworked. (Here one must remember that a fair appraisal of individual Serrurier pieces is difficult when they are viewed apart from their original settings.) Three years later, in another article on the use of metal – this time by Prince Karageorgevitch in *L'Art Décoratif* – are shown a Serrurier wall-bracket, two chandeliers, a standard- and table-lamp, and, most charming of all in the grace and wispiness of its wrought-iron supports, a dining-room lustre.

By 1905 the unbridled voluptuousness of Serrurier's Art Nouveau curves had given way in general to a more austere, disciplined geometry, though the transition was never so marked as in the work, for instance, of Van de Velde.

Very few of Serrurier-Bovy's furnishings have been seen outside of Belgium in recent years. Three of his light fixtures – two chandeliers and a table-lamp – were included in an exhibition on 'Lighting' at the L'Ecuyer Gallery in Brussels in 1967. The likely price range for these fixtures is BF7,800 to 13,200 ($260 to $440).

VAL SAINT LAMBERT

Virtually no biographical literature was available on the *cristalleries* of Val St Lambert until Dr Joseph Philippe's definitive book (*Le Val Saint Lambert*) on the firm's history was published in 1974. Yet the firm, which was founded in 1826 near Liège, had by 1880 been launched, in Dr Philippe's words, on 'what was probably the greatest period in the history of Val St Lambert; in the last twenty years of the nineteenth century and until 1914, some 5,000 employees and first-rate technical installations produced an enormous output using extremely varied decorative techniques.'

Internationally renowned – in particular for its crystal glassware, often similar in appearance to that of Baccarat or Neo-Renaissance glass – the firm played a full part in Belgium's Art Nouveau experience under various art designers, most notably Camille Renard-Steinbach, Dieudonné Masson and Léon Ledru. According to A. Defêchereux, ex-Works Director of the firm, the range of light fixtures around 1900 included lustres, branched candelabra with pendants, globes, screens, reflectors, and shades, either in cut crystal or frosted, wheel-cut, sandblasted, or acid-etched for decorative effect. A minority of these were in Art Nouveau designs, although very few seem to have survived.

A further link with Art Nouveau was through Val St Lambert's associations with Horta, Van de Velde, Serrurier-Bovy, and Wolfers, all of whom were to have designs for glassware executed by the firm. Horta, for example, had the reflecting crystal plates for his Hôtel Solvay (1903) chandeliers made at Val St Lambert, and it is probable that the shades for Serrurier-Bovy's lamps were also done there. In addition, Désiré and

Henri Muller (two of the Muller *frères*) were invited in 1906 from their Lunéville factory to work at Val St Lambert and to instruct the firm's glassmakers in the 'fluogravure' technique they had learned when students of Gallé. It is likely that some of the glassware resulting from this venture would have been incorporated into lamp shades.

VAN DE VELDE, HENRY

Polemicist of the old and theoretician of the new, Henry van de Velde, originally a pointilliste painter like his compatriot Van Rysselberghe, turned to architecture and, finally, to all aspects of design. Appalled by the eclecticism of late nineteenth-century interiors, he wrote, in his *Formule d'une Esthétique Moderne*, of 'the insane follies which the furniture makers of past centuries had piled up in bedrooms and drawing rooms . . . Processions of fauns, menacing apocalyptic beasts, benevolently hilarious cupids (bawdy in some cases and complaisantly anxious to please in others), and swollen-cheeked satyrs in charge of the winds.' His remedy for this was the pursuit of the right form – a form which was to be simple, truthful and absolute.

This manifested itself in the characteristic Van de Velde line, which was less pronounced than that of Guimard or Horta. His philosophy of the *Gesamtkunstwerk* ('total work of art') led to his designing in every medium and on every scale: jewels, silverware, bookbindings, tea services, buckles, ceramics, textiles, wallpapers, etc. A part of this versatility was to result in a wide range of light fixtures: candelabra for candle power and chandeliers and table-lamps for oil, gas, and electrically powered lighting.

Unlike Horta, Van de Velde did not design these solely for the interiors of his buildings – for example, his own villa at Uccle, the Esche house in Chemnitz, the Leuring house in Scheveningen, the Folkwang Museum in Hagen, or the Haby Barber Shop and Havana Co. Cigar Store in Berlin – though obviously they did comprise the major part of his lighting production. Julius Meier-Graefe commissioned him to design brass and copper chandeliers and table-lamps for his shop La Maison Moderne in Paris, as did Samuel Bing for his Maison de l'Art Nouveau. Some of these were illustrated in an article in *L'Art Décoratif* (1899) and show Van de Velde's interplay of curved lines and empty spaces; in the elliptical or flattened spherical shapes of the reservoirs of his oil lamps can be seen an expression of his view that an object's function should not be subordinated to its design.

Later fixtures – products of his sojourn in Germany – were stripped of their ornateness. Rigidly symmetrical, the charm and spontaneity of his earlier essays gone, these show the mood of the newly-emerging Van de Velde, precursor of the Bauhaus. Geometry abounds, and unconcealed rivets and clips join the fixtures' glass globes to their metal mounts.

There have not been many Van de Velde lamps or candelabra on the Art Nouveau market. It is the candelabra that are highly prized; a pair was sold for $1,575 (£785) in New York in 1975.

WOLFERS, PHILIPPE

Apprenticed into his father Louis Wolfer's atelier in 1876, Philippe Wolfers worked in the early 1880s in Neo-Rococo and *japonaiserie* styles before diversifying into precursory Art Nouveau floral designs by 1890. Celebrated principally as a jeweller, Wolfers extended his talents to such objects of vertu as bronze cachepots, vases in cut and cameo crystal, goldwork, marble statues, and a sculpted oak lectern. In the vanguard of those artists and designers who legitimized the use of ivory (obtained from the Belgian Congo) beyond its traditional role for such everyday accoutrements as boxes and buttons, Wolfers participated in the 1897 chryselephantine exposition patronized by Leopold II, exhibiting several ivory statues and objects, such as his 'Caress of the Swan', which is similar in inspiration to his 'Fairy with a Peacock' lamps.

His contribution to Art Nouveau lighting was probably limited to the two lamps illustrated, one of which, incidentally, inspired an almost identical figural lamp by the French sculptor Alexandre Falguière. After 1904 Wolfers concentrated on sculpture, although he did design a complete ensemble at the 1925 Exposition Universelle, in which were included a series of silver chandeliers. Totally non-functional, the bulbs positioned in the peacock's tail (ill. xxvi) show how quickly Wolfers had adapted the new electricity to his aesthetic needs. No form of combustion lighting would have allowed the incorporation of a concealed light source in this manner.

GREAT BRITAIN

The British contribution to lighting has been meagre, which is surprising in view of what British artist/craftsmen, such as Chippendale, Sheraton and Hepplewhite, achieved in other areas of the decorative arts. Light fixtures have always been of low-key, secondary importance in the British home: some quaint, some graceful, but, all in all, predictably non-experimental and dull.

The Art Nouveau period, which Great Britain is credited with having spawned through the doctrines of Ruskin, Morris and the Pre-Raphaelites, found lamp exponents well in the shadow of their European counterparts: no sculptural lighting, no beautiful Nancy glass lampshades, no fanciful fripperies à la Horta. Charles Eastlake's *Hints on Household Taste* (1868) was still not out of date; Rudyard Kipling's 'The God of things as they are' demanded an evocation of past glories and resistance to change.

Among the clutter in the average Victorian home, replete with its curios, bric-à-brac, and overall atmosphere of *horror vacui*, were to be found traditionally styled electroliers, gas pendants and candlesticks. These *The Studio* tried frequently to display to their best advantage, although without much enthusiasm. Chandeliers by George Walton, Harry Powell and J. E. C. Carr; electric candle sconces by Alexander Fisher, George Frampton and the Guild of Handicraft; candlesticks by Christopher Dresser, A. E. Jones and James Dixon; table-lamps by Edward Spencer and, from the 1880s, by Arthur Mackmurdo; newel posts by G. Wagge; billiard table lights by the Artificers' Guild: among these the common denominator was chaste tastefulness, rather than a 'new art'.

ASHBEE, CHARLES

Founder of the Guild of Handicraft in 1888, Ashbee cannot and *would not* (on occasion he spoke out vehemently against the style's excesses) be classified as a *bona fide* exponent of Art Nouveau. His work falls, rather, somewhere between Art Nouveau and the British Arts and Crafts movement: less flamboyant than the former yet less austere than the no-nonsense ruggedness of the latter. An architect (for example, 38 Cheyne Walk, London), designer, and, like William Morris before him, something of a peripatetic social reformer, Ashbee is now known principally for his silverware and jewellery, which are characterized by purity of design and linear elegance. His versatility was extended, though infrequently, to lamps, two of which are illustrated. The apparently limited number of such fixtures indicates, however, that these were special commissions rather than a standard part of his artistic repertoire.

Although several objects by Ashbee have appeared on the London market since 1972, none of his light fixtures have done so. It is therefore difficult to estimate what one, or a pair, of his silver candlesticks would bring, but this would not be less than £1,000 ($1,900) for a pair.

XVIII Ashbee. A table-lamp designed for Prince Ludwig von Hesse, 1900. The glass shade rests on a chased silver base set with amethysts. The Prince commissioned the lamp while Ashbee was collaborating with the architect Baillie Scott on his designs for the Darmstadt Art Colony.

XIX Mucha. This gilt-bronze bust may well have been used as a table-lamp.

XX Léonard. These two gilt-bronze dancers formed part of Léonard's *Jeu de l'écharpe* series. The light bulbs are hidden in the folds of the billowing scarves.

XXI Gurschner. A bronze and Turbo Marmoratus shell table-lamp.

XXII Gurschner. A bronze and nautilus table-lamp.

XXIII Loetz. A fine iridescent glass table-lamp attributed to Loetz; the silvered bronze base is unsigned.

XXIV Gurschner. An elegant bronze table-lamp, with a typically Art Nouveau housing for the glass shade.

XXV Korschann. A gilt-bronze table-lamp with a concealed inkwell.

XXVI Wolfers. A marble and bronze group called *La Fée au Paon* (peacock fairy). Electric bulbs are positioned in the peacock's tail so that the light rays are transmitted through the *plique-à-jour* 'eyes' to produce a heightened effect normally associated with jewellery. The statue now lacks the peacock's feathers that originally hung from the woman's outstretched left hand.

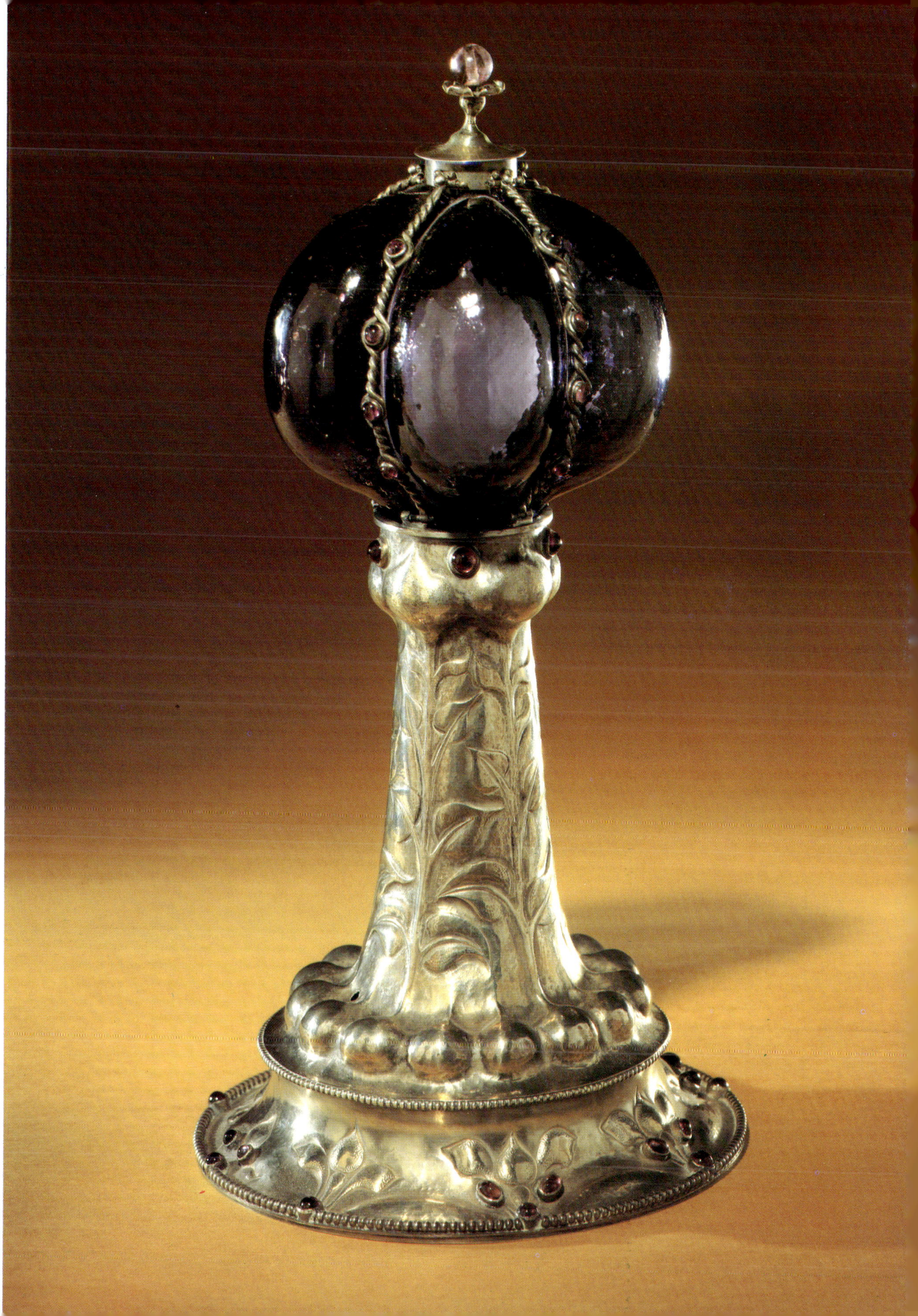

XIX

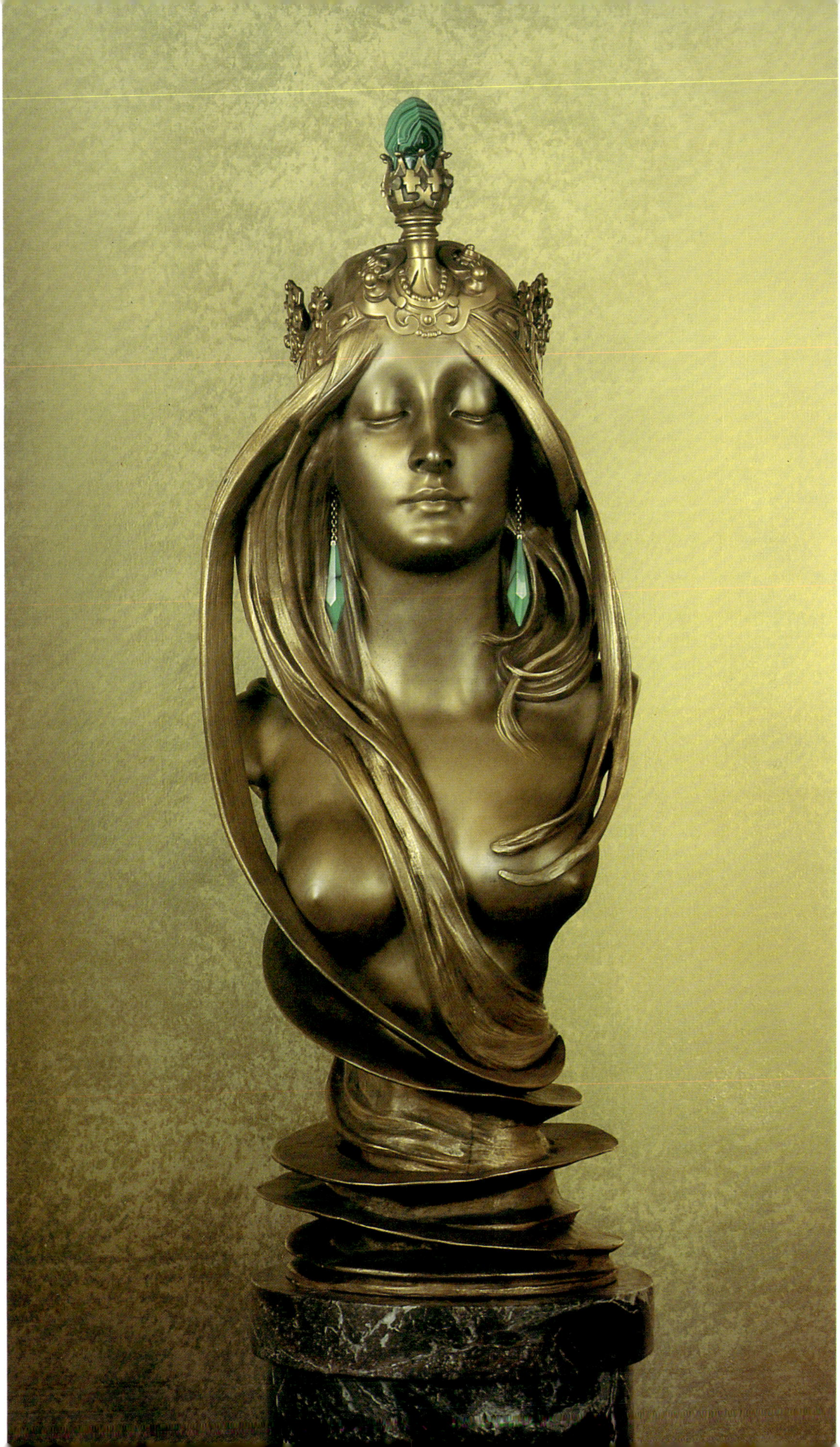

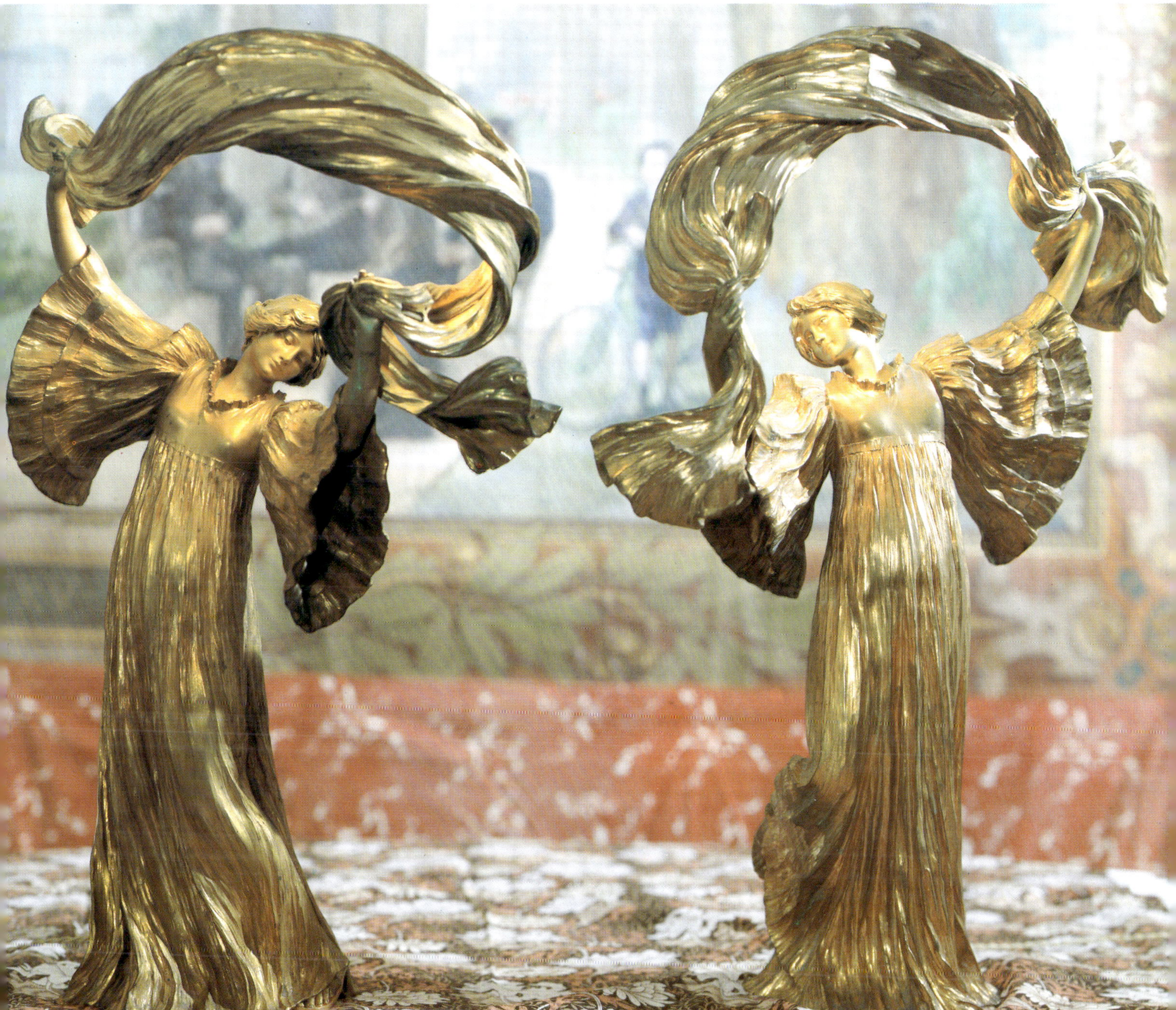

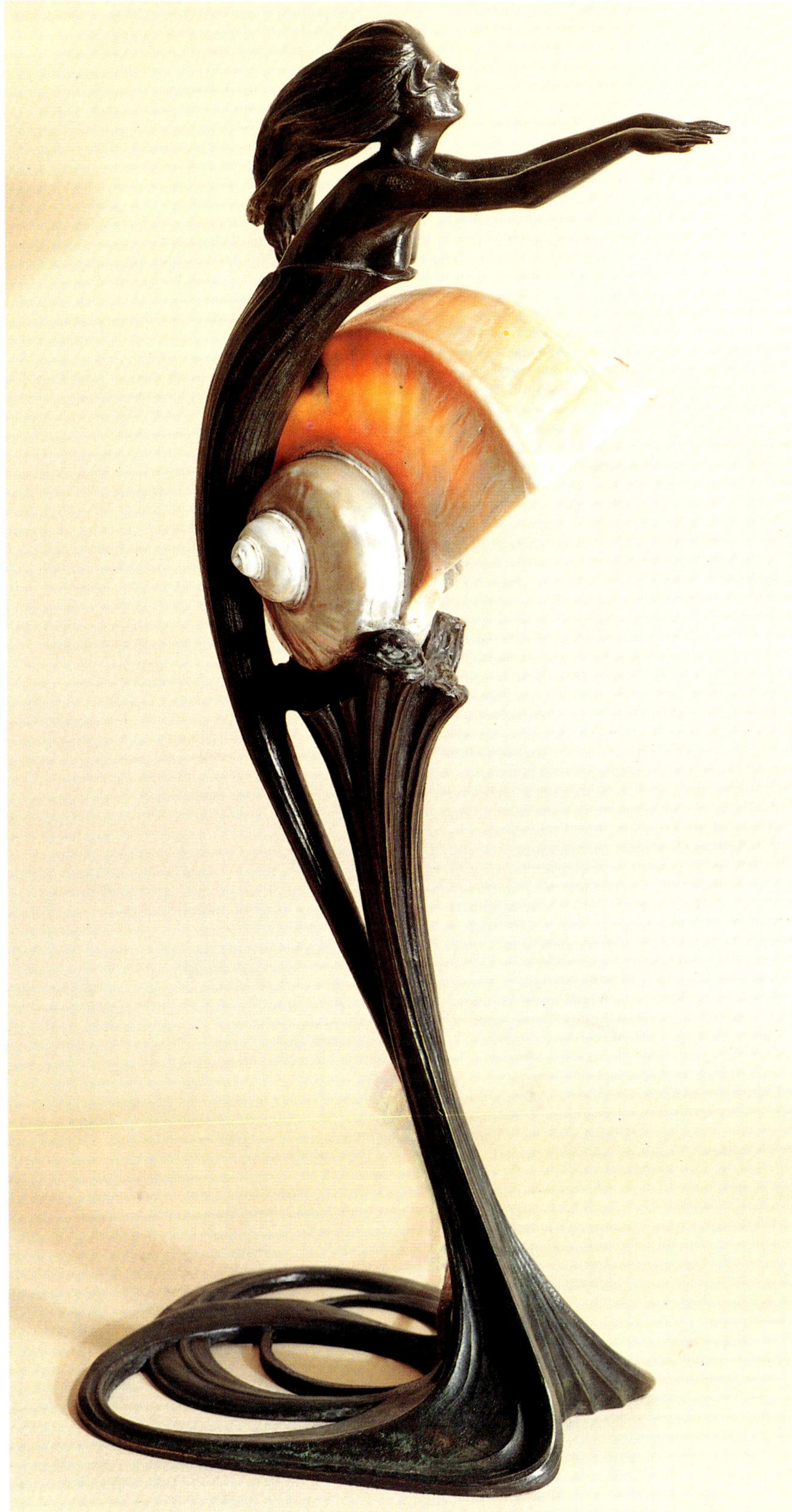

XXI

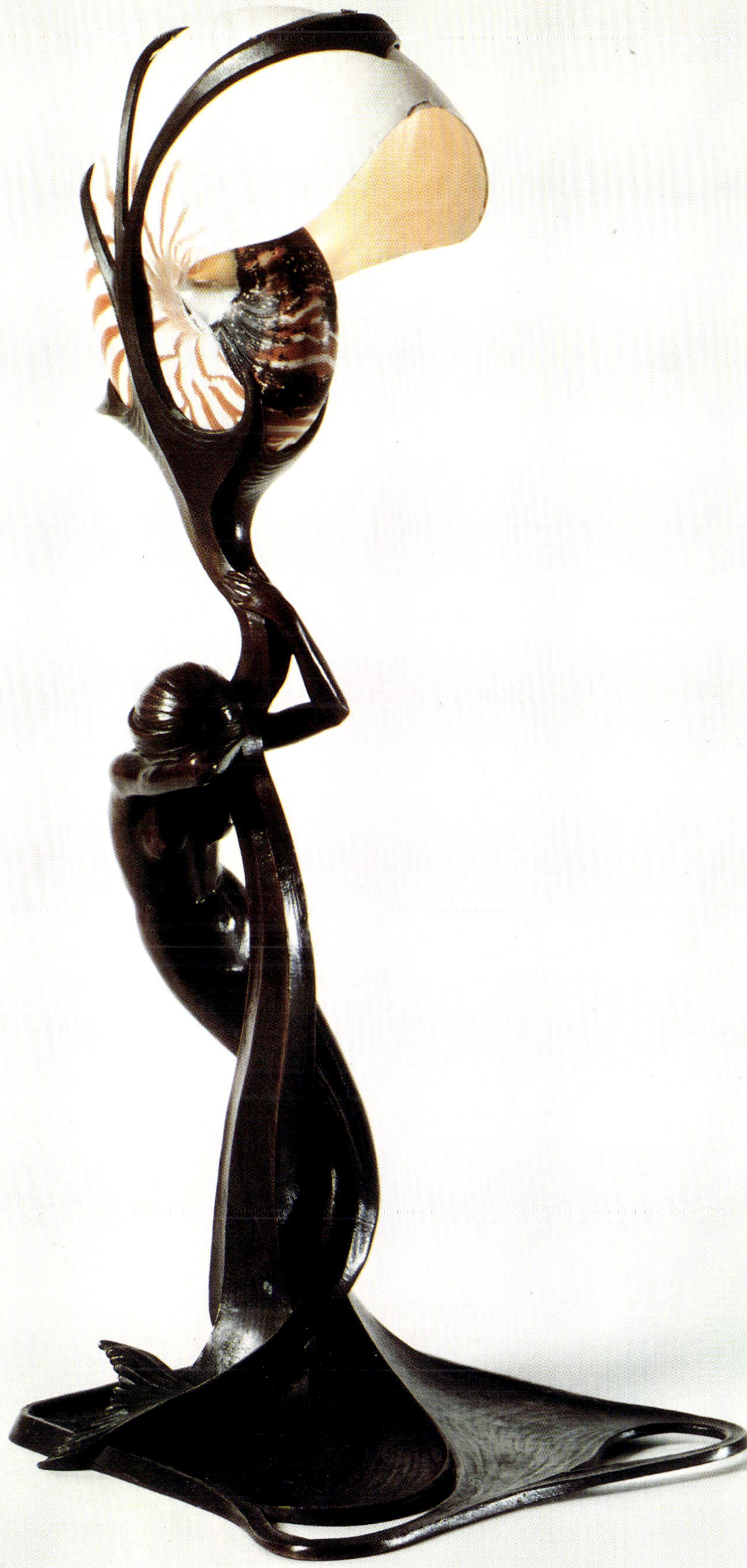

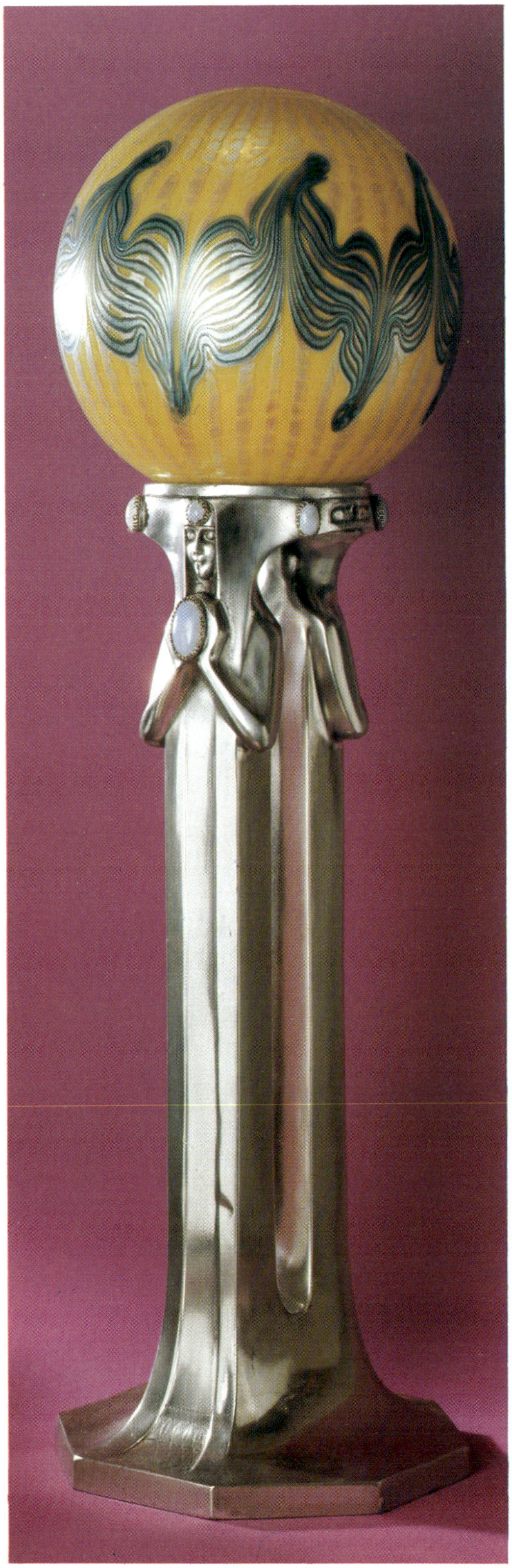

XXIII

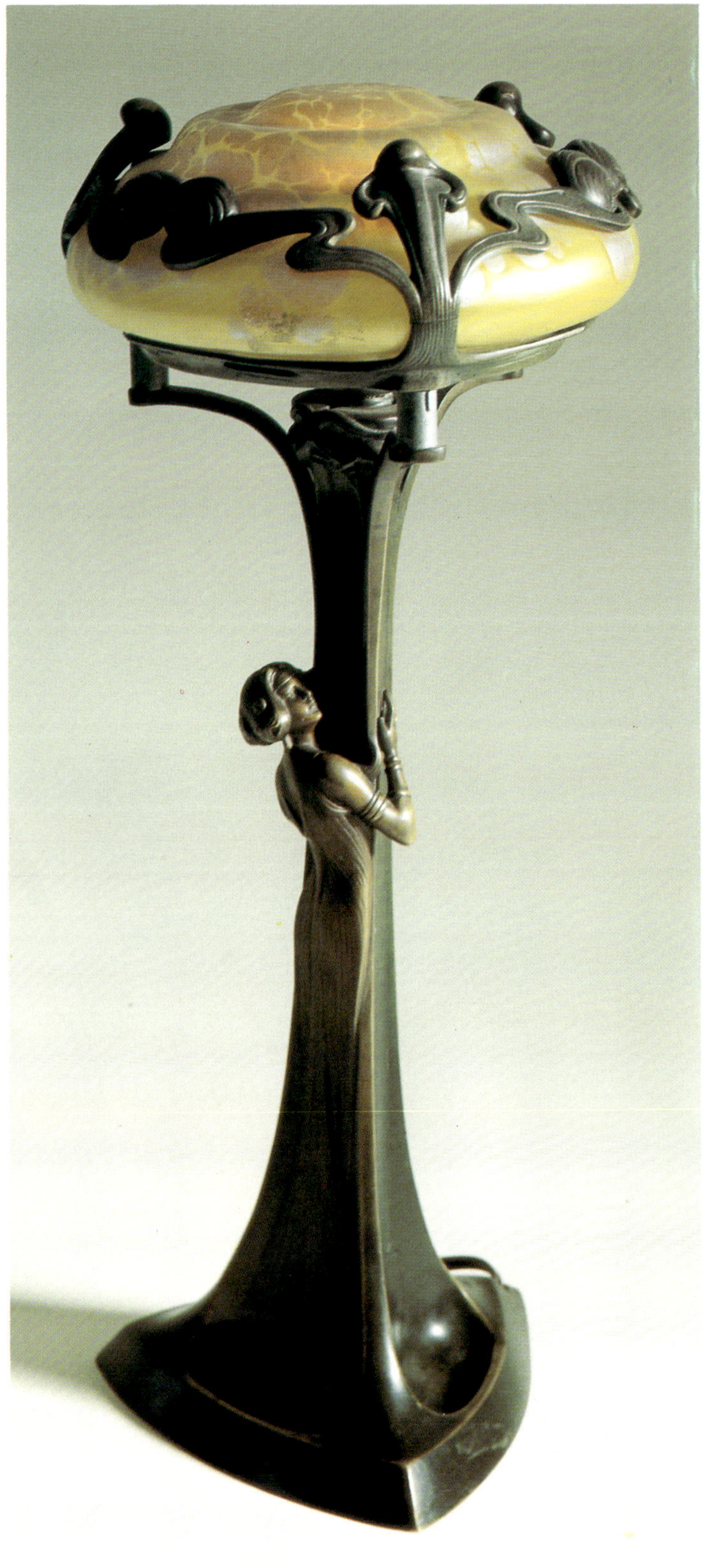

XXIV

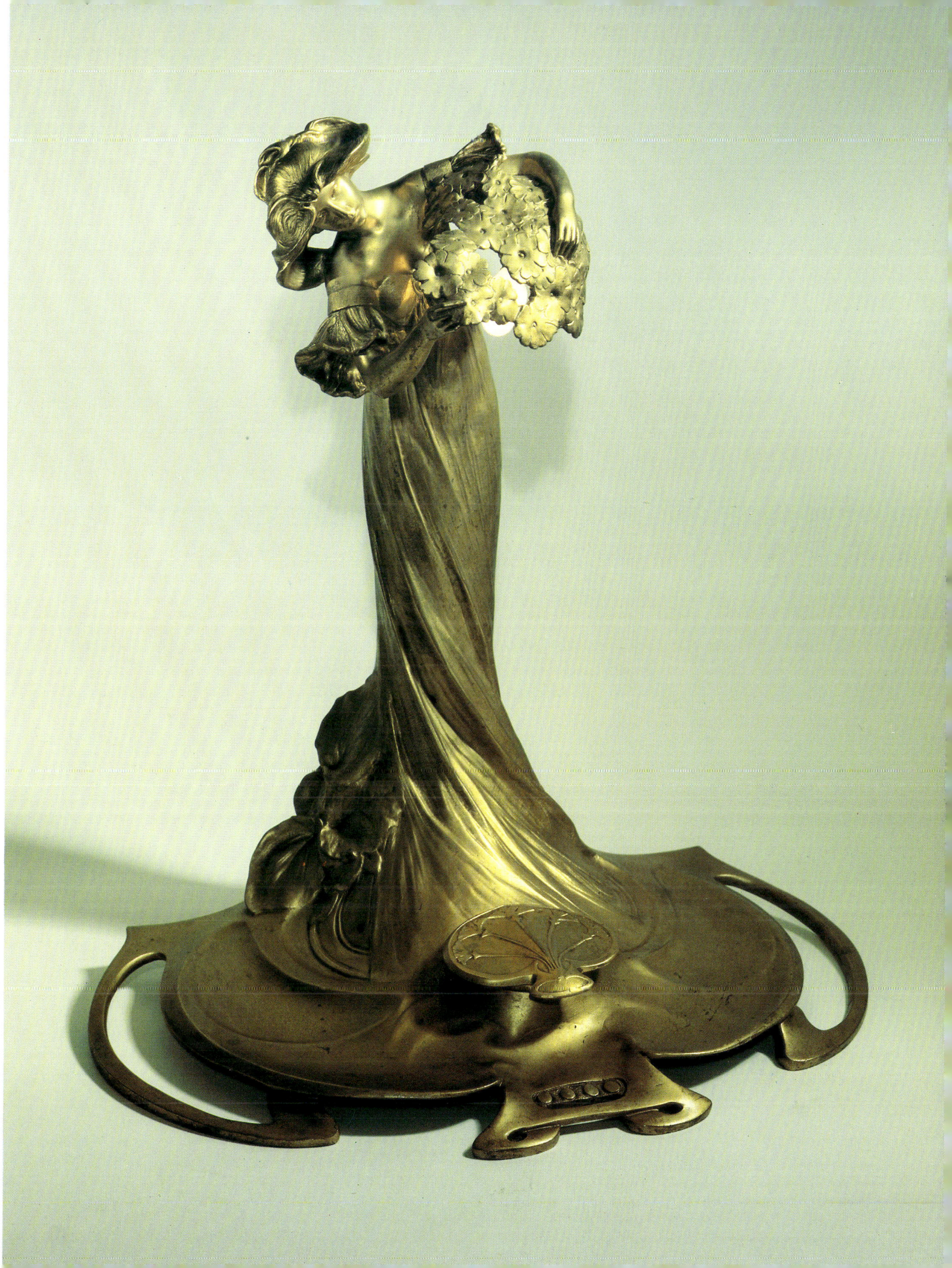

XXV

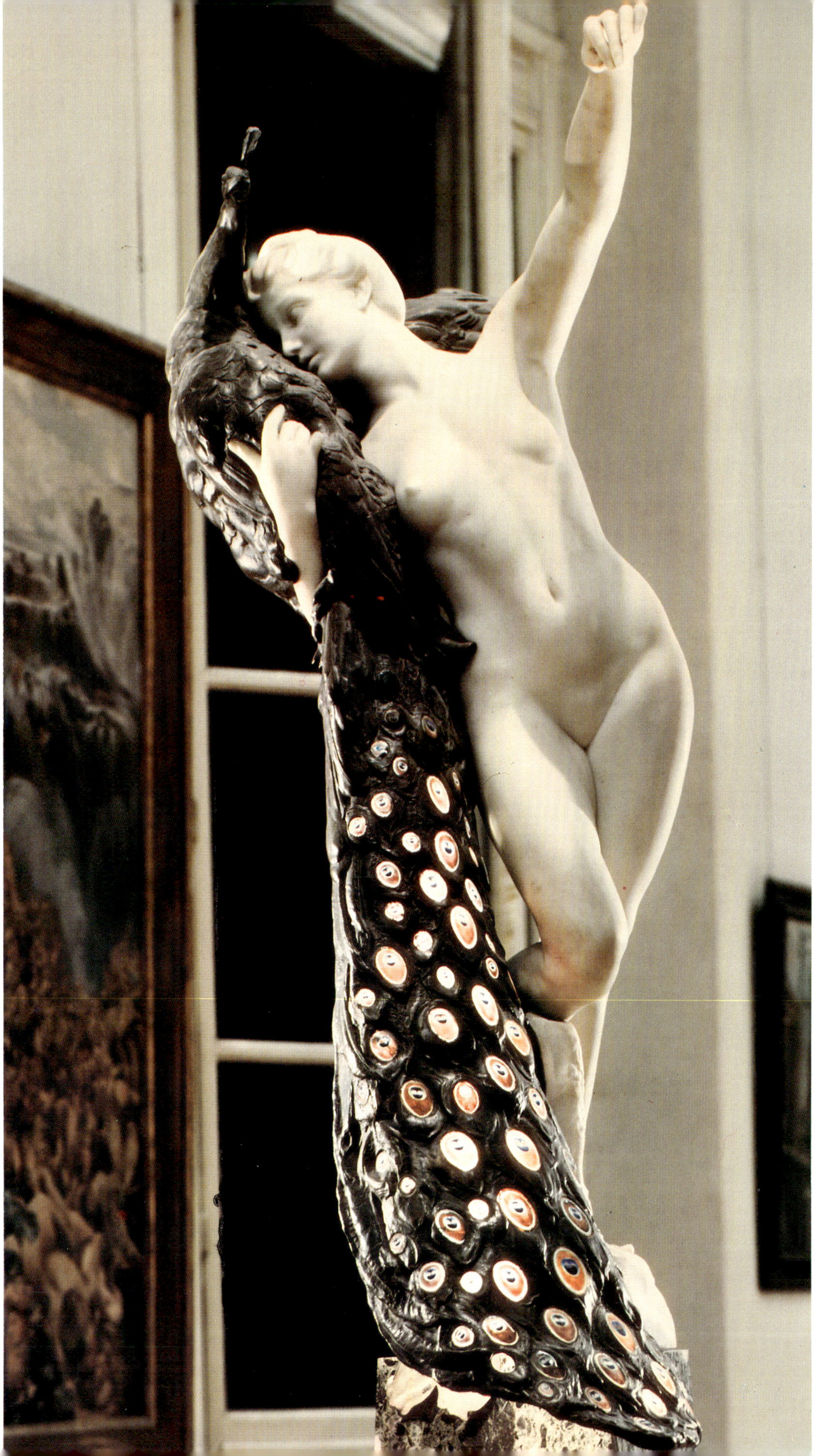

BENSON, W. A. S.

Benson was encouraged by William Morris in 1880 to set up a small workshop in Hammersmith, London, for the production of turned metal work. Although closely allied to Morris's aesthetic philosophies, Benson subscribed to one viewpoint which Morris consistently opposed – the use of mass-production machinery – and his designs for a wide range of household gadgets and utensils, such as coat-rack stands, firescreens, chafing dishes, music-stands, and electroplated tea kettles, were based on the potentialities of machine manufacture.

Benson is remembered primarily, however, as a designer and manufacturer of light fixtures. Working mainly in copper or brass, or a combination of the two, he produced a multiplicity of standard domestic lights, a range of which are illustrated in three catalogues that were published from his shop in New Bond Street, which he opened in 1887 and ran concurrently from then onwards with his factory at Hammersmith. Well-versed in the shibboleths of home illumination requirements, Benson offered specific fittings for each area of a house: the hall, corridors, stairwell, library, billiard-room, etc., and one of his catalogues contains a three-page list of suggestions for optimum lighting effects.

The lights themselves range considerably in style from traditionally styled electroliers and 'Flemish and Georgian pendants in brass with candle tubes' to the machine-made table oil lamp with its shade composed of a series of copper fins mounted on a brass frame (originally marketed at £4.15s.), a model of which is now in the Victoria and Albert Museum. The design for this lamp, while certainly not 'Art Nouveau' by the criteria now commonly applied, did constitute a 'new art' by English standards.

The shades of Benson's fixtures were in such diverse materials as satin-finished flint glass, glazed muffled glass, and silk with white flounces. Mountings were likewise varied. Brass, copper, steel or Florentine bronze, and the firm's new 'Orichalcum' metal were available to be used as specified by the customer, with frosted, antique, hammered, or electroplated finishes. The only contemporary, internationally recognized English designer of light fixtures, Benson sold his work through Bing's Maison de l'Art Nouveau in Paris and it was illustrated in *L'Art Décoratif* in 1898 and 1901. Invariably incorporating clean, simple lines (the *Magazine of Art* in 1896 described his work as 'palpitatingly modern'), most of his lamp designs are nevertheless traditional before they are modern, safe before they are adventurous.

A Benson table-lamp, with a conical shade set on a fluted brass base, was sold in 1974 in Versailles for FF 1,450 ($280).

KNOX, ARCHIBALD

Born and educated in Douglas, Isle of Man, Archibald Knox moved to London in the mid-1890s, where he found employment in Dr Christopher Dresser's design studio, and later in that of Arthur Liberty.

In 1899, when Liberty authorized the firm's range of 'Cymric' silverware and jewellery, Knox was one of the artists commissioned to produce designs. Because of Liberty's strict policy of anonymity, Knox's name does not appear either in the firm's catalogues or on individual pieces, but it is known that he produced more than 400 designs for the company. Therefore attribution is usually limited to the formula 'Probably designed by A. Knox', although his authorship is certain in several pieces.

The Celtic inspiration for Liberty's Cymric silverware was singularly appropriate to Knox who, through his Manx upbringing, had been steeped in Celtic art, and the disciplined interlacing of ornamentation found on Manx and Cornish crosses and in illuminated manuscripts is evident in his work. Knox's designs were so crisply defined that all but the most costly and prestigious could be die-struck. In 1903, when the firm's 'Tudric' pewterware was launched in the same style, Knox extended his designs to the new alloy.

Among the range of his spectacular gem-set jewellery and pewter and silver tableware, were several candelabra and candlesticks, always of firm line and boldness.

The prices of Knox candlesticks or candelabra fall within the same range as that of his other pewterware objects, from £50 to £80 ($95 to $155). Those that have enamelled decorations are likely to be more expensive.

LIBERTY'S

'The absence of ledgers, day book and correspondence relating to the Cymric and Tudric schemes has made it usually difficult and frequently impossible to document the authorship of designs. As is by now well-known, the firm never published the names of the artists working for them in their own catalogues.' (*Liberty's 1875–1975*; exhibition catalogue, Victoria and Albert Museum, July–October 1975, p. 15.)

Despite the policy of blanket anonymity, it has been possible for Mrs Shirley Bury, of the Metalwork Department at the Victoria and Albert Museum, to assess, with a degree of confidence, that most of the light fixtures (candlesticks and candelabra) marketed under the Liberty brand-name were designed certainly by Archibald Knox and, most probably, also by Rex Silver. Various other designers, such as Christopher Dresser, Oliver Baker, Bernard Cuzner and Jessie M. King, were occasionally commissioned to produce designs for the Liberty range of Cymric and Tudric ware.

The Cymric silverware, with its Celtic motifs, came first, in 1899. This was mostly executed by the firm of W. H. Haseler of Birmingham by a mass-production, die-stamping process, after which the metal was often given a 'hammered' finish to lend it a hand-crafted appearance. Another Birmingham company – the silversmiths W. Hutton & Sons – likewise supplied Liberty's with both silver flatware and hollow ware, though not in comparable quantities.

In order to provide a cheaper line than silver, Arthur Liberty extended the same designs to his Tudric pewterware. Pewter, an alloy of tin and copper which, prior to its revival and legitimization by Art Nouveau exponents, had been considered as *ersatz*, was to reach a wider buying public. It was Knox and Silver, in their clean and utilitarian Celtic designs for pewter candlesticks and candelabra – often with *repoussé* or *martelé* finishes and gem-set – who helped significantly to elevate the objects' worth above the alloy's innate value.

One pair of Liberty & Co. pewter candlesticks, impressed Tudric, sold for £55 ($110) in London in 1974. The same pair brought $305 (£150) in New York in the next year.

MacDONALD, FRANCES and MARGARET

The 'Glasgow Four' evolved from both marital and creative liaisons: Margaret MacDonald married Charles R. Mackintosh and her younger sister, Frances, married Herbert McNair. The sisters worked independently and also together in producing a wide range of art- and craft-objects: watercolours on vellum, painted gesso and mother-of-pearl plaques, 'Honesty' and 'Vanity' mirrors in beaten tin, and embroidered and linen appliquéd panels. These were often incorporated in the interiors of the houses designed by their architect husbands.

Their distinctly attenuated style was on the fringe of Art Nouveau, and on occasion generated an almost mystical and ghostly – even ghoulish – effect. Although acclaimed in Germany and Austria, this received a hostile response in London. An example of this style can be seen in the *repoussé* back-panels of their candle sconces – a charming form of ambience lighting which they appear to have made their own preserve. In addition, Frances produced candlesticks in beaten brass.

None of the MacDonald sisters' light fixtures has come on to the Art Nouveau market in recent years. It is therefore difficult to estimate what such objects would fetch, but certainly this would be considerably in excess of the objects' intrinsic value.

MACKINTOSH, CHARLES RENNIE

Mackintosh's contribution in the field of domestic lighting evolved from his concept of a totally integrated environment; to this end he turned his hand with equal readiness to friezes, plaques, ladderback chairs, hall chimes, silverware, and chandeliers to ensure that everything was *en suite*. In both the clean, yet austere, interplay of the horizontals and verticals of his architecture and the same variables evident in his mural decorations – the latter softened with stylized motifs of Celtic and medieval Scottish mythology – can be seen the Mackintosh idiom, one which was to act as a lodestar for the Vienna *Secession* at the same time as it steered away his compatriots.

The light fixtures in Mackintosh's buildings all bear an individual stamp, although they are, on average, less identifiably 'Mackintosh' than most of his decorative objects. They can be seen in Glasgow, at the School of Art, Mackintosh's studio flat at 120 Main Street, the house that he designed at 34 Kingsborough Gardens, and in the inimitable Ingram Street tea-rooms of Miss Cranston. Outside Glasgow, there are examples in 'Hill House' and 'Windyhill'.

For the most part these fixtures are chandeliers: clusters of sheet steel lamps in the Glasgow School of Art Library, brass chandeliers in the Board Room in the same building, sheet metal and coloured glass suspended lights in the entrance hall at 'Hill House', the large (and less successful) crystal chandelier in 'The Willow' tea-rooms.

For his own studio flat he designed two pairs of candlesticks; and another pair (1904–05), with ebonized wooden columns and silver nozzles, were shown in the 1968 Mackintosh exhibition at the Victoria and Albert Museum, where a rare and later (*c.* 1917) wooden standard lamp from 78 Derngate Street, Glasgow, was also displayed.

His preferred materials were sheet metal and brass, often inset with panels of coloured glass. It is unfortunate that the finished articles are infinitely inferior in their execution to his original designs. Mackintosh's brief stopped short of production; but the exposed channels of the H-frame lead cames that house the glass panels and their shoddily soldered joints represent a stark affront to the crispness and clarity of his blueprints. Anybody who has examined the virtuosity of the leading in a Tiffany Studios' glass lampshade would rightly be appalled.

Mackintosh's furnishings fetch premium prices on today's market. An armchair of his brought £9,200 ($18,000) at auction in London in 1975. It is unlikely, however, that any Mackintosh light fixtures will appear on the market; most of them are still in their original settings in buildings which have had a preservation order placed on them.

SILVER, REX

After having opened his own studio in 1880, Arthur Silver was commissioned by Liberty's, up until his untimely death in 1896, to provide wallpaper, chintz, and cretonne designs. On his death, management of the studio passed to Harry Napper and later to his eldest son, Reginald (Rex). It was he who became an important designer of textiles, silver and pewter for Liberty's around 1900.

Rex Silver, at twenty years of age one of the first London designers (along with Bernard Cuzner and Jessie M. King) to be incorporated into Liberty's Cymric scheme, was joined by Archibald Knox, with whom he shared a close affinity, as can be seen from the two artists' surviving designs. Like Knox, he designed such household utensils as silver clocks, bowls and candlesticks, the latter possessing considerable elegance and dignity. Attribution is still exceedingly difficult. Information made available to Mrs Shirley Bury of the Metalwork Department at the Victoria and Albert Museum since the 1975 Liberty's centenary exhibition suggests that Knox may well have worked for a time in the Silver Studios; if this is true, then designs previously attributed to Rex Silver may, in fact, have been made by Knox.

FRANCE

In deciding whom to include from the multitude of French *fin-de-siècle* designers and artists who applied themselves to lighting, I have drawn the line *above* Gilbert Péjac and G. Guinier and *below* Lucien Alliot. Analysis of the annual Parisian Salon catalogues shows that electricity drew on virtually every talent in Paris, and in Nancy its appeal was almost as pervasive. Of those whose work is not covered here, the following deserve at least mention: Eugène Colonna, who designed various lamps and candlesticks for La Maison Moderne; De Vez (pseudonym of De Varreux, director of the Pantin Cristallerie), D'Argental, Delatte, and Richard, for their cameo table-lamps; Eugène Vallin and Jacques Gruber at Nancy for, respectively, their billiard-table lights and chandeliers; Alexandre Charpentier and Villé Vallgren for their gilt-bronze wall-brackets; Georges Gardet for his illuminated *animalier* bronzes; Firmin Bate for his charming *flambeaux*; the five sculptors in the Moreau family; and Théodore Lambert for various fixtures. Of special note, however, are the lamps of Péjac and Guinier, both of whom exhibited regularly at the Salons and at the 1900 International Exposition.

ALLIOT, LUCIEN

A student of the sculptor Barrias, Lucien Alliot exhibited his busts, statuettes, and groups through the Société des Artistes français Salons from 1903. (As late as 1934 he was elevated to the Société's jury on sculpture, a post he held till 1939.) Although he is best known for his 1905 'Violoncelliste' statue and 1920 'A l'Enfance' public park monument, both in plaster, he did a substantial number of small bronzes – often silvered or *vert-de-gris* – which were wired for electric lighting. These occasionally appear for sale in the Paris flea-markets and in major auction houses. His preferred theme was the standard *femme-fleur*, whom he often depicted as draped and holding light sources disguised as musical instruments, such as frosted glass cymbals or drums, which when illuminated emitted a pleasant yet non-functional light.

Since he was not an important sculptor, Alliot's lamps fall within the lower price range of Art Nouveau objects. His signature on his bronzes is often misread, and appears in auction catalogues as 'Allio*n*'.

An Alliot sculptural lamp brought FF950 ($185) in Nancy in 1973. In 1975 a larger model fetched FF1,550 ($315) in Paris.

BOUVAL, MAURICE

Well to the fore among those bronze-workers who, at the turn of the century, 'adapted' traditional sculpture into *garnitures de cheminée*, inkwells, letter openers, etc., Bouval is, if anything, underrated. He was a champion of the Art Nouveau woman-flower hybrid, and among the many small objects in his repertoire, there are several that bear the stamp of the *petit-maître*.

After studying under the grand-master Alexandre Falguière, Bouval exhibited through the Société des Artistes français and La Maison Goldscheider. His bronzes, which were cast by at least three different founders – Colin, Jollet, Thiebaut *frères* – combined sensuous nymphs, water lilies, lotuses, and poppies with a sometimes strong suggestion of symbolism and the supernatural. In the heavy-lidded eyes of his 'Ophelia' bust, the mystique of his 'Le Secret' statuette (no doubt inspired by Fix-Masseau's on the same theme several years earlier), and the trance-like state of the maidens in his 'Dream' and 'Obsession' candelabra, there is something of Poe's hallucinatory fantasy.

Bouval designed a wide range of light fixtures: wall-brackets, candelabra, candlesticks (such as his bronze 'Tristesse' exhibited at the 1897 Salon of the Société des Artistes français, and the pair of gilt-bronze *flambeaux* shown by Goldscheider at the 1900 international exposition), and table-lamps.

Bouval's bronze and gilt-bronze figures are expensive. Most small and medium-sized ones bring more than $750 (£400) in New York, and if they incorporate electric bulbs, the price is likely to be in excess of $2,000 (£1,100).

BRANDT, EDGAR

It was between 1900 and 1905 that Edgar Brandt laid the foundation for his subsequent emergence as the pre-eminent ironsmith of the 1920s. At the age of twenty, and while still in the shadow of Emile Robert, he began to exhibit his ironwork through the Société des Artistes français, the Salon d'Automne and, by 1910, the Société des Artistes Décorateurs. His delicacy of design and technical dexterity developed rapidly and were increasingly acclaimed by the critics. Wrought-iron doors, grille work, firedogs, lamps and candelabra proved enormously popular; it was only his essays in the fields of jewellery and, briefly, wooden furniture that met with some criticism. Brandt's early light fixtures were similar in concept to the rest of his metalwork repertoire. Botanically inspired, the mounts for his chandeliers combine linear fluidity with leaf-and-bud decoration, his favourite motifs being eucalyptus and maidenhair fern. It was during this period (in 1905 a chandelier by Brandt with a blown Daum shade was illustrated in the December issue of *L'Art Décoratif*) that Brandt and the Daum brothers set up the reciprocal commercial arrangement whereby the latter would produce the glass shades for Brandt's light fixture mounts, and vice versa. This partnership was to last – apart from the hiatus created by World War I – well into the Art Déco era.

A pair of Brandt wall-brackets was sold at Versailles in 1972 for FF800 ($160). Brandt's work tends to obtain higher prices when it incorporates Daum glass shades.

CAUSSÉ, JULIEN

Caussé rarely deviated from his chosen themes: women and flowers. Best known for his 'Fée des Glaces' (Ice Fairy), Caussé's repertoire of small bronzes was marketed through the Société des Artistes français and the Maison Eugène Blot, and consisted of busts, statuettes, visiting-card trays, and sculptural lamps in bronze, marble, stone and pewter.

His lamps, often with mythological or allegorical titles, are invariably of a young woman with electric bulbs housed around her head or body. The placing of the bulbs often seems arbitrary – as if, after completion of the sculpture, they had been tacked on simply to brighten the whole composition. Examples of such lamps, like those of Alliot, find their way at regular intervals into flea-markets and leading auction houses.

In 1973, a three-light Caussé metal lamp entitled 'Le Chardon' (The Thistle) brought FF 800 ($160) in Paris.

CHALON, LOUIS

Chalon was an artist whose talents in the fine and applied arts ranged considerably wider than the bronzes and sculptural lamps for which he is best known. A student of Jules Lefebre and Boulanger, Chalon was initially a painter, exhibiting classically inspired canvases at the annual Salons of the Société des Artistes français from the early 1880s. By 1900, as shown by an article in the *Revue des Arts Décoratifs*, he had also become an accomplished illustrator (for *Le Figaro* and for editions of Rabelais and Balzac), a gem-setter, a couturier, ceramicist and sculptor. In 1898 he was asked to do a series of *trompe-l'œil* illustrations intended to give the impression of white-and-blue porcelain, and decided, after several unsatisfactory attempts, to model them first in painted wax. The result was so charming that further models for other objects followed, and these, in turn, became the maquettes for an extensive range of bronzes, which were often cast by the founder Louchet. Of such early sculptural attempts, the critic in *L'Art Décoratif* wrote in 1901 that Chalon was 'One of the hopes of the applied arts. The first works coming from his hands both have personality and are unforeseen. They recall the colourist rather than affirm the sculptor. The exactitude of proportion is frequently sacrificed to the aim of *sveltesse* and slender elegance; thus the attempt to adapt to the three-dimensional is not always successful.'

In the world of Art Nouveau small bronzes, however, proportionality was not of overriding concern; Chalon's portrait busts, vase of the Hesperides, inkwells, clocks, and chased and silvered watering can give evidence of a talent and style that are easily mistakable for those of Salon colleagues such as Bouval, Michelet, Théodore Rivière, and Caussé.

The *femme-fleur* was a popular theme in Chalon's lighting pieces. Half-naked bronze nymphs or naiads bear torches or are enveloped by flowers whose petals, predictably, house electric bulbs. These, like his other objects, were frequently given symbolist titles such as 'Thoughts', 'Repose', or 'Towards the Light'. In 1902 he designed two lamps in marble: 'Butterflies' and 'Woman with Poppies'.

Chalon's bronzes, including his lamps, are expensive. Prices in London range from £300 to £500 ($575 to $950) for a small or medium-sized Chalon object.

CHÉRET, JOSEPH

Joseph Chéret, younger brother of the famous poster designer, Jules, was a sculptor who served his apprenticeship under Vallois and Carrier-Belleuse (whose daughter he married). He made his Salon debut in 1863, and in 1887 became director of the modelling studio at Sèvres, a post he held until his death.

A transitional artist, his style was partly Neoclassical and partly Art Nouveau. His designs for bronzes, executed by the Paris founder Soleau, included putti and cherubs in full or high relief, who frolic among irises and water lilies (whose corollas sometimes house electric bulbs). He designed several light fixtures for Soleau – mainly wall-brackets, two of which were entitled 'Enfants aux colliers' and 'Empire'.

Though he died in 1894, several of his works are signed and dated 1900, and even 1904. Soleau evidently saw, after Chéret's death, that his themes were increasingly in vogue, and therefore had several of the original range of bronzes recast from maquettes still in his foundry. This is substantiated by an article in *Art et Décoration* on the electric light fixtures at the 1900 Exposition Universelle; reference is made to a Soleau exhibit 'from a model by Joseph Chéret'.

The scarcity of Chéret's sculpture adds to its price. The fuchsia lamp illustrated was on sale in Paris in 1975 for FF6,500 ($1,400).

DAMPT, JEAN-AUGUSTE

A generation older than most of those who applied their talents to the Art Nouveau movement around 1900, Jean-Auguste Dampt had already, by 1876, attended the Schools of Fine Arts in both Dijon and Paris, and made his debut at the Salons. Primarily a sculptor, he switched readily from marble to stone to wood to ivory, and proved one of the period's most versatile mixed-media practitioners, exhibiting furniture, sculpture and light fixtures at the annual Salons of the Société Nationale des Beaux-Arts and 'L'Art dans Tout' exhibitions.

Remembered mostly for his superlative 1894 'La Fée Melusine et le Chevalier Raymondin' (a group of a knight in steel armour kissing a jewel-encrusted ivory maiden) and his wood-and-ivory 'Paix du Foyer' statuette four years later, Dampt was to establish himself with the series of orchid chandeliers and wall-brackets that he was commissioned to design by the Maison Beau for the latter's display at the 1900 international exposition. The critics were jubilant: Monsieur Beau – who had, in addition to Dampt, the talents of Péjac and Giraldon to draw on for the designs of various chandeliers that he marketed through the exposition – promptly had the Dampt series mass-produced. This event was commented on by an art critic in *L'Art Décoratif pour Tous*, in 1902 (*i.e.*, two years afterwards when the same range of lights were reintroduced, this time by way of the Société Nationale des Beaux-Arts):

> It is disturbing to have to use the word 'chef-d'œuvre' to qualify contemporary productions, but one must say that Dampt has produced some definitive works. This year he exhibits a lamp in gilt-bronze and cut glass for electric lighting. This

> is the property of a manufacturer who, without doubt, will reproduce it in large quantities. The thought of vulgarization is, of course, alarming, as this piece would certainly be more appropriate in a museum than as one of an edition of industrial bronze light fixtures.

This highlighted the dilemma facing all contemporary critics: how to lead the craftsman into the technological age, while reconciling themselves to the fact that the object would subsequently be reproduced by assembly-line methods to the point of vulgarization.

Very little of Dampt's work has reached the market in recent years, so it is difficult to estimate its value. Certainly those fixtures of his orchid series which have survived – one is in a Hamburg museum, others in a private collection in Germany – are worth at least FF 7,000 ($1,450) each.

DAUM, AUGUSTE and ANTONIN

Jean Daum fled his native Bitche in Lorraine when it was annexed by Germany in 1870 and settled in Nancy. It was here, following a series of unsuccessful business ventures, that he emerged in 1878 in the unlikely role of head of the Verrerie de Nancy. Joined later by his two sons, Auguste (in 1879), and Antonin (in 1887), Daum extended the firm's initially rather dull table- and domestic glassware range into the field of art glass.

To Auguste fell the administrative and financial responsibilities, and to Antonin, trained as an engineer, the production. It is a misconception, therefore, to picture the Daums, like Gallé, as artist/craftsmen who executed their own designs in glass. Professional men (though they no doubt quickly acquired a working knowledge of the various glassmaking techniques), theirs was the task of assembling as creative and balanced a team of designers, artists and artisans as possible. Antonin himself, in fact, was to refer on several occasions to his own manual maladroitness.

During its early years, the firm included such widely known Art Nouveau exponents as Jacques Gruber (from 1894 to 1897), Henry Bergé (from 1900), and Amalric Walter.

No doubt initially influenced by Gallé, the Daums' early production of art glass was generally parallel, though inferior, to Gallé's: for example, vases, bowls, *solifleur* vases, and lamps were executed by cameo, engraving and enamelling techniques. Gradually, however, a more sophisticated and individual repertoire of shapes and finishing techniques emerged: 'martelage' (a hammered finishing effect), 'jaspé' (mottled glass), 'intercalaire' and *pâte de verre*. Daum *frères* also gradually developed their own palette. More sober than that of Gallé, its emphasis was usually on the autumnal range: ochres, oranges, sepias and burgundies.

Although Gallé's pre-eminence must at first have seemed daunting, it was the Daums' lamps – produced mainly from 1893 in acid-etched cameo (and often finished on an engraver's wheel) – that first established the firm's innovative qualities. They were widely acclaimed by the critics for their *lampes-fleurs* at the 1900 international exposition, and in an article in *L'Art Décoratif* (1903) Maxime LeRoy wrote, 'although inspired directly by Gallé, their contrivances for electric lights show the utmost originality'. In 1908, an enthusiastic critic wrote in *La Revue Lorraine Illustrée*, 'Inimitable: the happy and multiple combinations that come out of their studios . . . on the shades flights of bats, coleoptera and lepidoptera which come as if attracted by the light. Also, on a wrought-iron base, an eglantine in full bloom, and, on a hemispherical shade, the petals of a hedgerow rose.'

This touches on the two dominent themes in the firm's designs for its lamps. First, insects and night-creatures – which had until then been considered as too distasteful a theme for the decorative arts – and second, flowers: marguerites, crocuses, gentians, columbines, hyacinths and umbels are just a few of the floral anthology reproduced faithfully on their lamps.

While the Daums had a business arrangement with Louis Majorelle whereby they provided all the glass for his lamps and he the metalwork for theirs, they also had certain mounts for their light fixtures (and other glassware) executed from 1905 by Edgar Brandt, and, less frequently, by André Groult. In these last two cases, the bases appear to be supplementary to the shades and the finished objects have the earmarks of Daum creations. With Majorelle, however, and particularly in some flower-form lamps that bear the signatures of both ateliers, the central design concept appears to have been derived from that part of it executed in metal.

Examples of all forms of Daum *frères* light fixtures appear regularly in the major Art Nouveau centres. Prices range from FF 2,200 ($465) for small night lights to FF 4,500 ($950) and up for medium-sized cameo table-lamps.

DE FEURE, GEORGES

Georges de Feure was the most versatile of the Art Nouveau artists who made contributions in the decorative arts. Of Dutch parents, he became a protégé of Cheret's in Paris in 1890, and his boundless talent reached fruition in his appointment as head of the design department of Samuel Bing's Maison de l'Art Nouveau – a department that also included Eugène Colonna and Eugène Gaillard.

De Feure's style was based on safely proportioned masses to which was applied exquisite, yet conservative, ornamentation. From his lithographed posters, book illustrations, and gouache textile designs, to his jewellery, sculpted wooden furniture and wall hangings, the common denominator is refinement.

His range of designs for candelabra, candlesticks and table lamps executed by Bing's studios was wider than one might expect from the few that have been rediscovered to date. Some were illustrated in an April 1901 article in *L'Art Décoratif* on Bing's pavilion at the 1900 international exposition, with the following critical comment: 'the candelabra represented here, for example, show a union of very simple and rational elementary lines with those more fantastic, daring, and, needless to say, more exquisite in detail. Even the candlestick consisting of a straight stalk is a delicious object made with an exuberance of imagination in its simplicity.'

An article in *L'Art Décoratif pour Tous* in the following year shows a further range of his light fixtures: one a gilt-bronze three-branched electric light candelabrum, another a candlestick of stylized floral design with the calyx as a wax pan, and a third a bronze table-lamp with twin shades in puffed silk. All are very feminine; ideal to provide the soft ambience lighting for a boudoir.

De Feure did not remain in the commercial sphere after World War I, but took up the appointment of Professor of Decorative Arts at the National School of Fine Arts in Paris.

There have been several pairs of de Feure silvered two- and three-branched candelabra on the market recently in Paris and Brussels. In 1976 one pair sold for FF 2,625 ($525), another for FF 2,375 ($475).

DE JARNY, PAUL

Paul Brindeau de Jarny, brother of the painter Edward de Jarny, is lighting's 'Invisible Man'. First exhibiting his metalware in the Salon of the Société Nationale des Beaux-Arts in 1901, he was still a Salon participant well into the 1930s. Yet, amazingly, virtually none of his prodigious output has been rediscovered.

A colleague of Brandt and Schenck, de Jarny designed and executed a wide range of home metalwork appliances that included keys and key escutcheons, doorhandles, *portemanteaux*, and – by far the most numerous – light fixtures. Models of these, in cast- and wrought-copper, wrought-iron and brass, were displayed at the Salons almost every year (at the 1908 Salon d'Automne alone, for example, de Jarny exhibited a chandelier, two wall-brackets, a desk-lamp, two *flambeaux*, and a candlestick). The themes, often in series, were drawn from nature. Ivy, camellia, dandelion, mimosa, vine, and plane tree were used as the basic designs for chandeliers, table-lamps, etc.; and de Jarny even devised a special twisted metal chain (to support his chandeliers) which he patented and exhibited separately from his lamps in each year's Salon.

Described by Léon Rioter in a 1902 *Revue des Arts Décoratifs* article as being without peer in his knowledge of the plastic qualities of the materials he used, de Jarny received similarly favourable reviews from other critics, although some found his style rudimentary and brusque. Where, then, have all these lamps gone? It is extraordinary, considering the quantities in which they were produced, and the sometimes exquisite quality of design, that de Jarny's lamps have defied discovery in the recent Art Nouveau revival. One reason may be that de Jarny neglected to sign his work effectively: in the case of one table-lamp that I have seen, the artist's name is scratched amateurishly on the metal underside of the base with a sharp instrument. It could easily have been erased; and indeed this may be what happened to the bulk of his output.

DUFRÈNE, MAURICE

So promising was Dufrène's talent that, in 1900, immediately on graduating from the Paris School of Decorative Arts, he was invited by Meier-Graefe to join the design staff of his La Maison Moderne, a position Dufrène held until the shop closed some years later. Few designers – perhaps only de Feure – were as successful in the range of work they undertook. His output in the early 1900s was prodigious, and he maintained his momentum well into the post-war era (see page 168). Since Dufrène applied himself to all aspects of interior design – from porcelain tableware to furniture, wallpapers, brocades, and tooled leather handbags (and much more besides) – it was natural that, as an *ensemblier*, he should have turned his versatility to home illumination.

Few, if any, of Dufrène's light fixtures appear to have survived, although at least a dozen of them were illustrated in contemporary decorative arts magazines between 1900 and 1913. Their theme is characteristic of all of his work (except for one of two chandeliers illustrated in *Deutsche Kunst und Dekoration*, 1902/3, in which the tangled flower supports remind one more of Guimard or Horta at their most rampant). Usually he showed quiet refinement and simplicity of form allied to a sober palette.

Dufrène's systematic progression from 1900 to 1925 can clearly be seen. Early table-lamps, in which patinated mounts housed enamelled reservoirs and pleated cloth shades, tend towards curvilinearism and floral stylization. By 1910, however, the foundations of his Art Déco designs are visible in the upturned shades of some of his table-lamps and in their sharply reduced ornamentation.

Dufrène's lamps were exhibited in La Maison Moderne (along with lamps by Paul Follot, Crespin, and Abel Landry), and at the Salon d'Automne, the Société Nationale des Beaux-Arts, and the Société des Artistes Décorateurs.

No Dufrène light fixtures have been placed on the Art Nouveau market in recent years, so it is difficult to predict what they would bring. His work, however, is of comparable value to that of de Feure.

FLAMAND, G.

Another of the legion of *bronziers* who turned their hand to small domestic ware around 1900, Flamand was less widely known than most. He does not appear to have exhibited at the annual Paris Salons at all, which meant that his work was unlikely to receive much appraisal from those art critics whose job it was to cover these exhibitions for the contemporary decorative arts reviews. It seems likely that he was not based in Paris, for the standard and style of his works were at least as good as many of the objects that were illustrated or reviewed in the editorial columns of such magazines as *L'Art Décoratif*.

His output could not, however, have been unsubstantial, for several leading European Art Nouveau collections now contain small Flamand gilt-bronze vases, silvered bronze night-lights, table-lamps, and wall-brackets. One of his pieces, entitled 'Le Fée Electricité', is something of an anomaly: it is not, as one might expect, a gilded fairy brandishing a naked bulb to herald in the new century, but, of all things, a small inkwell.

The theme of his light fixtures tends to be predictable: graceful young maidens support the nozzles for candle holders or electric sockets.

Flamand bronzes do not fetch high prices. In Paris a small Flamand table-lamp is likely to range in price from FF 1,300 to 1,750 ($275 to $365).

FOLLOT, PAUL

Joining Landry and Dufrène in 1901 as a designer for La Maison Moderne, Follot showed sense and sensibility in the range of domestic ware he designed. These qualities persisted throughout a career that lasted well into the 1920s.

Light fixtures were part of the range of furnishings that he designed for the music rooms, boudoirs, dining-rooms, etc., exhibited at La Maison Moderne, the Salon d'Automne, and the Société des Artistes Décorateurs. The materials he favoured were chased bronze and stained glass panels (the latter manufactured by the Maison Foy); in several chandeliers and table-lamps he used these in combination. When three-dimensional glass was required – for example, in domed shades – it was provided by the Daum *frères*. 'Safe' but uninspiring, his lamps were, on average, less successful than his furniture, which was often made of exotic woods with olive tree or ebony marquetry.

FRÉMIET, EMMANUEL

Frémiet's long career began in 1843 when he first exhibited his bronze animal groups at the Salon des Artistes français. He was the nephew and pupil of the celebrated sculptor François Rude.

Frémiet's association with both Art Nouveau and the realm of domestic lighting was a peripheral one. He is included here, however, because among the menagerie of marabou storks, butterflies, pelicans, orang-utangs and dragons that adorn the friezes, column capitals and antechamber floors of his clientele's buildings are at least three examples of his sculptural lighting. The one illustrated shows his pioneership in the use of the electric light in a way that would have been impossible with any form of combustion lighting at that time.

Two other lamps, both chandeliers, are illustrated in an 1898 *Art et Décoration* article on Frémiet by the critic Paul Vitry. One attractive aspect of Frémiet's work – conspicuously lacking in the *fin de siècle* applied arts – is his humour. Other than the grotesqueries and mask-jugs of the Martin brothers, there was virtually no lightheartedness in Art Nouveau.

GALLÉ, EMILE

Master glass craftsman, ceramicist, cabinet-maker, marquetarian in both glass and wood, and author (his dissertations on the applied arts were published, after his death, under the title *Les Ecrits pour L'Art*), Gallé was the founder and driving force of the School of Nancy, which was formed in 1901. With nature as his inspiration, Gallé used an unmatched gamut of glassmaking techniques: enamelling (often *champlevé*), cameo (also known as *verre doublé*), *pâte de verre*, and – now considered the most collectable –

marqueterie sur verre. These were used to produce innumerable vases, lamps, perfume burners, snuff bottles, etc., that depicted all aspects of botanical, marine and entomological life.

Gallé's lamps constituted a major part of his glass production and included many of his most virtuoso pieces. All forms of decorative lighting were undertaken in the Gallé studios, from large chandeliers down to minute night lights, the technique most frequently employed being cameo glass. Gallé himself tried to participate in or oversee the entire production process while personally designing and executing all his major pieces. He used glass as a three-dimensional medium in which to express his affinity for naturalism, symbolism and surrealism; many of his creations were inspired by specific verses by contemporary writers such as Baudelaire, Mallarmé, Hugo, Maeterlinck, Zola, and his friend Robert de Montesquiou. Such lines became, in turn, vitrified citations that appeared on certain pieces known, consequently, as '*verreries parlantes*'.

The wooden, bronze, and wrought-iron mounts for Gallé's lamps were executed in a studio adjoining his *cristallerie*, while those (less frequently) in silver were commissioned from various workers in precious metals.

When Gallé died in 1904, the administration of his firm fell to his son-in-law, Pédrizet-Gallé, while Victor Prouvé took over the leadership of the School of Nancy. Without the inspirational genius and overall generalship of Gallé, the army of by then over 300 employees was put to reproducing commercially, and in bulk, many of Gallé's earlier creations. The firm ceased operating at the outbreak of World War I.

Despite the large number of Gallé lamps on the market, prices continue to remain high. A standard Gallé cameo table-lamp, which fetched FF 7,450 ($1,490) at auction in 1974, had by 1977 doubled in price. Several rarer pieces brought between FF 43,750 and FF 52,500 ($8,750 and $10,500) in Paris in 1976. A pair of mould-blown Gallé table-lamps sold in 1977 in the US for over $35,000 (£20,000).

GUIMARD, HECTOR

Believing, like Horta, that a building should constitute a complete environment, Guimard designed façades, furniture and even doorknobs, so that everything should be harmonious. At the 1903 Salon d'Automne and the Société des Artistes Décorateurs, he declared that he was an 'architect of art', a claim so preposterous to many of his contemporaries that general appreciation of his importance in the decorative arts has largely been posthumous. A graduate of the School of Decorative Arts and the School of Fine Arts, both in Paris, Guimard is best known for his series of cast-iron entrances for the Paris Métro stations. These, in their voluptuous and organic curvilinearism, are representative of his general style, which he claimed was determined by the three principles of logic, harmony and sentiment.

For the ensembles for such commissions in Paris as the Castel Béranger and Castel Henriette, Hôtel Mezzara, and the houses at 60 rue la Fontaine, 142 avenue de Versailles and 122 avenue Mozart (where he himself lived), Guimard designed numerous light fixtures. Some of these, which were executed under his direction in his own studio, are still *in situ*, while others are in private collections. Surprisingly, they lack the characteristic boldness of his other furnishings. One series of chandeliers, for example, consists of hanging strands of crystal rods interspersed with glass beads and long rectangular panels of blue and green transparent glass. The effect is Byzantine or Hispano-Moorish, quite incongruous with the abstract naturalism of, say, his pearwood cabinets or cast-iron cachepots. A standard floor-lamp now in a Paris collection, however, is more successful, incorporating an inverted metal shade on a sculpted wooden mount: a means of illumination that anticipated a style popularized by Art Déco lighting exponents.

Very little of Guimard's work has reached the Art Nouveau market in recent years. One of his Métro cast-iron panels brought £380 ($750) in London in 1975. It is probable that his chandeliers would bring at least £1,000 ($1,900) each.

JONCHERY, CHARLES

Jonchery was a student of Aimé Millet and Antoine Gauthier whose sculpture was exhibited at the Salons of the Société des Artistes français from 1883 to 1922. Despite such protracted exposure, however, very little biographical information exists on him; less, certainly, than is required to chronicle the history of an Art Nouveau artist whose small bronzes are still made available to collectors at public auctions and through antique dealers. Among his range of *objets d'art* were portrait medallions, busts, garniture clocks, candelabra and table-lamps. These were in plaster, bronze or marble. In 1903, Jonchery exhibited a table-lamp entitled 'The Wave'. Often identifiable by the characteristically insouciant expressions on the faces of his Art Nouveau maidens – a dominant theme – his work was not considered important by his contemporaries.

Jonchery's objects do not bring very high prices. A typical woman-flower bronze table-lamp fetched FF2,450 ($490) in Paris in 1976. A spelter three-piece garniture mantel set, comprised of a clock and two candelabra, brought $595 (£340) in New York in 1977.

LANDRY, ABEL

Born in Limoges, Landry attended that city's School of Decorative Arts before transferring to the School of Fine Arts in Paris, from which he graduated as an architect. Following a brief stint as a landscape painter and a sojourn in England during which he met and was influenced by William Morris, Landry returned to Paris to pursue his vocation as an architect. He received commissions for villas, apartments, and the building for Meier-Graefe's La Maison Moderne on the rue des Petits-Champs; and the last commission no doubt helped to influence Landry's decision to extend himself into the realm of interior decoration. He designed wallpapers, desks and chairs, marble chimney mantels and stained glass windows, some of which were executed and marketed through La Maison Moderne itself alongside the work of such colleagues as Van de Velde, Dufrène, Orazi and Follot.

Landry's style, similar to that of de Feure (critics frequently referred to their communality of taste), lacked superfluous ornamentation and was therefore easily adaptable to mass-production. An article in *The Studio* in 1904, referring to an ensemble of his exhibited through a group that called themselves 'la Poignée', praised his furniture for its 'simplicity and its fine and elegant appearance [which] is quite refreshing after the abracadabrant experiments with which we are, alas, only too familiar.' His designs for lamps were similarly refined. Wrought-iron chandeliers, gilt and silvered bronze ceiling-lamps, table-lamps and *flambeaux* were exhibited – in addition to La Maison Moderne – at the Société des Artistes Décorateurs and the Salon d'Automne between 1906 and 1913, and were marketed, after Meier-Graefe's shop closed, by Maison Déroullia et Petit, Grands Magasins de Printemps, and Maison Ballauf et Petitpoint.

The shades for such fixtures varied. Pleated cloth, panels of coloured glass, enamel and aquamarine crystal, are among the materials listed in contemporary Salon catalogues. For a good cross-section of Landry's earlier lamps see *Deutsche Kunst und Dekoration* (1902/3), pp. 179, 551 and 555.

Very few of Landry's light fixtures appear to have survived. None has reached the market in recent years, so it is difficult to predict what they would be worth today.

LAPORTE-BLAIRSY, LÉO

In the realms of Art Nouveau sculptural lighting, Léo Laporte-Blairsy was without peer – not so much for the innovative flair he showed in his compositions or for the technical virtuosity of their execution (although both of these are factors), but primarily because he was one of the first to use the newly commercialized incandescent bulb in a way that would have been impossible with combustion lighting. To place a gas mantle or paraffin wick inside his 'Balloon Seller', for example, would have been impossible. Like Emmanuel Frémiet and Gustav Gurschner, Laporte-Blairsy was quick to understand the electric light's infinite aesthetic possibilities for his chosen *métier*, sculpture – but he took them further than anyone else.

Born in Toulouse, Laporte-Blairsy was trained, like so many of his contemporaries, by Falguière, and made his debut at the Salon of the Société des Artistes français in 1887. Initially a sculptor and engraver of rather large monuments and busts, he later decided to reduce the scale of his work because, according to a critic in *L'Art* (1902), he felt that 'the twentieth century, to the gates of which electricity had triumphantly advanced, would revolutionize everything.'

This transition must have taken place by the late 1890s, as the sculptures that he exhibited from 1898 were mainly on a small scale. Not only lamps, but statuettes, vases, letter-openers and épergnes were produced in bronze, marble, plaster, and, for the Sèvres Manufactory, in white biscuit porcelain. In one year – 1903 – the Salon catalogue lists objects by Laporte-Blairsy in gold, silver and translucent enamel. Most of these were marketed by M. Houdebine, although one lamp in 1904, *La Voie Lactée*, was marketed by the founders Susse *frères*.

His lamps, or more accurately, illuminated sculptures, were his main area of concentration. The themes he used, described in 1903 by de Felice as 'luminous fantasies', represented a strange mixture of the anecdotal, the eclectic and Art Nouveau. Some, such as *La Fillette au Ballon*, which depicts a young girl holding up a balloon that she has just bought from the Magasins du Louvre, tell a story; others, fashioned either as Breton women or as a Greek dancer, are historically inspired; yet others, such as his *femme-fleur* wall-brackets, umbel and peacock table-lamps, are pure 1900. A critic in *Art et Décoration* in 1902 wrote:

> Laporte-Blairsy borrows from every age in history, all periods of legends, all the memories of decor and models in each of life's ages to raise them to the most logical and natural degree, and with a gentle grace, by the beauty of dazzling light.

Documentary evidence is available of at least seventeen different Laporte-Blairsy light fixtures, the whereabouts of many of which are now unknown. These are as follows:

Table-lamps: *L'Enfant au Ballon*, *Une Mime romaine*, *La Voie Lactée*, *La Marchande de ballons*, *La Porteuse de Seaux*, Statuette à lanterne (untitled), *L'ombellifère*, Greek dancer (untitled), *Femme à la Coquille*, *La Fée au Coffret*, *Vestale*, *Les Paons*, *Femme Chrysanthème*.

Wall-brackets: *Le Gui* (mistletoe), *Rose de Noël.*

Night-lights: *L'enfant à la lanterne*, *La Fillette au ballon*.

Laporte-Blairsy survived World War I and continued to exhibit at the Salons. In 1922 he showed a statuette that *The Studio* critic described as a fine 'Blairsy-Laporte'. He died the next year.

Laporte-Blairsy's sculptural lamps are in great demand. A silvered bronze version of his *La Voie Lactée* fetched £1,000 ($2,000) in London in 1974. A *Femme à la Coquille* lamp was sold in Paris in 1976 for FF9,625 ($1,925).

LARCHE, RAOUL

The son of a craftsman, Raoul Larche was a student of both Alexandre Falguière and Eugène Delaplanche at the School of Fine Arts in Paris, before making his debut, in 1881, at the Société des Artistes français. Though an accomplished sculptor, he was, like so many of his colleagues at the turn of the century, eclipsed by Rodin's shadow and appears to have adjusted his output towards mass-production castings of small bronzes rather than unique commissions.

An undated catalogue of a posthumous exhibition of Larche's works gives a full survey of his career, which was cut short in 1912 when he was run down by a car. The exhibition offered hundreds of examples of Larche's paintings and sculpture, the latter as varied in its subject-matter as in its materials. Busts of mythological deities, groups of peasant girls, figurines of sword-bearing youths and of naiads clasping conch- and triton-shells, were executed in stone, white biscuit porcelain (for the Sèvres Manufactory), pewter, bronze, and terracotta. Among the objects shown were eight light fixtures, cast by the founder Siot-Décauville, and listed as follows:

Table-lamps: *Libellule*, *Les abeilles*, *La danse*, *Loïe Fuller*, *L'éclair*, *Roses Tremières*, all in gilt bronze.

Ceiling-lamps: *La Comète*, *Les papillons*, both in bronze.

The list disproves the popular misconception that Larche's only sortie into the field of sculptural lighting was his lamps of Loïe Fuller.

The prices of Larche's 'Loïe Fuller' gilt-bronze table-lamps have rocketed. A single-bulb version which brought £1,300 ($2,600) in London in 1973 was on sale in New York in 1976 for $6,650 (£3,800). A two-bulb lamp, one of which sold in London in 1972 for £460 ($950), brought $8,750 (£5,000) in New York in 1976. Recent forgeries are ruining this market. However, a gilt-bronze casting of *Libellule* sold at Christie's New York in 1977 for $4,400 (£2,525), and a gilt-bronze signed Loïe Fuller sold at Monte Carlo in late 1977 for FF65,000 ($13,000).

LEDRU, AUGUSTE

Ledru studied under the sculptors Augustin Dumont and Jean Bannassieux. Along with Joseph Chéret and Raoul Larche, he was among the first artists to concentrate on that aspect of Art Nouveau which venerated the female form. Indeed, he had an overwhelming penchant for the motif of naked women; by 1893 his pewter objects were already garnished with naked bodies, some of which clasped the floriform nozzles of candlesticks or, sprouting dragonfly wings from their backs, acted as wall-brackets for electric lights.

Few Ledru bronze objects have survived, and of these only one or two are light fixtures. A casting of the illustrated Ledru candleholder brought FF1,675 ($335) in auction at Versailles in 1975.

LEGRAS AND COMPANY

This crystal company was founded in 1864 by Auguste J. F. Legras in Saint-Denis, near Paris. By 1900, under the management of François-Théodore Legras (who was succeeded, in turn, by Charles Legras in 1909), the firm was producing a wide range of tableware – mainly vases and, to a lesser extent, table-lamps – in cameo, enamelled, and intaglio-carved glass.

The lamps incorporate pleasant subject-matter – for example, pastoral scenes or seascapes – but are disappointingly predictable and unimaginative in form. They are mainly baluster-shaped columns on flared feet supporting domed shades. Their unvarying shape places them in that group of French table-lamps whose identity is virtually impossible to determine without looking at the signature, and which art critics frequently label disparagingly as 'imitation Gallé'.

Legras' colours, however, are softly pleasing. Because of their autumnal palette, the Legras landscapes stand out in relief against acid-etched pastel grounds to produce effects which, though never sensational, are totally balanced.

The Legras firm closed at the beginning of World War I and reopened afterwards under the name Verreries et Cristalleries de Saint-Denis et de Pantin Réunis.

Prices for a standard Legras cameo table-lamp of between 15 and 20 inches in height ranged between FF 3,075 and 4,375 ($615 and $875) in Paris in 1976.

LÉONARD, AGATHON

Agathon Léonard (real name Léonard-Agathon van Weydeveld) was born of Belgian parents in Lille, where he attended the Academy of Fine Arts. Settling in Paris, he became a member of the Société des Artistes français in 1887 and also, in 1897, of the Société Nationale des Beaux-Arts. Creator of portrait medallions, groups and statuettes in rose quartz and green Egyptian marble, *flambé* earthenware, bronze, ivory, and plaster, he is now known almost exclusively for his '*jeu de l'écharpe*' ('scarf game') series of female figurines. These – ten maquettes of which were first shown at the 1897 Salon of the Société Nationale des Beaux-Arts and which were illustrated in the catalogue as a 'project for the decoration of the foyer of a dance hall' – were later commissioned by the Sèvres Manufactory to be modelled in white biscuit porcelain for their pavilion at the 1900 International Exposition. Pieces could be bought either as a complete set or individually, and the project was so successful that the founders, Susse *frères*, subsequently obtained the right to cast the originals in bronze.

Among the various poses of the dancers – one, for example, is playing a tambourine; another (*La Cothurne*) seems to be adjusting her sandal – are two of women who hold aloft billowing scarves in which are hidden electric light bulbs. Though it is natural to associate these figures with Loïe Fuller, there is no documentary evidence to support the claim, listed in many auction catalogues, that these models are of her. It seems highly improbable that, in a group of ten dancers, two would be of Loïe Fuller and the rest an 'accompaniment'.

The two figurines that are wired for electricity in the *jeu de l'écharpe* series fetch considerably more than those that are not. As there are so few available models, prices tend to be artificially high, not less than FF 17,500 ($3,500) for a small gilt-bronze and ivory model.

MAJORELLE, LOUIS

Born in Toul, although in fact a Nancéien, Majorelle was studying painting in Paris under Jean Millet when his father died in 1879 and he was recalled to Nancy to run the family cabinet-making business. Although now celebrated principally for his furniture, Majorelle designed not only pianos, desks, nests of tables, armchairs in mahogany, amaranth and tamarind, but also wrought-iron banisters and light fixtures. The latter became possible when Majorelle extended his studio to include a metal workshop where the ormolu and iron mounts of both his own lamps and those of Daum were cast or wrought. Majorelle's lamps represent the epitome of refinement and good taste. A critic in a 1908 *Revue Lorraine illustrée* article wrote:

> Some of the flower lamps that he has created are exquisitely original. Here, for example, is a water lily in which the frosted crystal centre is designed to house the bulb. In another are three candleholders, of unequal height, set beneath lobed dandelion leaves. Finally, there is a sinewy candelabrum comprised of three magnolia flowers, and of a perfect elegance.

Although most frequently of floral inspiration (including the orchid and honesty flower), some Majorelle table-lamps were of geometric form (see, for example, two illustrated in *L'Art Décoratif*, December 1904). Quite uncharacteristic of Majorelle's style were the series of gilt-bronze *femme-fleur* wall-brackets commissioned by the restaurant Lucas Carton in the Place de la Madeleine, Paris. (Most of these are still *in situ.*) His light fixtures, like all his work, were marketed through his own shops, and through the annual Salons. In 1902, for example, he displayed three bronze and glass table-lamps, two wrought-iron lamps, and three wrought-iron candlesticks at the Salon of the Société des Artistes français.

Majorelle's working alliance with the Daum *frères* is well known, the latter providing all the shades for those Majorelle fixtures which included glass. What is less widely known, however, is that Majorelle produced a series of lamps with cloth shades, often on gilt-bronze and wrought-iron bases identical to the ones he used for some of his glass-shaded fixtures. Two undated Majorelle sales catalogues (probably *c.* 1910) illustrate a range of such cloth table-lamps, showing that Majorelle, like Tiffany, interchanged certain bases and shades. This also explains why some of his bases that turn up in the Paris flea-markets are missing their presumed glass shades: they may, in fact, originally have had cloth.

There are very few Majorelle light fixtures in general circulation in the Art Nouveau market. Models tend to be expensive: upwards of FF 26,250 ($5,250).

MULLER FRÈRES

No fewer than nine Muller brothers and one sister were, at various times up until 1914, employed as either artists or artisans in the Muller glass works. The family having settled in Lunéville in 1870, the two eldest brothers, Désiré and Eugène, found employment at the Gallé studio in nearby Nancy, where three other brothers – Henri, Victor and Pierre – were later likewise to undergo their apprenticeships. It was due to Henry's urging – he was the most entrepreneurial of the family – that the Mullers established their own design studio. This they founded in rue Sante-Anne in Lunéville, though the actual glass was blown for them, under their direction, at the Hinzelin Gobeleterie in the neighbouring town of Croismare. Jobs were apportioned according to individual abilities; for example, Emile and Eugène designed the shapes for the glassware, which the other brothers and the sister executed by various techniques, the most common of which entailed cameo glass (sometimes incorporating up to seven differently coloured layers) that was subsequently acid-etched or wheel-cut to obtain the required definition.

Among the wide range of glass tableware produced by the firm – pitchers, *solifleur* vases and bowls – were innumerable table-lamps, chandeliers and night lights. Since the Mullers were disciples of Gallé, it is not surprising that their designs were of similar floral and entomological inspiration. Insects, bats and butterflies crawl, fly and flutter among fuchsias, convolvuli, lianas and bramble in a kaleidoscope of colours and in a style which, even in the 1930s, was more Art Nouveau than Art Déco. The firm's chandeliers, of which a large number have survived, can be seen in shops in Paris's rue St-Denis and rue St-Honoré, Manhattan's Madison Avenue, and Brussels' avenue Louise. The firm continued its increasingly commercial production until the outbreak of World War I. The war caused a severe disruption of operations and a subsequent dispersal of the family, but in 1919 the liaison with Hinzelin was re-established and production recommenced. The work force at one time numbered 300 before the firm finally closed in 1936.

A 27-inch high Muller *frères* cameo table-lamp sold in London in 1973 for £800 ($1,600), while a smaller one fetched £230 ($460). In 1977 the price range for standard Muller table-lamps and hanging shades was from £300 to £1,000 ($525 to $1,750).

ROBERT, EMILE

Robert is often credited with initiating the renaissance in the art of wrought-iron which took place late in the nineteenth century after a lapse of almost a whole century. Apprenticed in the family ironmongery, Robert was one of the last to use the forge (the oxyacetylene blow-lamp became commercialized in the early 1900s), combining hammer, anvil, chasing tool, burin and creative flair to produce a wide gamut of domestic metalware: grilles, balustrades, consoles and vase mounts. He exhibited through the Société des Artistes français.

Robert also turned his hand to all forms of light fixtures, especially chandeliers. As he was of an earlier generation than the Art Nouveau artists and craftsmen, the bulk of his lighting creations were designed for gas and paraffin, rather than electric light, but several of his chandeliers include mechanisms for both paraffin and electric bulbs.

Robert had to collaborate with other craftsmen when his lamp designs included non-metal components: earthenware reservoirs were provided by Bigot and glass shades by Laumonnerie. The themes for his lamps were, as in all his work, mainly vegetal. Clusters of flowers – often umbels or thistles – spring from the interlacing mounts that housed reservoirs or light sockets in such profusion that they often appear overworked and cluttered. There is a Victorian fussiness about Robert's earlier work, but after 1900 his designs became less ornate – for example, the two table-lamps illustrated in *L'Art Décoratif*, January–June 1903, which have a linear conception.

Very little of Robert's ironwork has been rediscovered. A pair of his wall lights was on sale at the flea-market in Paris in 1976 for FF450 ($90) each.

SAUVAGE, HENRI

As an exponent of Art Nouveau, the architect Sauvage was best known for the pavilion he designed for Loïe Fuller at the 1900 Exposition and for his villa for Majorelle at Nancy. He did, however, design complete *ensembles* for the Café de Paris and the interiors of most of his buildings: for example, the *Logements Hygiéniques* and the Maison de Rapport, both of which were commissions from the Paris housing authorities.

Sauvage appears to have designed only a few lamps, but their number is in inverse proportion to their quality of design. At the 1902 Salon of the Société Nationale des Beaux-Arts, he exhibited a five-branched lustre and a table-lamp that were described in *L'Art Décoratif pour Tous* as 'complementing an ensemble of immense artistic merit'. The lustre, which was illustrated in the June issue of *L'Art Décoratif* of that year, consists of curved glass panels housed in a gently voluted bronze frame, while the table-lamp shown here is one of the most unpretentiously elegant objects to emerge from the whole epoch. Two other table-lamps that I have seen are of similar floral inspiration and charm.

SCHENCK, EDOUARD

Along with Brandt and de Jarny, Schenck was one of the dominant metalworkers in the early 1900 Paris Salons. Drawing on both the world of entomology – the coleopter, capricorn and stag-beetle – and that of botany – the oak, rose, colchicum and iris – Schenck produced a wide range of metal domestic ware. Andirons, screens, *jardinières*, chimney ornamentation, and lamps were designed as insects and flowers in hammered or *repoussé* wrought-iron, both often patinated and inlaid with cabochons of *flambé* earthenware or panels of coloured glass. In lighting Schenck designed and executed chandeliers, wall-brackets and lanterns, many of which were exhibited at the Salons d'Automne. Six of these are illustrated in a 1906 *L'Art Décoratif* article by the critic Roger de Félice on the ironwork of Schenck and Brandt. Largely complimentary in his appraisal of their aesthetic worth, Félice suggests, though, that they are a trifle too robust and crude in the vigour of their execution. Considering the nature of the craft in question, this was perhaps an unfair comment, no doubt elicited by viewing Schenck's metalwork in juxtaposition with that of Brandt.

Schenck continued to produce light fixtures into the 1920s (see page 184), when he was joined by his son Marcel.

Schenck's metalwork is rarely found today. It would not, however, fetch high prices on today's Art Nouveau market because of Schenck's heavy style.

SCHNEIDER, CHARLES and ERNEST

In 1903 the Schneider brothers established a crystal factory at Epinay-sur-Seine, about seven miles from Paris. To Ernest, the elder brother, fell the managerial responsibilities of the firm, to Charles the directorship and supervision of the art glass and crystal department, a position he held from the firm's inception until the outbreak of World War II. (The firm still exists, though in 1962 it moved to Lorris, near Orléans.)

It was therefore Charles Schneider who was responsible for the wide range of art glass tableware made during the early 1900s. Vases, *compôtes*, wine glasses, table-lamps, etc., were produced in a wide range of techniques; among the best known are the cameo, enamelled and mottled 'intercalaire' varieties. Schneider's designs for table-lamps and chandeliers tend either to be geometric or to depict tableaux from nature: the latter, for example, consisting of landscapes in which woods or lakes stand out against lighter coloured grounds. These light fixtures are often housed in wrought-iron mounts into which the glass was sometimes blown.

Identification and attribution of Schneider's glassware can be confusing since the firm employed at least four different methods of signing its work, and these often in combination. First, the word 'Schneider' was sometimes used as a script signature (with variations – e.g., the word was sometimes preceded by a representation of a vase); secondly, and presumably only for selected pieces that Charles Schneider himself made, the word 'Charder' (composed of *Char*(les) (Schnei)*der*) is used; thirdly, at some stage part of the production was marketed under the name of *Le Verre français*; and, fourthly, some pieces are marked only with a small piece of striped glass (the French word for this is '*filigrane*'). This, in the French tricolors of red, white and blue, is embedded into the cameo piece. In some table-lamps the base is signed 'Charder' and the foot engraved 'le verre français'.

Often lumped into the category of 'commercially inspired imitations of Gallé', Schneider's lamps are, however, increasingly sought by today's collectors. Their cameo lampshades have recently begun to fetch high prices. Until 1974, the price for a standard Schneider table-lamp ranged in Paris from FF350 to 800 ($70 to $160); by 1976 prices had more than trebled.

SELMERSHEIM, TONY and PIERRE

Tony Selmersheim and his younger brother Pierre designed numerous forms of illumination throughout careers that were to span three decades. Tony was initially in partnership with the much-celebrated architect, Charles Plumet, and collaborated with him on the decor of various buildings. Furnishings, such as chaises longues, buffets, chiffoniers, and light fixtures, were shown at the exhibition of L'Art dans Tout group (previously 'The Six'), as well as through the Société Nationale des Beaux-Arts and the Salon d'Automne.

Selmersheim's lamps – wall-brackets, candlesticks and chandeliers – have a spontaneous charm. One of these, shown at the 1904 Salon d'Automne, elicited from the critic Léon Rioter an accolade that was astonishing in its imagery, considering the quiet simplicity of the chandelier:

> at the centre of the nearly cream ceiling is a gilt and matt copper lily pad lustre with vast leaves that have elastic loops revolving around them to evoke the

> tranquil current of pools or rivers where water nymphs live. In the midst of the flowers hidden among the enlacements of these lakeside flora are bulbs that emit a soft light, as if one were dreaming in the gently rocking waves.

A critic in *L'Art Décoratif* in 1899 had, perhaps, said it better when, in the concluding paragraph of an article on that year's L'Art dans Tout Salon, he described a ceiling light and two wall-brackets shown by Selmersheim:

> if I have not commenced with these, it is because I cannot find adequate words to express their beauty. Suffice it to say that I know of nothing in the modern applied arts field to surpass them. For those who want to know how beauty can ally itself with an object, go and see: they will learn how.

Pierre Selmersheim, an architect, worked independently and placed more emphasis than his brother on the smaller range of household appurtenances. His garniture clocks, inkwells, *vide-poches*, and all forms of light fixtures were displayed through the Société Nationale des Beaux-Arts and the Société des Artistes Décorateurs. At the former in 1902, he included a bronze electric table-lamp, a paraffin lamp and a wall-bracket; at the latter, in 1906, a table-lamp and two flambeaux. By 1910 he commissioned out his designs for execution by Socard and the Gallé firm.

No Selmersheim lamps appear to have been rediscovered. They would probably fall into the medium price range for such Art Nouveau objects, between FF2,100 and FF3,300 ($440 and $700).

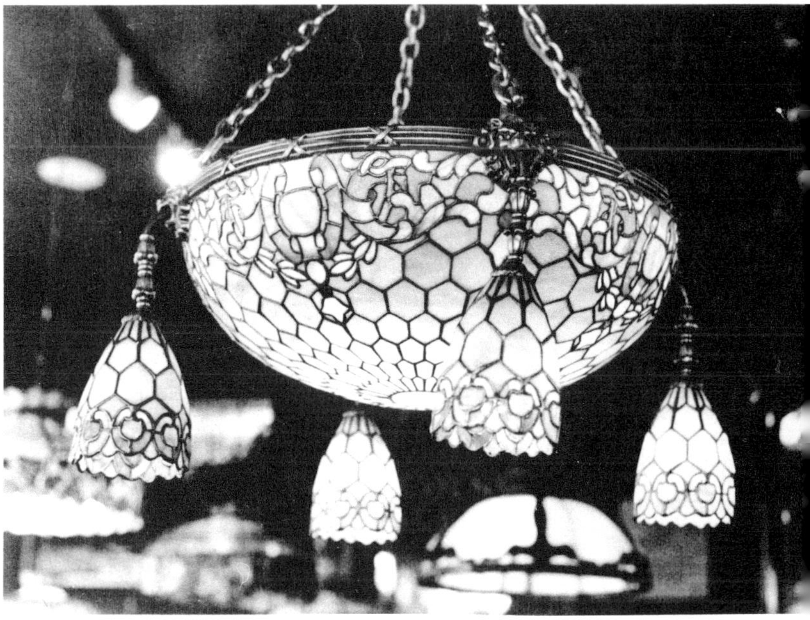

U.S.A.

Duffner and Kimberly
This hanging lampshade was advertised in an undated sales catalogue as 'Dome number 1003, 27″ × $8\frac{1}{2}$″, $315.' (1)

Handel
Below, a leaded glass lampshade with winged scarab repeating design. (2)

Right, a reverse-painted parrot lampshade. (3)

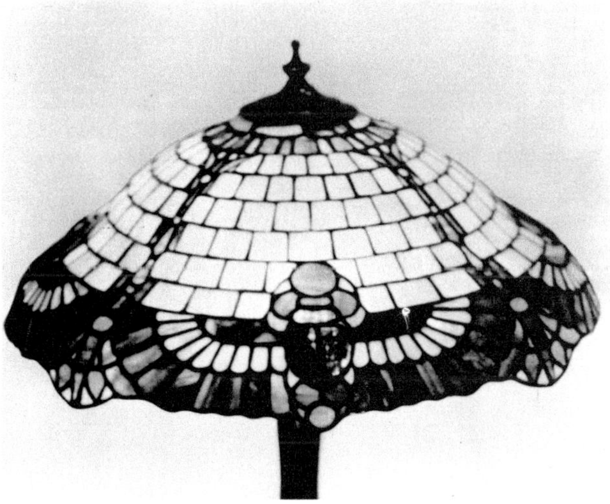

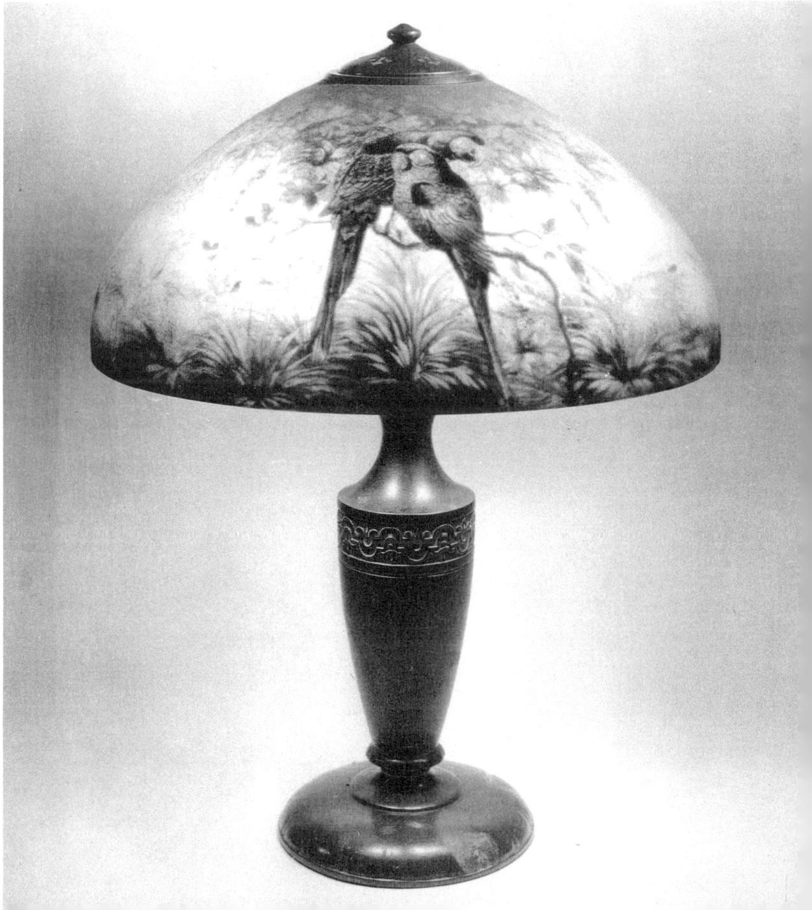

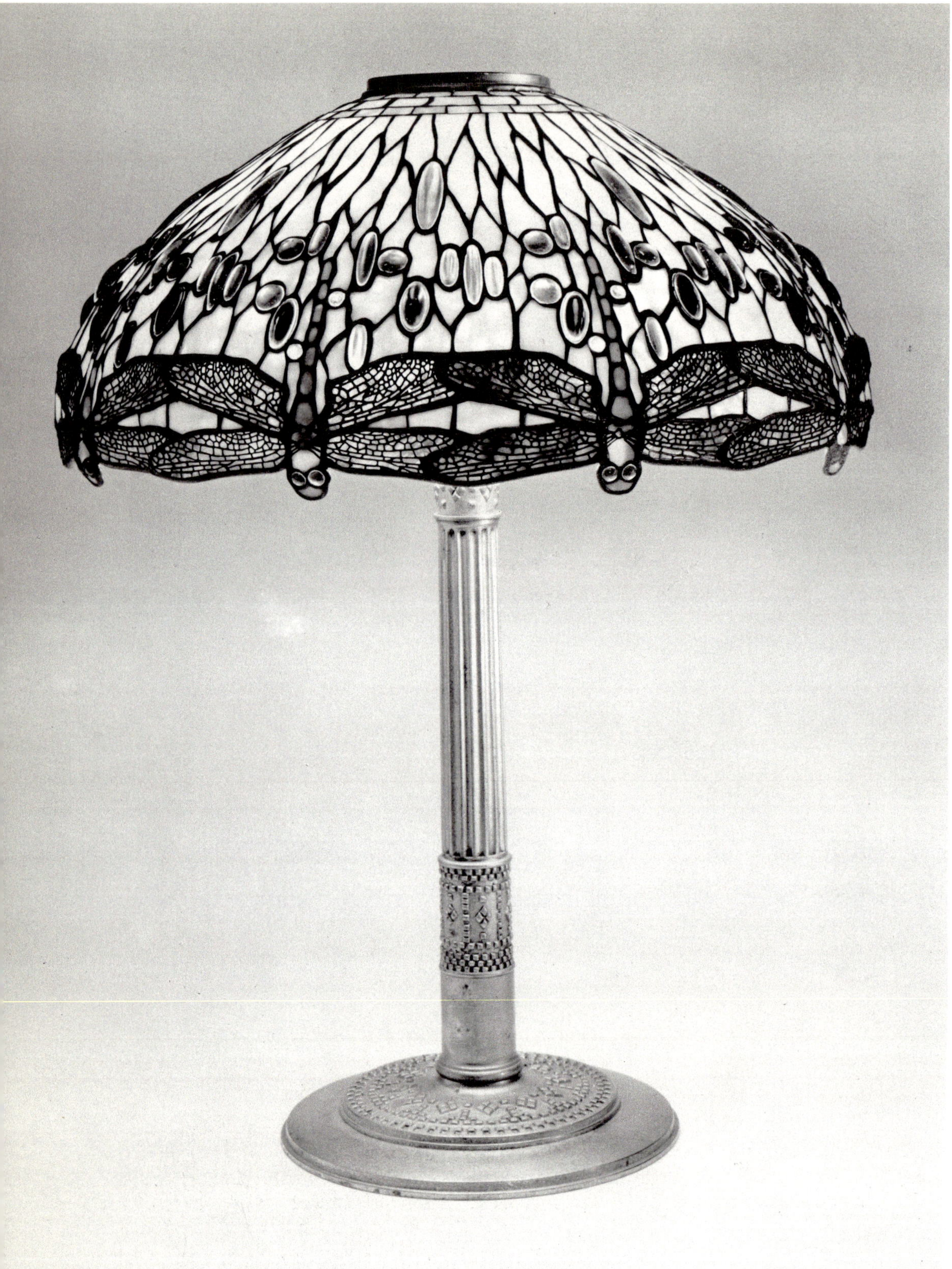

TIFFANY
Left, a dragonfly lamp incorporating glass cabochons. The dragonflies' wings are composed of single pieces of glass overlaid with patinated bronze filigree. (4)

Below, a glass and bronze daffodil lamp with lily pad base, the conical shade with yellow daffodils on a mottled green ground. (5)

Right, a unique magnolia floor-lamp by Tiffany Studios, certainly one of the most important lamps of the period. (6)

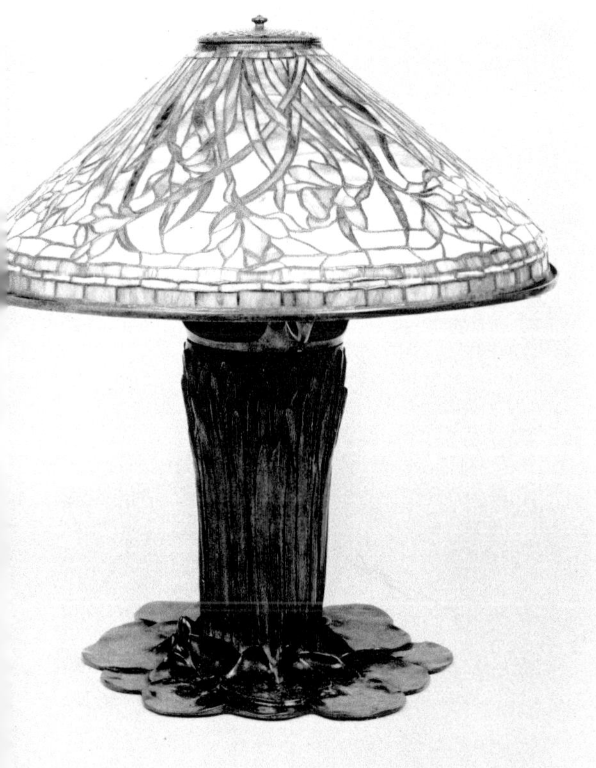

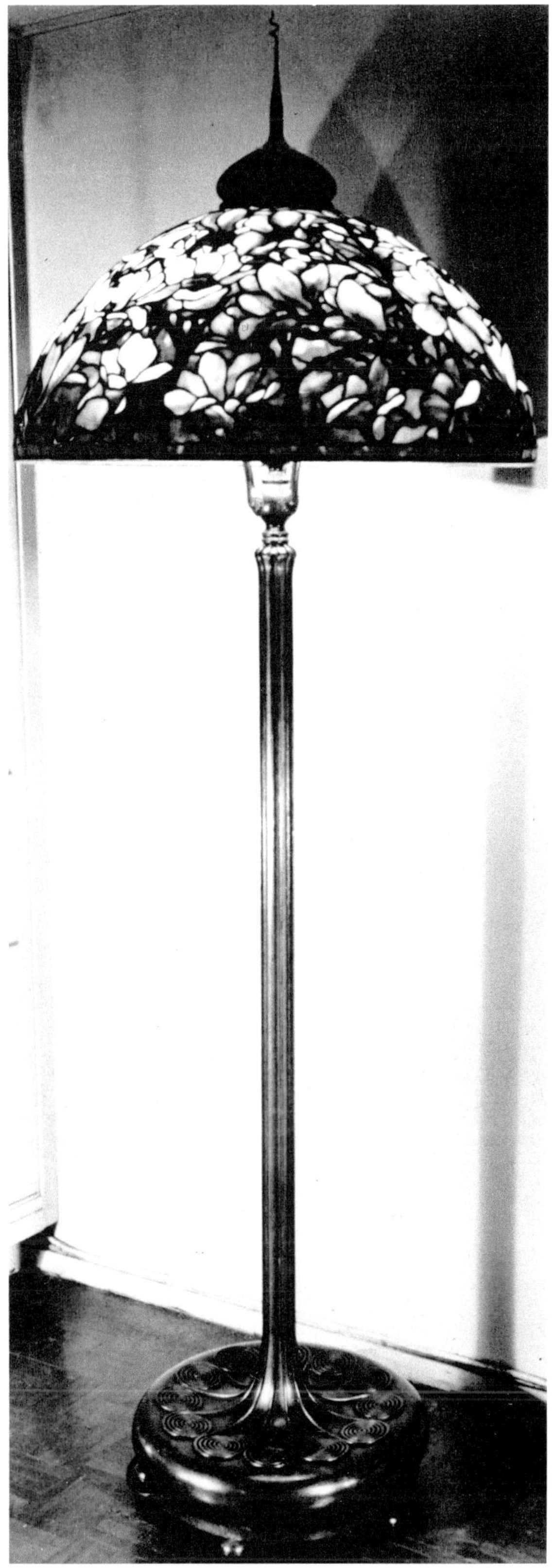

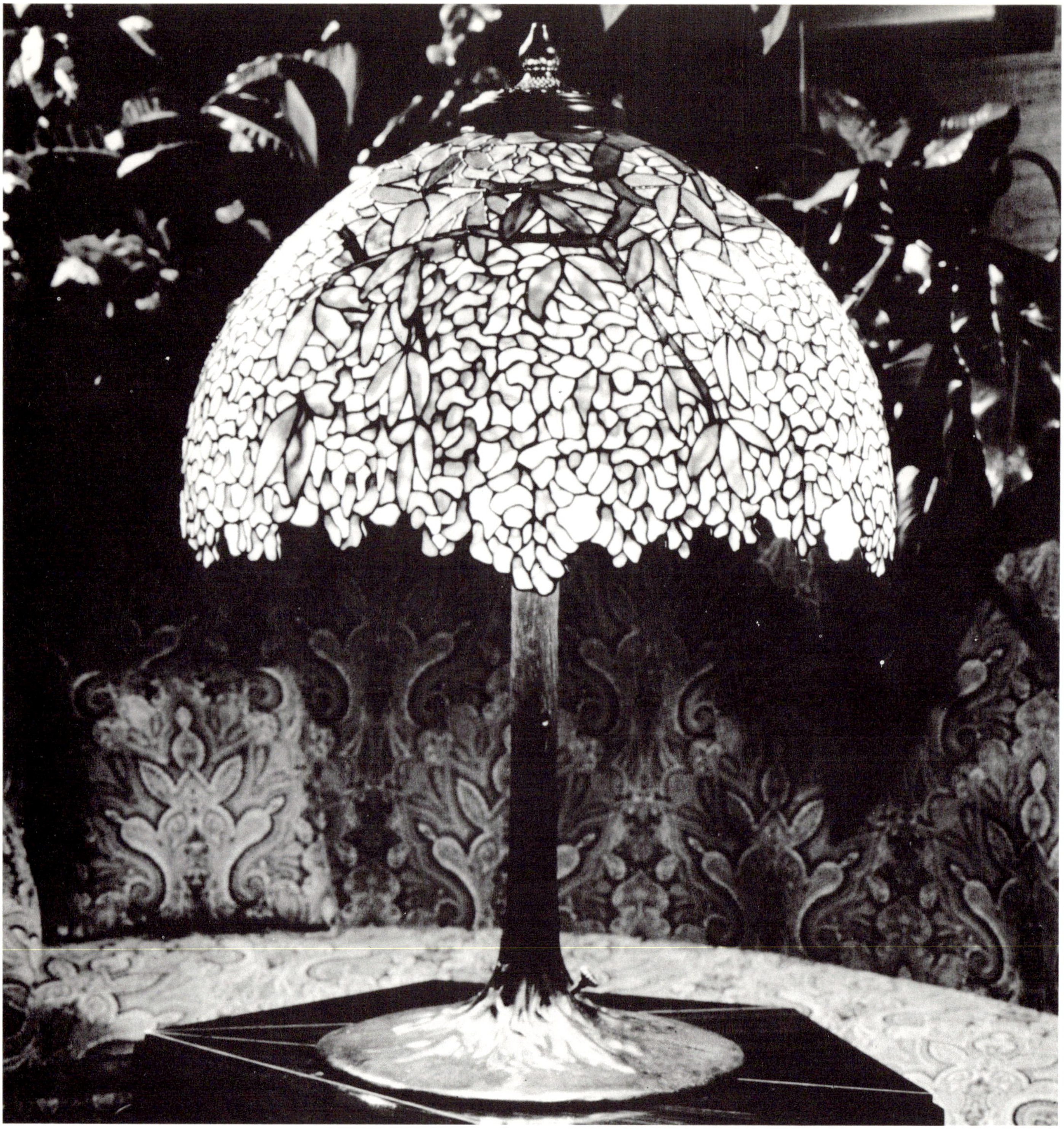

TIFFANY
A laburnum table-lamp, often mistaken, despite the difference in colour, for the more widely known wisteria. (7)

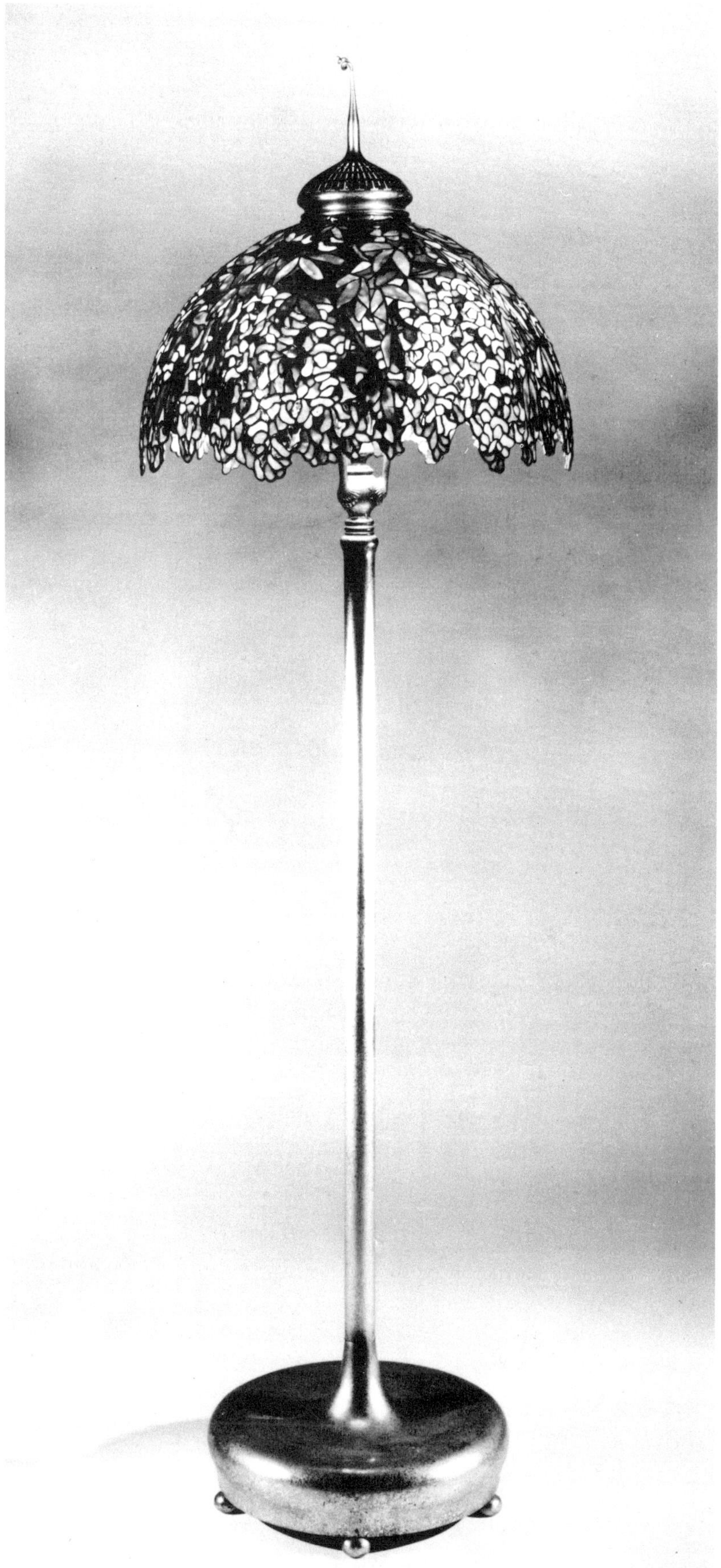

TIFFANY
A laburnum leaded glass and gilt-bronze floor-lamp, *c.* 1910. (8)

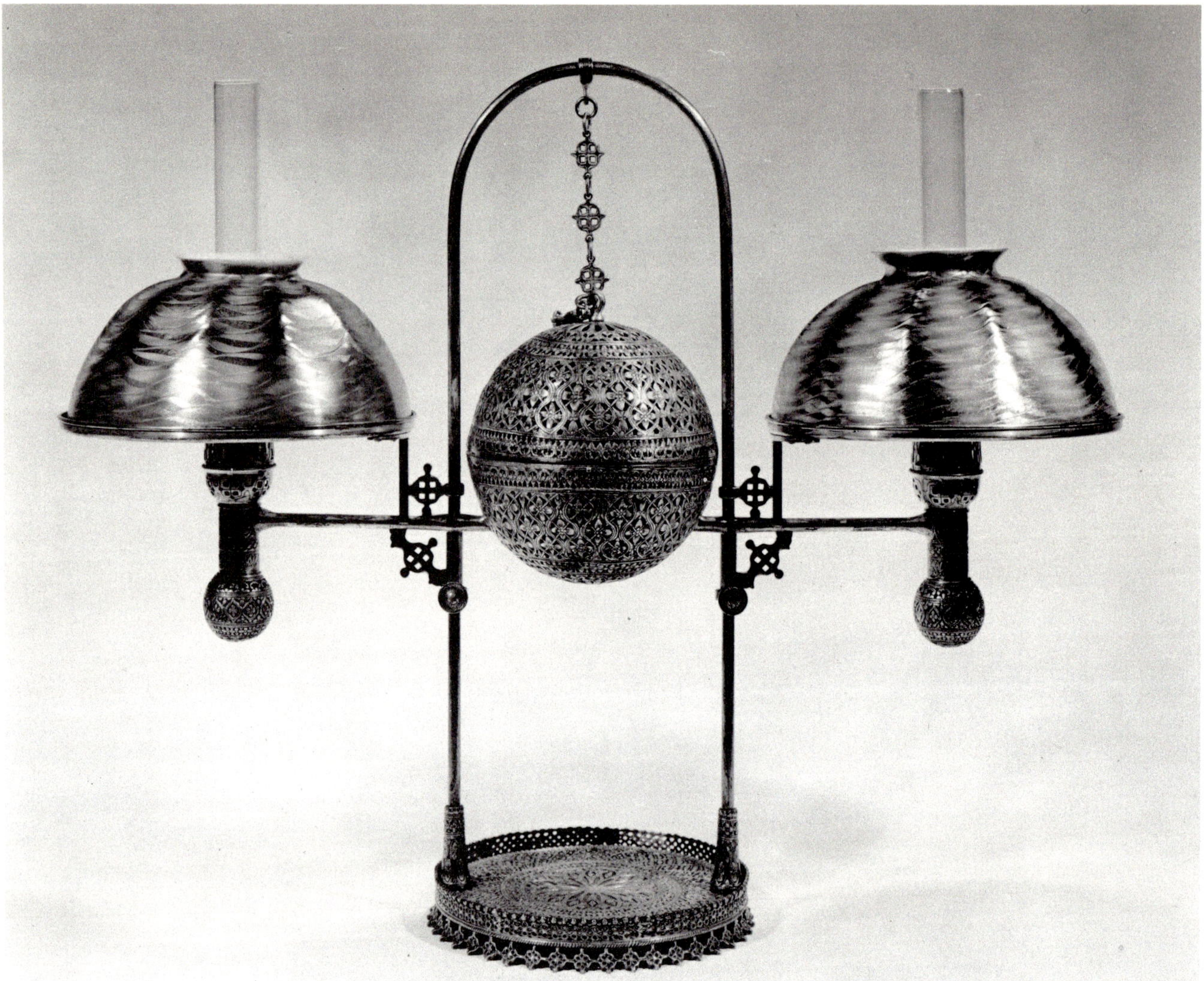

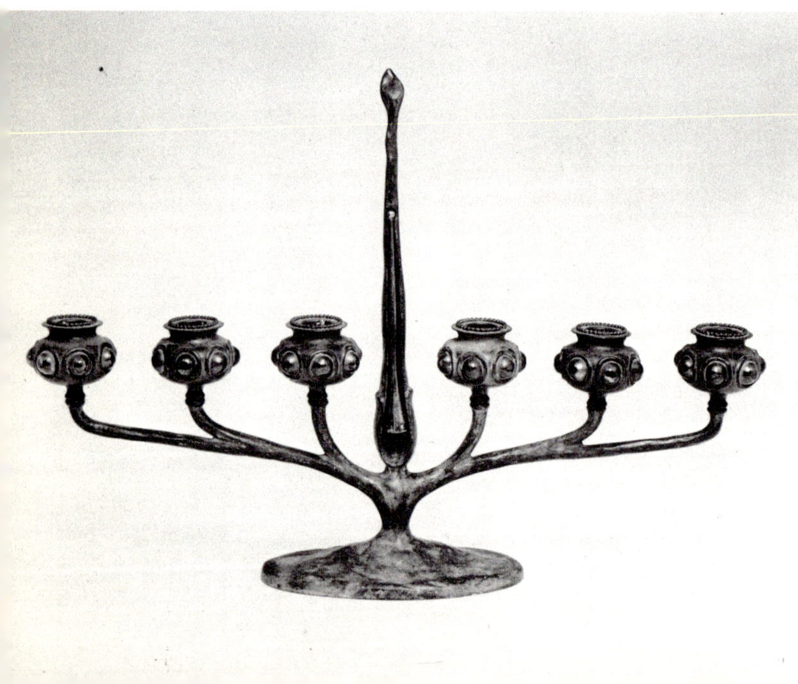

TIFFANY
Above, a silvered-bronze and Favrile glass student oil-lamp. (10)

Left, six-light candelabrum of glass and bronze. The central floriform handle contains a snuffer. (9)

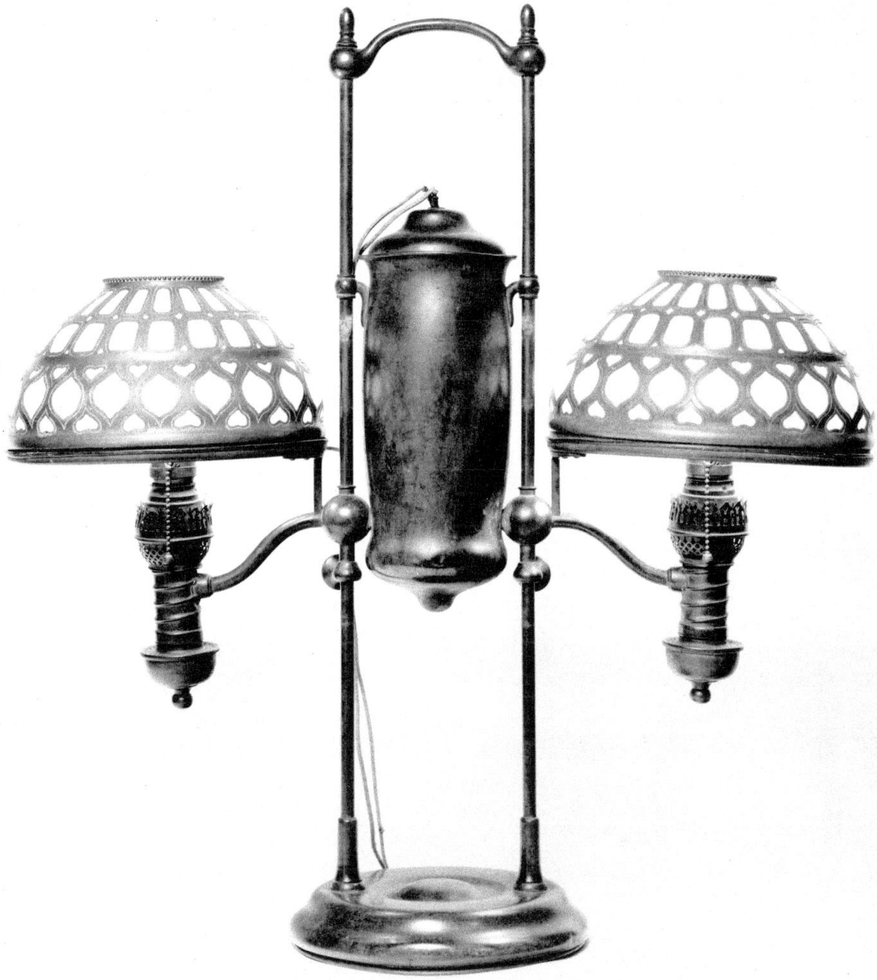

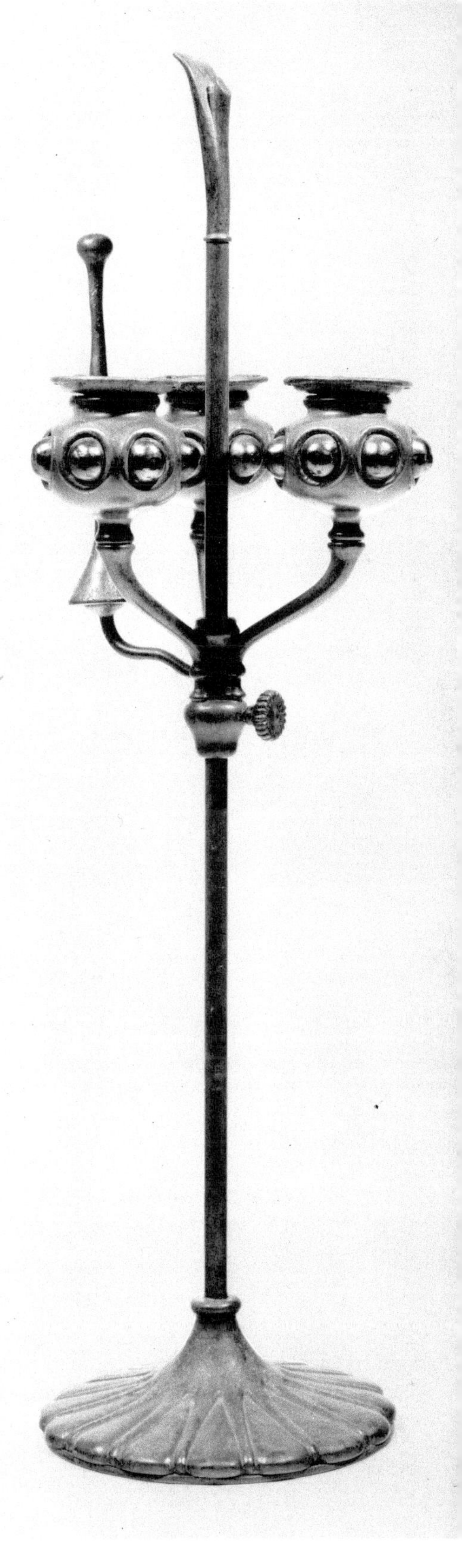

TIFFANY
Above, a student oil lamp of blown glass and bronze (later converted to electricity). (11)

Right, a three-branched candelabrum, with snuffer. (12)

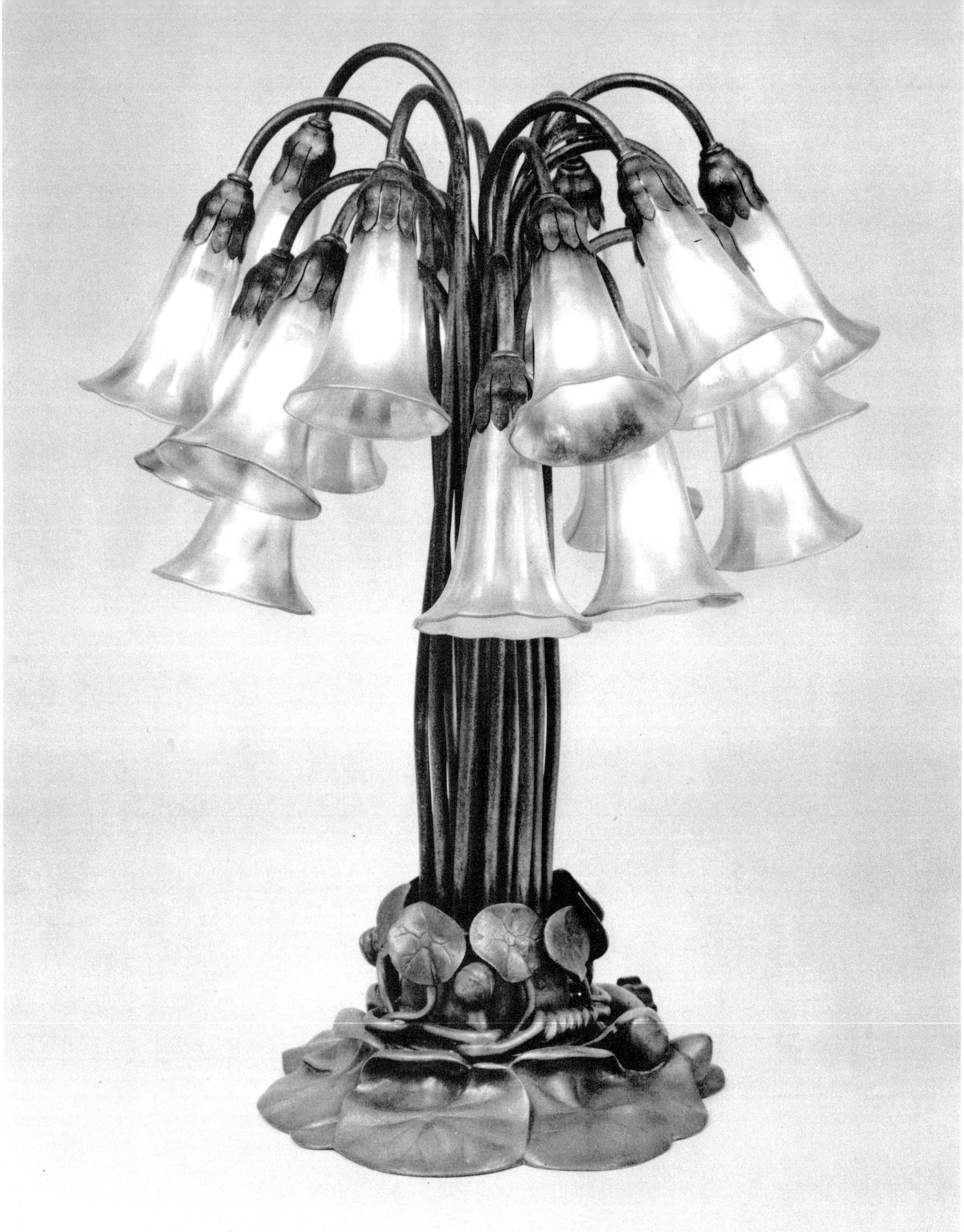

TIFFANY
A sixteen-light lily table-lamp. (13)

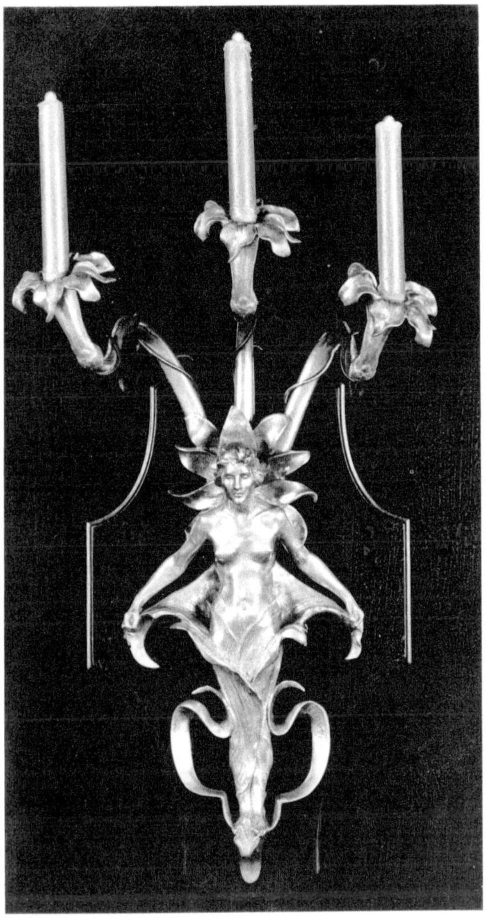

BELGIUM

DUBOIS (PAUL)
A bronze three-branched wall-sconce, *c.* 1900 (14)

DUBOIS (FERNAND)
A five-branched silvered bronze candelabrum which was shown with a matching wall sconce at the 1902 Turin International Exhibition in a Horta *ensemble*. The candelabrum was first exhibited in pewter in the 1899 Salon of La Libre Esthétique. (15)

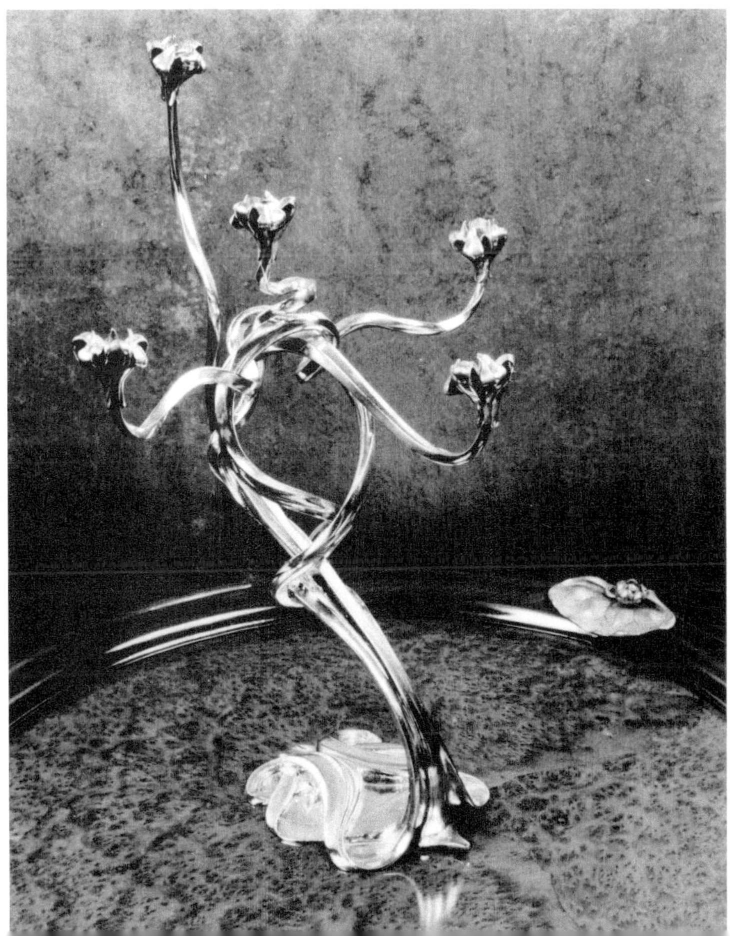

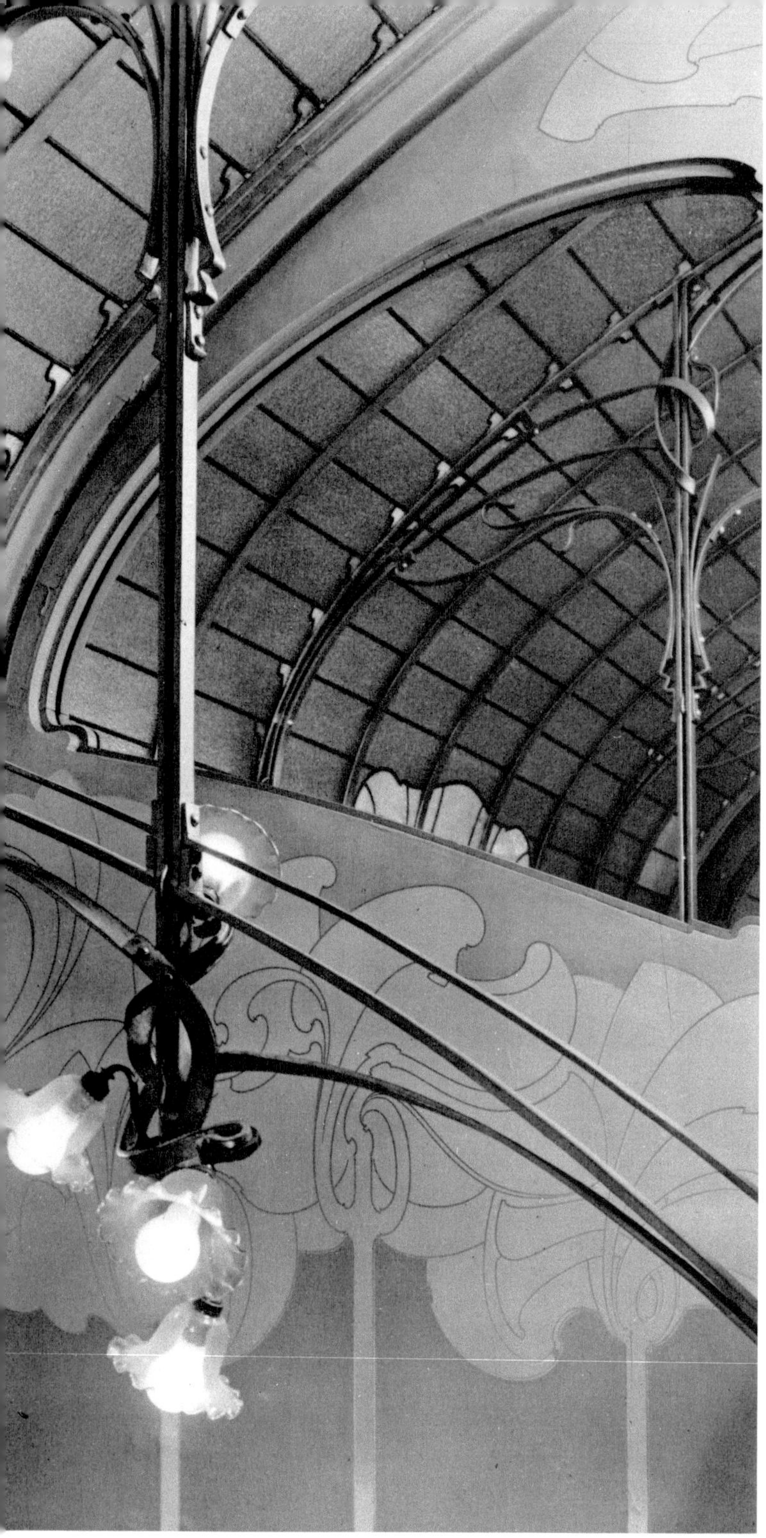

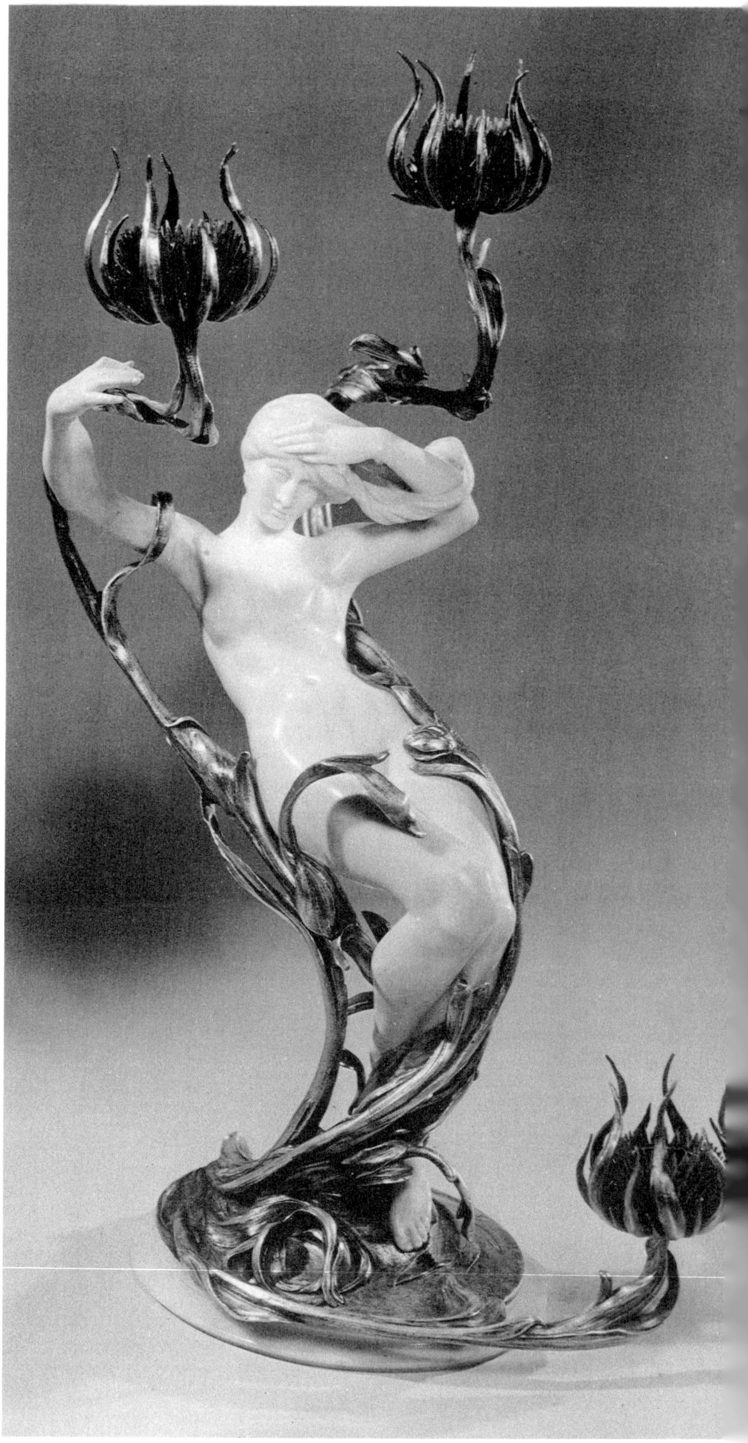

Horta
A gilt-bronze chandelier designed for the Hôtel Solvay, Brussels, 1903. The crystal shades are believed to have been made by Val Saint Lambert. (16)

Rombaux/Hoosemans
In this best-known of the Rombaux and Hoosemans candelabra, the ivory maiden is held by silver thistle stalks. (17)

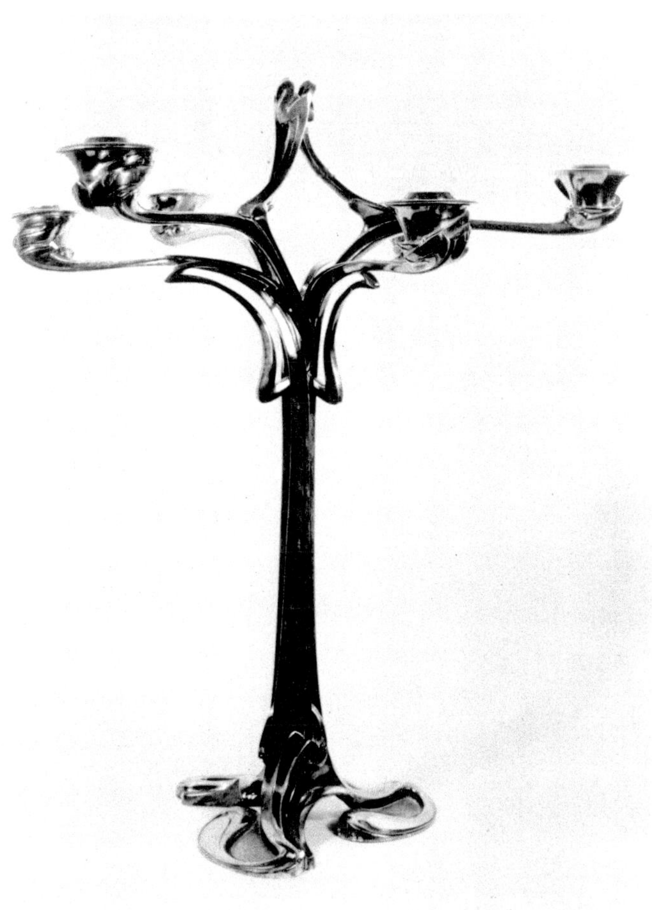

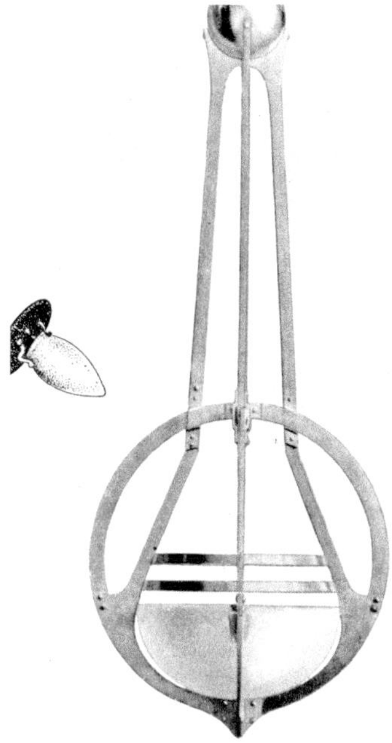

VAN DE VELDE
Above, a six-branched silvered-bronze candelabrum of 1902. (18)

Above right, a metal and blown glass chandelier, *c.* 1906. The Spartan design seems to predict van de Velde's later association with Gropius and the Bauhaus. (19)

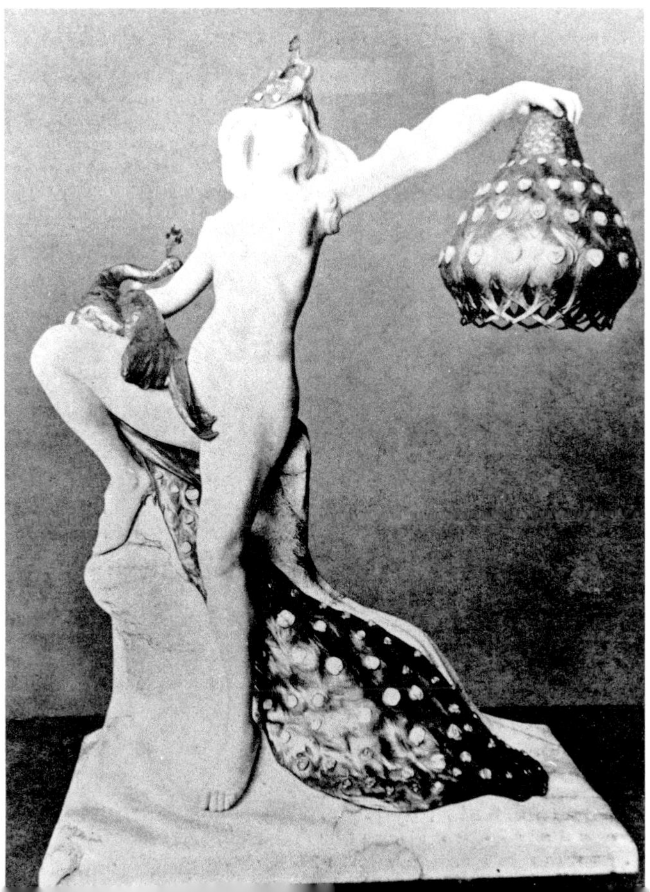

WOLFERS
This version of Wolfers' peacock lamp caused a sensation at the 1901 Salon National des Beaux-Arts. It was illustrated in three contemporary magazines and the critic C. Saunier stressed the unsuitability of the subject matter for lighting purposes. Compare colour illustration XXVI. (20)

GREAT BRITAIN

Ashbee

Right, this silver table-lamp was illustrated in *L'Art Décoratif* in 1899. Ashbee designed very few lighting fixtures, and in this case at least was clearly unable to solve the wiring problem. (21)

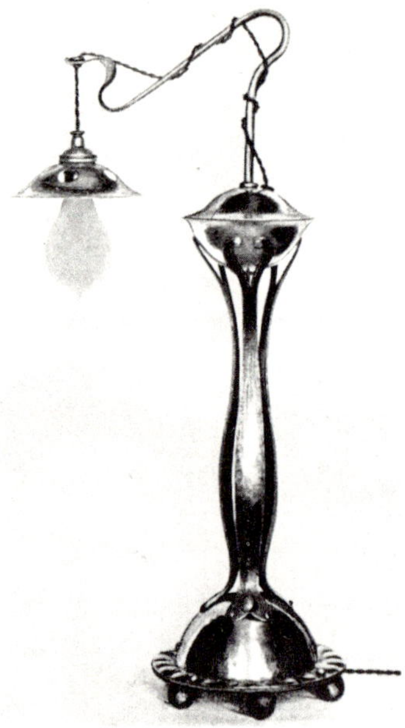

Benson

Far right, a copper and brass table-lamp incorporating glass shades. (22)

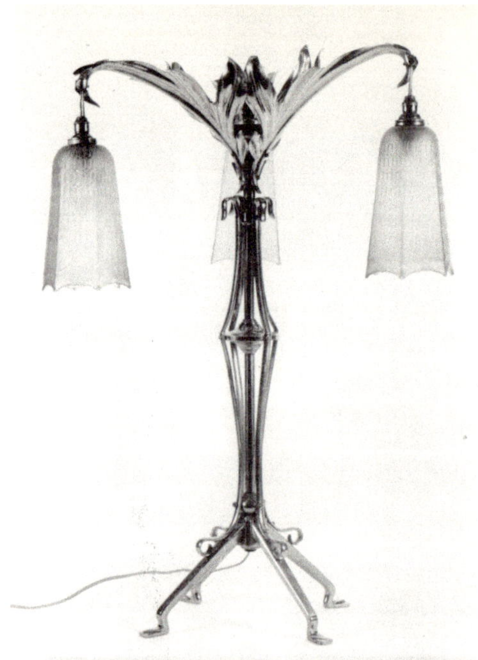

Knox

Below left, a Liberty & Co. Tudric pewter candlestick, probably designed by Knox, 1903. (23)

Below right, a pair of Tudric pewter two-branched candelabra designed in 1905 and illustrated in the Liberty catalogue, No. 119 (1906), p. 79, no. 1. (24)

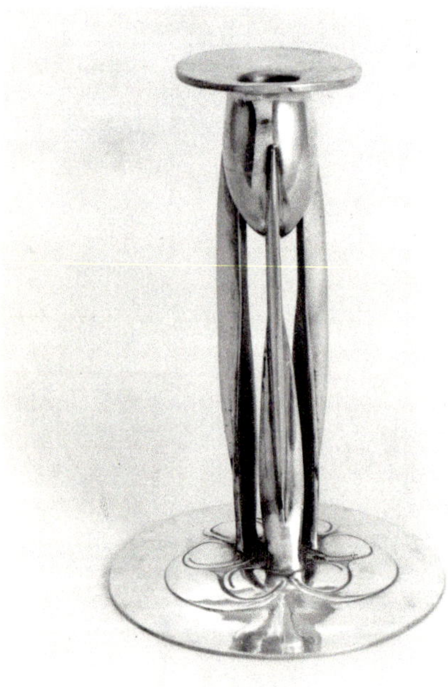

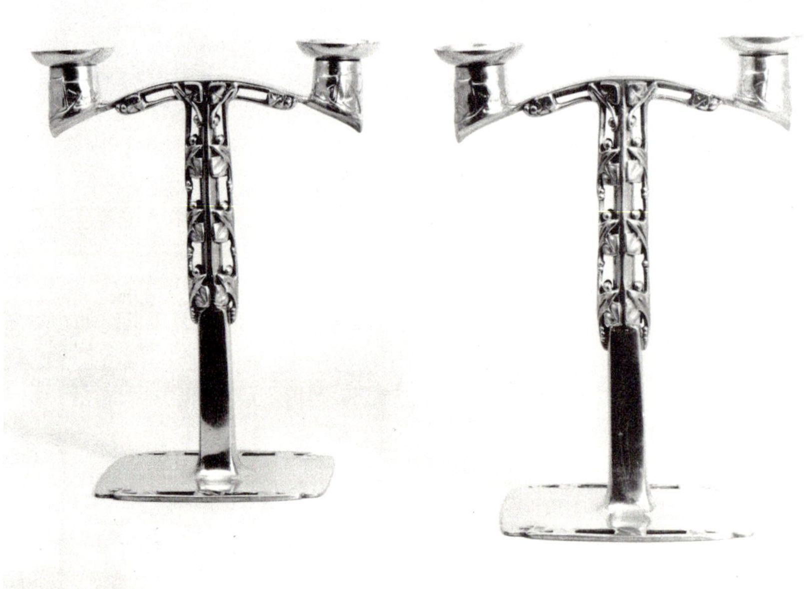

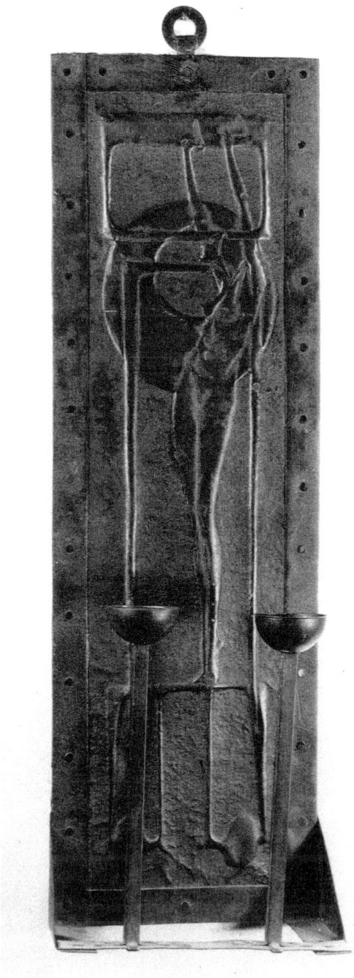

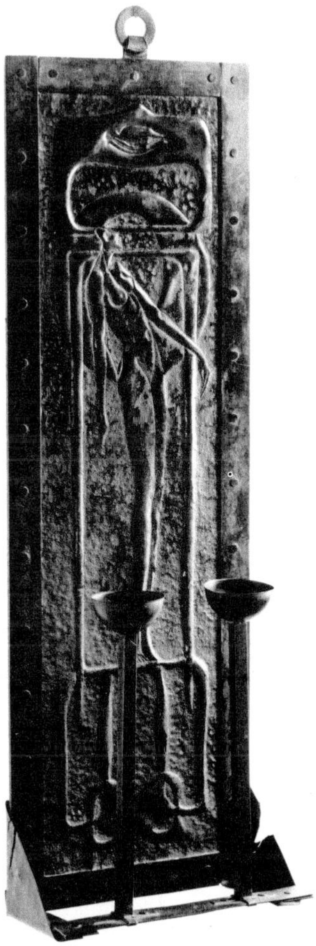

MacDonald
A pair of beaten brass candle sconces, entitled 'Morning' and 'Night', *c.* 1897. A similar pair was illustrated in an article by Gleeson White in *The Studio*, XI (1897). (25, 26)

Mackintosh
Right, watercolour and pencil design for ten pendant light fittings for Miss Cranston's Argyle Street Tearooms, Glasgow. (27)

Right below, watercolour, ink and pencil design for pendant light fittings. (28)

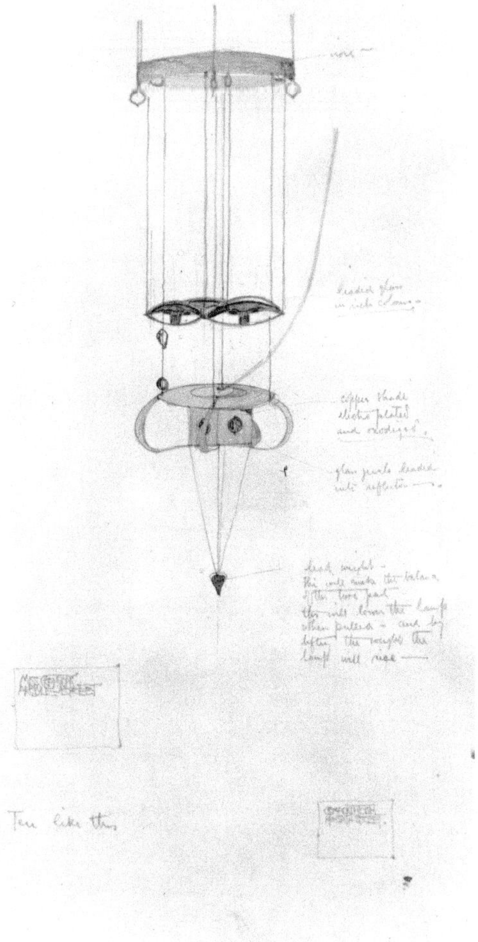

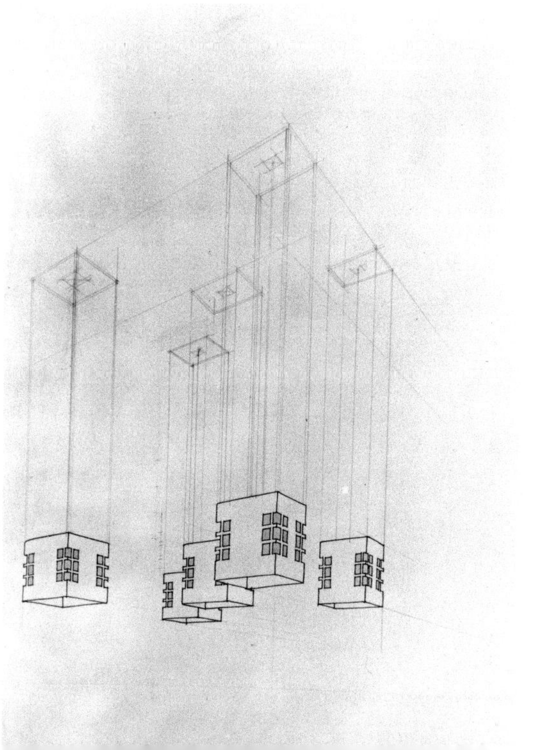

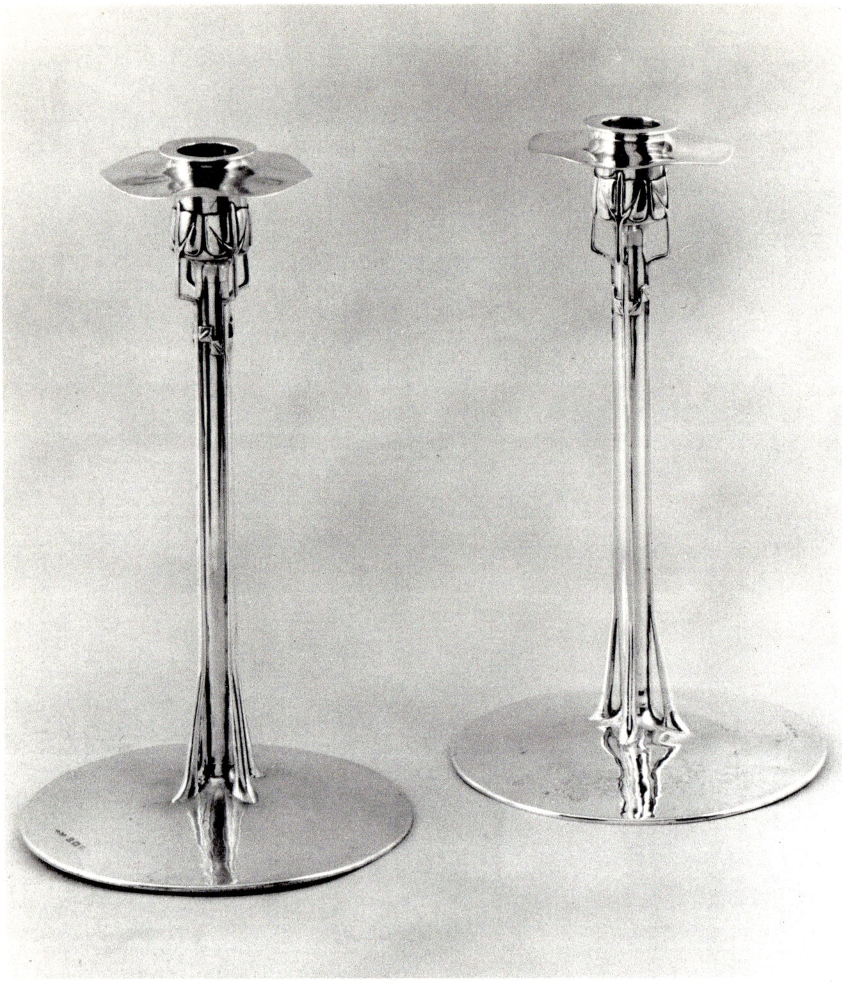

SILVER

Left, a pair of 'Conister' Cymric silver candlesticks designed for Liberty & Co., *c.* 1899. (29)

Left below, designs for Silver's 'Pollock' and 'Conister' Cymric silver candlesticks. (30)

Below, design for 'Thousla' Tudric pewter candlestick, Liberty & Co., *c.* 1900. The inscription reads: 'not used thus – but simplified'. (31)

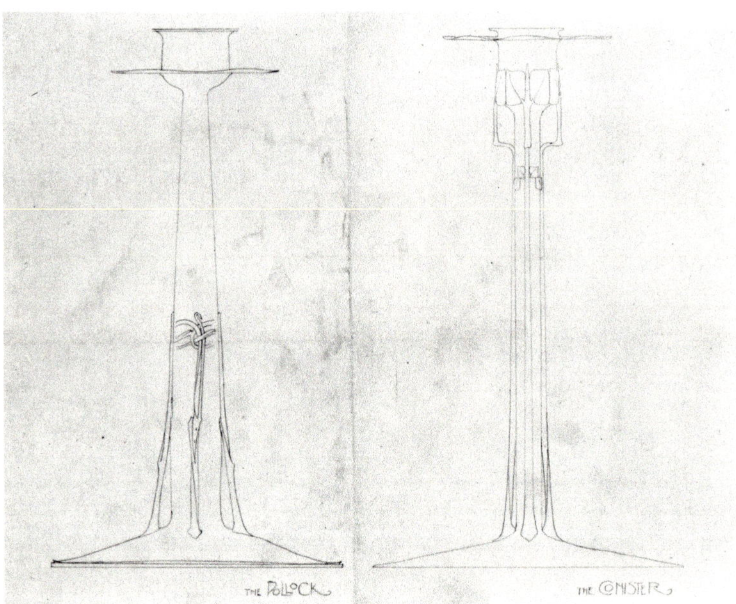

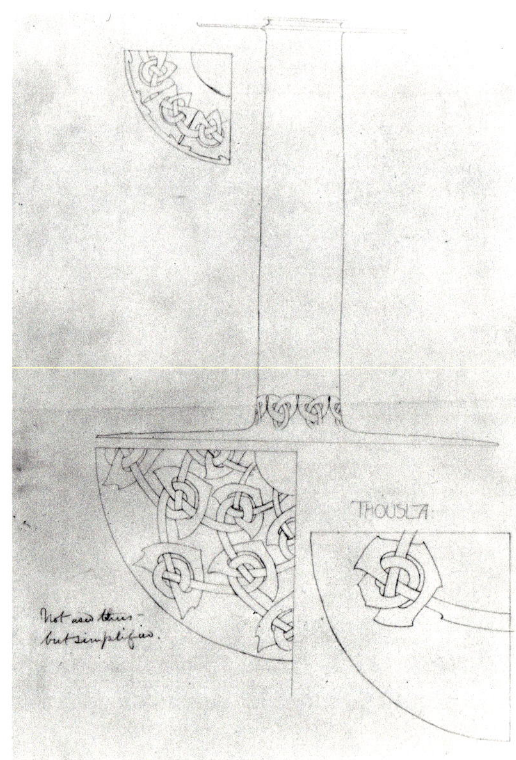

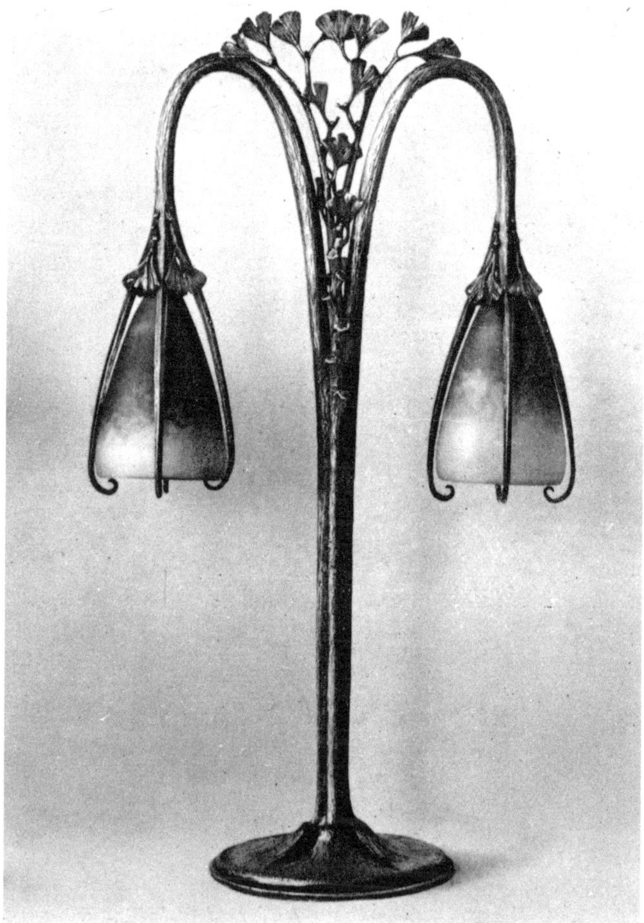

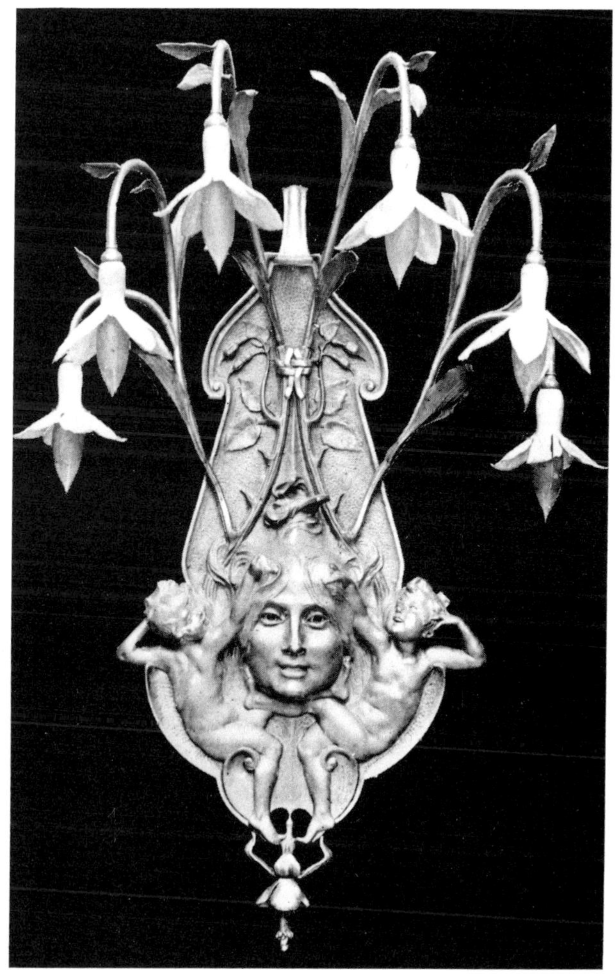

FRANCE

Brandt
Wrought-iron table-lamp with blown glass shade by Daum An identical model was illustrated in *Art et Décoration* (July–December 1920), p. 47. (32)

Chéret
This charming fuchsia wall-bracket by Joseph Chéret was reissued after his death by the founder Soleau for the 1900 International Exposition and again in 1904. (33)

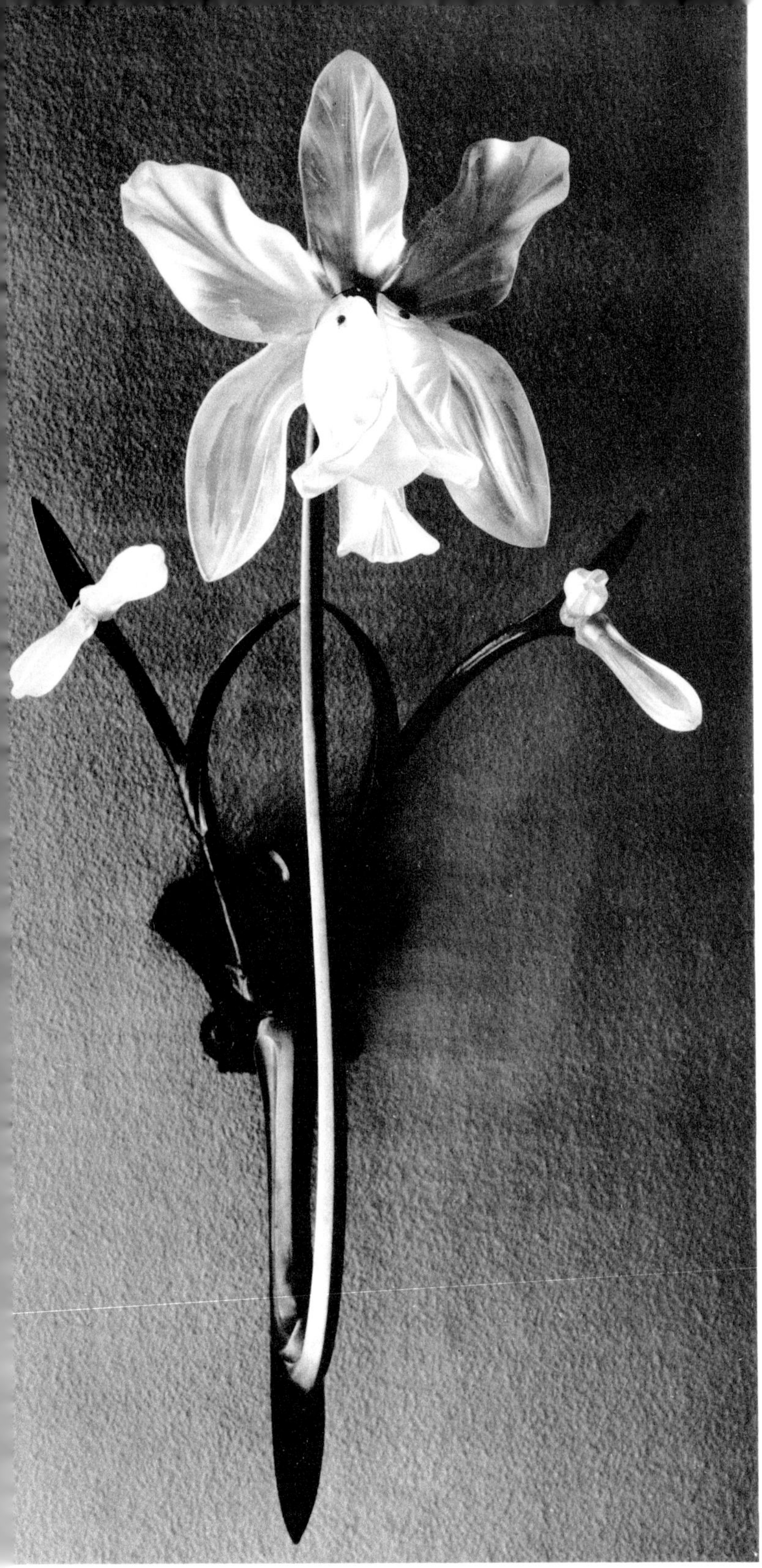

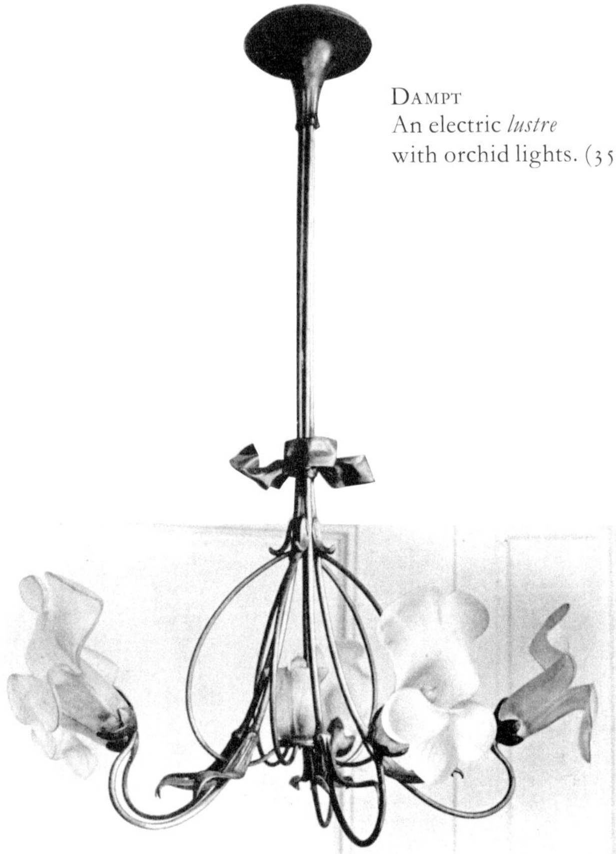

Dampt
An electric *lustre* with orchid lights. (35)

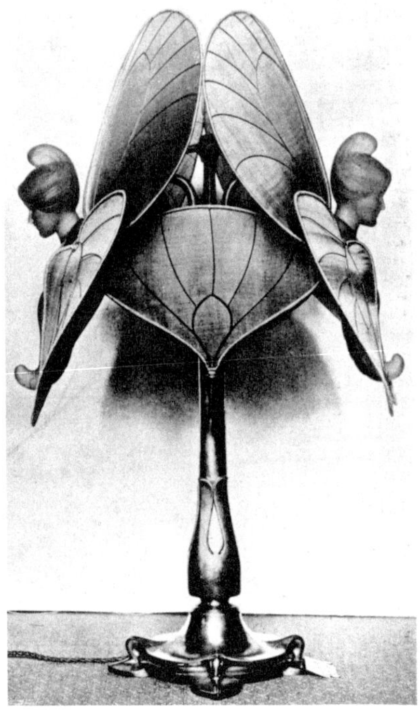

Dampt
This wall-bracket was one of a series of orchid fixtures designed for the Maison Beau and exhibited at the 1900 International Exposition. (34)

Dampt
Contemporary photograph of a rare and vanished table-lamp. (36)

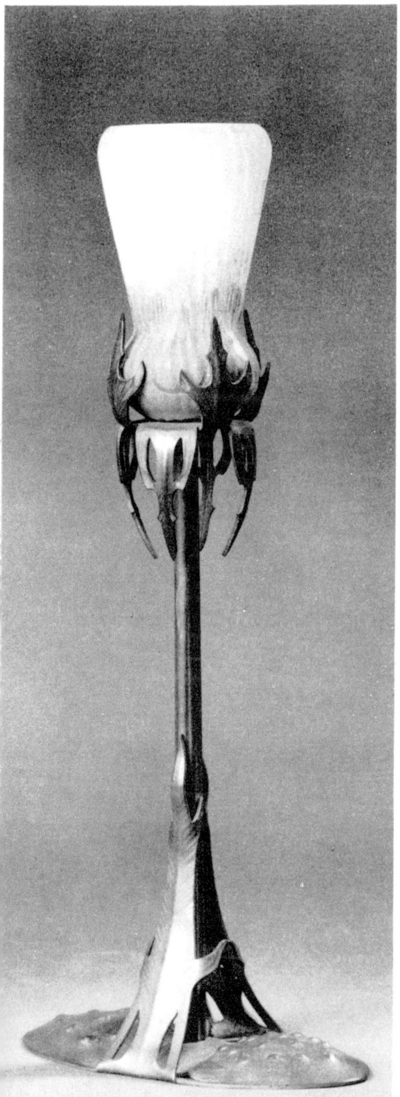

DAUM
A 'thistle' table-lamp with wrought-iron mount by Majorelle. (37)

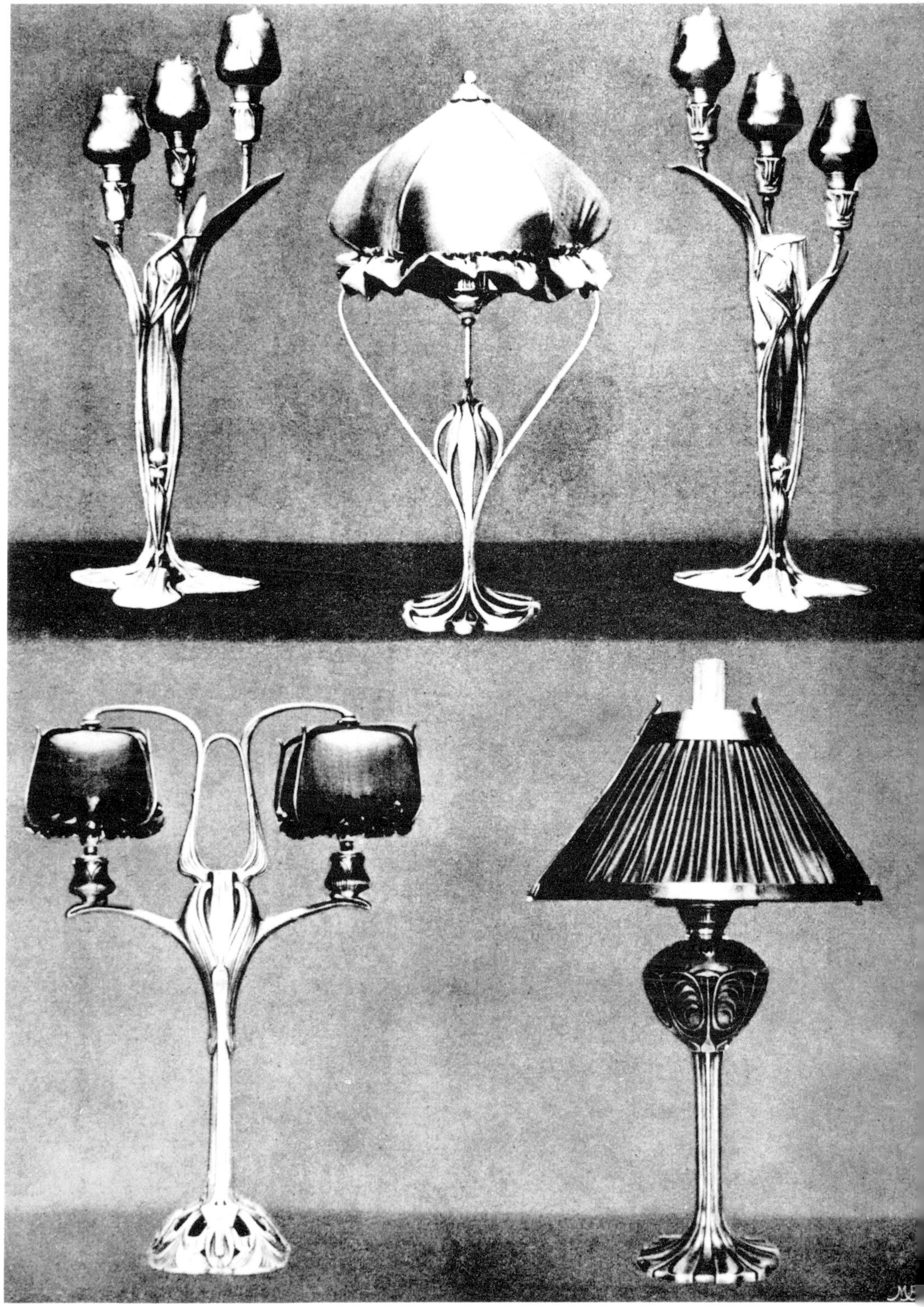

DE FEURE
A selection of light fixtures by de Feure for Bing's L'Art Nouveau shop. The pair of three-branched candelabra incorporate Tiffany Favrile shades which de Feure obtained through Mr Bing's association with Tiffany. The cloth shades on the three table lamps suggest that they were designed for a woman's boudoir. (38)

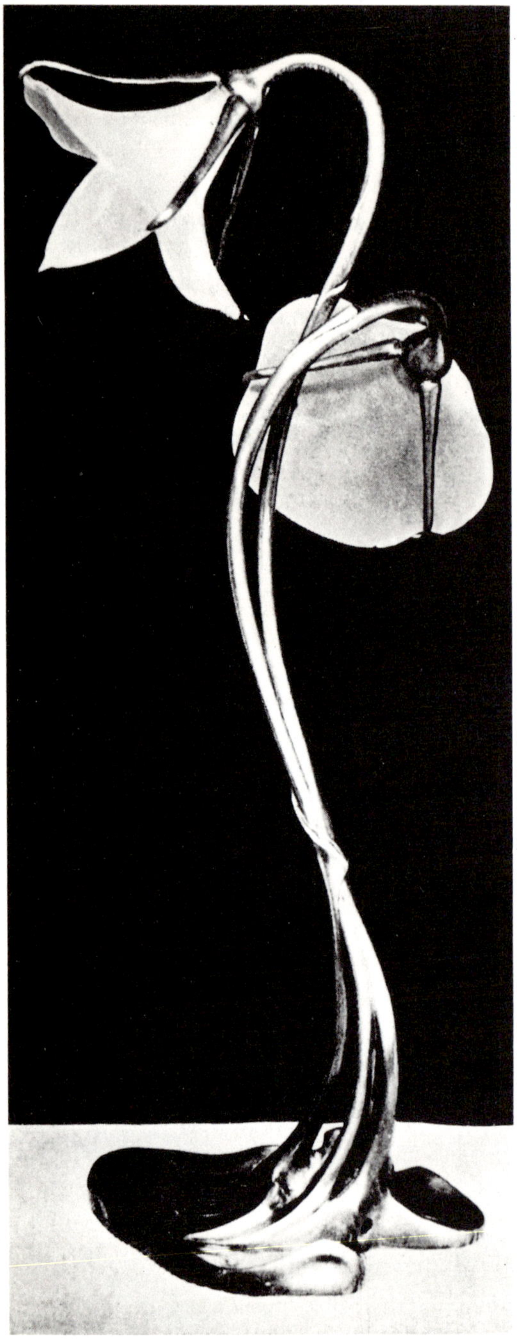

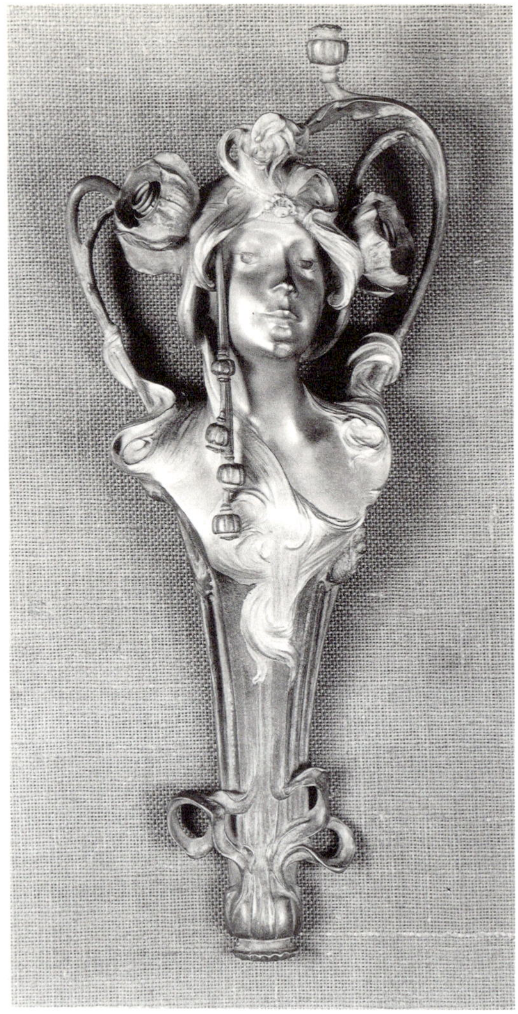

FLAMAND
A rare bronze electric wall-sconce, *c.* 1900. (40)

DUFRÈNE
This bronze lamp was shown in the 1901 Salon of the Société des Artistes Décorateurs. (39)

FIX-MASSEAU
Pierre Fix-Masseau was a prominent sculptor whose defence in the early 1890s of sculptors who undertook commissions for such household objects as lamps and centrepieces helped to pave the way for the subsequent glut of these objects on the market. His candlestick of 1897 (opposite left) resembles a gargoyle on a Gothic church. (41)

FRÉMIET
This gilt-bronze group entitled 'Baboons with Soap Bubbles' (opposite right) was commissioned by Sarah Bernhardt for her *hôtel particulier* in 1899. The bubbles contain electric bulbs. (42)

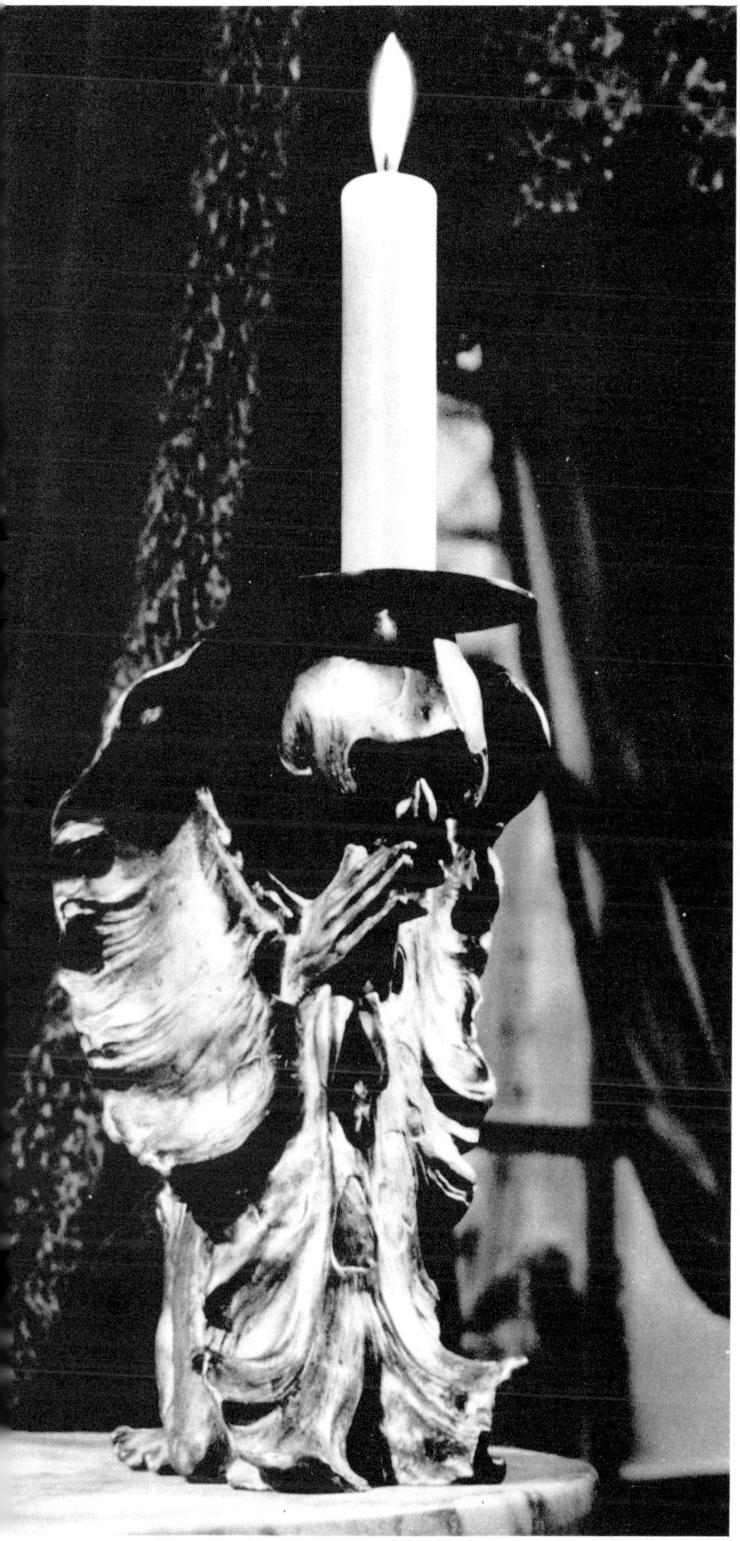

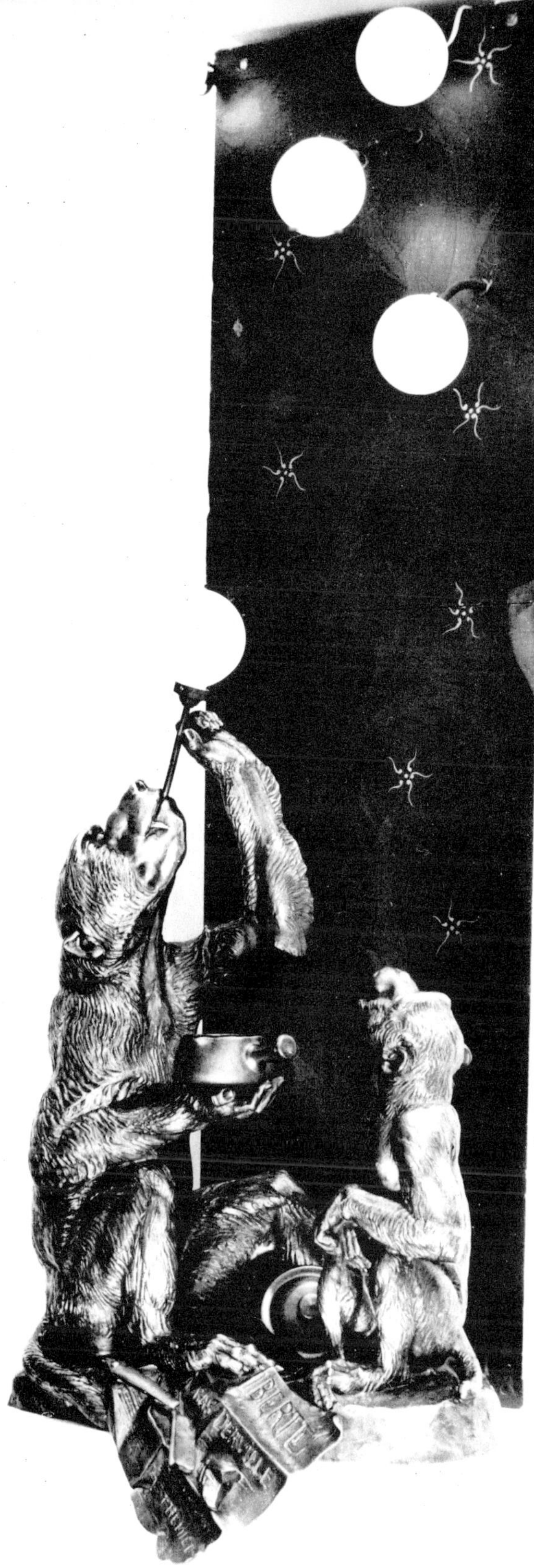

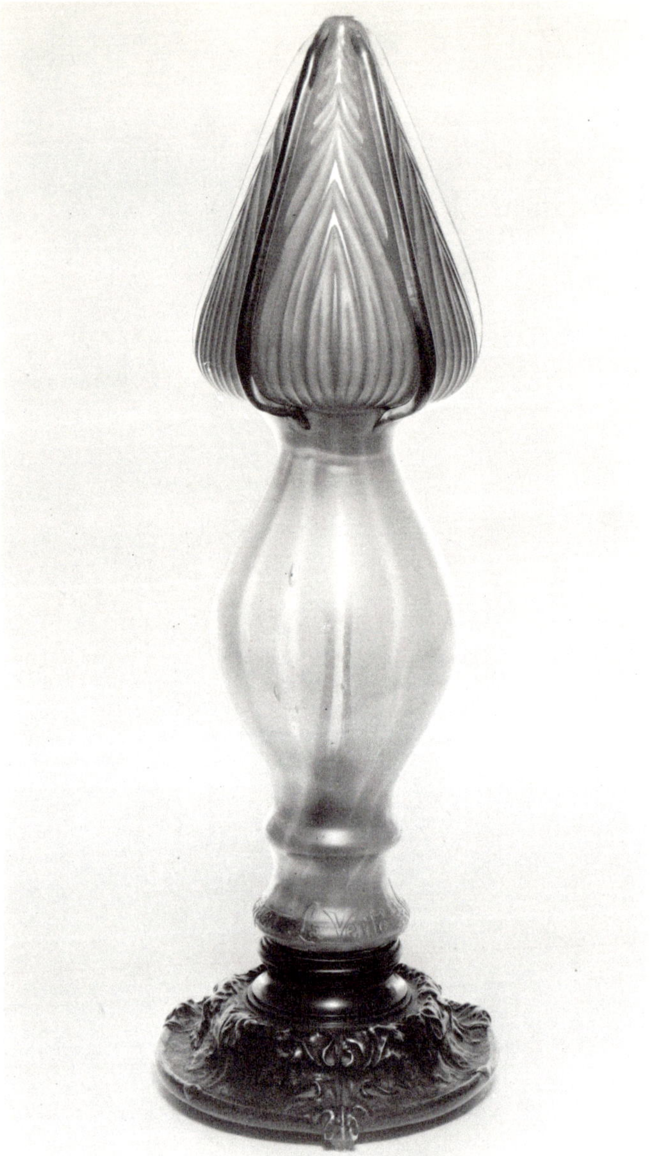

GALLÉ
A small table-lamp in the form of a palm-shoot, bearing on its base the inscription 'La vérité s'allumera comme une lampe' (Truth will shine like a lamp). (43)

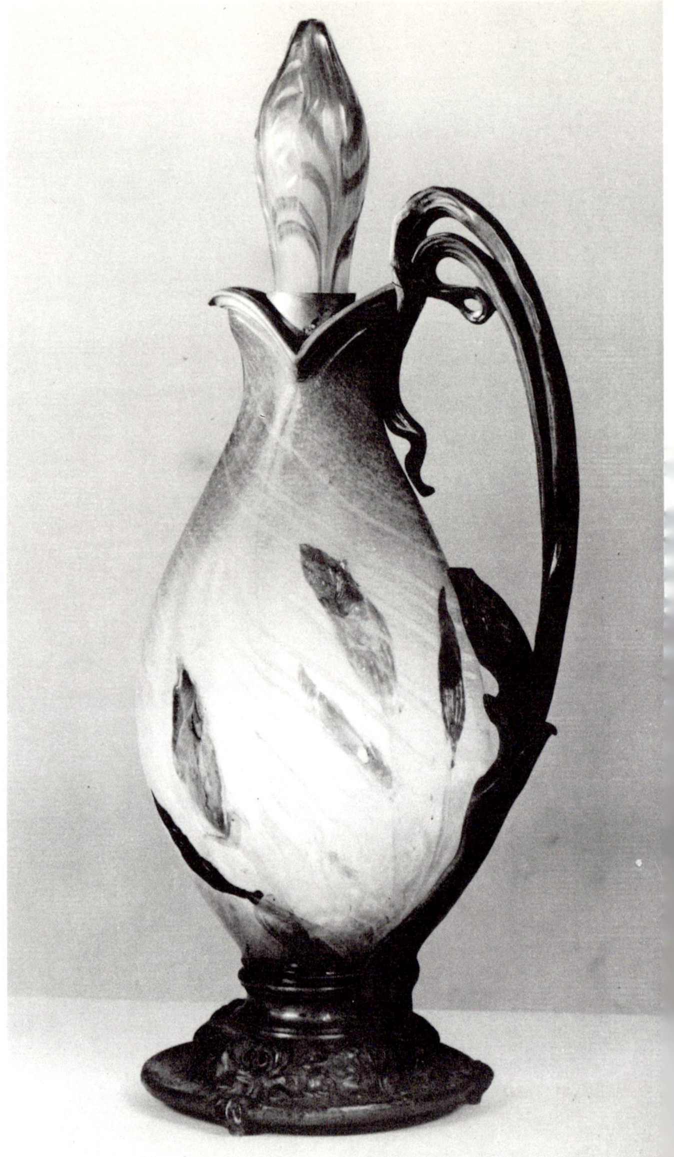

GALLÉ
A cameo flagon table-lamp bearing the inscription 'Lumière, tu ne seras pas éteinte' (Light, you will not be put out). (44)

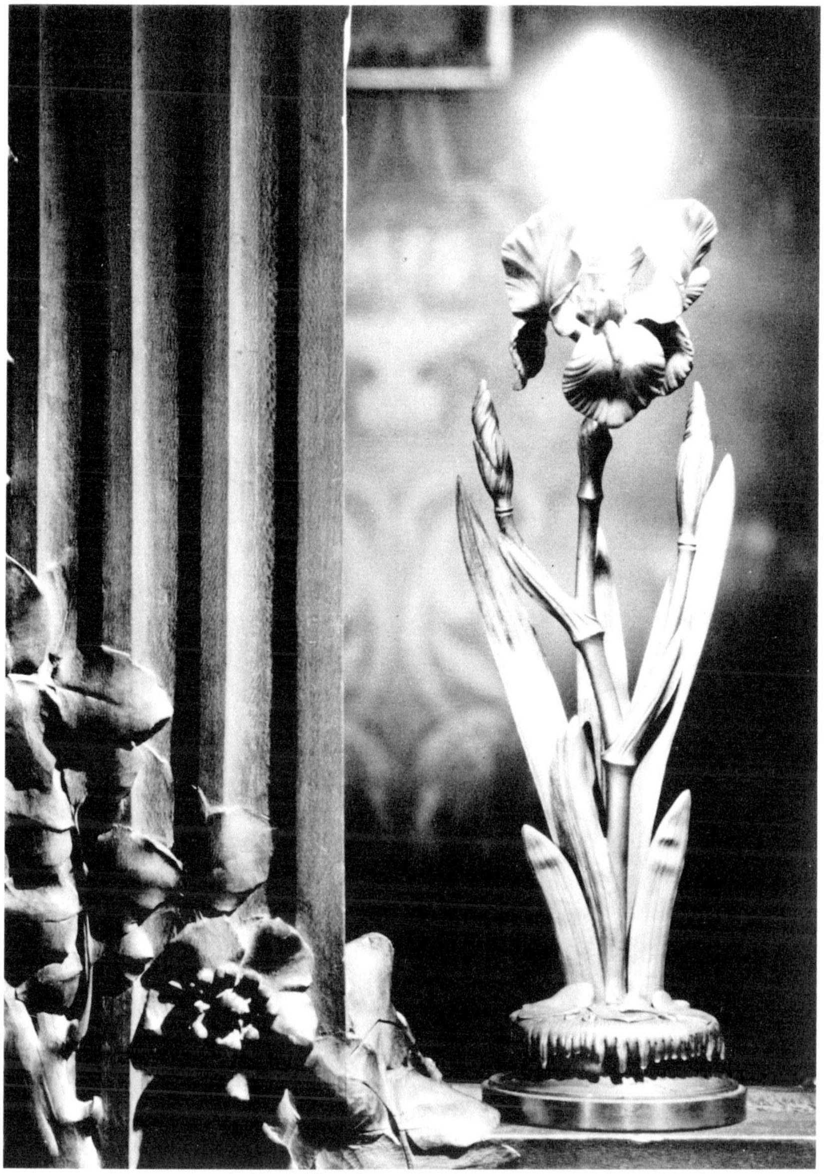

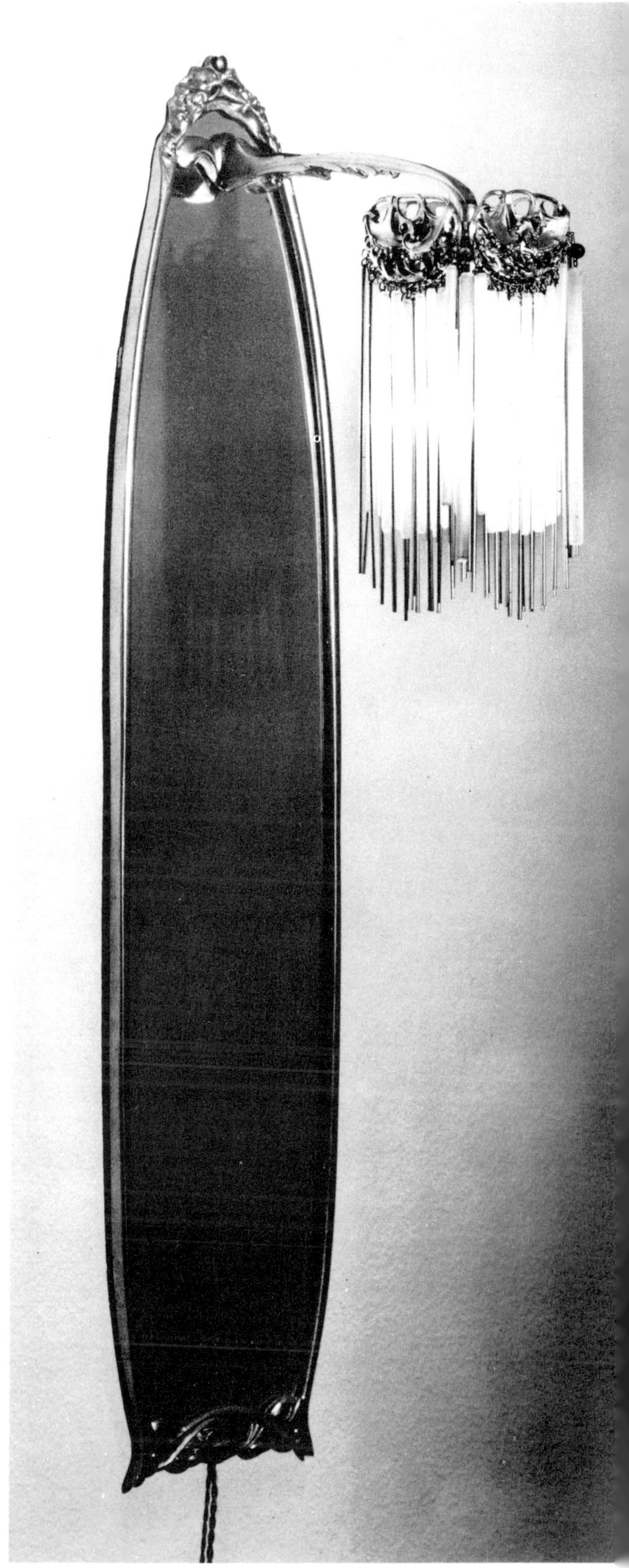

GALLÉ
Iris table-lamp. (45)

GUIMARD
A mirror/lamp combination which emphasizes the Art Nouveau concept of integrated wholes. (46)

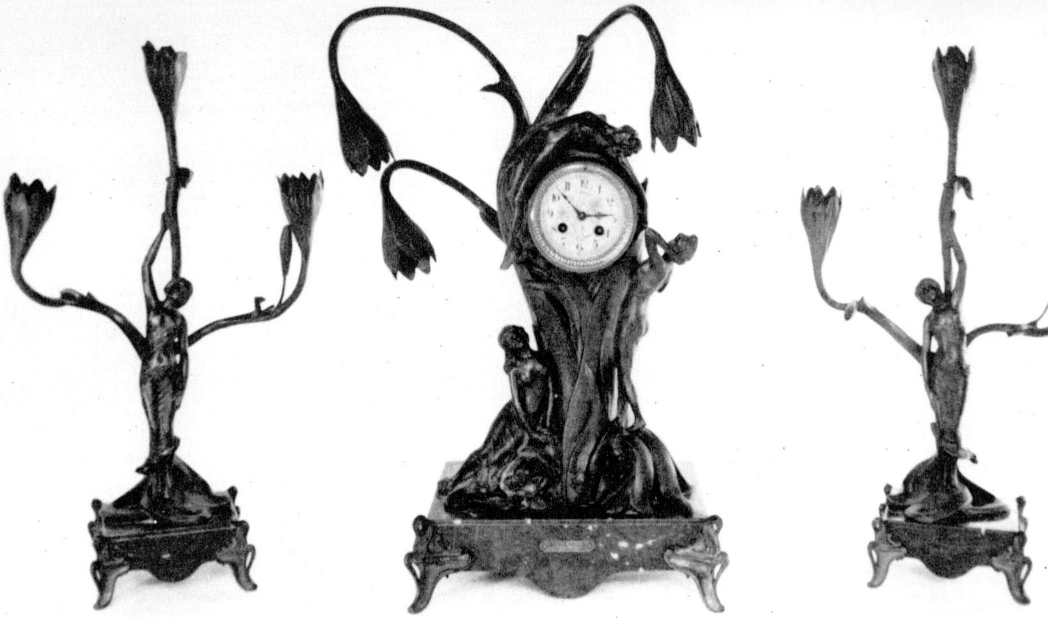

LANDRY
Right, a gilt-bronze model of this chandelier was incorporated into a children's bedroom which Landry exhibited at the Société des Artistes Décorateurs in 1906. It was illustrated in *L'Art Décoratif* in the same year. (49)

JONCHERY
A mantel set, including a pair of gilt-bronze candelabra, showing Jonchery's predilection for the *fin-de-siècle* 'Woman' theme. (47)

Left, a typical *femme-fleur* table-lamp; in this case the young woman holds a flower in which the electric bulb is set. This lamp was illustrated in the *Revue des Arts Décoratifs* (1901), p. 262. (48)

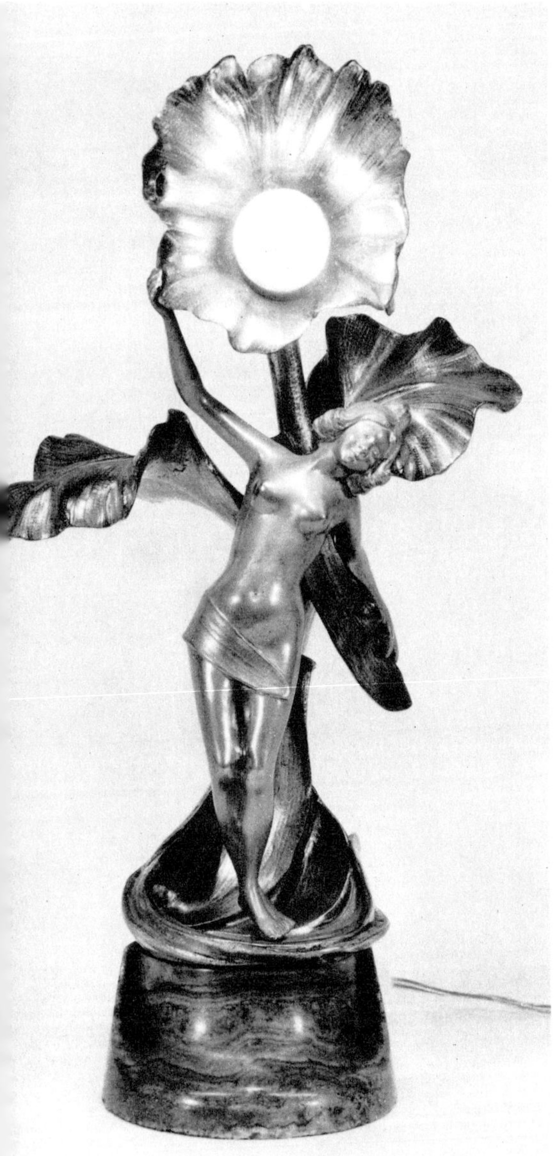

LAPORTE-BLAIRSY
Right, 'Femme à la Coquille' (Woman with shell), a lamp designed to be placed on a piano to project light onto the sheet-music. (50)

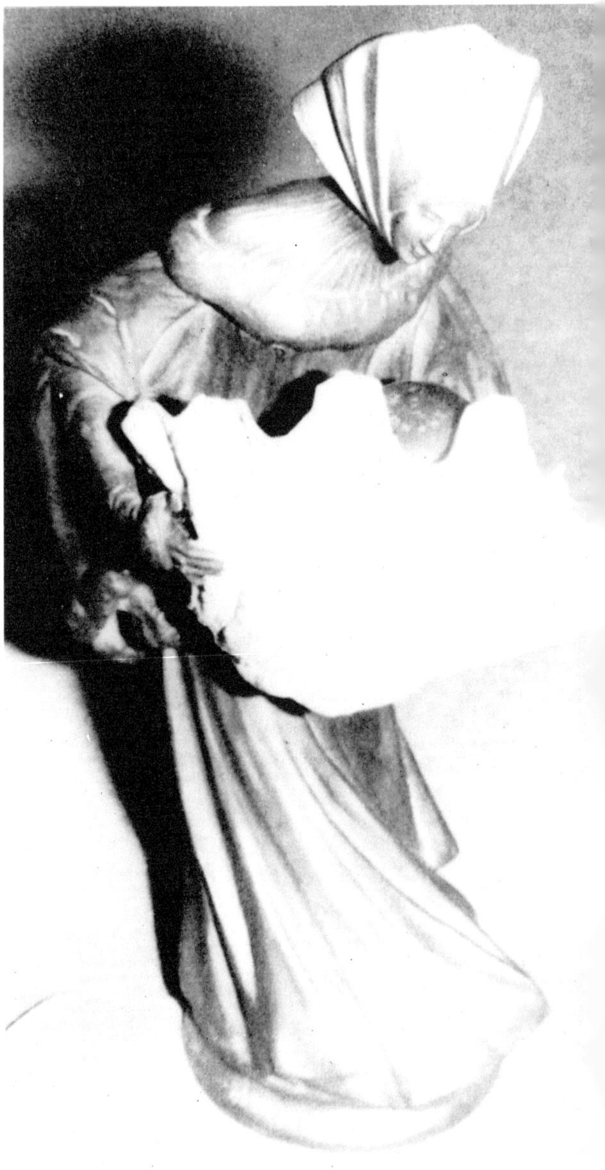

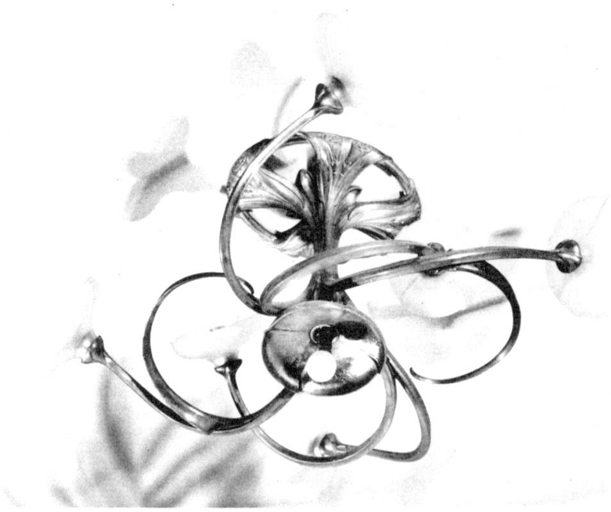

Laporte-Blairsy

Below left, 'La Fée au Coffret' (Fairy with casket), a bronze and glass table-lamp marketed by Eugène Houdebine and illustrated in *L'Art* (January–June 1902), p. 46. (51)

Below, 'La Voie Lactée' (The Milky Way). A patinated bronze model of this lamp was first exhibited at the Société des Artistes français in 1904 and then reproduced in both bronze and silvered bronze by the founders Susse *frères*. The globe, which houses the bulb, is of etched blue glass. (52)

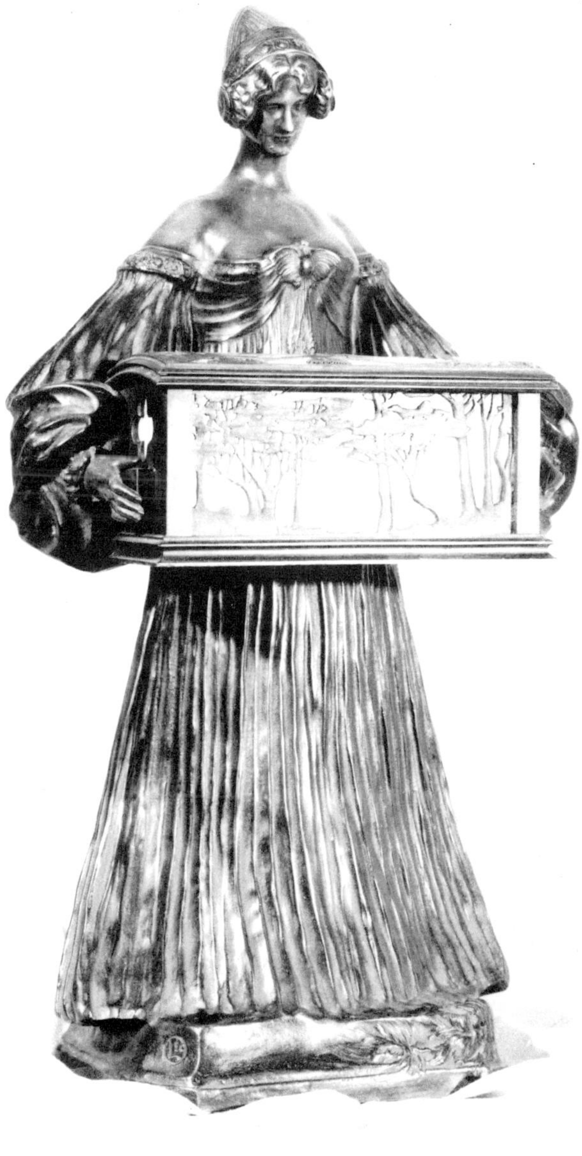

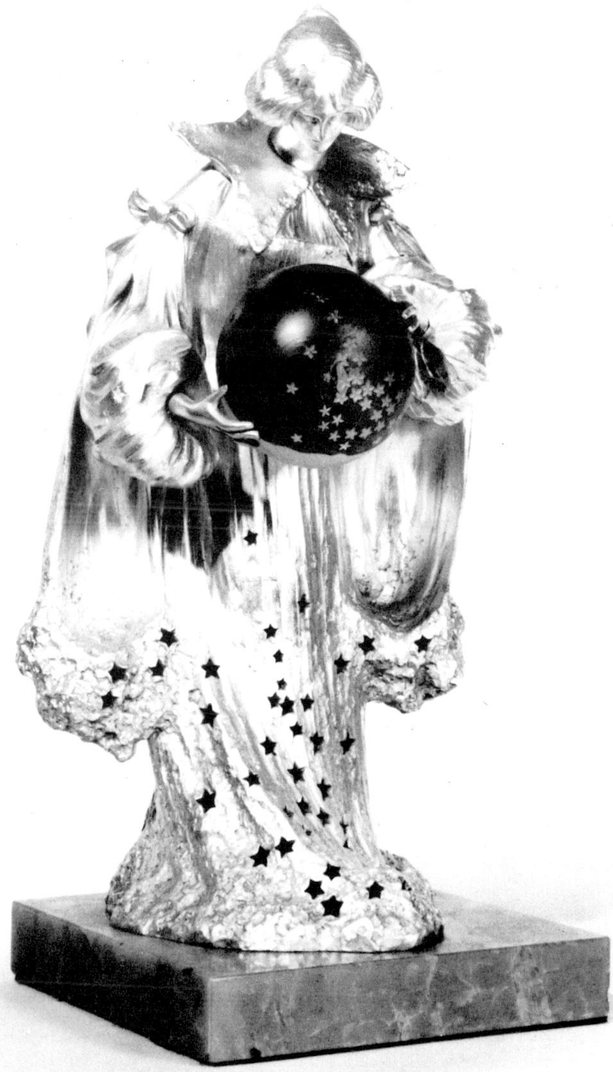

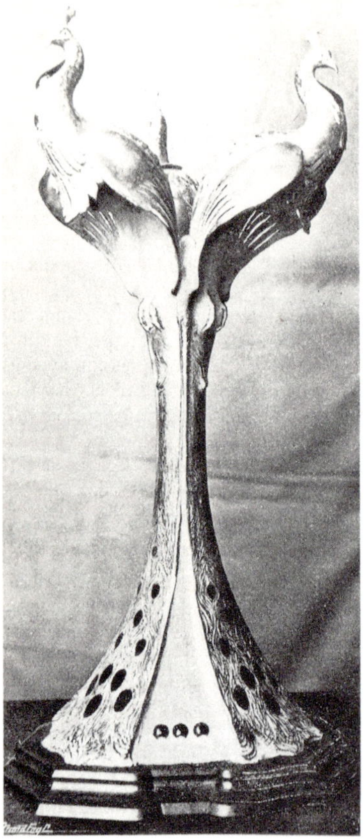

Laporte-Blairsy
'Les Paons' (The peacocks), a bronze floor-lamp first exhibited at the 1901 Société des Artistes français and later marketed through Houdebine. The bulbs are concealed behind the peacocks' plumage. (53)

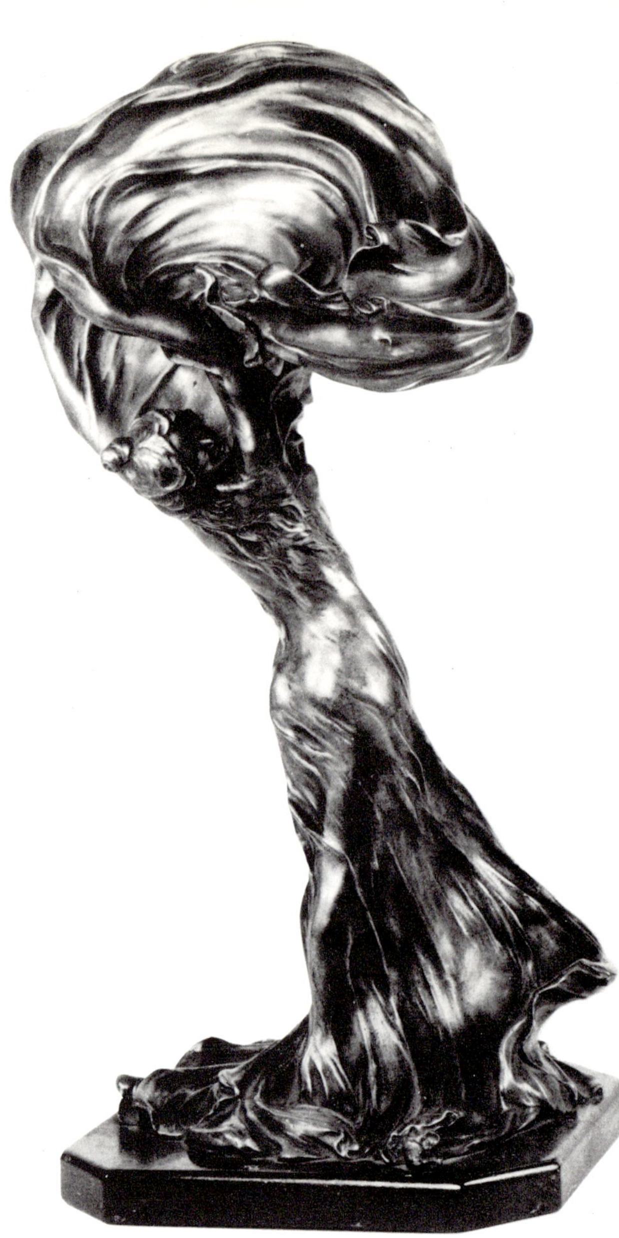

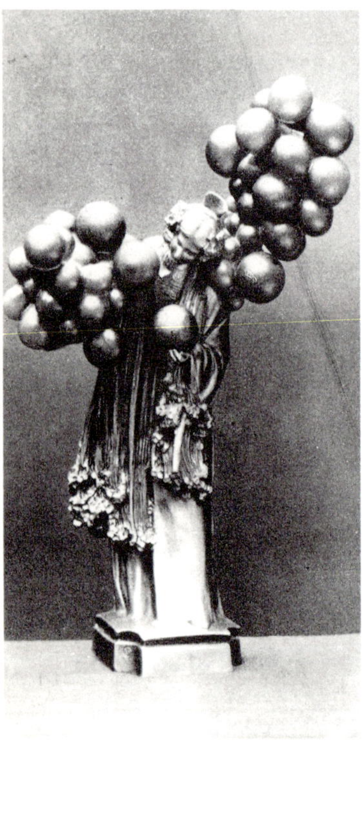

'La Marchande de ballons' (The balloon seller). This remarkable bronze lamp in which the balloons are in moulded pink glass, would have been inconceivable for combustion lighting: a naked flame placed inside the lamp would have cracked the glass. (54)

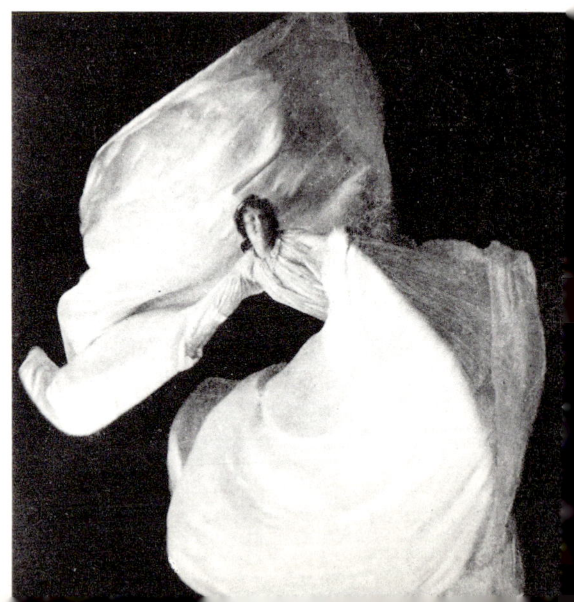

Loïe Fuller (1862–1928), the first dancer to make artistic use of the incandescent filament bulb. Her performances at the Folies-Bergère inspired numerous artists and sculptors to seek to re-create her lighting effects on paper and in metal. (56)

Larche
Three 'Loïe Fuller' lamps.
(55, 57, 58)

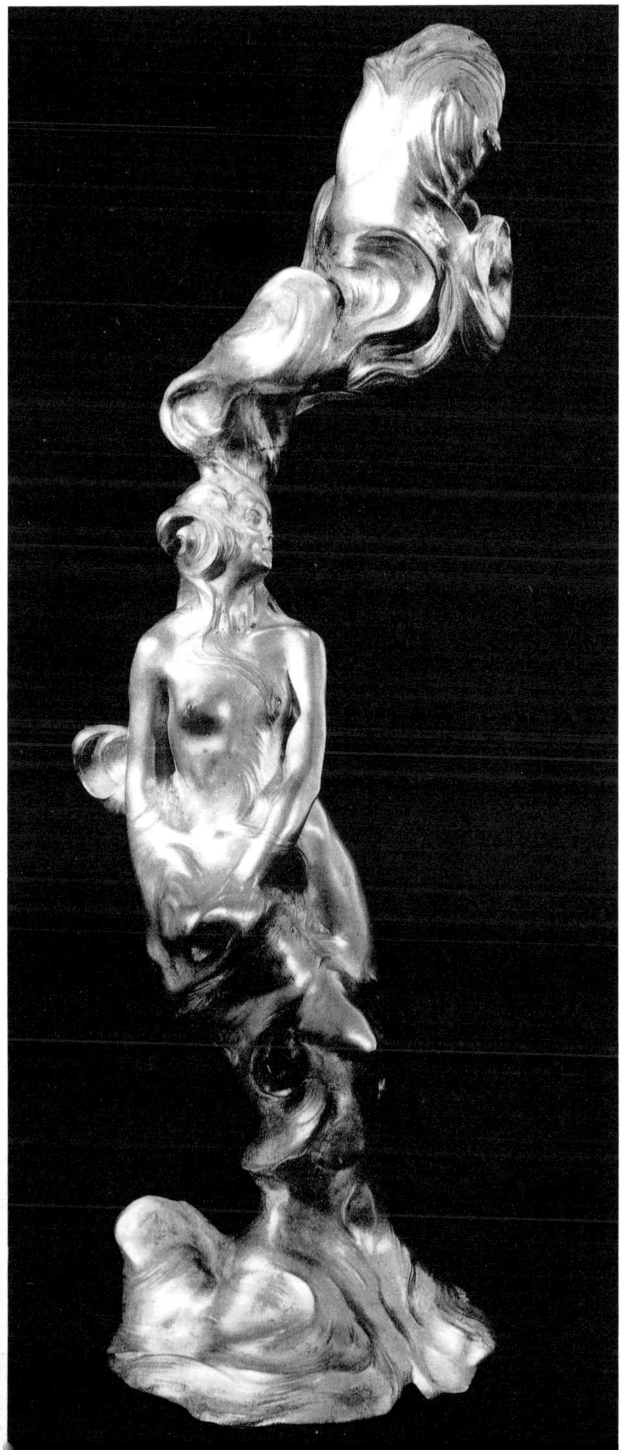

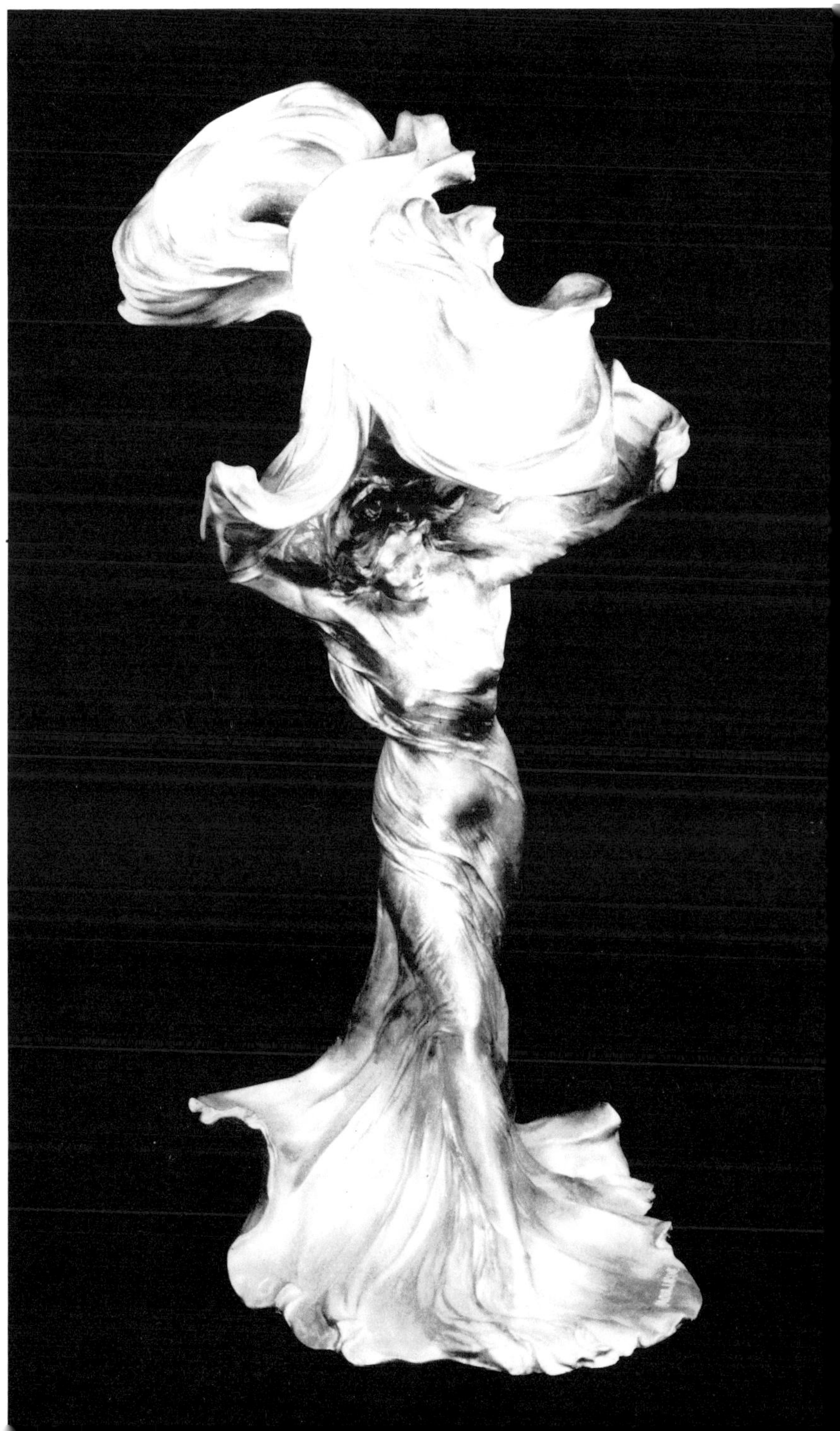

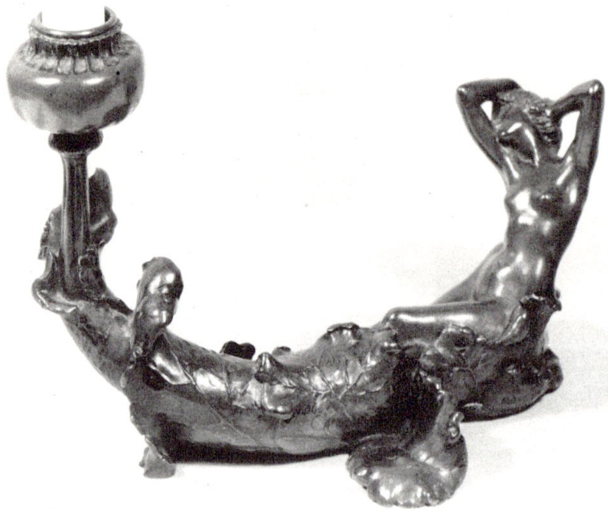

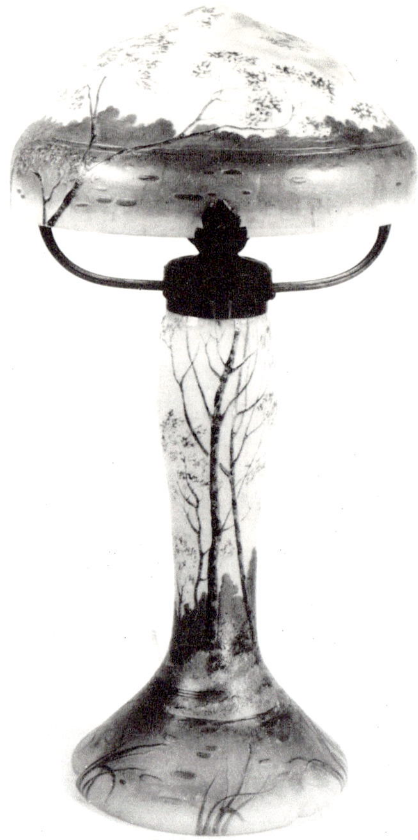

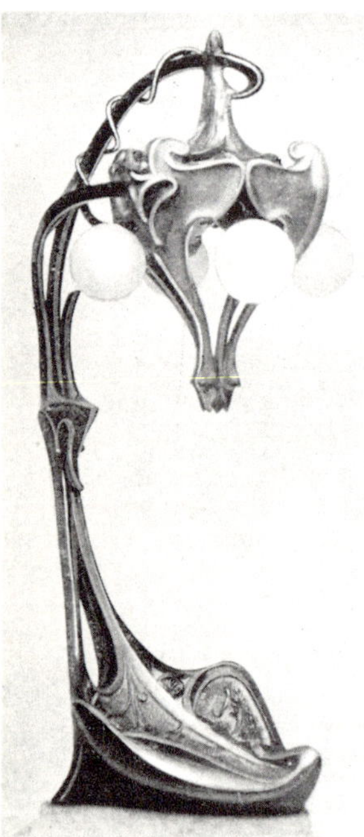

LEDRU
A charming bronze candlestick, with the nozzle cast as a poppy. (59)

LELEU
This bronze table-lamp, 'Le Liseron', designed as a convolvulus, was described by a critic in 1901 as 'certainly one of the more successful designs for the electric light to have emerged in the last few years.' (61)

LEGRAS
A triple-overlay cameo glass table-lamp depicting a riverscape. (60)

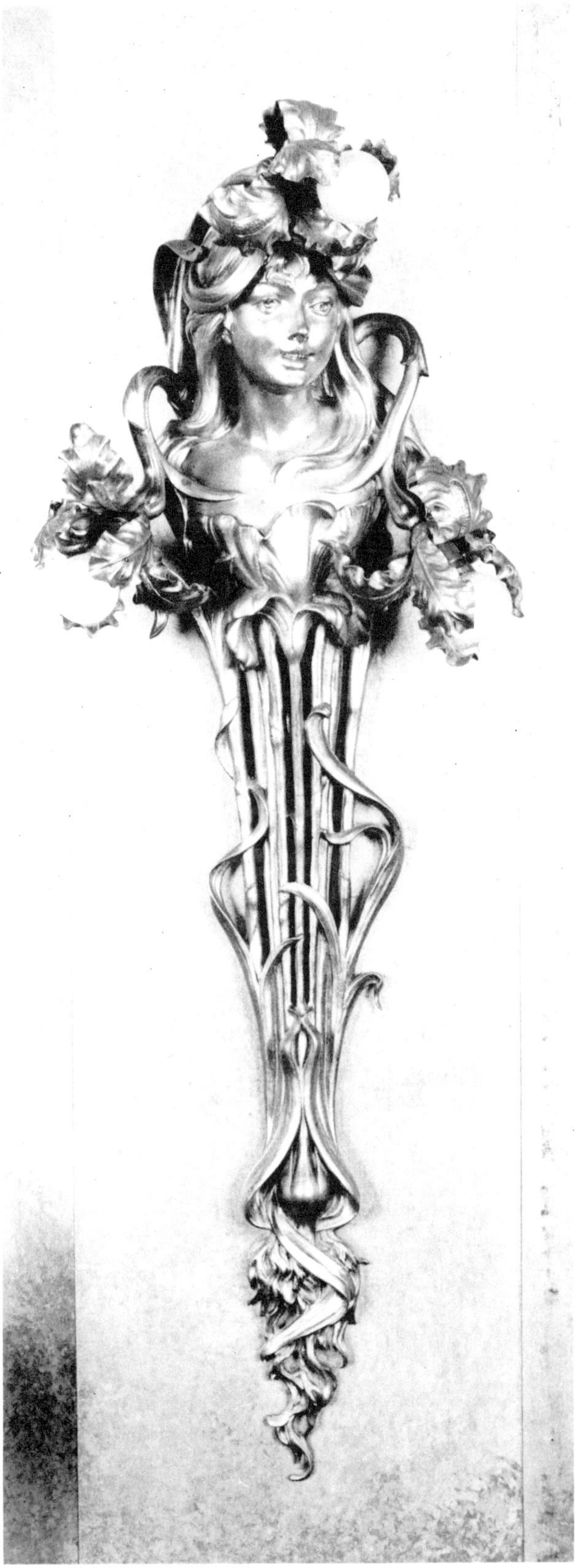

MAJORELLE

Left, one of the gilt-bronze wall-brackets commissioned by the Lucas Carton restaurant in Paris. The *femme-fleur* theme is uncharacteristic of Majorelle's work. (62)

Below, a magnolia table-lamp with glass shade by Daum *frères*. (63)

Below right, a water lily (*nénuphar*) table-lamp with Daum shade. (64)

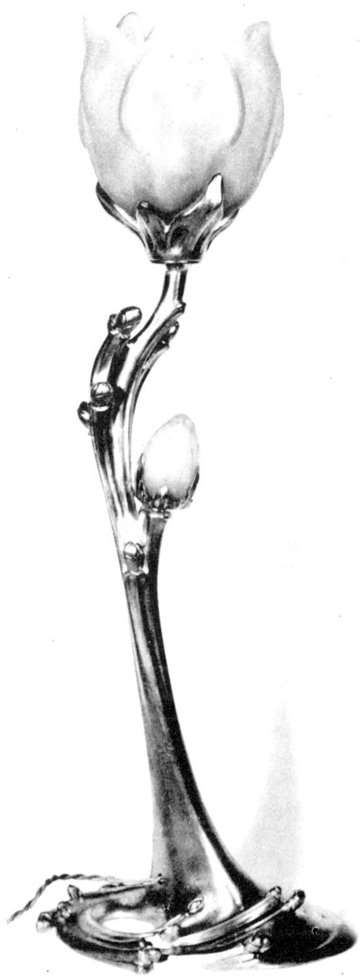

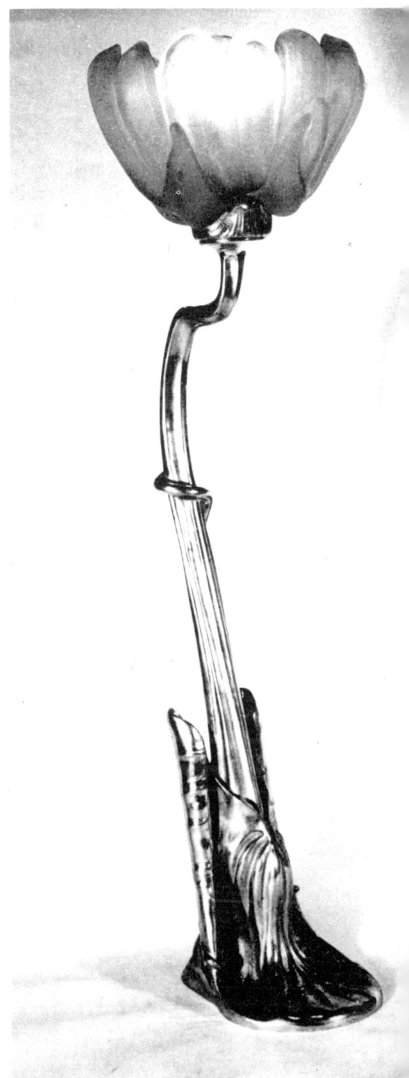

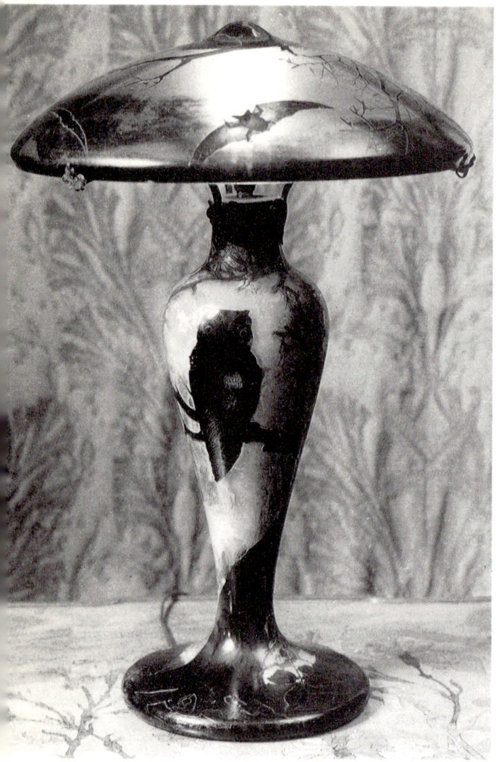

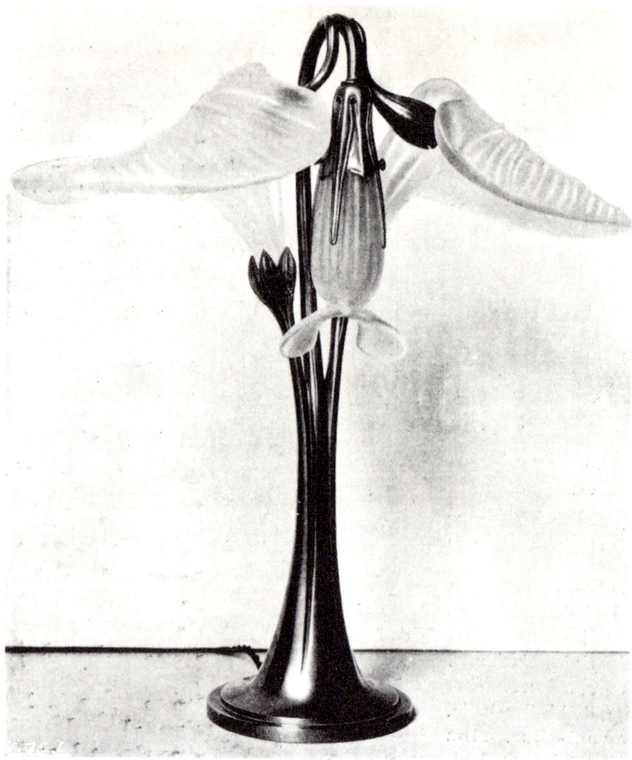

MULLER *frères*
This cameo table-lamp (far left shows the Art Nouveau pro clivity for nocturnal creatures (65)

SAUVAGE
This floral table-lamp was firs exhibited at the Société Nationale des Beaux-Arts in 1902. There is a model of it (lacking one glass shade) in the Musée de l'Ecole de Nancy. (66)

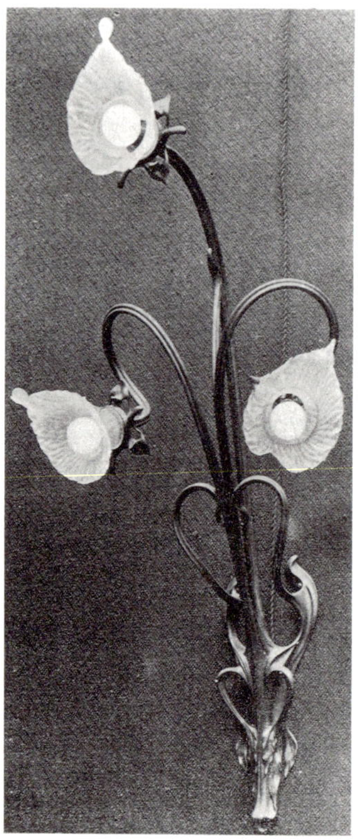

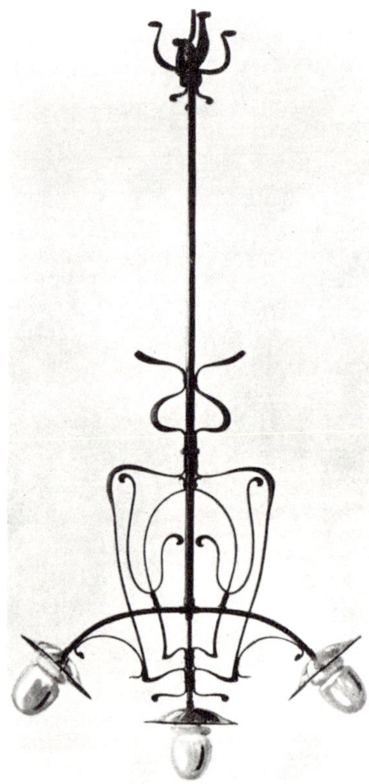

SELMERSHEIM
Metal and glass wall-bracket by Tony Selmersheim, shown at the 1901 *L'Art pour Tous* exhibition in Paris. (67)

SERRURIER-BOVY
A wrought-iron chandelier de signed *c.* 1901. (68)

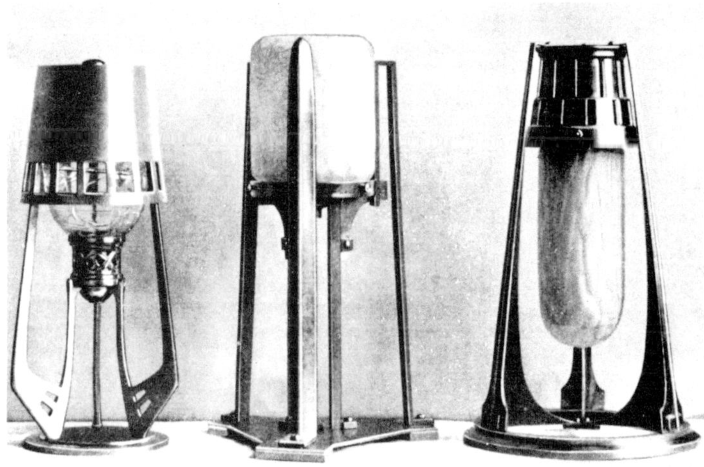

GERMANY

Behrens
Above, a selection of table-lamps, illustrated in *Deutsche Kunst und Dekoration* (1902/03), p. 432. (69)

Right, a bronze and glass table-lamp, 1902. The sweeping design of the shade is similar in concept to the winged women that Behrens incorporated into the fountain in the hall of the German pavilion at the Turin International Exposition in the same year. (70)

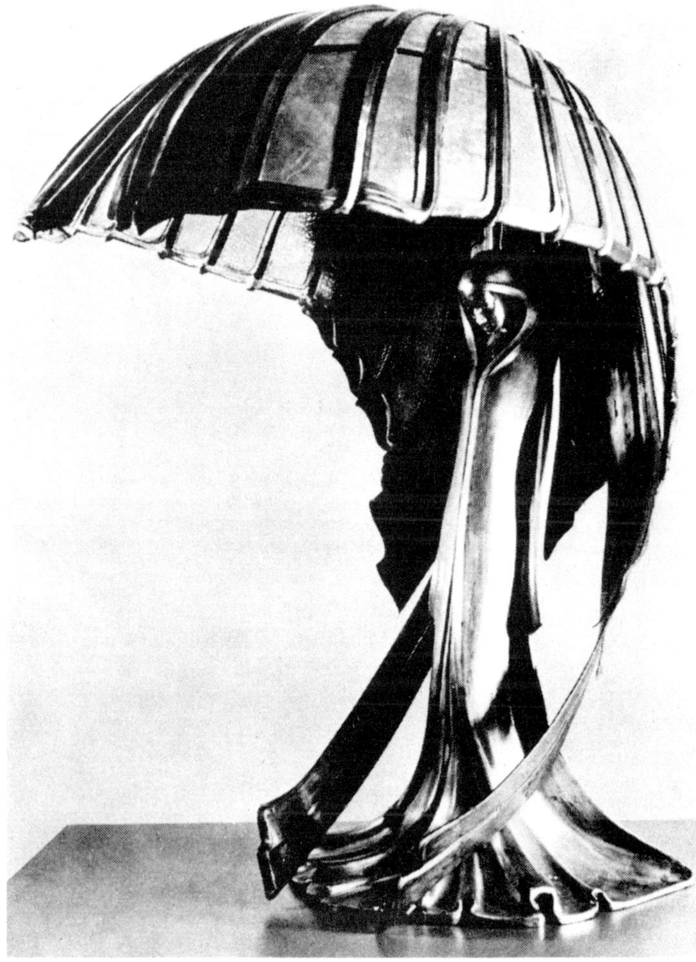

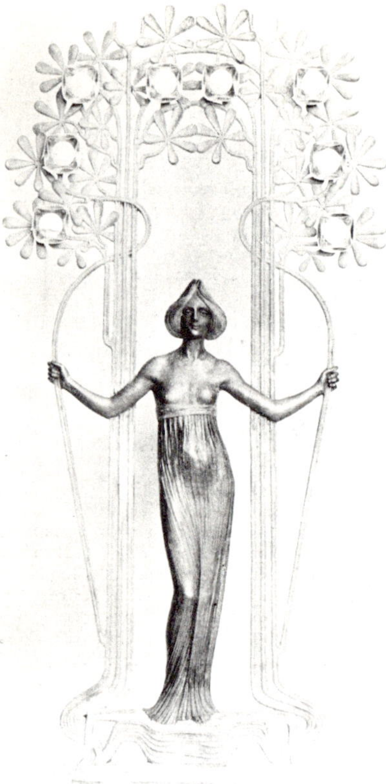

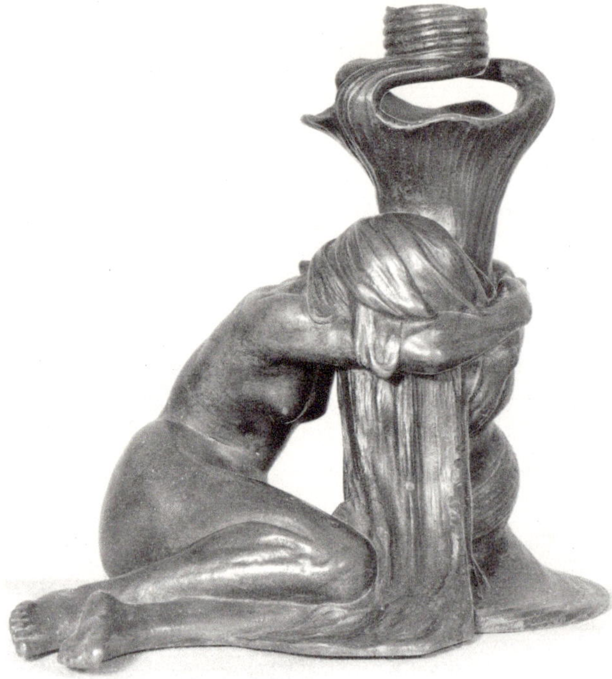

GURSCHNER
Left, a bronze wall-bracket exhibited at the 1900 International Exposition by a Herr Foerster, the dealer who handled Gurschner's works. The fixture was favourably noted by the critic Gustave Soulier in an article in *Art et Décoration* on the lighting at the Exposition. (71) Right, a rather rough-hewn electric candle holder exploiting the Art Nouveau 'Woman' theme. (72)

LOETZ
An iridescent glass and metal table-lamp attributed to Loetz. (73)

OLBRICH
Left, design for a candelabrum, and right, design for a gas wall-bracket; both 1901. (74, 75)

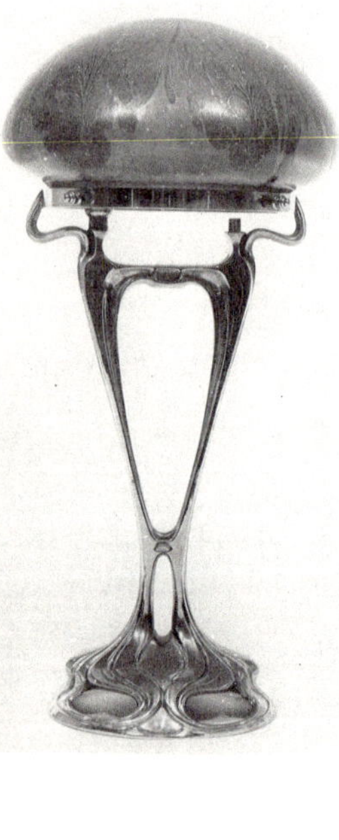

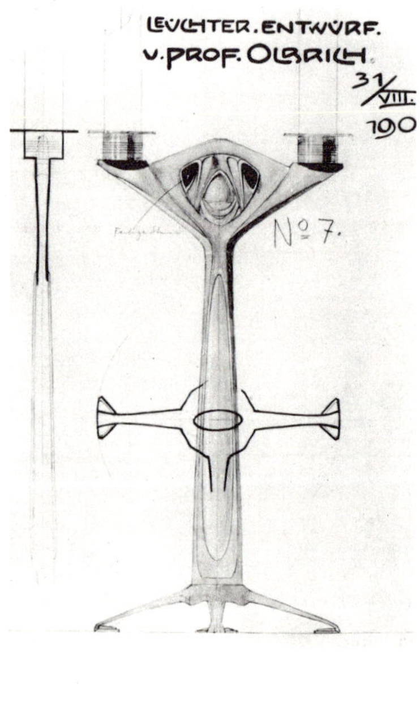

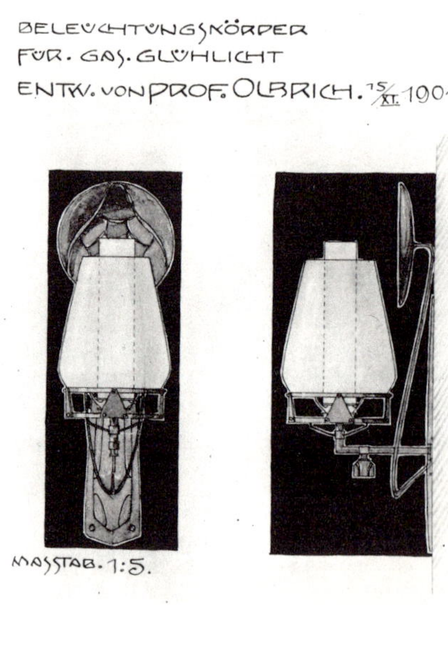

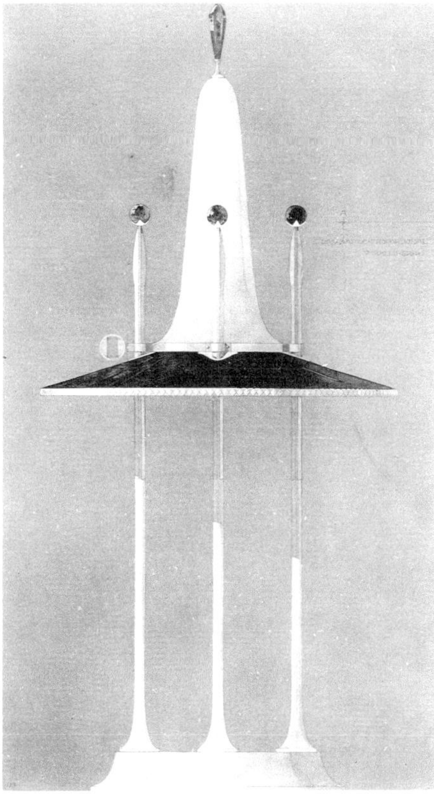

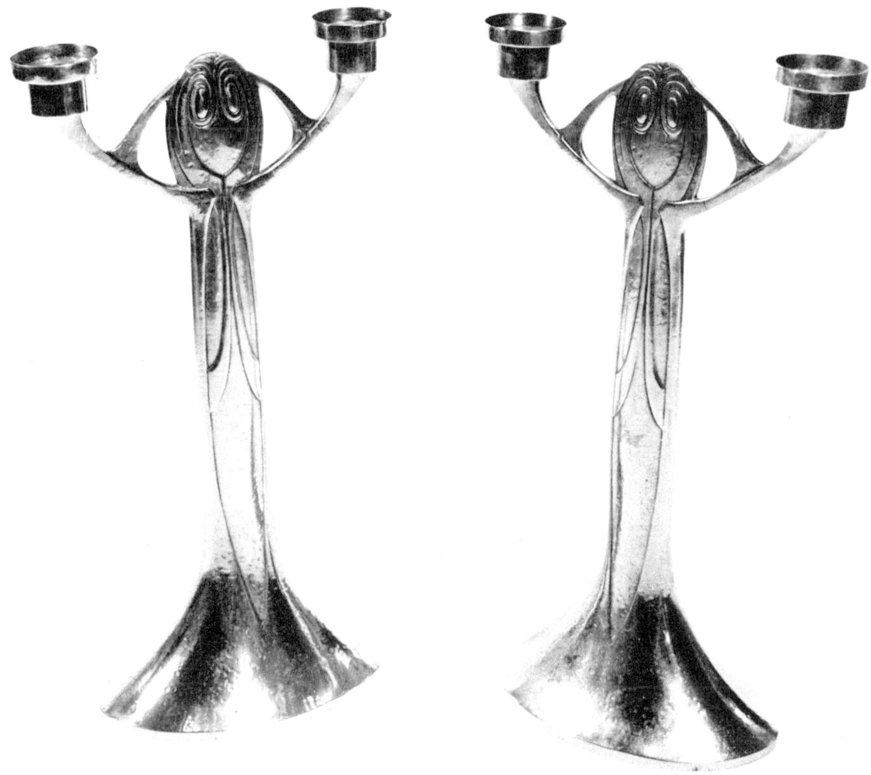

OLBRICH
Left, sketch for a lighting fixture, and right, a pair of pewter candlesticks designed 1901 and shown in 1904 at the Darmstadt Art Colony exhibition. (76, 77)

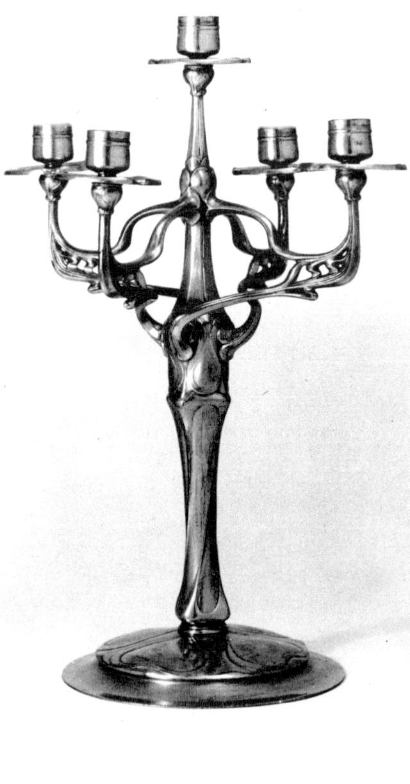

Pewter candelabrum marketed under the 'Osiris' name by Walter Scherf & Co., Nuremberg. (78)

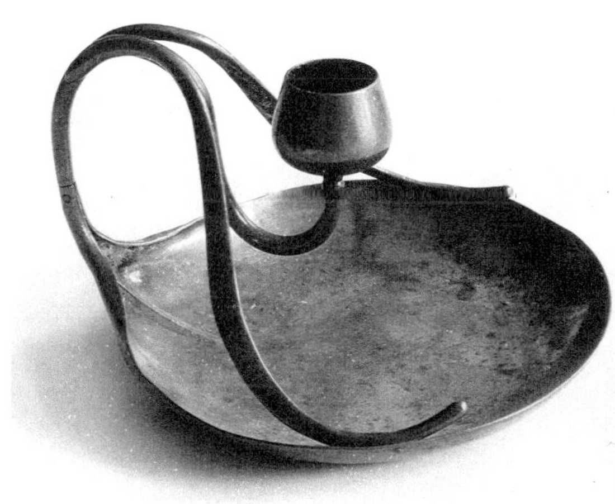

RIEMERSCHMID
A bronze candlestick, *c.* 1900. (79)

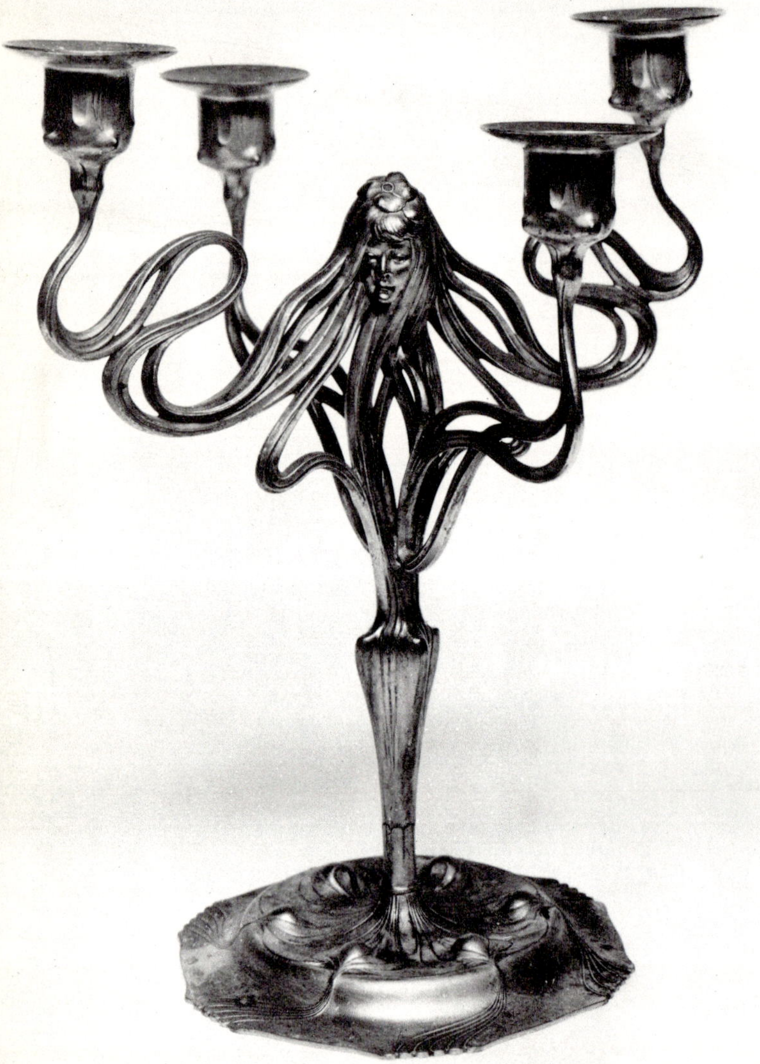

Schmitz
A bronze four-branched candelabrum, stamped 'Orivit' on the base. (80)

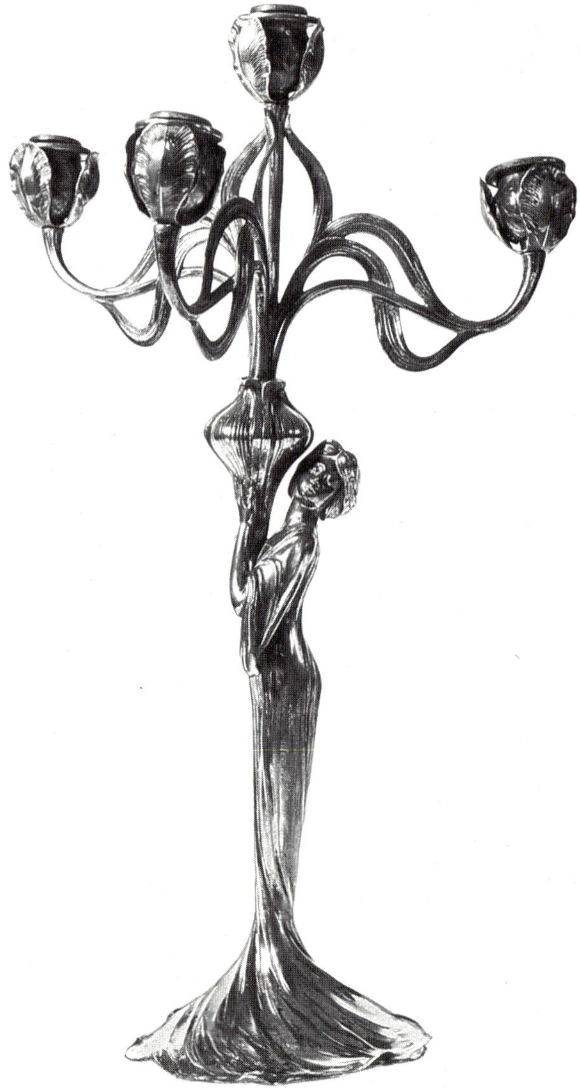

W.M.F.
A candelabrum in silvered metal, *c.* 1900. (81)

GERMANY, AUSTRIA, CZECHOSLOVAKIA

The designs for light fixtures that were based on the *Jugendstil*, the German/Austrian form of Art Nouveau as promoted in the pages of *Jugend* (hence its name), was based largely on the same themes that pervaded all Art Nouveau. More austere than that of its neighbours to the west and south-west, *Jugendstil* lighting was, for this reason, less distinctive. (One startling exception to that rule was Gertraud von Schnellenbühel's frenetic twenty-four branched candelabrum now in the Munich Stadtsmuseum.)

Austria's breakaway Secession group of young artists and craftsmen do not appear to have placed any specific emphasis on domestic illumination above that of their other furnishings and appliances executed largely by the Wiener Werkstätte. Only Gustav Gurschner, in fact, can be described as having been a specialist lighting exponent, though the architect Josef Hoffmann did design certain lamps in his chequerboard idiom (the original Hoffmann lighting is still *in situ* in the Stoclet Palace in Brussels), as did his fellow founder-member of the Secession, Koloman Moser. Little is known of the Viennese Rubenstein whose charming 'Daphne' table-lamp was exhibited at the 1900 International Exposition, or of Peter Tereszczuk, who sometimes incorporated Gallé shades into his anecdotal bronze-and-ivory lamps.

Fixtures of note not included here because they were peripheral to the main stream of *Jugendstil* activity are as follows: the chandeliers of Professor Bruno Paul; the 'Osiris' pewter candlesticks by Walter Scherf & Co., of Nuremberg; table-lamps by Richard Müller of Dresden and Albin Müller of Magdeburg; the ceiling lights of Professor Bernhardt Pankok of Stuttgart; and the candlesticks by A. Reiman and Otto Schulze, both of Berlin.

BEHRENS, PETER

Peter Behrens, exemplar of mixed-media versatility, was an architect, designer and painter, who applied himself to all forms of design, from houses to wood engravings, glassware, furniture, carpets and much more besides. After the triple security of three *Kunstgewerbeschule* degrees (from Karlsruhe, Düsseldorf and Munich) and further itinerant learning in Holland and Paris, he returned to Germany where, in 1893, he became a founder-member of the Munich Secession. With Richard Riemerschmid, Behrens brought German industrial design to its acme far ahead of the rest of the world (his avant-gardism was to influence the work of Walter Gropius, Mies van der Rohe and Le Corbusier, all of whom worked for him), and emphasized simplicity and functionalism rather than the floral vernacular preferred by most of his colleagues.

Behrens' designs for light fixtures show (except, most notably, in his table-lamp incorporating a stylized Art Nouveau woman) his predilection for clean, straight lines. This conservatism is evident in his metal and opalescent glass night light, silver candlesticks, ceramic table-lamps, and arc lamps designed for A.E.G. (Allgemeine Elektrizitäts Gesellschaft) in Berlin.

GURSCHNER, GUSTAV

Gurschner has been the victim of neglect for far too long. Largely unknown, rather than passed over, his *petits bronzes*, like those of Laporte-Blairsy, have lacked an effective publicist, especially in the realm of lighting. Born in Muhldorf (Bavaria), Gurschner's formal education included art school in Bozen and the Imperial Arts and Crafts School in Vienna, the city where he was finally to settle. His work was included in the inaugural exhibition of the Vienna Secession in 1898, after which he participated in numerous exhibitions both in Vienna and internationally: for example, Munich, Paris (including the 1900 Exposition) and Monte Carlo. His reputation grew accordingly.

In the early part of his career he devoted himself to monumental groups and portrait busts, but he then turned his hand to smaller, domestic objects, such as bronze ashtrays, door-knockers, ladies' hand-mirrors, inkstands, pen trays, and sweetmeat dishes, most of which were marketed by the Viennese A. Forster. A pen sketch in *The Studio* 1909 Yearbook informs the reader that Gurschner's most recent work in sculpture had been (*i.e.*, by 1909) the memorial to commemorate the meeting between King Edward VII and the Emperor Franz Josef at Marienbad in 1905, and that he had also designed and executed prizes for the Gordon Bennett and Herkomer automobile races.

Gurschner appears to have had an immediate affinity for the newly commercialized incandescent filament bulb and its potential for incorporation in, and enhancement of, his bronzes. (The word 'enhancement' is used deliberately here, as most of Gurschner's lamps are more illuminated than illuminating.) Even his use of bare-breasted young women – potentially so hackneyed a theme – as the central figures in many of his lamps, largely survives any stricture, for his figures, like those by Korschann, Bouval and Chalon, have a quiet dignity and a poetic charm. Another favoured theme – this one shared by Tiffany – was seashells, such as the Chambered Nautilus and Turbo Marmoratus, to house the electric bulb: the shells' translucency produced a richly luminescent effect when backlit.

It is not clear who provided the glass shades for certain of Gurschner's lamps. There is no documentary evidence that Gurschner himself worked in this medium (although the small staff in his *atelier* did, under his guidance, extend themselves into the fields of jewellery and, fleetingly, furniture), and the iridescent lustre in one of the shades strongly suggests that it may have been by Loetz.

Gurschner also designed and executed candlesticks – for example, a silvered bronze pair entitled 'The Wind' – and several wall-brackets, the latter often with naked bulbs.

Gurschner's bronze table-lamps, particularly those that incorporate seashells, are now collectors' items. Prices in excess of $4,400 (FF 22,000) have been paid for them in New York.

J. P. KAYSER SOHN

The pewter foundry of Kayser Sohn was founded in 1862 in Krefeld-Bochum by J. P. Kayser of Kaiserwerth. Following extension and modernization of the firm's facilities in 1885, the founder's son, Engelberg Kayser, set up a studio in 1900 in Cologne, where the models for the foundry's pewterware were designed. Experimentation in new techniques resulted in the adoption of a new mixture of copper and antimony which gave the alloy a silvery brightness and also endowed it with extra durability. Most objects made from this material were marked 'Kayserzinn' (*i.e.*, Kayser pewter).

The firm participated in the German Art Nouveau movement, producing pewter domestic ware such as *jardinières*, salvers, cigarette lighters, and a large range of candlesticks and candelabra, some of which were marketed through Liberty's in London. As in the case of Liberty's Tudric range of tableware, Kayser Sohn was to benefit from the turn-of-the-century relaxation towards an *ersatz* material whose intrinsic value was minimal.

Kayser Sohn pewterware falls into the same price range as Liberty & Co.'s Tudric ware. Kayser Sohn candlesticks fetch between £50 and £80 ($95 and $150).

KORSCHANN, CHARLES

Born in Brno, Moravia (now Czechoslovakia), Korshann led a nomadic life, with sojourns, following his graduations from both the Vienna and the Berlin Schools of Fine Arts, in Paris (1894–1906), Berlin and Frankfurt (1906–14), Cracow (1914–19), and finally Brno. A sculptor and medallist, he designed during his stay in Paris a series of Art Nouveau *petits bronzes*, many of which were cast for him by the Paris foundry of Louchet.

His various objects in bronze and plaster, such as inkwells, clocks, portrait busts (in 1904 he did a bust of Alphonse Mucha for the Moravian Museum in Brno), centrepieces and lamps, were exhibited through the annual salons of the Société des Artistes français from 1894 to 1905. A favourite motif was the *femme-fleur*, and his objects are frequently adorned in low- or high-relief by flower-enveloped maidens who, in the case of his table lamps, take on the role of caryatids supporting cloth or glass shades. Characteristically more coy and demure than most of the semi-divine Dianas that clambered, sprawled or reposed on *fin de siècle* bronzes, Korschann's young women seem somewhat inhibited: whereas they *appear*, on first glance, to be topless, closer inspection reveals a discreet hairline high on the breasts that identifies the V-necks of their diaphanous robes.

The prices of Korschann's small bronze and gilt-bronze objects range between £300 and £500 ($575 and $950). They fetch more if wired for electricity.

LOETZ-WITWE

Like Kayser Sohn, the firm of Loetz-Witwe was to be a family affair. Established in Klostermühle in Bohemia in 1830 by Johann Loetz, management passed, on his death in 1848, to his widow ('Witwe'), who was followed, in turn, by their grandson, Max Ritter von Spaun, in 1879.

It was under the latter's modernization programme that the firm expanded into international recognition, capturing Grand Prizes at the 1889 and 1900 Paris expositions. Early imitations of semi-precious stones – for example, chalcedony, jasper and aventurine – provided a popular line of glassware, and this was followed by the firm's iridescent range, such as the *Verres papillons* first presented to the public in an 1899 Paris exhibition.

On the basis of Tiffany's technique for iridescent glass, the firm produced a wide range of glass tableware in the Art Nouveau style at the turn of the century. Bowls, *solifleur* vases, rosewater sprinklers, candlesticks, and lamps were designed and executed in a palette that included peacock green and blue, gold, and yellow lustres – often in trailing or splashed patterns, and overlaid with silver.

It is incredible that a firm of the stature of Loetz-Witwe could have allowed so much of its glassware to leave the factory unsigned, a situation which makes attribution exceedingly difficult. Those objects that were signed (it has been suggested that these were for the foreign market only, a stipulation laid down by Tiffany to avoid confusion with his own iridescent glassware) often had their bases engraved 'Austria' with the firm's mark of a pair of crossed arrows in a circle.

There can be little doubt that Loetz made shades for bronze sculptors such as Gurschner, but, on the other hand, nothing is known about who supplied the metal mountings for Loetz's own range of light fixtures (and general tableware). It is amazing that the designer of the base in a stunningly beautiful lamp (illustration XXIII) should not have insisted on having his name appear somewhere on the object.

For the rest, the problem of identification is enormous. This is true also of glass lampshades made by the firm under commission from various lamp-makers; in this case, where only a part of the final object was made, Loetz's already established reluctance to sign their glass was, if anything, reinforced.

The prices that Loetz lamps bring depend partly on how authentically they can be attributed to the firm. Loetz shades are keenly sought: prices in Paris in 1975 ranged between FF 2,625 and 5,250 ($525 and $1,050).

MUCHA, ALPHONSE

The question whether Mucha can be included among Art Nouveau artists who contributed to lighting depends in whether a specific gilt-bronze bust which he made around 1900 was originally intended to house an electrical fixture. Having examined one casting of this bust (only five Mucha busts in all have been rediscovered), I am convinced by various features that indeed the bust was at one time a lamp.

It is not surprising that Mucha, like so many of his contemporaries, should have felt the challenge of electricity, and that he too should have exploited his particular talents in order to salute the advent of a new era.

The four large Mucha busts (the fifth one that has been rediscovered is smaller) are probably worth not less than £40,000 ($75,000) each.

OLBRICH, JOSEPH

Pre-eminent architect and co-founder of the Vienna Secession with Josef Hoffmann and Koloman Moser in 1897, Olbrich is remembered primarily for his buildings, such as the Vienna Secession Exhibition Hall (1898) and the houses for an artists' colony on Darmstadt's Mathildenhöhe, the latter by invitation of the Grand Duke Ernst Ludwig of Hessen. His creative talents, however, like those of Hoffmann, Moser and Otto Wagner, were to be deployed in a wider range than architecture alone: jewellery, pewter tankards, silver tableware, the interiors of yachts and villas, etc. In lighting he is best known for his pewter candelabra, of which a substantial number still exist. In addition, in a retrospective exhibition of his work at the Darmstadt Hessisches Landesmuseum in 1967 were shown several of his aquarelle and pencil sketches for electric ceiling-lamps, silver and pewter candelabra, brass table-lamps, and gas wall-sconces, most of which were designed for the interiors of his buildings and in some cases cast in limited numbers for the general public. Never over-elaborate, his designs are both functional and clean-cut, with echoes of Mackintosh and the Viennese School's proclivity for the cube and the rectangle.

A pair of Olbrich pewter candlesticks were sold in London in 1972 for £750 ($1,500).

RIEMERSCHMID, RICHARD

A founder-member of Munich's *Vereinigte Werkstätten* (United Workshops), Riemerschmid was well equipped to carry out the group's objectives: to co-ordinate the activities of artists, designers and craftsmen in the *Jugendstil* movement. Himself an architect, designer and painter, Riemerschmid played an important role in Teutonizing the various influences from abroad; and his Anglomania is expressed in the sober and functional lines of his silver flatware cutlery and his furniture – clearly conceived for industrial reproduction. This emphasis is also visible in his range of candlesticks and candelabra, which are unsensational yet have a quiet dignity.

His designs for the chandeliers for his interiors, likewise executed by the Werkstätten, tend to be less restrained; indeed, they are rather cluttered. For example, in his music room, shown at the German Art Exhibition at Dresden in 1899, the chandelier consisted of a large circle of approximately twenty small shades, each suspended by interlacing electric wires. The overall effect is one of a confusedly woven spider's web. In another ensemble, this time for a bachelor's bedroom, a similar reticulated effect is obtained with the wiring; and in the entrance hall of a cottage in Ulm, the functionalism of the wires as power conduits is too undisciplined, giving the impression that Riemerschmid never finally resolved the issue of how best to incorporate them satisfactorily into the overall effect. His strong belief in functionalism precluded his disguising them.

SCHMITZ, FERDINAND HUBERT

Little is known about Schmitz beyond his connection with the firm of 'Orivit' in the Rhenish town of Köln-Ehrenfeld. He was not one of the important *Jugendstil* exponents, and among the few surviving examples of his work are several pairs of candelabra (see illustration 80). Orivit was an artwork metalware firm which Schmitz evidently joined sometime before 1901, for after that date the firm's trademark was either 'Orivit' or 'Schmitz Edelzinn'. Among other things the plant produced pewter dishes and mounts for pottery bowls; and I have seen two table-lamps signed 'Orivit', both of which – of extraordinarily fine design – have silvered bronze mounts that support glass shades.

The Schmitz candelabrum illustrated brought $350 (£200) in New York in 1976.

WÜRTTEMBERGISCHE METALLWARENFABRIK (W.M.F.)

South-east of Stuttgart, on the road to Ulm, lies the town of Geislingen, where this firm (Württemberg is the district in which Geislingen lies) was founded in 1853 by Daniel Straub. Initially called the 'Straub & Schweitzer metalwork factory', and later 'Straub & Son', the firm amalgamated in 1888 with a competitor named Ritter to form the present-day company.

The firm's production was quick to diversify, the metalwork section being supplemented – and nowadays overhauled – by a glass and crystal works at Göppingen. It is only the former that concerns us here. Around 1900, when W.M.F. was employing about 3,000 people, a wide range of metal domestic ware – in silver, nickel, pewter, copper and brass – was manufactured and then marketed through sales outlets in cities such as Cologne, Vienna, Berlin and Warsaw.

Traditionally inspired styles – for example, Neo-Renaissance and Rococo, until 1900 the cornerstone of W.M.F.'s output – were largely shelved a few years later to concentrate on *Jugendstil*. It was during this period that the firm mass-produced silvered metal and pewter domestic ware – centrepieces, *tazzas*, claret jugs, goblets, mirrors, etc. – in the prevailing Art Nouveau vernacular; and candlesticks and candelabra constituted a large proportion of this range of utensils. These, often composed all too predictably of draped women supporting twisting stems that culminated in scroll motif candle-nozzles, seem plagiarized versions of their French *femme-fleur* counterparts. Idiomatically, they are unquestionably 'Art Nouveau' and, in a market where demand outstrips supply, consistently fetch good prices at today's auction houses.

The prices that W.M.F. objects will bring have risen steadily over the last few years. A pair of silvered metal candelabra brought £320 ($650) in London in 1974, while a small silvered metal table-lamp was sold for $665 (£330) in New York in 1975.

4

Art Déco Lighting

XXVII Gallé. This charming wall-fixture, at the Musée de l'Ecole de Nancy, consists of blown glass gourds hanging from a wrought-iron trellis.

XXVIII Korschann. A small gilt-bronze night-light.

XXIX Bouval. One of a pair of silver candelabra entitled 'Obsession' and 'Dream', illustrated in the August issue of *L'Art Décoratif*, 1900. The same figures were later cast in gilt-bronze and wired for electricity.

XXX Guimard. One of the famous Métro entrances designed by Guimard and erected in all areas of Paris.

XXXI Gallé. 'Corolla', a blown cameo glass table-lamp with bronze base. The veins on the glass are etched.

XXXII Bouval. 'Le Chardon', a bronze thistle table-lamp, *c.* 1900.

XXXIII Anonymous. An unsigned chandelier incorporating two face-to-face dragonflies; the blown glass shade is contained in the circle described by the insects' abdomens.

ART DÉCO

XXXIV Argy-Rousseau. A *pâte-de-verre* night-light, *c.*1925, with moulded grotesque masks in low relief. The base is of wrought-iron.

XXXV Gray. A tubular ceiling-light.

XXXVI Ruhlmann. This alabaster 'bedhead' wall-bracket was first exhibited in a bedroom in *loupe d'amboine* at the 1925 International Exposition.

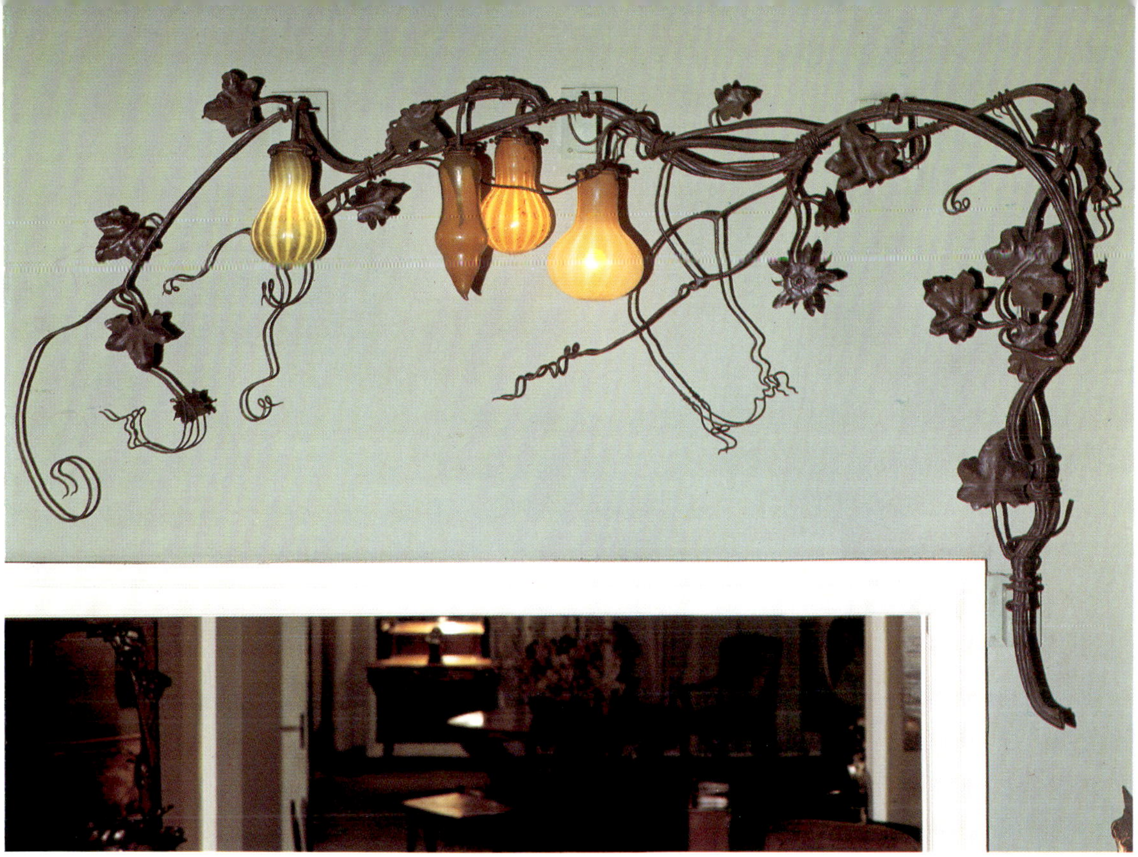

XXVII

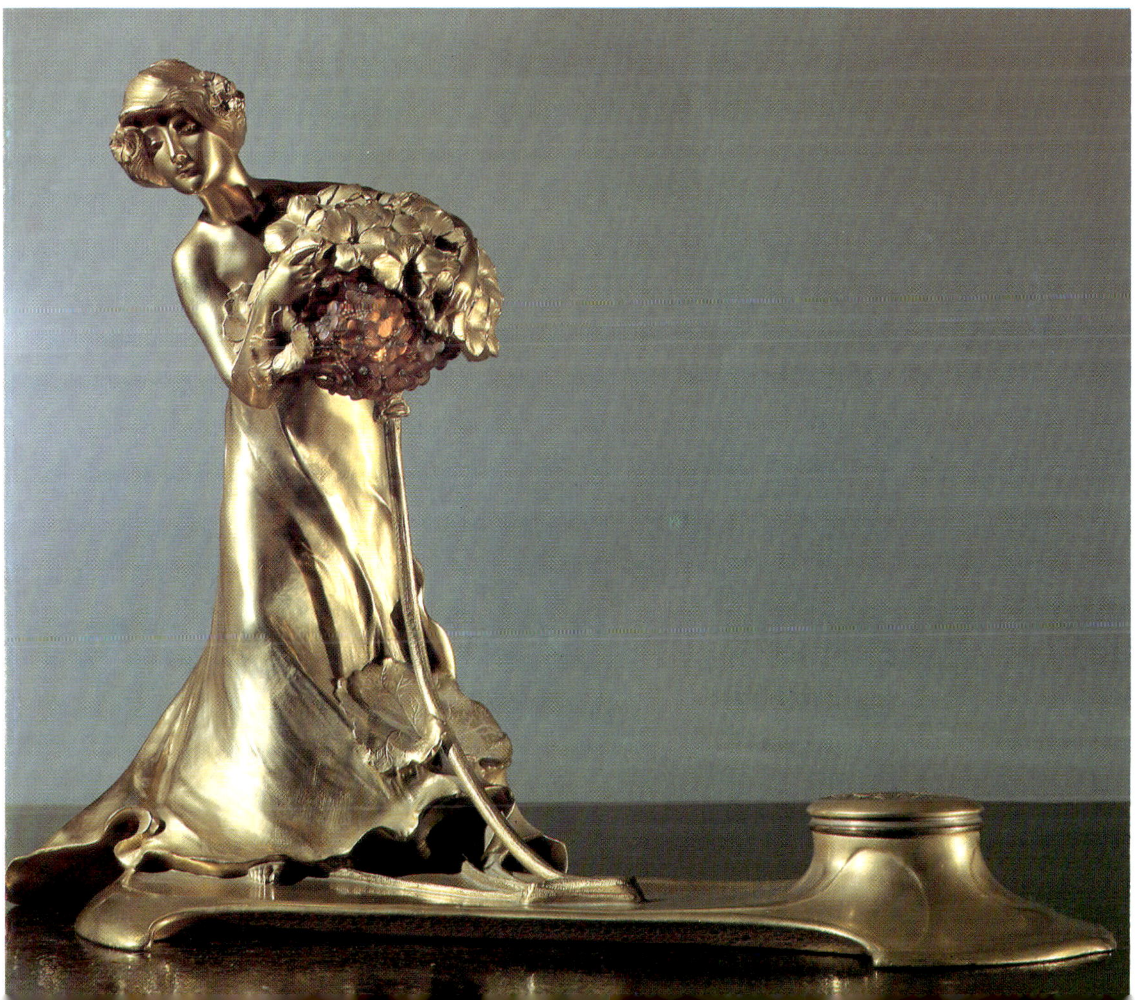

XXVIII

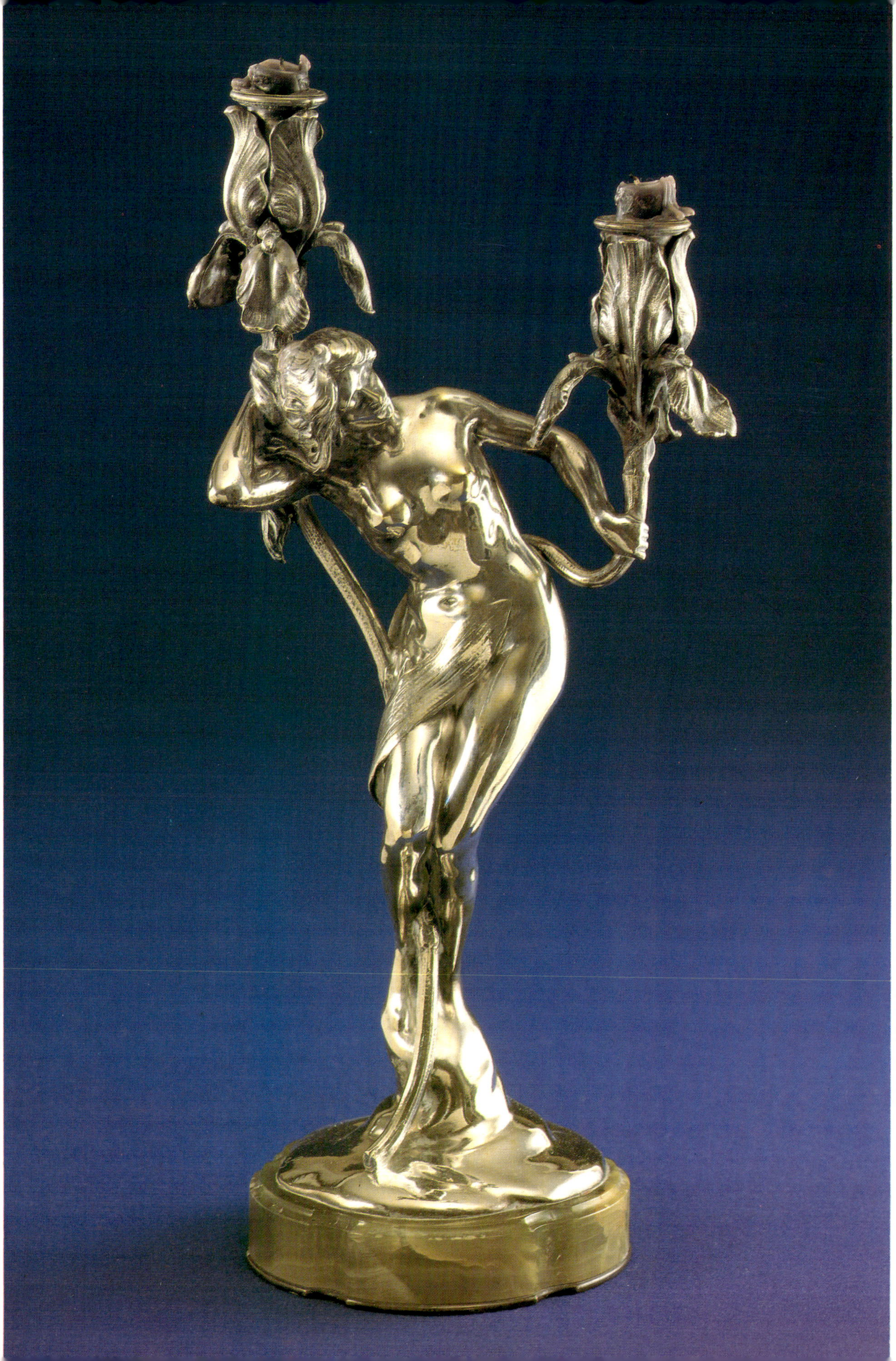

XXIX

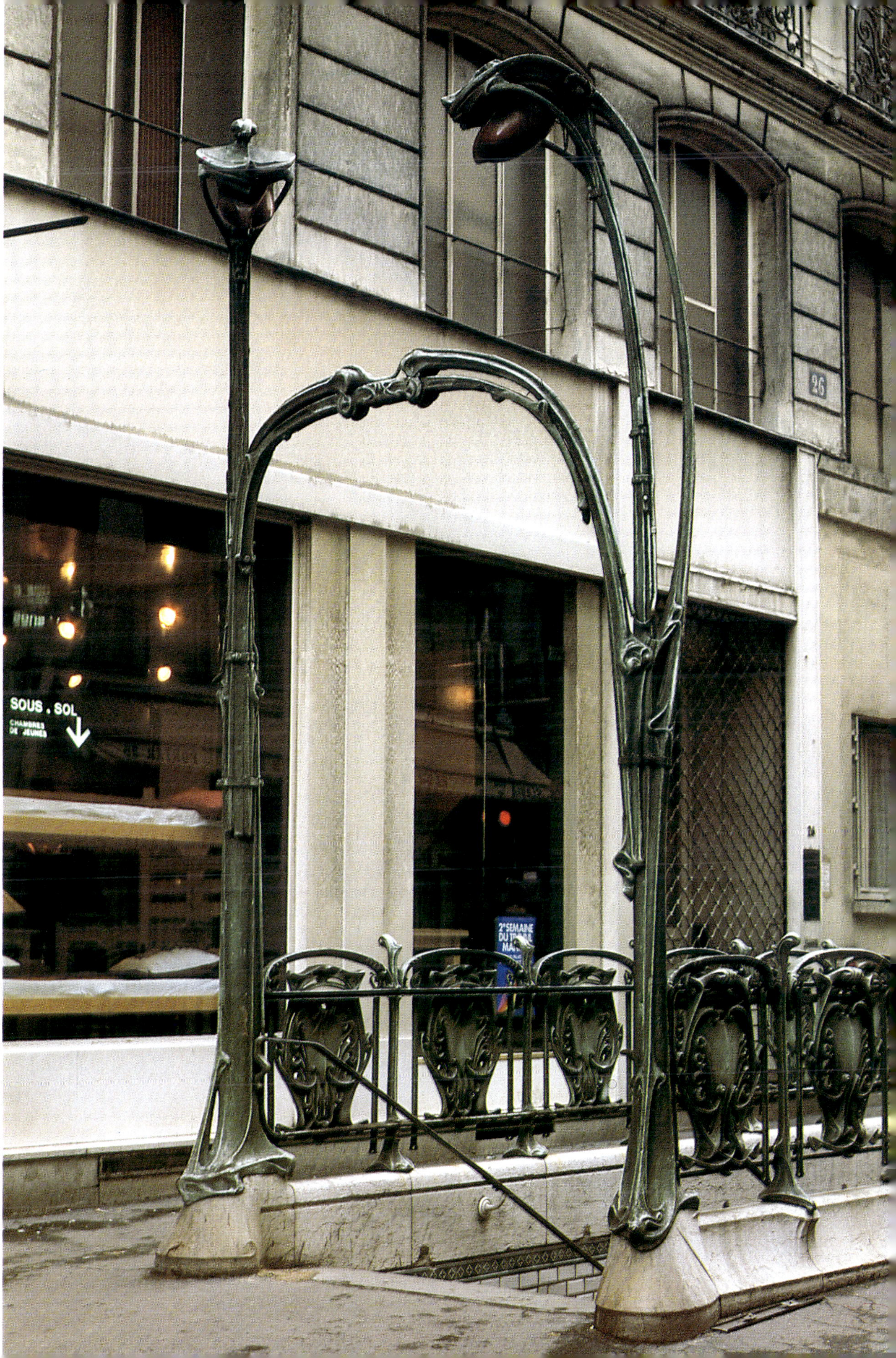
SOUS . SOL
CHAMBRES
DE JEUNES
26

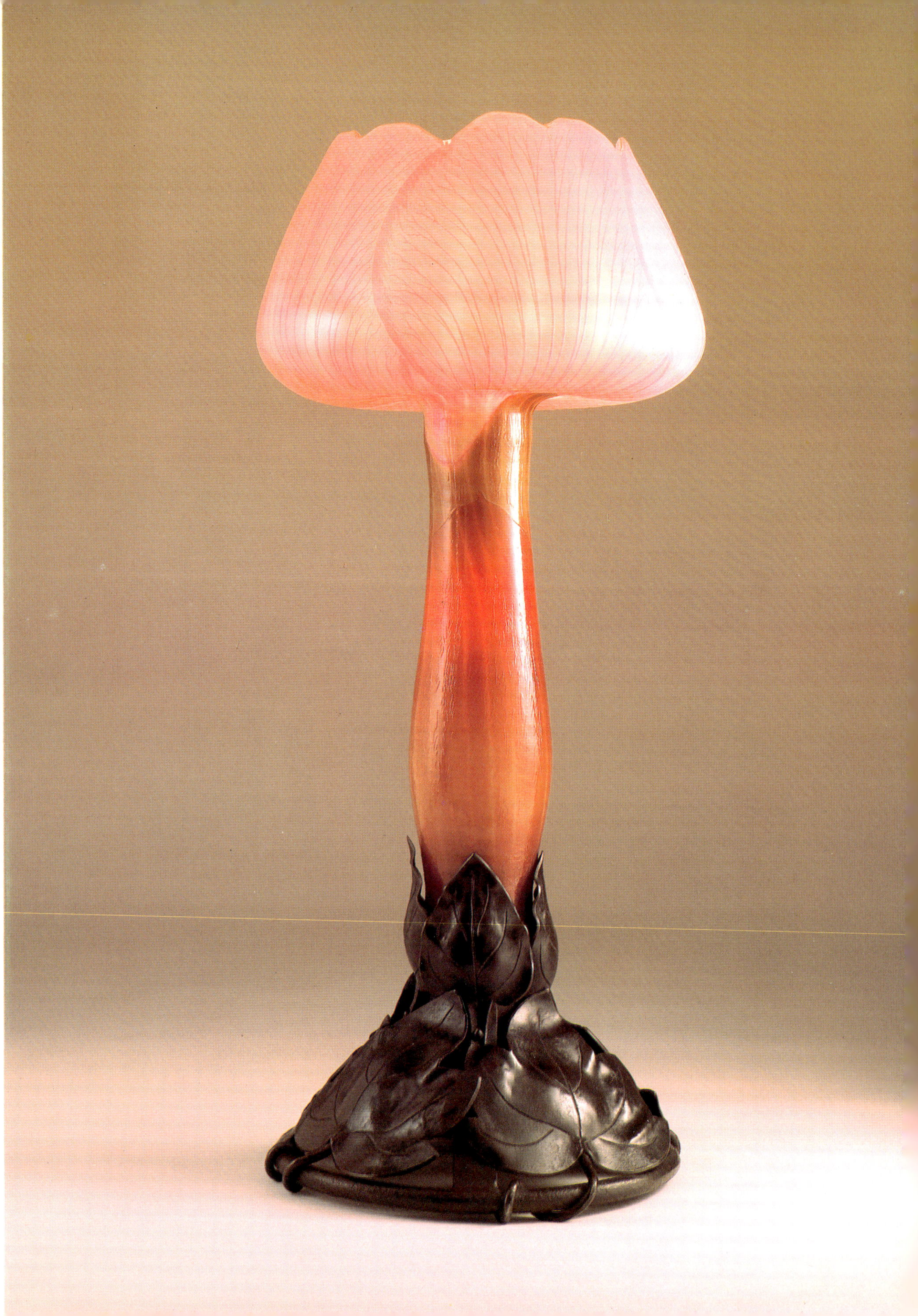

XXXI

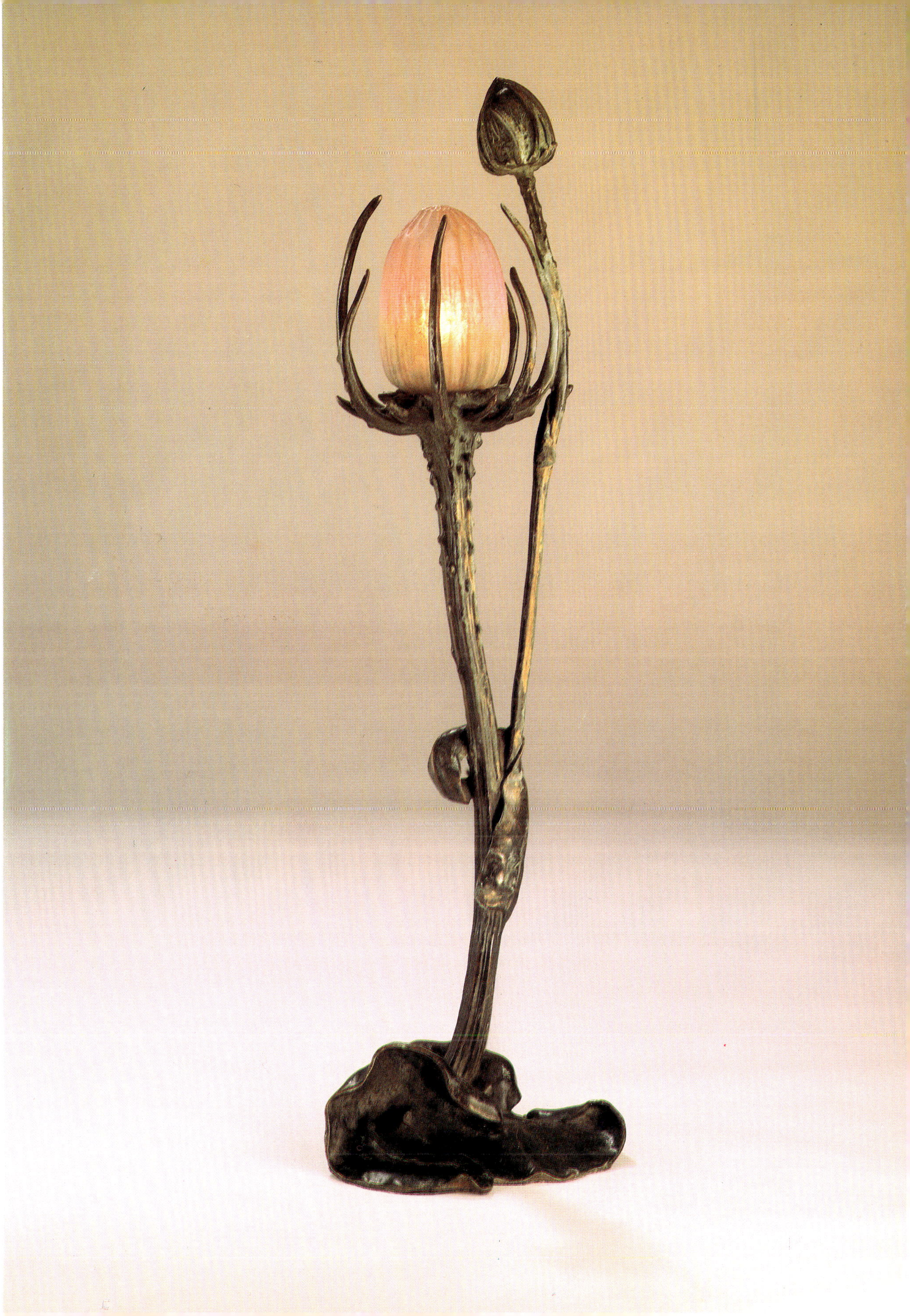

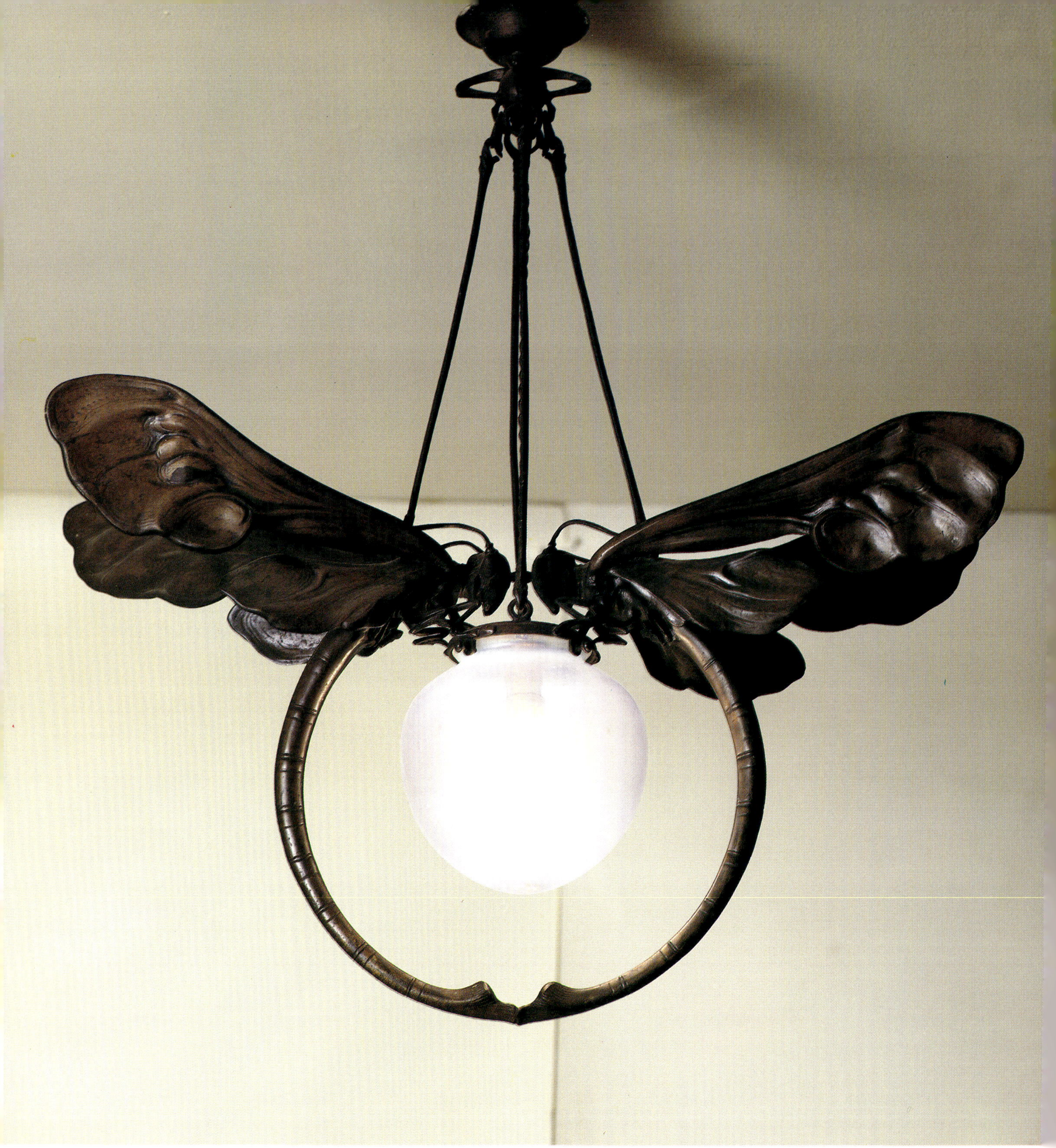

XXXIII

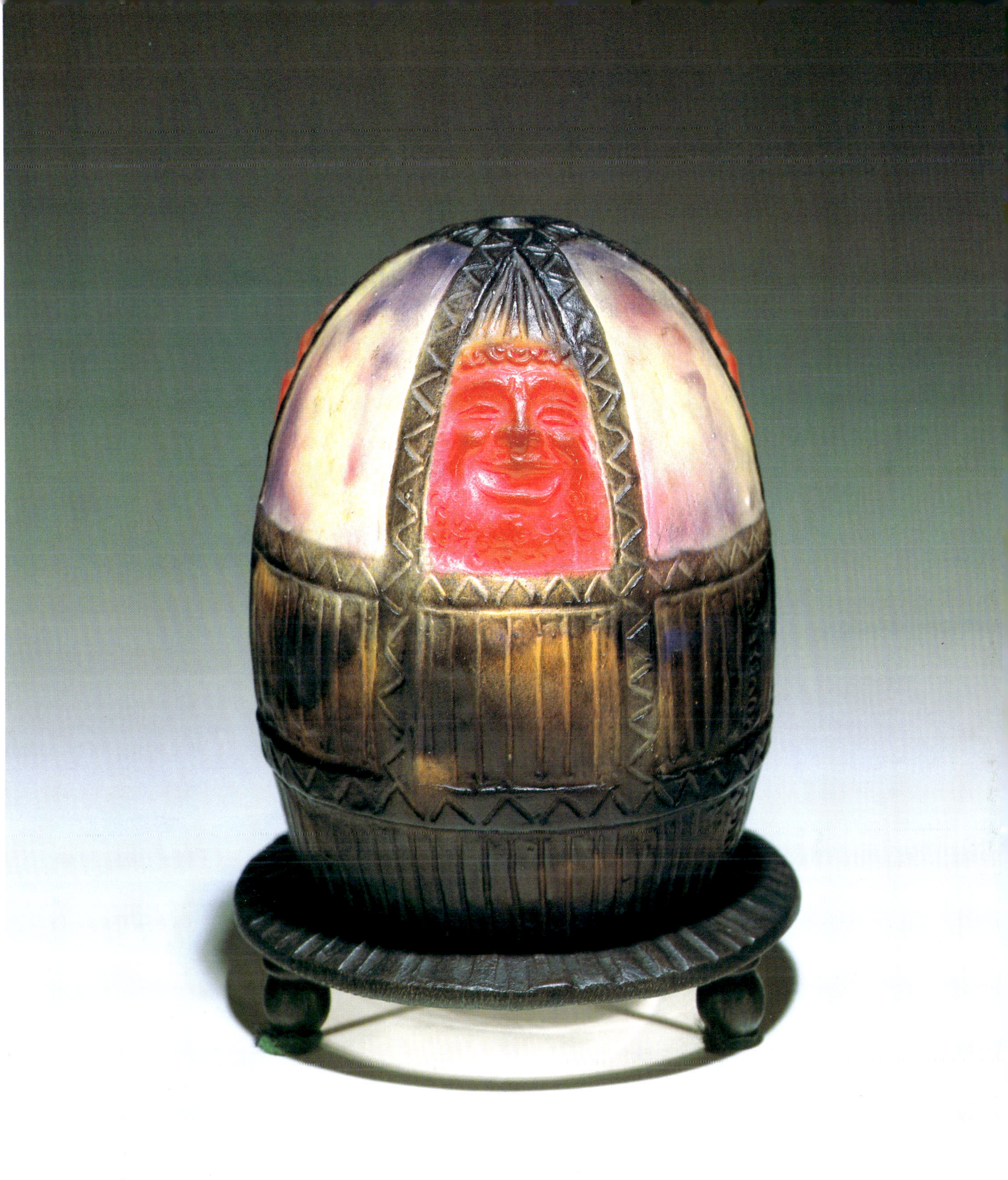

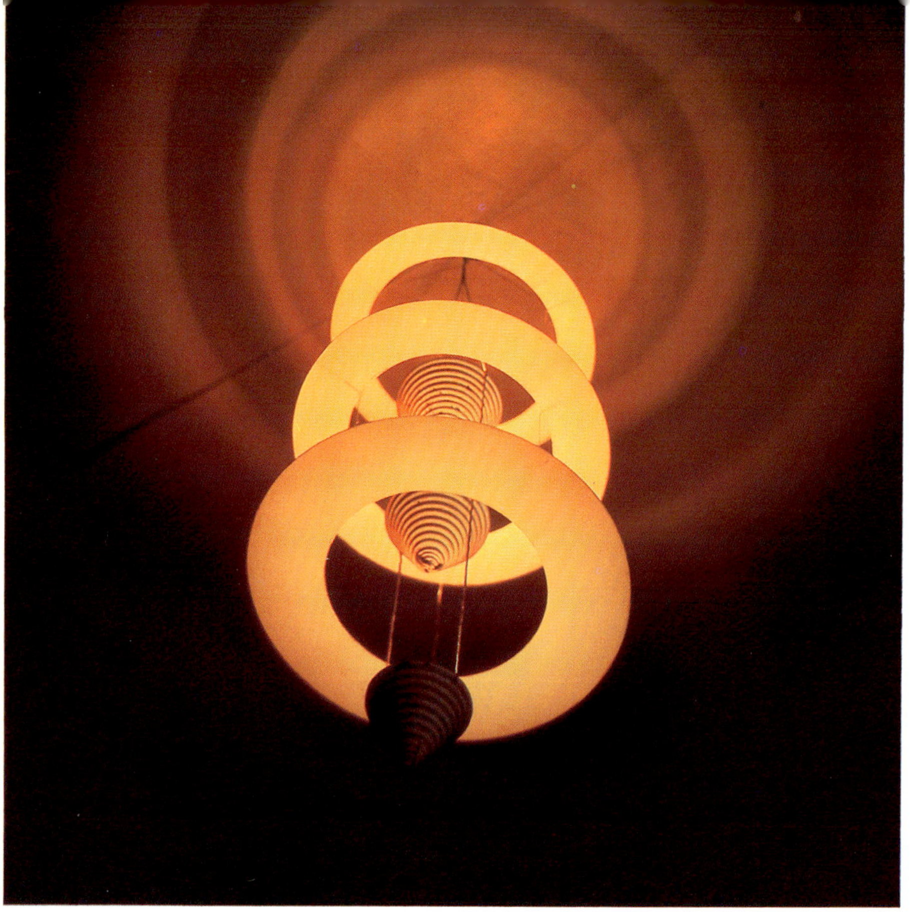

XXXV

XXXVI

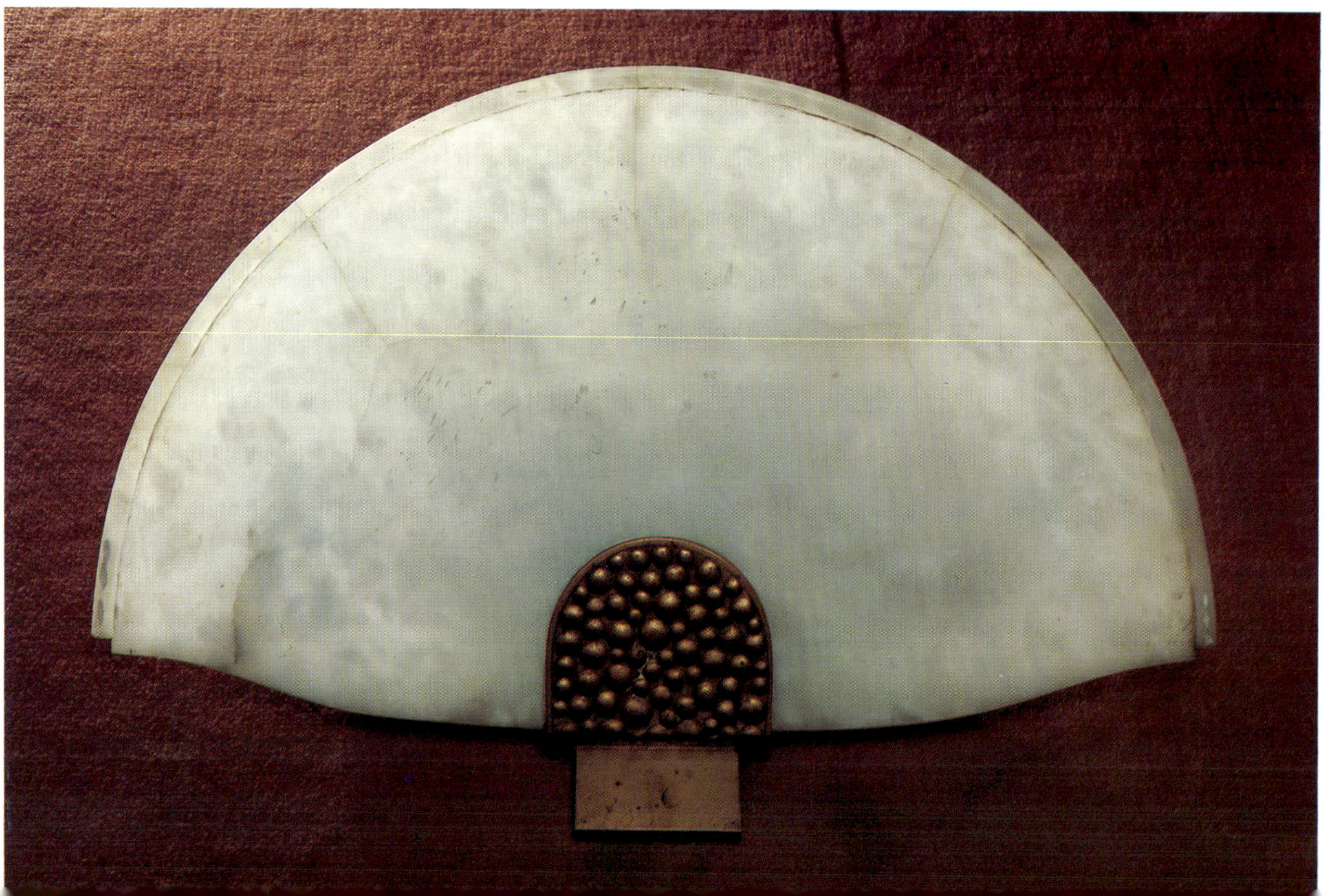

Art Déco lighting

For the decorative arts, World War I constituted the dividing line between the 1900 and the 1925 aesthetics. Art Nouveau had reached its highpoint at the 1902 Turin International Exposition, and by 1913 it was drained of new ideas or departures.

The philosophy of the 1920s, expressed in a number of parallel movements such as the Odeonesque, Jazz style, Modernist, represented the antithesis of Art Nouveau. At the 1925 Exposition Universelle des Arts Décoratifs et Industriels Modernes in Paris, the term Art Déco was coined and became the umbrella name for all similar movements. Its philosophy was summed up in an article in *The Studio* (1930):

> Furniture has an architecture of its own, of which the principles have been gradually evolved down the centuries. These laws cannot be disregarded except at risk of the gravest mistakes, the chief of which is to make a piece of furniture the fantasy of the hour, and not a lasting thing; tempting its owner, a few years later, to banish it to an attic corner as something intolerable. I number amongst my acquaintances one of the '1900 men', the whole of whose furniture was made for him in his enthusiasm for the generous but fallacious theories of that time. It is appalling, and one wonders today how people can still live in such a setting.

Art Nouveau had, according to this view, violated the very basis of design: in its fetish for ornamentation it had disguised the object's function. Francis Jourdain, from the early 1900s an apostle of purity of form and one of the most articulate publicists of Art Déco, described the new mood as follows:

> It is more and more apparent that simplicity is not synonymous with poverty and that civilization, if it has other needs than barbarism, has also different aptitudes. It is more sensitive to the beauty of proportion, harmony of surface, volume and line, and more offended by obvious and exterior ornamentation. It appeals to the intelligence.

The characteristics of the new epoch became simplicity of line, richness of material, and sobriety of decor. Beauty demanded the perfect adaptation of an object to its use. It is as well, therefore, to warn those readers who, as lovers of Art Nouveau, presume that Art Déco lamp designs are based on the same aesthetics, that they may be in for a shock.

The difference in lighting between the two periods could hardly, in fact, have been more pronounced. Gone, first of all, were the spectral delights of Art Nouveau lamps: the azure blues, moss greens, magentas and lavenders. In their place came achromatism: the glass lampshades relying on factors other than colour for their effect. (Glass was universally considered to best meet the light-diffusing qualities required for artificial illumination.) By etching, enamelling, or sandblasting the glass, the glass artist could orchestrate the light; by pressing or engraving it he could achieve sculptural effects; and by combining such processes, he could obtain any number of nuances. In place of the spectrum there were milkiness and limpidity, infinite richness and imagery.

Gone, also, in large part, were the major turn-of-the-century motifs: the flower, the volute and the insect. Art Déco exponents turned to sunbursts, crescents and the zigzag (though such motifs were incorporated into light fixtures far less frequently than into other home appurtenances). Even 1900 'Woman', although not rejected, underwent a metamorphosis: her languorous looks hardened into those of a woman of action. The statuettes of the Austrian Preiss and the Rumanian Demêtre Chiparus, for instance, portray clean-spirited youth frozen in athletic pose. No longer a lotus-eater, woman busied herself by *doing* things, as well befitted a member of the fast-moving age of jazz, open sports cars and air travel.

Even the materials changed. Bronze, the indisputable champion of the Art Nouveau era, fell totally out of favour. In its place were painted metal, alabaster, marble, lacquer, mirror, and sharkskin. No longer was nature found to be alluring: now designers looked to the Pre-Columbian pyramids at Chichen Itza and Tikal for their inspiration. Seldom before had an art movement, conceived in part by its immediate predecessor, turned so fully on this parent.

In lighting, the distinction was further compounded by the new 1920s philosophy of the role that illumination was to play in a modern interior. During the 1900s, designers had concentrated on turning lamps into *objets d'art*. The fixture's primary function, *i.e.*, its ability to provide the required amount of light for the specific situation, had become obscured in the preoccupation to make the lamp itself beautiful. Such non-functionalism was, to the 1920s purist, symptomatic of the whole Art Nouveau *malaise*, and one to which he would certainly not himself fall prey. A light fixture had a specific and very important part to play in an ensemble: it had to ensure a logical distribution of the light; one that would meet, in each instance, the requirements of visibility and ambience. A fixture's elements were therefore to be subordinate to its lighting function. No longer were the rays to be imprisoned behind panels of opalescent glass or have to manoeuvre their way out from behind openwork bronze shades. The light wanted to search out dark cornices, to chase away the shadows, and, above all, to be free.

The 1900 *art* of lighting thus gave way to the 1920 *science* of lighting. Lamps became simply vehicles: the means whereby the light could be relayed to wherever it was needed. This explains why Art Déco lamps often appear, to the uninitiated, to be upside down! The inverted shade's function is to project the light onto the ceiling which, in turn, softens and diffuses it.

The reason that the light was reflected off a secondary source (such as a ceiling) and not seen directly, was explained by Desny in a January 1929 article in *Lux*: 'It is very wrong to think that a room is well-lit because one is dazzled by the intense burst of the luminous points of light. The essential, to the contrary, is that there is no specific point to tire the eye.' From this it was logically argued that, if a lamp's *raison d'être* was solely to project the light and concentrate the attention of the inhabitants of a room *away from* itself, it would itself cease to be a distinct element in the interior design of that room. Lamp exponents were, in theory at least, faced with a choice: either to make their models as quietly functional and unostentatious as possible, or to do away with them entirely and find a means of illuminating the objects to be viewed themselves – for example, walls, ceilings, lintels and fountains. The reason that most Art Déco fixtures continued, however, to contain a measure of ornamentation was that neither alternative was in practice found to be satisfactory. As lamps were still needed to provide localized light for reading purposes, etc., so most exponents refused to take their designs to the extremes of excessive logic to which, say, Jacques Adnet, with his frosted, naked tubes, took his. On those occasions when circumstances called for the use of a visible fixture, then the latter would be visibly worth looking at; and whereas its appeal was less spontaneous than that of its Art Nouveau predecessor, it was aesthetically more subtle. As Graham Dry, an antique dealer in Munich, recently wrote to me: 'A good Art Déco lamp does not have to be lit in order to justify itself. It is pure form, and can exist on its own terms. An Art Nouveau lamp, on the other hand, had to be lit in order to exist. Light was needed to bring it to life.'

So the 1920s lamp survived as an *objet d'art*, while its ability to meet various illumination needs was continually extended. Perzel and Sabino, for example, at various times offered no fewer than five different forms of lighting – direct, semi-direct, mixed, semi-indirect, and indirect – the subtleties of which were, no doubt, lost on most of their customers. The visible fixture remained, though, as a reminder of the past, and the new fascination was with a new development: invisible lighting. As M. J. Wetzel wrote in an article in *Lux* (April 1928), 'It is an advantage to hide the light source, as the effect is more striking when one cannot see its origin. Hence the disappearance of bulbs into walls, ceilings, and behind pilasters where they are masked by diffuser screens.'

Art Déco lighting was best seen, paradoxically, when it was not seen! Architectural lighting had arrived. Designers of both visible and hidden lighting had ample opportunities to display their creations: a 'Grand Competition of Light' was arranged in Paris in 1924 by the Syndicated Union of Electricity; in 1925, the International Exposition provided another excellent showcase (for a review of these lamps, see G. Janneau's *Le Luminaire et les Moyens d'éclairage*, the first of three booklets that he published on 1920s illumination). In the 1930s five Salons of Light were held: in 1933, 1934, 1935, 1937 (as part of that year's International Exposition: see G. Henriot's *Luminaire Modern*), and 1939.

In addition, there were, of course, the annual Salons and those floating museums of interior design, the ocean liners. Ships such as the *Normandie*, *Ile de France*, *L'Atlantique*, *Empress of Britain*, and the Swedish *Kungsholm* provided top designers with *carte blanche* to experiment with the most modern lighting effects. Mention should also be made of the Roxy Theatre and Radio City Music Hall in New York, and the Savoy Hotel in London.

The transition from direct to indirect lighting led to a spate of interest in this new art form. Groups such as the *Société pour le Perfectionnement de l'éclairage* formed to gather and disseminate information for the householder on the fundamentals of hygienic and psychological illumination; the International Commission of Lighting, which had last met in 1921, reconvened quickly in Bellagio in 1927 to proclaim the new aesthetic as its own; and magazines were launched to inform an expanding readership on recent developments. The speed at which the latter took place provides the best indication of the enthusiasm that had been generated. In 1912 there were only three specialist lighting reviews in the world: the *Illuminating Engineering Society* in the U.S., *Good Lighting* in Great Britain, and *Licht und Lampe* in Germany. By 1928, however, this number had grown to fifteen, with additional magazines in Austria, Belgium, Italy, Japan, Argentina and France. Of these, the one that most concerned itself with the alliance of lighting and Art Déco was *Lux*, published in Paris from 1928.

Articles by leading Art Déco exponents, such as Genet & Michon, Perzel, Lacroix, and Printz, covered all aspects of lighting from shop windows to illuminated monuments and tennis courts, with each writer defining his own guidelines for optimum decorative or utilitarian effect. Due to its proximity to the Paris Salons, *Lux* quickly established itself as *the* mouthpiece on lighting while promoting, in addition, the science of photometry. The latter, for long a *bona fide* discipline, but one that had been considered largely theoretical and thus impractical for anything other than laboratory purposes, took on a new, greatly enhanced status. Photometric units such as footcandles, lumens, lux and intensity were measured. So were angles of reflection. So, too, were the coefficients of the transmission of light. Even the size of retinal images was recorded. This preoccupation with photometry created, in turn, a new vocation: that of the lighting engineer. The need to define, from an optical viewpoint, the brilliance of the surfaces to be lit, the distribution and accentuation of shadows, which colour (if any) to use, and the position, number and power of the light sources, led to the need for a specialist technician – one to whom both the architect and the interior decorator could turn. The lighting engineer was to serve such a purpose. He was to apply, in each new setting, whatever physiological, psychological and artistic considerations were necessary. The foremost of the 1920s lighting engineers were three Parisians: André Salomon, Jean Dourgnon, and Juget. Salomon, a director of the Entreprise Perfecla, emerged as the period's leading spokesman on lighting. Expounding frequently on his philosophies in both *Lux* and *Art et Décoration*, he was consulted at some time or another by most of the leading architects and designers – Mallet-Stevens, Herbst, Guévrékian, and Chareau – to advise them on their illumination requirements. In 1929 Dourgnon invented the *Tigralite*, a device to be fixed in the corner of a room to project the light on to the ceiling.

The most important of the Art Déco adherents who designed various forms of light fixtures are discussed in the following section. My choice of whom to include is based on the same criteria that I applied to lighting practitioners in 1900. Readers will notice, however, that, unlike the Art Nouveau section, there is no breakdown of designers by country. The reason for this is that, of those people who involved themselves with the genesis and subsequent growth of the Art Déco style of decorative lighting almost all were French and based in Paris. A breakdown by country would therefore be inappropriate. Of those who designed lamps and who are not covered individually in the text, mention should be made of the following:

In France, Jean Goulden, the silversmith and enameller, who designed some cubist table lamps; Tony and Jacques Socard, who made leaded glass lamps; Charles Piquet, the metal worker, who made wrought-iron floor-lamps; André Hunebelle, the glass artist, who designed etched and engraved lamps; A. Kelety, the sculptor, whose illuminated bronze women acted as night lights: Rapin, whose translucent porcelain *vases lumineux* were marketed through the Sèvres Manufactory; and Jean Puiforçat, the eminent silversmith, who exhibited some small table-lamps of characteristically crisp design at the Salons. There were many others besides; e.g., Raoul Lamourdedieu, Théodore Rivière, Paul Iribe, Fargette, Adrien Robert, Gilbert Poillerat, Jacques Gruber, and Auguste Fabre.

In England, the firms of Waring & Gillow, Heal & Sons, Troughton & Sons, and, for a long time specialists in home illumination, Best & Lloyd.

In Germany, K. J. Junker, Wilhelm Wagenfeld and Marianne Brandt designed lamps which, executed by the Bauhaus, are astonishingly modern by today's standards. A range of the work of other designers, such as F. A. Breuhaus and the Handwerker- und Kunstgewerbeschule, is illustrated in contemporary issues of *Innen Dekoration* and *Deutsche Kunst und Dekoration*.

In Italy, the firms of Venini, at Murano, and Veronese marketed a range of quasi-Art Déco illuminated vases and table-lamps; while in Belgium, mention should be made of Val St Lambert, for whom Léon Ledru designed some very neat shades.

Far fewer lamps from the 1920s have been rediscovered by today's dealers and collectors than from the 1900s. The reason for this is twofold. First, a lot of Art Déco light fixtures do not appear incongruous or *démodé* in a 1960s or 1970s interior and therefore tend not to reach auction rooms very frequently. Secondly, and allied to this, is the fact that such fixtures are not easily recognizable as 'Art Déco' – a problem brought about by the fact, as mentioned previously, that lamps from the Art Déco period frequently do not contain the characteristic geometric, sunburst, or chevron motifs that make other Art Déco objects so readily identifiable. We can therefore assume that somewhere there are a great many collectable but as yet undiscovered lamps from the period.

5

The Art Déco Designers

The Art Déco designers

ADNET, JACQUES

Following his graduation from the School of Decorative Arts in Paris, Adnet exhibited at the annual Salons through such studios as 'La Maîtrise' and Saddier and Sons until, in 1928, he took over the direction of the Compagnie des Arts français, through which he was subsequently to have his designs executed. Imbued with Le Corbusier's dictum that a house is a '*machine à habiter*', his light fixtures – mainly chandeliers and desk lamps – showed the same philosophy of stark functionalism that he applied to all aspects of his ensembles, such as his tubular chromed ladies' dressing-tables, mobile drink cabinets and furniture in such intoxicating woods as bubenga and white peroba.

Based on sharp geometric design principles, Adnet's light fixtures show an exciting kineticism and spirit of invention – a panache, even – which is heightened by the freshness that his use of nickel imparted to the design. In one chandelier the metal rods that protrude from a central column to house the tubular frosted bulbs are perpendicular to the column, in another they are triangular, while, again, in a third the rods and tubular bulbs are opposed to each other in zigzag fashion. Almost nowhere is there a concession to ornamentation, the influence of contemporary *machinisme* being ever-present.

None of Adnet's light fixtures has apparently been rediscovered. They would be likely to fetch between FF 1,750 and 2,625 ($350 and $525) each.

ARGY-ROUSSEAU, GABRIEL

A graduate of the Sèvres School of Ceramics, Argy-Rousseau opened his own studio at the end of World War I, specializing in *pâte-de-verre* and *pâte-de-cristal* glassware. Nobody was to use the Salon forum more assiduously. Exhibiting every year in the Salon des Artistes français (from 1919), and in the Salon d'Automne and the Société des Artistes Décorateurs (both from 1920), his range of glassware *objets* was predictable from year to year: vases, bowls, plates, medallions, pendants, *bonbonnières*, etc.

Art Déco

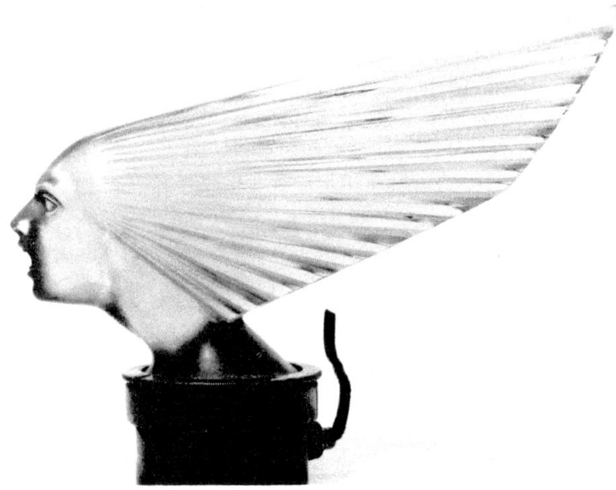

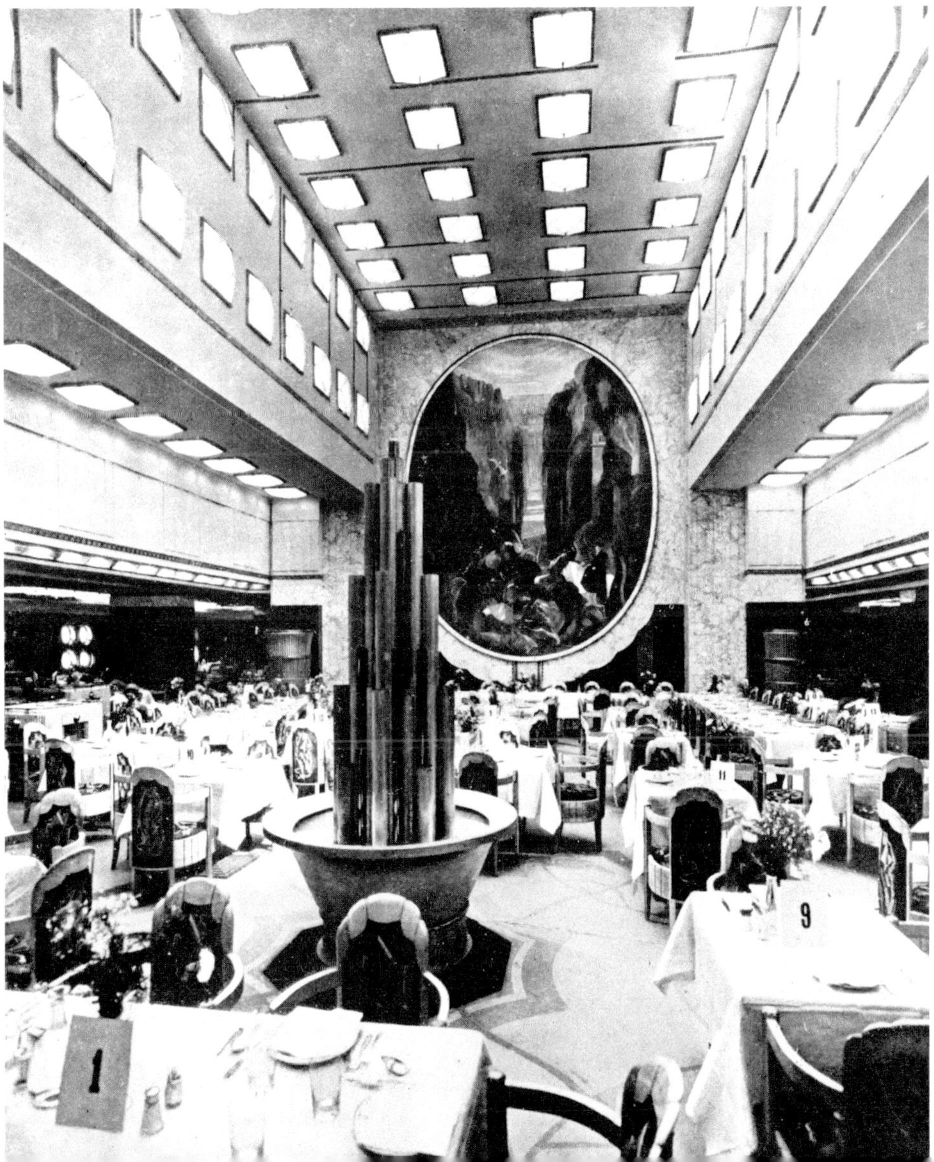

This 'Spirit of the Wind' car mascot by Lalique captured the 1920s image of 'Woman' as an Art Déco design element. With parted lips and streaming hair held by the wind, the figurehead symbolized the emancipated jazz-age woman of action. The mascot was illuminated by a bulb placed at its base. (82)

The first-class dining-room of the Ile-de-France, *the famous French transatlantic liner of the 1920s. Designed by the architect Patout, the ceiling* dalles *of light were by Lalique. The lighting in the lounge and reading-room was designed by Süe & Mare and Leleu respectively.* (83)

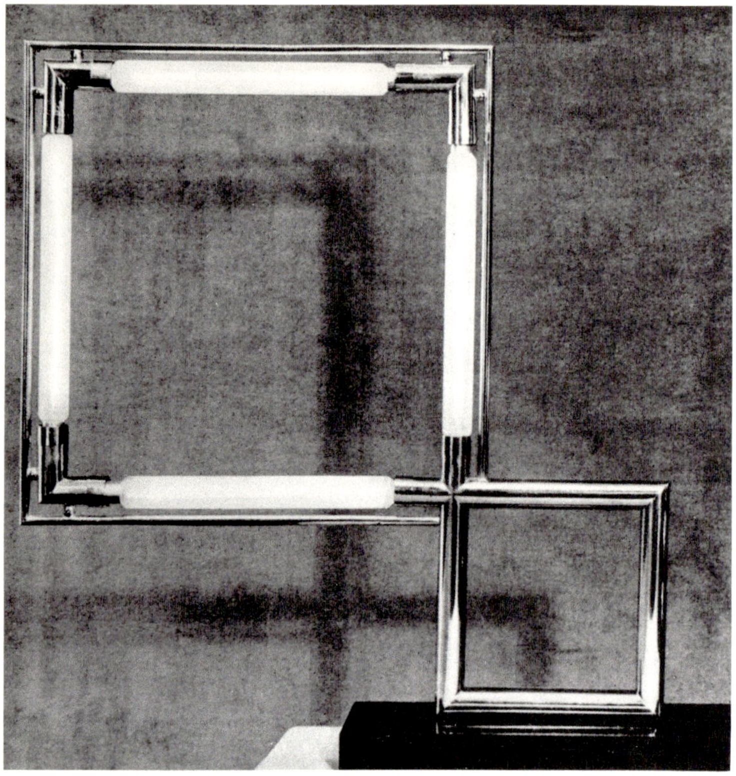

ADNET
Above, desk-lamp (1929) of tubular frosted glass and nickelled copper mount. The base is ebony. (84)

Right, table-lamp (1929) consisting of four balls superimposed perpendicularly; the top one of frosted glass, the lower three of nickelled copper. The base is ebony. (85)

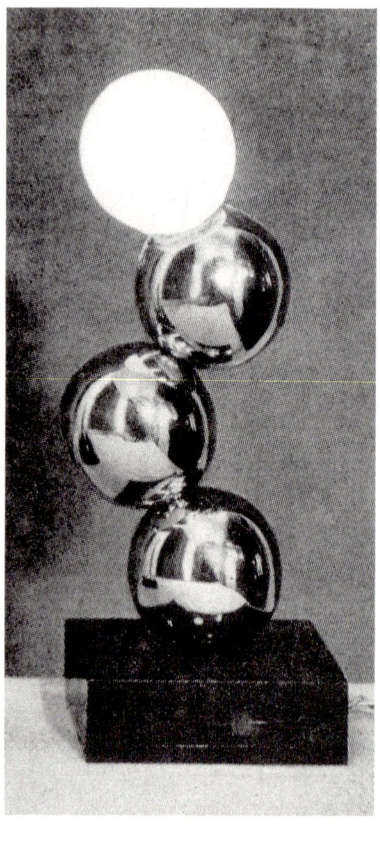

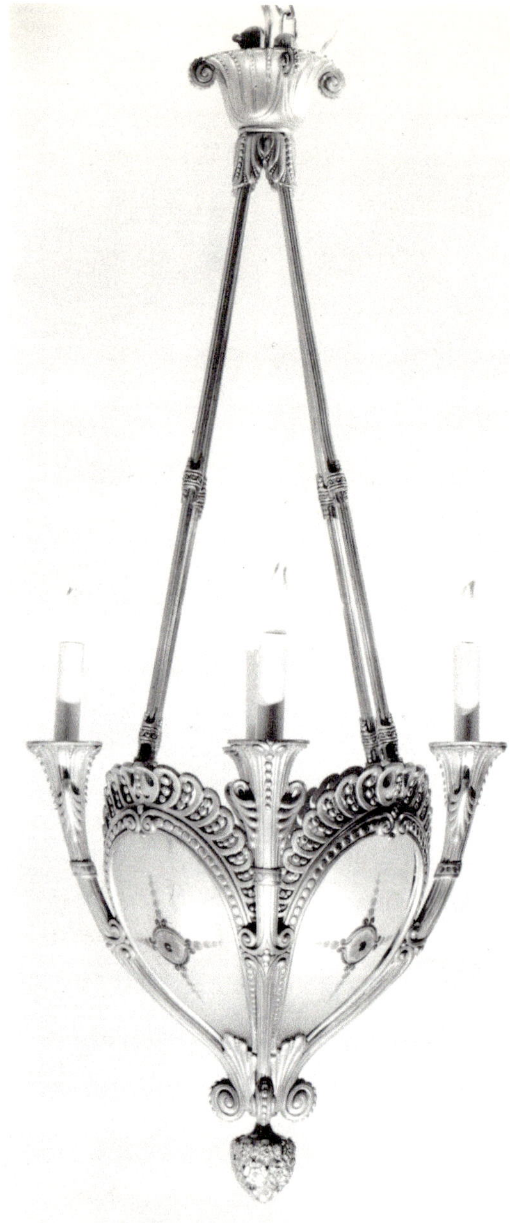

ARGY-ROUSSEAU
An ormolu mounted *pâte-de-verre* chandelier, *c.*1925. (86)

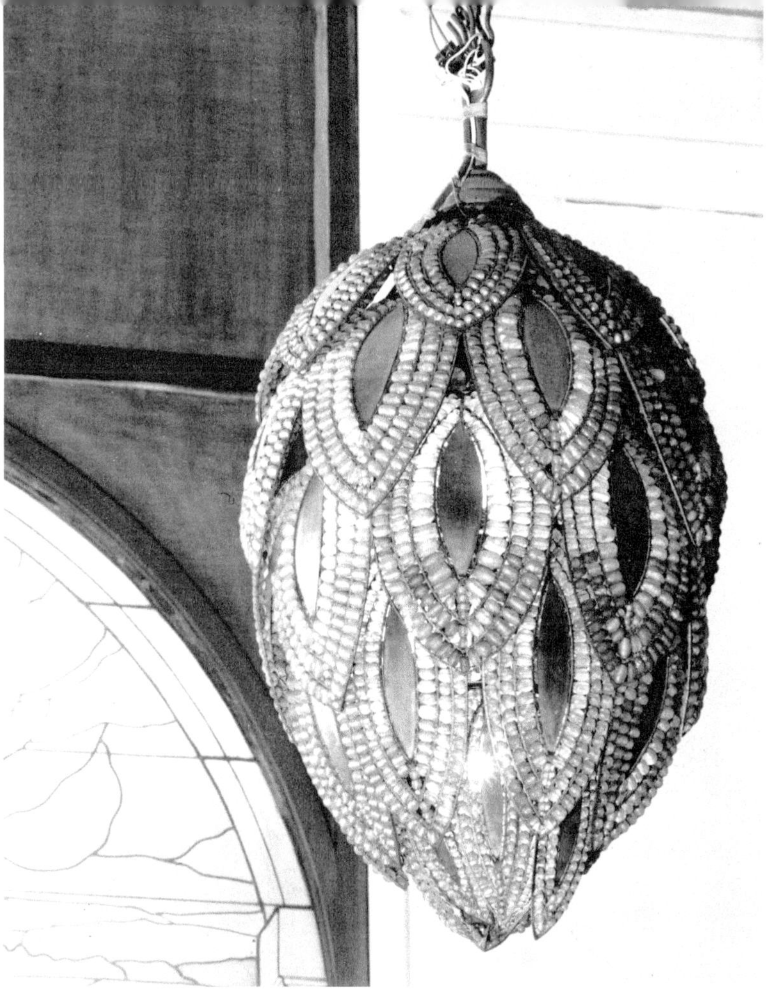

Baguès
This chandelier is in the shape of a pine-cone with five overlapping rows of seed pods in chromed metal bordered by crystal pearls. It was exhibited in the Pavilion of Elegance at the 1925 Exposition Universelle. (87)

Buquet
The name of the designer of this very important Art Déco lamp has, until recently, remained unknown. Thanks entirely to the research of Mr Eric Philippe of Arcueil, France, it can be identified as Edouard-Wilfrid Buquet, a Frenchman whose patent for the design of this 'Angle poise lamp' was granted on 11 July 1927 by the Department of Commerce and Industry in Paris. Its rotative abilities made this the most practical lamp of the period, and the most popular. It was used by, among others, the following architects and decorators in their interiors: Marcel Breuer, Louis Sognot, Maurice Barret, Joubert & Petit, Lucien Rollin, Suzanne Guiguichon, Marcel Coard, and Jean Sedlak. From 1928 to 1937 the lamp appeared in all the French publications pertaining to the decorative arts; for example, *Mobilier et Décoration*; *Art et Décoration*; *Art et Industrie*; *L'Amour de l'Art*; *L'Art Vivant*; *L'Illustration*; and *Décor d'aujourd'hui*. In the February 1959 issue of *L'Oeil* there appeared the following: 'Equilibrated lamp, 1925: this lamp, which is no longer made, was of a truly functional design: ingenious, practical and of a plastic value which evokes the research of contemporary sculptors.' Buquet's name, however, is not listed in any reviews of the period, although he made each of his lamps by hand and to different specifications. (89)

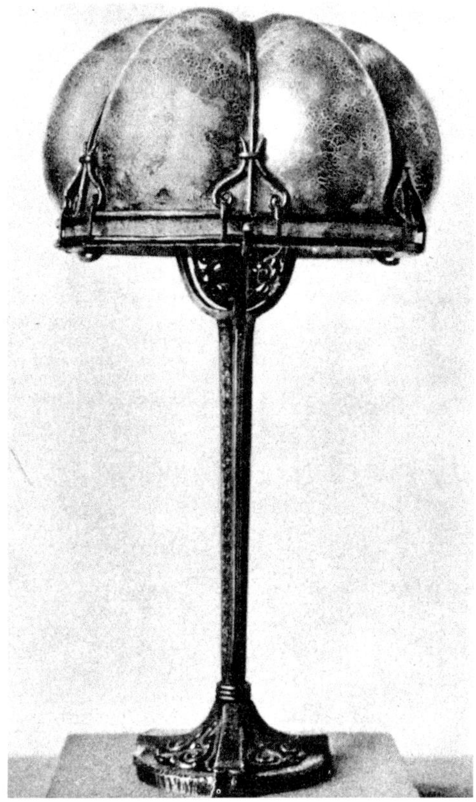

Brandt
A wrought-iron and glass table-lamp, *c.* 1922. The glass, probably by Daum, was blown into the mount – hence its 'imprisoned' look. (88)

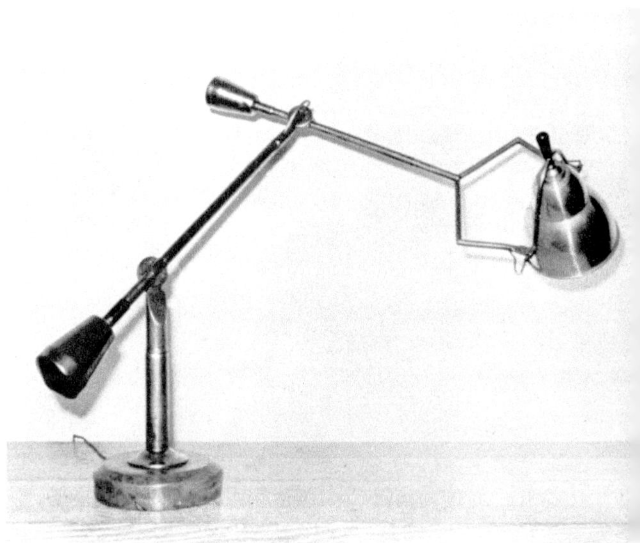

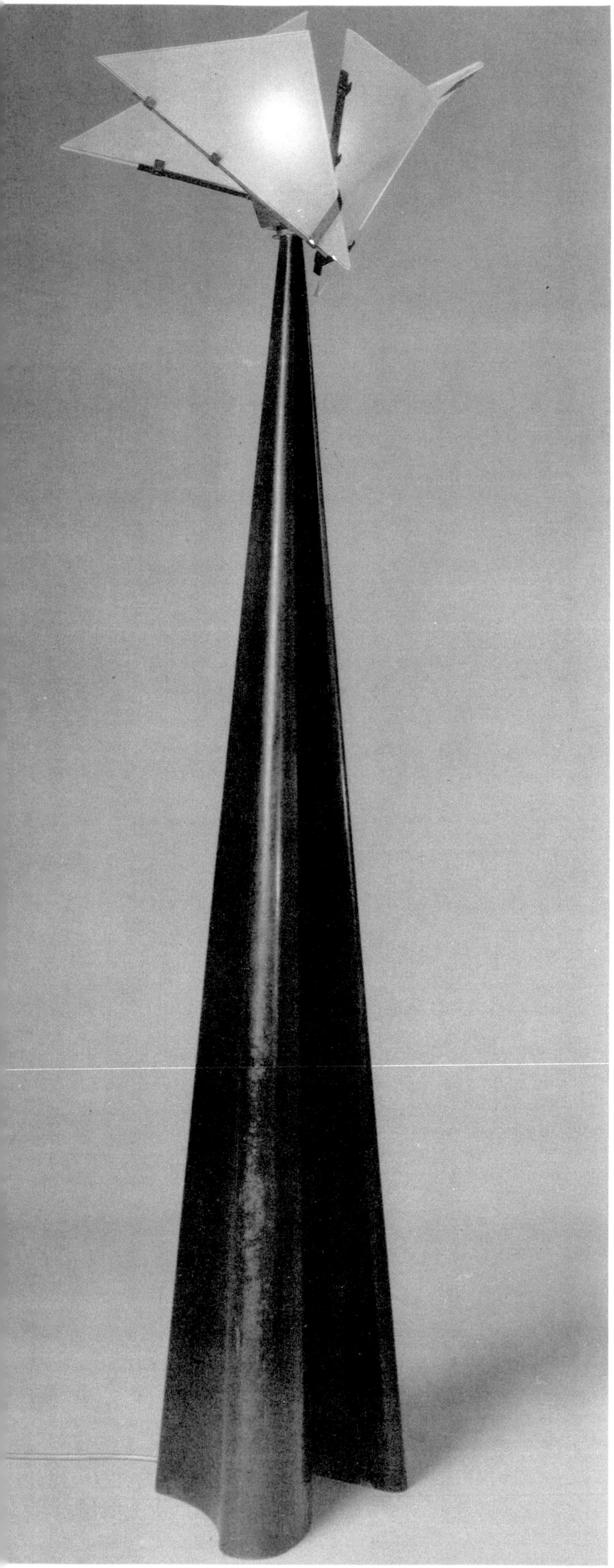

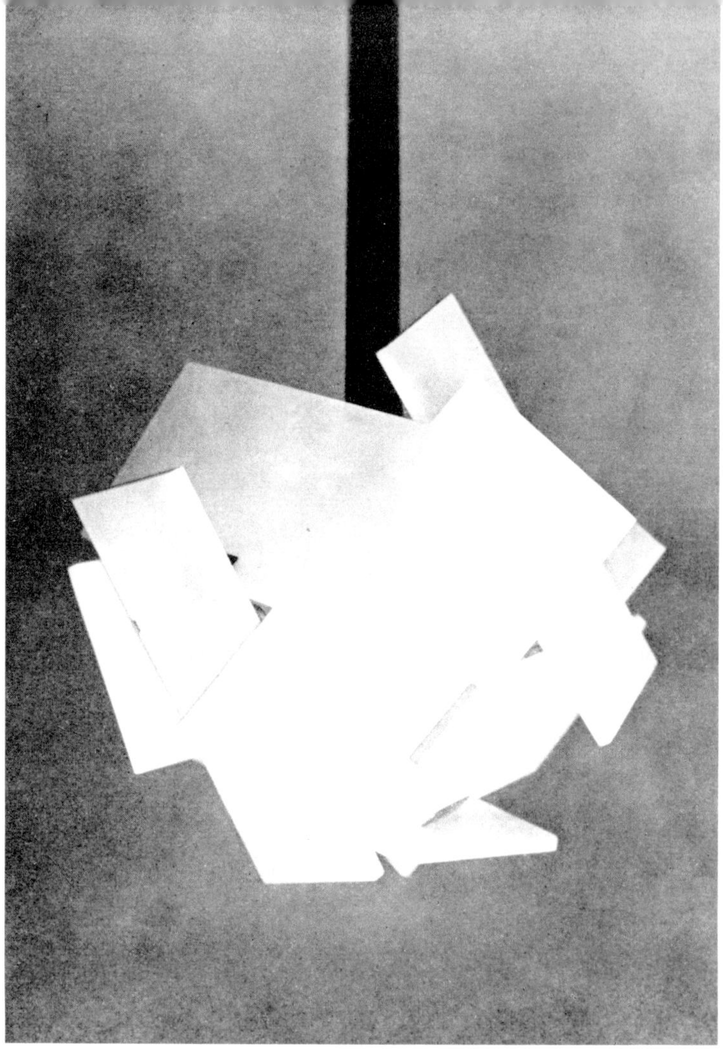

CHAREAU

Left, Pierre Chareau's ingenious polygonal floor-lamp: slices of alabaster are supported by a wooden base. It was shown at the 1924 Salon d'Automne. (90)

Above, the chandelier version of Chareau's floor-lamp. Here the slices of alabaster are linked to the central ceiling shaft by metal clips. This model was shown at the 1927 Exposition des Cinq and later used in the salon that Chareau designed in Mallet-Stevens' house in the rue Mallet-Stevens. The third in the series – a table-lamp on the same theme – can be seen in *Lux* (December 1928), p. 187, or *Art et Décoration* (January–June 1925), p. 156. (91)

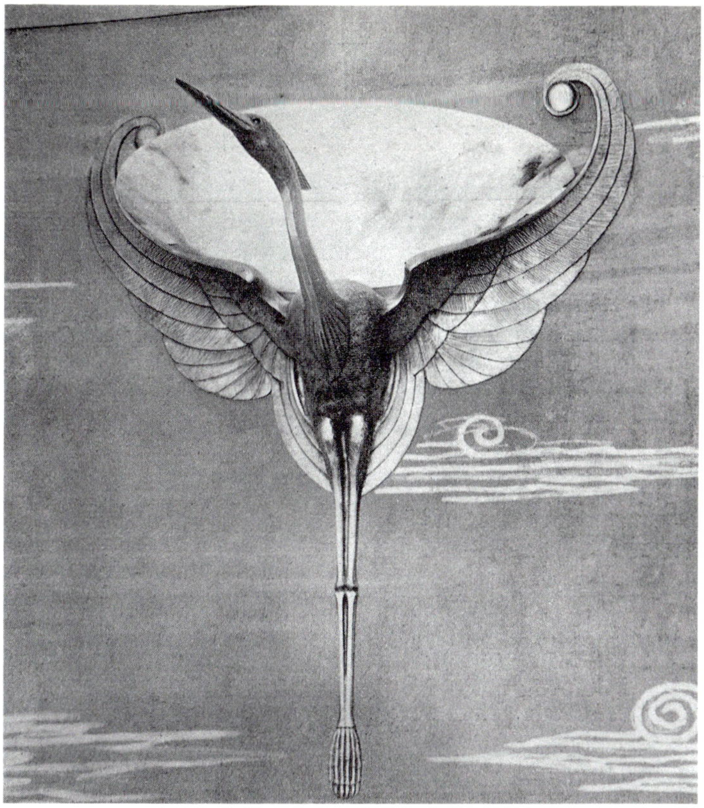

CHEURET
'Stork' wall-bracket in bronze and alabaster, 1922. The stylized stork was to be the theme, again, for the bronze mount of a mirror that Cheuret exhibited at the 1924 Société des Artistes français. (92)

DAMON
A chromed-metal swivel reading-lamp exhibited at the Salon d'Automne in 1928. (93)

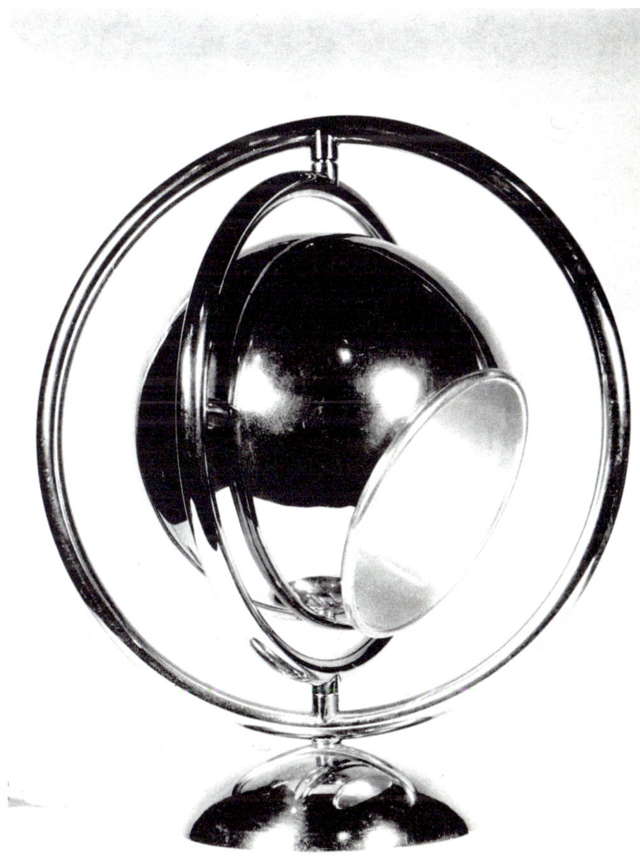

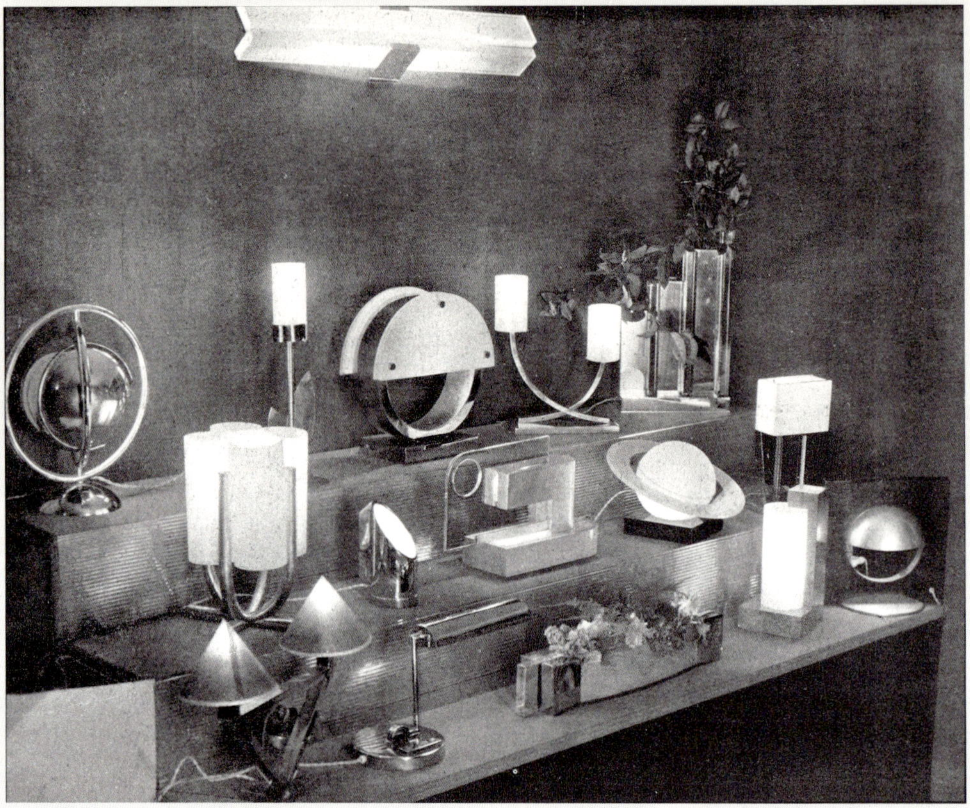

LUMINAIRES
MODERNES
VERRES
DIFFUSANTS

Nouveaux Magasins d'Exposition
4, Av. Pierre-1er-de-Serbie
PARIS (XVIe)

Téléphone : PASSY 61-46

USINE A BOULOGNE

DAMON

Damon
A wide range of the light fixtures marketed by Damon's studio. Included are several Lacroix lamps and Gorinthe's 'Saturn' table-lamp. (94)

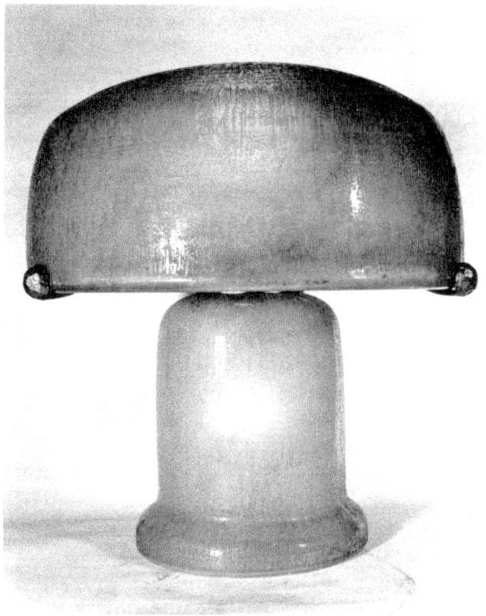

DAUM
An etched Daum mushroom table-lamp, 1933. (95)

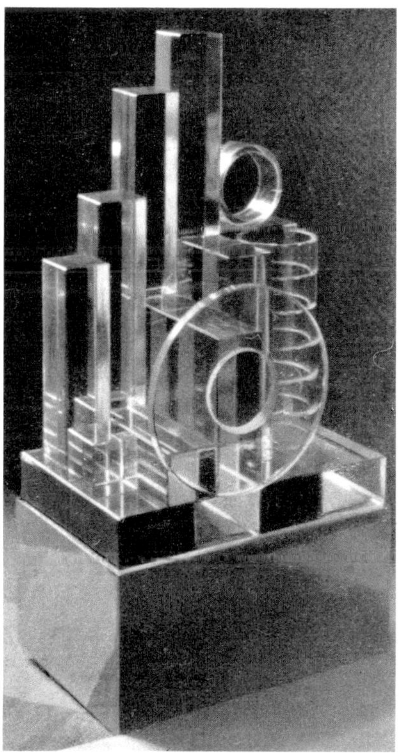

DESNY
A *bibelot lumineux*, which Desny called 'architectural lighting in miniature'. (96)

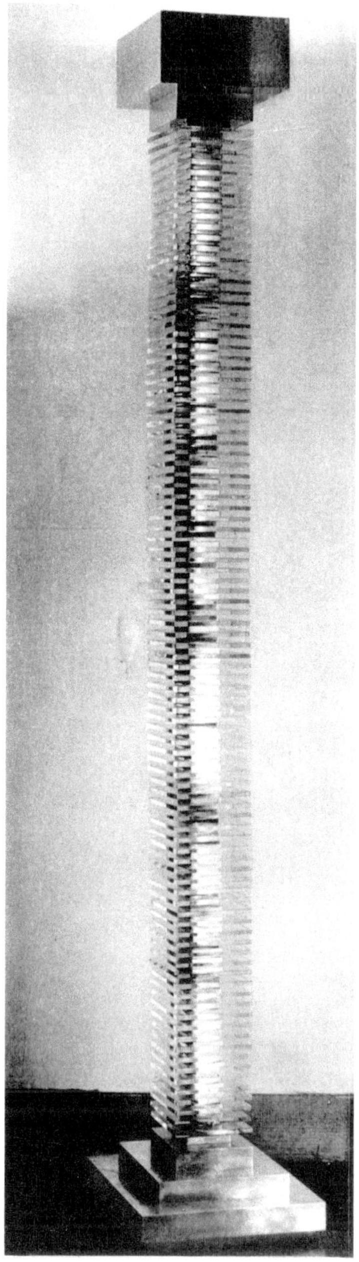

DESNY
Above, this floor lamp consists of a series of superimposed square sections of clear glass, each attached to a central column. Some light was emitted at intervals along the column and this played softly around the edges of the glass sections for decorative effect, but the lamp's main function was to provide indirect lighting, the latter supplied by the bulb housed in the cubic reflector at the top. (97)

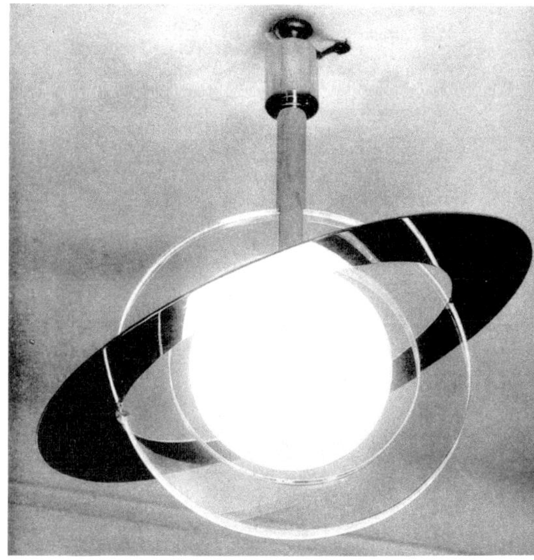

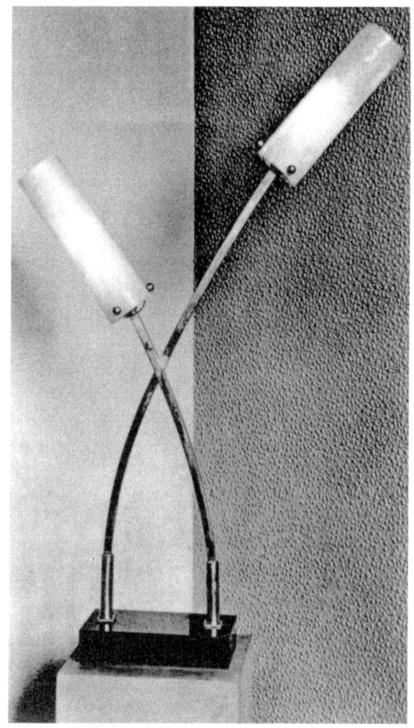

D.I.M.
Top, this 1930 *suspension* is entitled 'Saturn'. A very similar design, as a table-lamp, was produced by Gorinthe and marketed by Damon in the same year. (98)

Above, this Joubert and Petit lamp – more likely to have been intended for a pedestal than a table or desk – was marketed by D.I.M. The theme of cylindrical glass shades on attenuated arms was a popular one, used also, e.g., by Lacroix. (99)

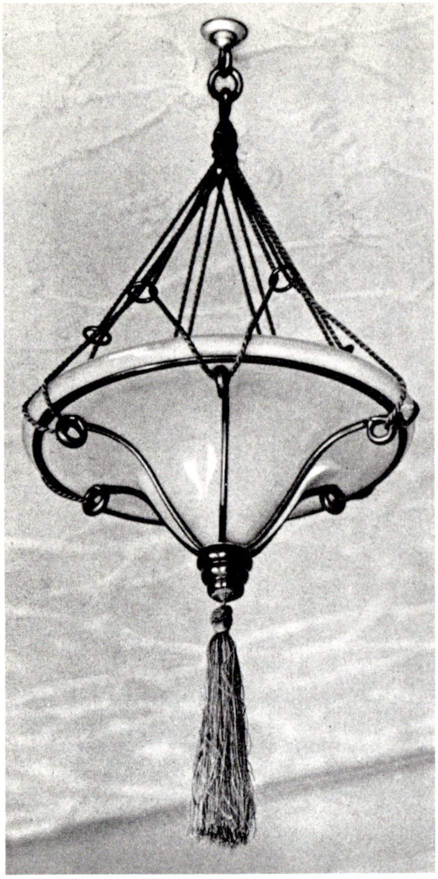

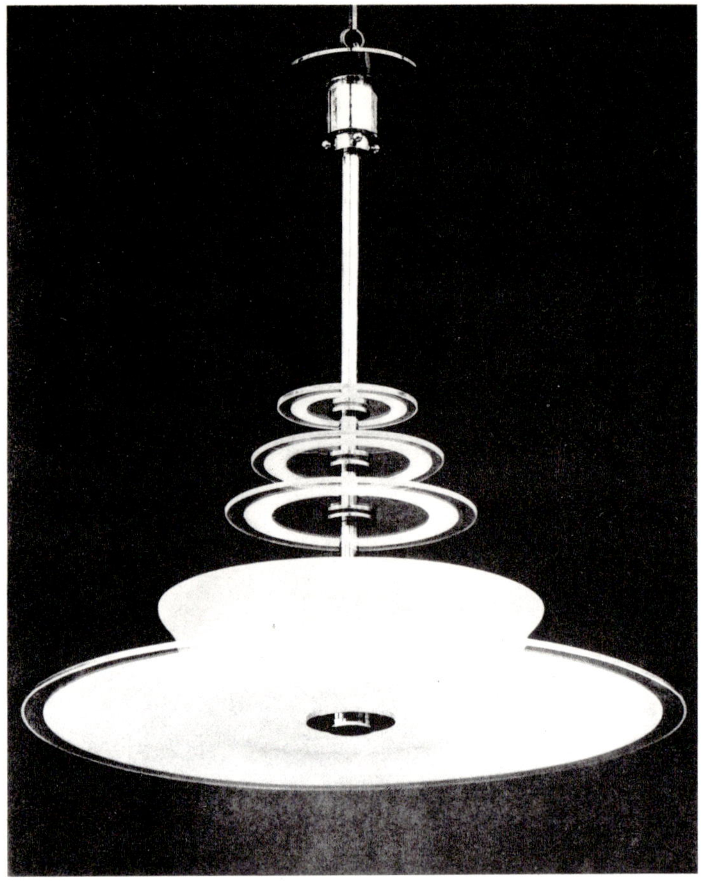

Dufrène
This 1920 chandelier consisted of an inverted glass bowl housed in a bronze mount, suspended by a network of silk cords culminating, at the bottom, in a silk tassel. (100)

Etling
A glass *bibelot lumineux* of a woman in diaphanous robes, reminiscent of Lalique's 'Suzanne au Bain' and similarly lit from within the base. (101)

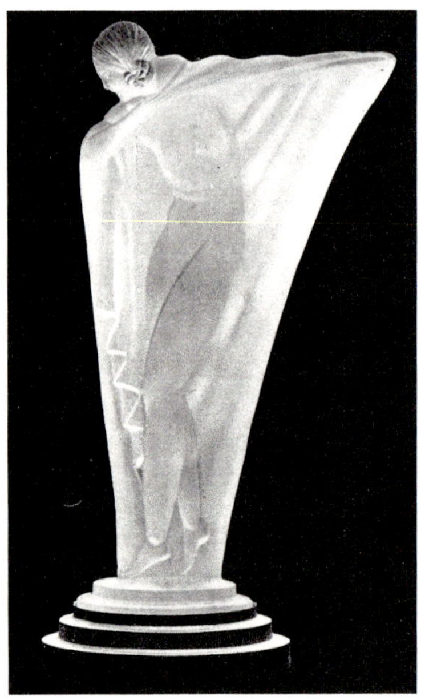

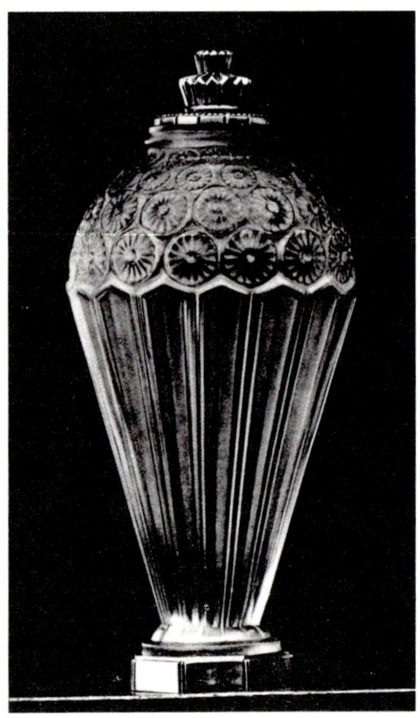

GENET & MICHON
A table-lamp in pressed glass (left below) shows Genet & Michon's minimization of visible metal mounts. A wide range of similarly designed fixtures was marketed in the late 1920s. The shape of the lamp and its stylized floret *motif* give the impression of an illuminated bouquet. By 1930, however, Genet & Michon had modernized their designs considerably. The chandelier at left is one of several of overall truncated cone shape that incorporated a series of glass discs, varying from two to six in number. (102, 103)

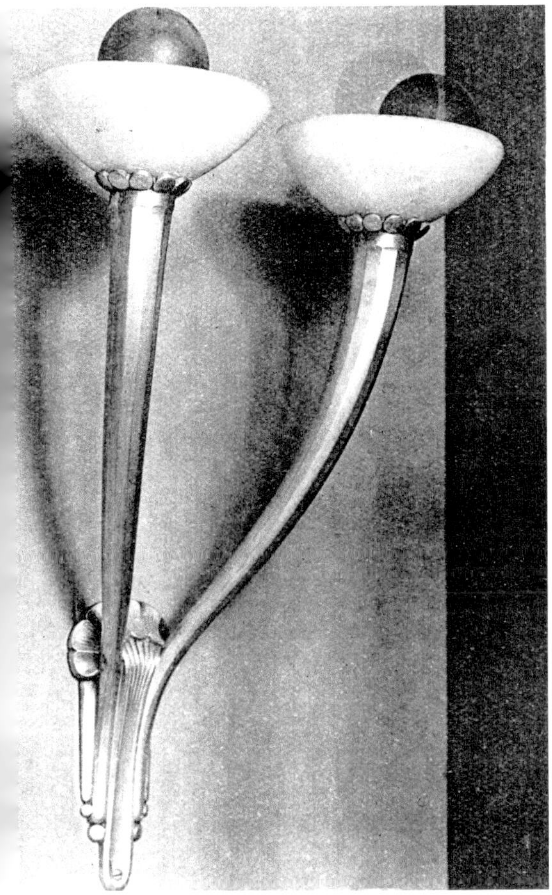

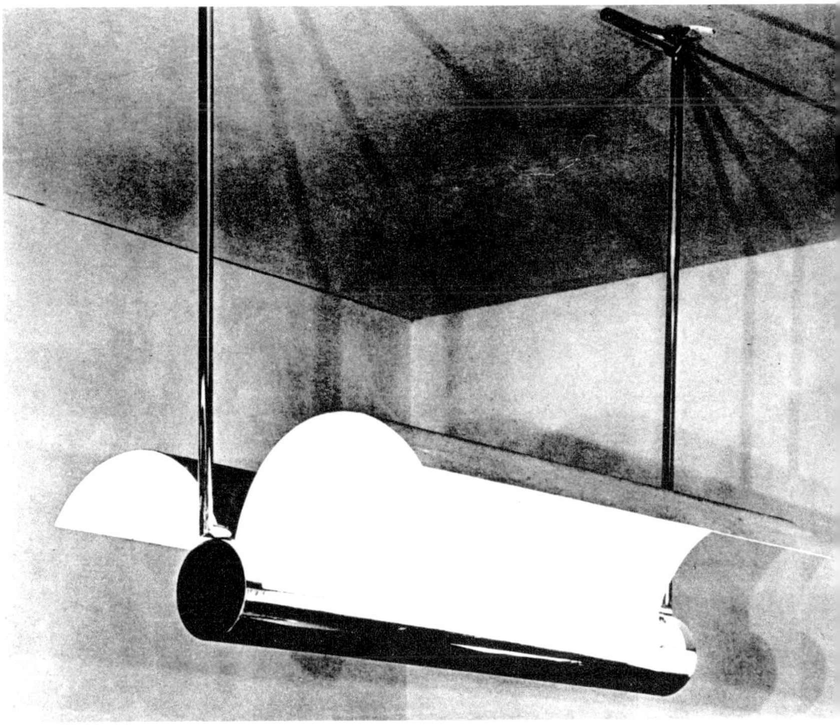

HERBST
This dining-room ceiling fixture was first exhibited at the 1928 Salon d'Automne. The curvature of the two wings was determined by the lighting engineer, André Salomon, to ensure the correct reflection of the light's rays on to the table below. If the guests were to be dazzled, this would only be by the cuisine. (105)

JOURDAIN
This ceiling fixture was designed for the Mallet-Stevens house. The bulbs are situated in the ends of the four inverted arms to project the light on to the ceiling for indirect illumination. (106)

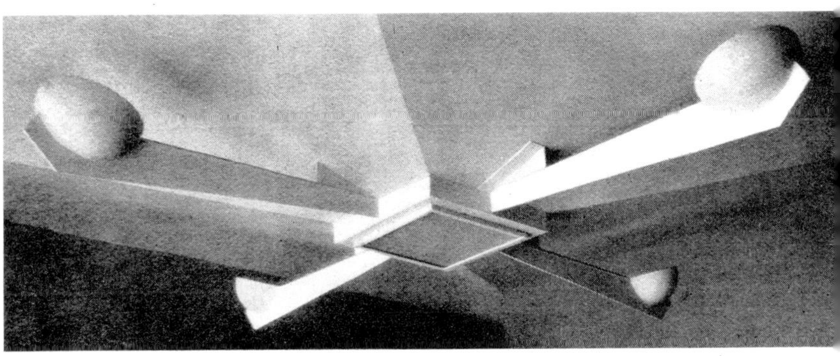

GIGOU
An elegant wall-bracket in chased gilt-bronze, shown at the 14th Salon des Artistes Décorateurs, 1923. More than a whiff of Louis XVI, but certainly not incongruous in a 1920s interior. (104)

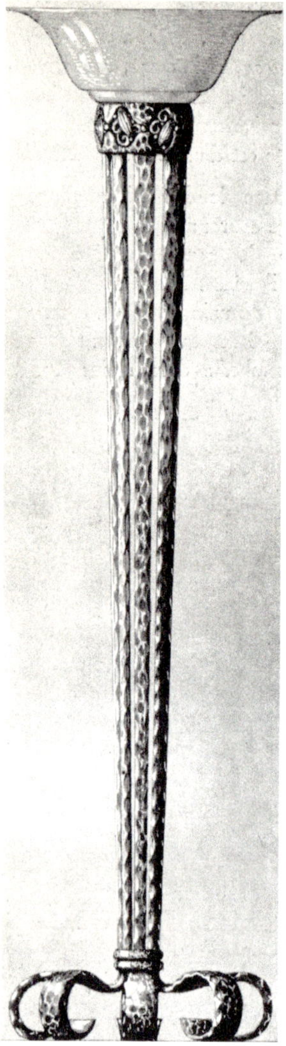

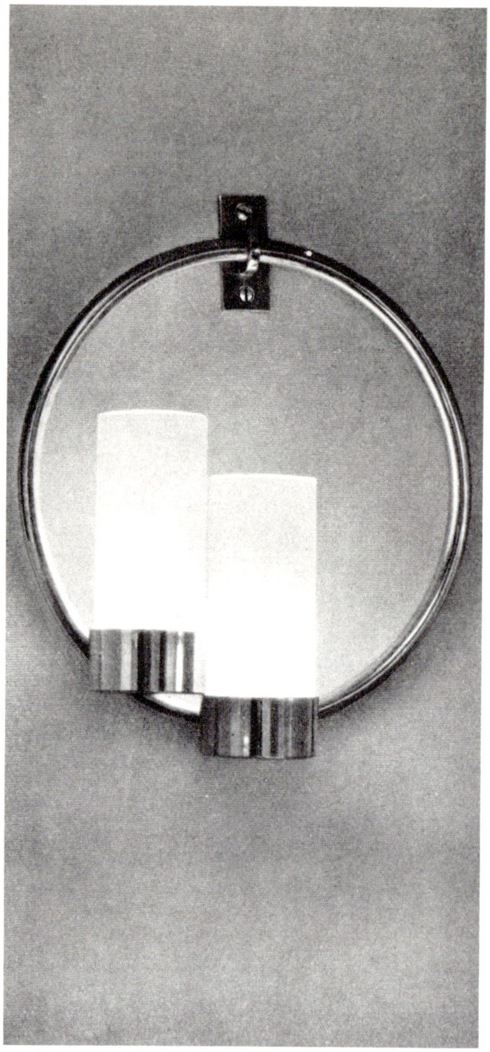

Kiss

Far left, this 1925 floor-lamp shows a heavy *martelé* finish to the wrought-iron characteristic of the work of Michel and Jules Nics. Most of Kiss's light fixtures are far more ornate, with the result that any initial clarity of design is lost in a maelstrom of whorls and volutes. The floor-lamp shown is, in its elegance, an exception. (107)

Lacroix

Left, this wall-bracket, in nickelled copper and tubes of frosted glass, was designed for a child's bedroom and first exhibited at the Salon of the Société des Artistes Décorateurs in 1929. (108)

Below left, this desk lamp by Lacroix, 1928, shows his remarkable versatility and modernity. Made of nickelled metal, it is rotatable. (109)

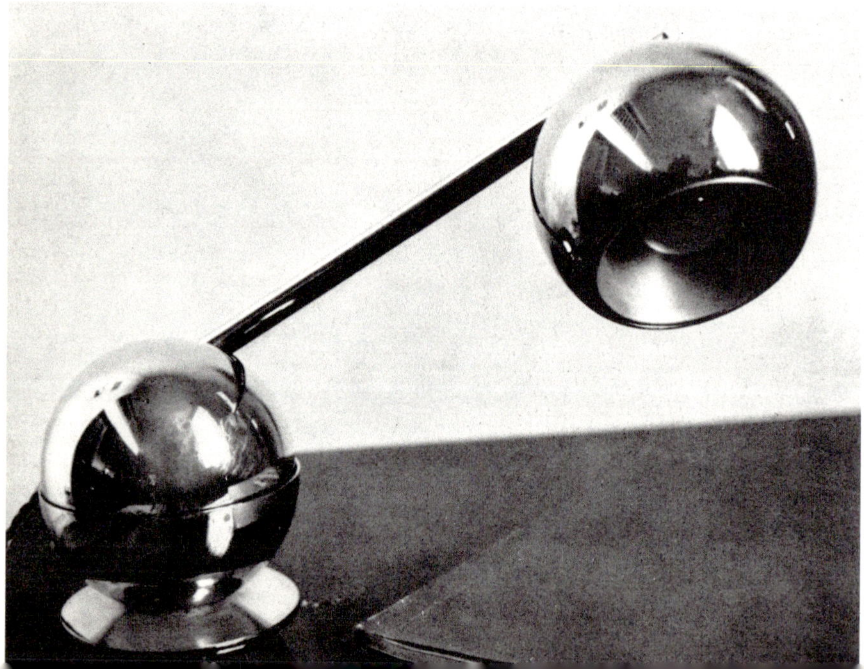

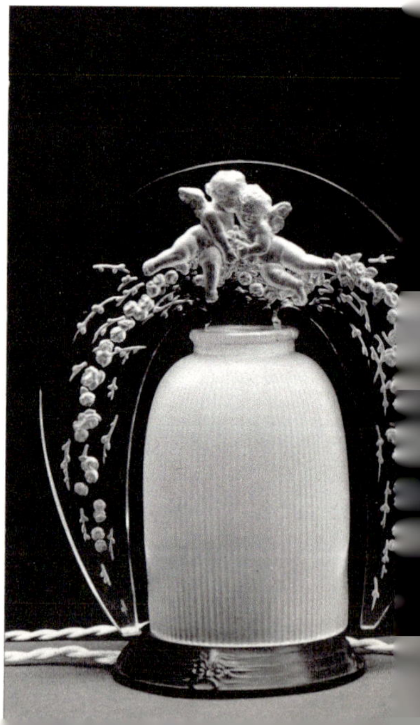

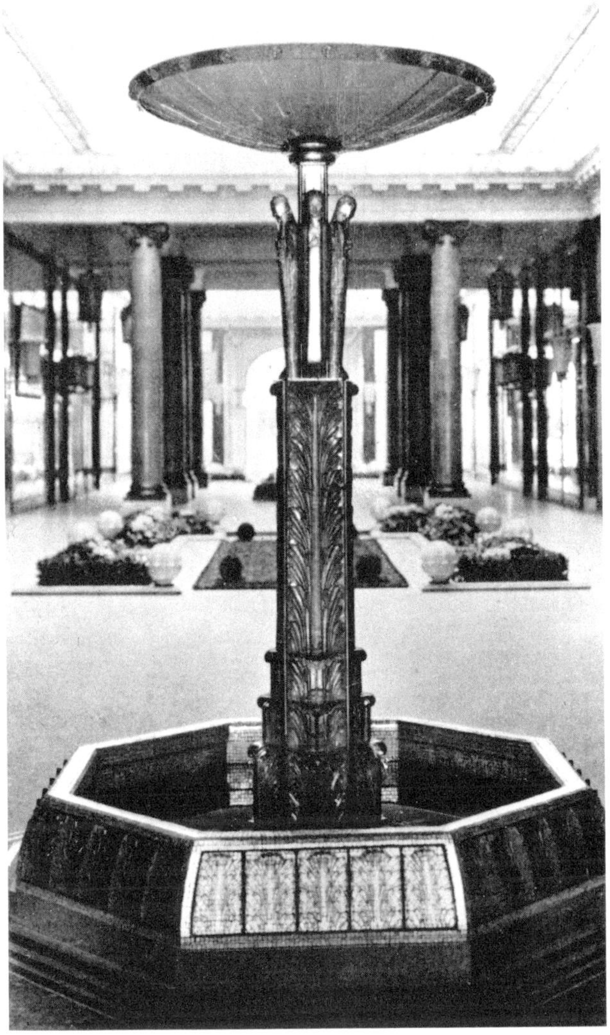

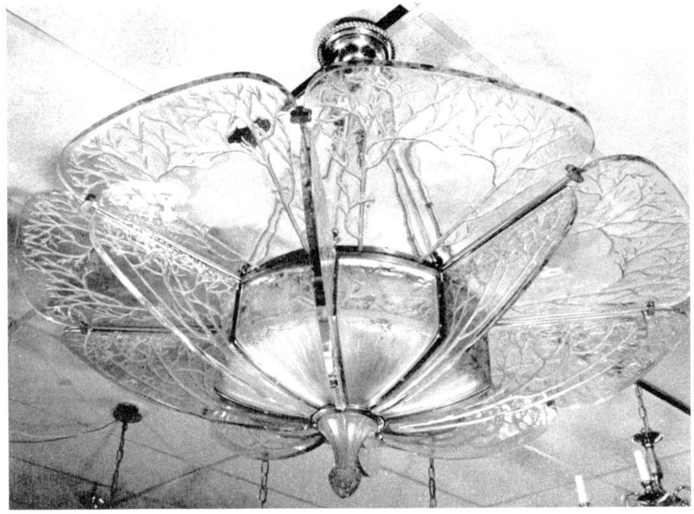

LALIQUE
Below left, three night-lights, *c.* 1921. The central shaft is in frosted glass in order to conceal the bulb within it. Lalique designed a wide range of these *objets*, varying the designs on the parabola-shaped decorative flange accordingly: for example, birds of paradise, swallows, putti, and blossom-bearing branches. (110)

Left, architectural lighting. This fountain by Lalique was one of several commissioned for the Champs-Elysées arcades, Paris. It is in moulded glass with four madonna-like figures positioned immediately below the top inverted glass bowl which houses the bulb, for indirect lighting. Another, and larger, Lalique fountain is situated on the Champs-Elysées on the corner of the Avenue Franklin D. Roosevelt. (111)

Above, a glass ceiling fixture. (112)

LE CHEVALLIER
An intriguing table-lamp in aluminium, *c.* 1929. This model has a much more finished appearance than most of Le Chevallier's lamps. (113)

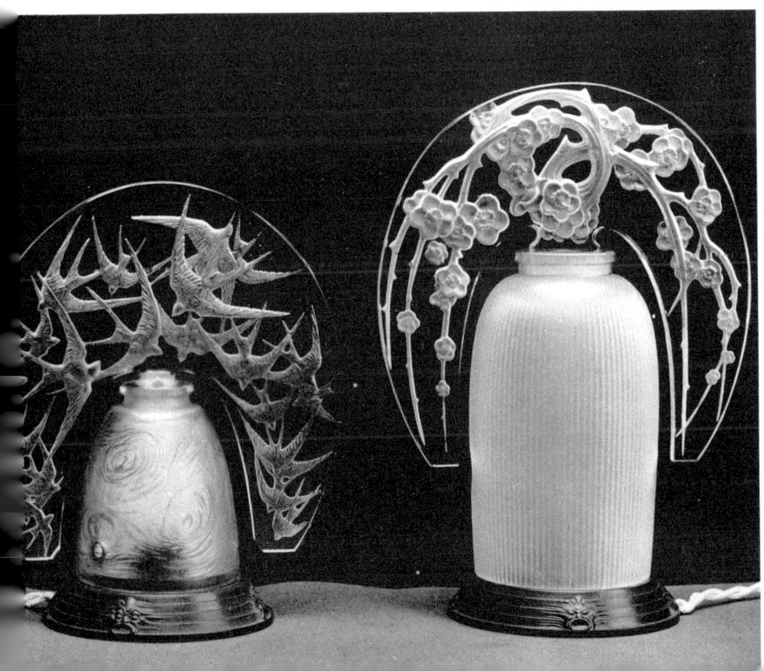

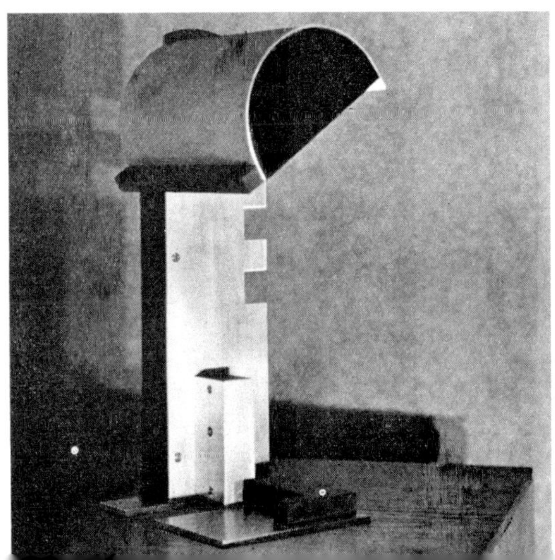

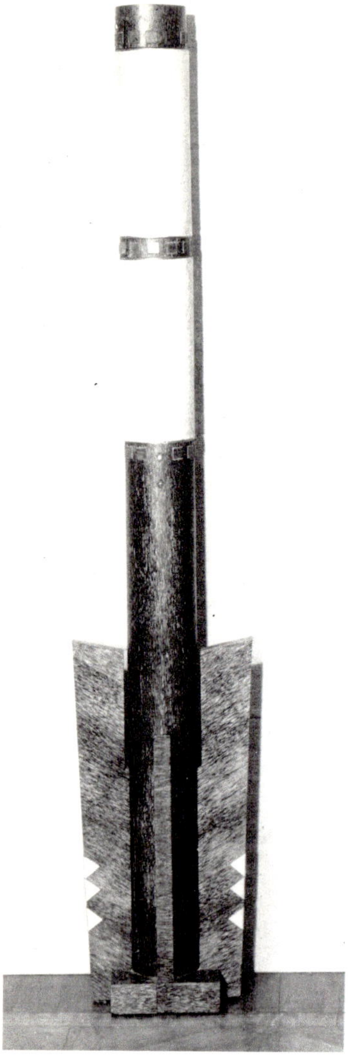

LEGRAIN
Floor-lamp in ground glass, the mount covered in parchment. (*Musée des Arts Décoratifs*) (114)

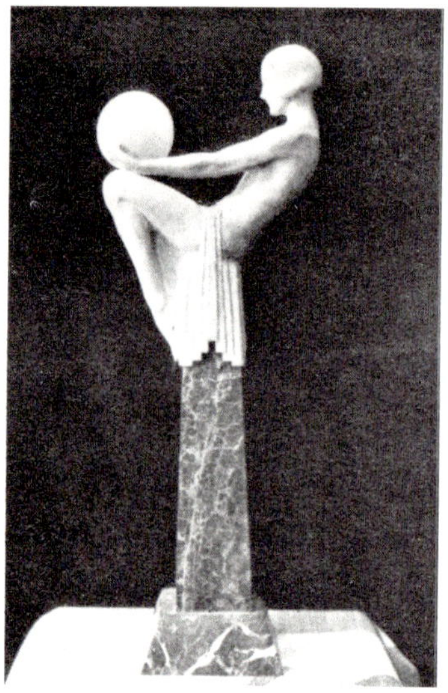

LE VERRIER
A *bibelot lumineux* in which the ball that the woman clasps on her knees lights up. This is a typical example of the Le Verrier range of *petits bronzes*. (115)

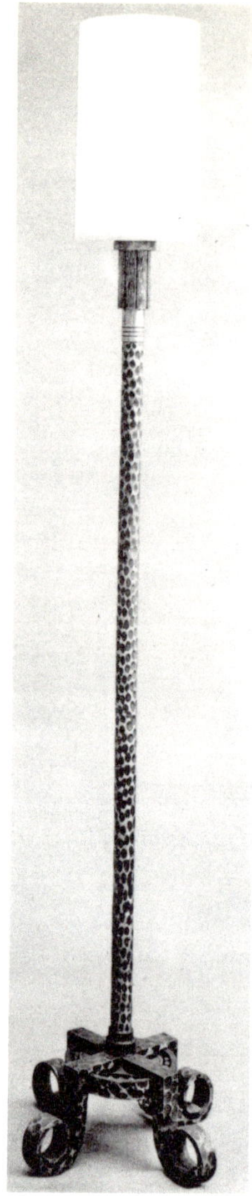

NICS
This neat and elegant floor-lamp by Michel and Jules Nics shows the *martelé* finish that they invariably applied to their wrought-iron. (116)

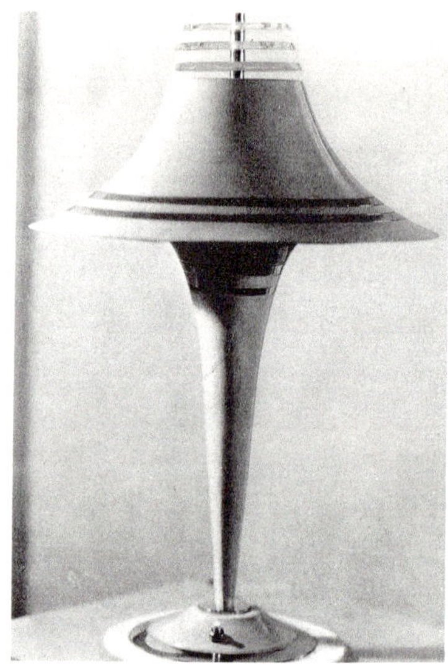

PAUL
This ultra-modern copper table-lamp was exhibited in the Pavilion of Light at the 1937 International Exposition in Paris. (117)

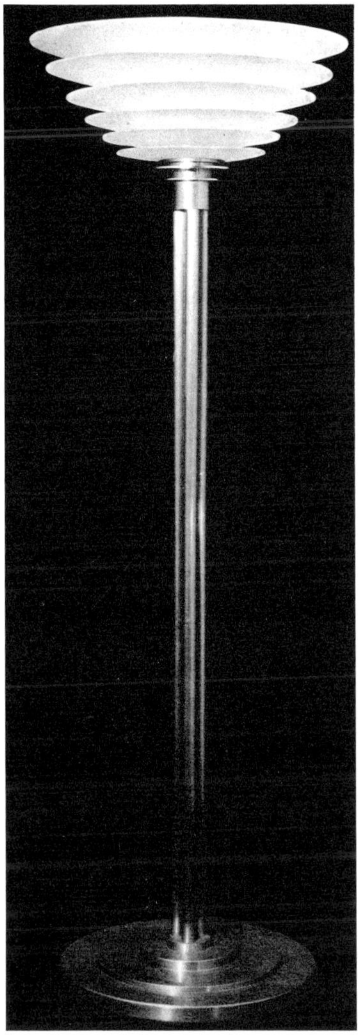

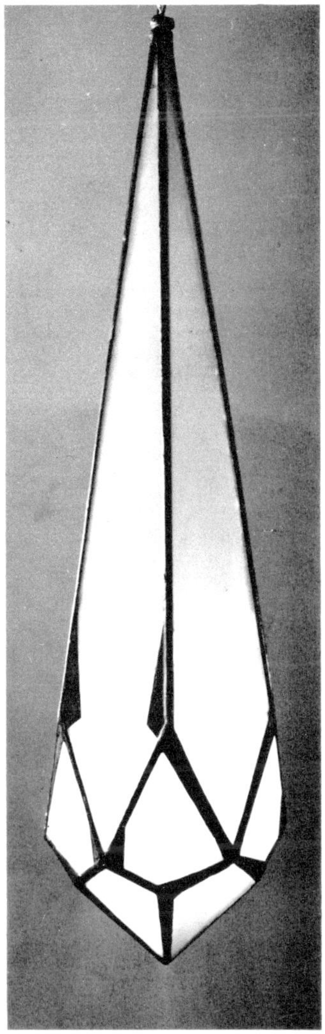

PERZEL

A floor-lamp shown at the 1930 Salon d'Automne. The slightly convex glass discs are arranged to provide 'semi-indirect' illumination. (118)

An early Perzel *suspension*, showing his use of glass of uniform opacity, and therefore diffusion, housed, in this instance, in lead. (119)

Below left, an illuminated table, with a frosted glass top and cylindrical column of opalescent glass housed in nickelled metal. The light source is in the column and those rays that are emitted vertically are refracted prismatically through the faceted piece of crystal. On the table top is a small statuette of a tennis player. (120)

RATEAU

In this bronze floor-lamp, in patinated *vert antique*, the reflector is supported by pheasants. The base consists of four outsized seeds of grain in a modern adaptation of the classical 'ball and claw' foot. (122)

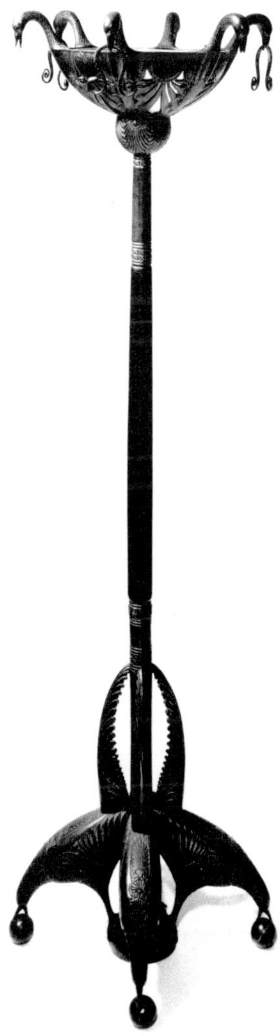

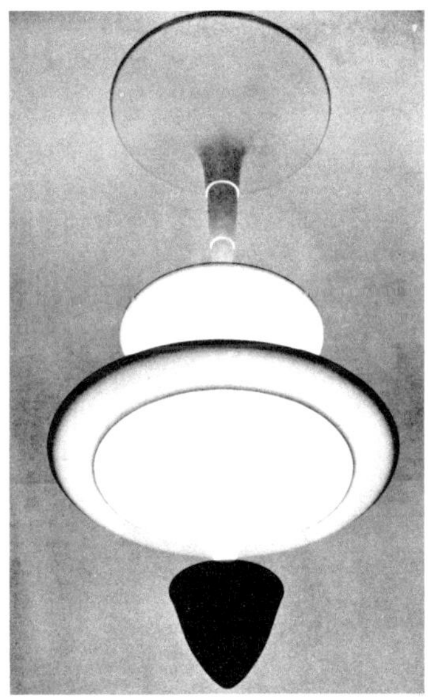

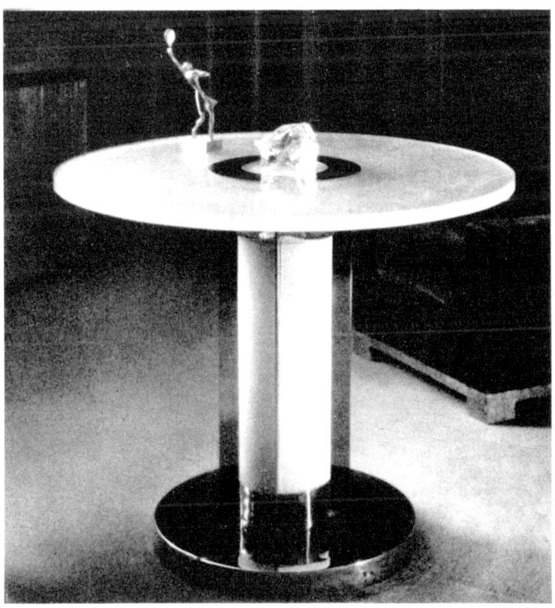

PRINTZ

This chandelier, first shown at the 1928 Salon d'Automne, was designed for a living-room for the Princess of Auvergne. It was made entirely of 'turtle-dove grey' metal, its shape being determined by the calculation of the curvature of its surfaces. (121)

RUHLMANN
Sketches of a *vase reflecteur* and a candelabrum, among many to be found in Léon Moussinac's *Croquis de Ruhlmann*, published in 1924. (123, 124)

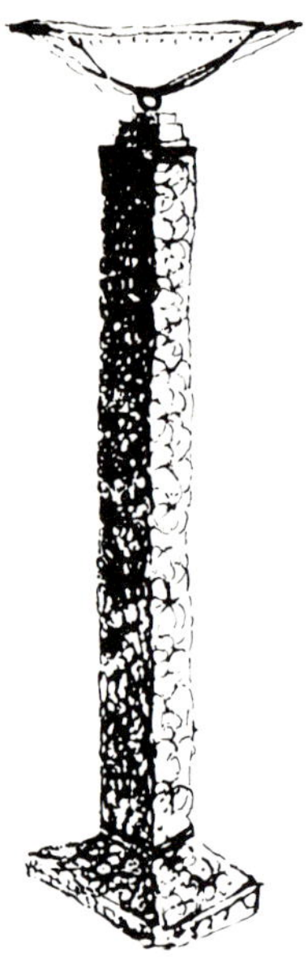

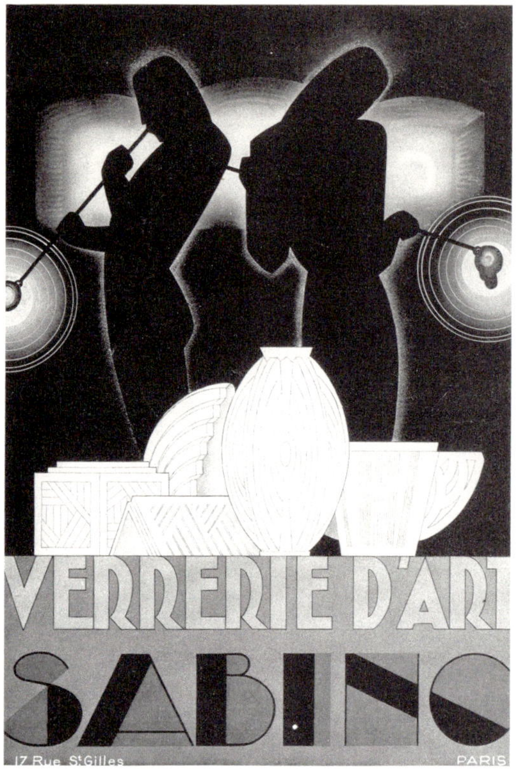

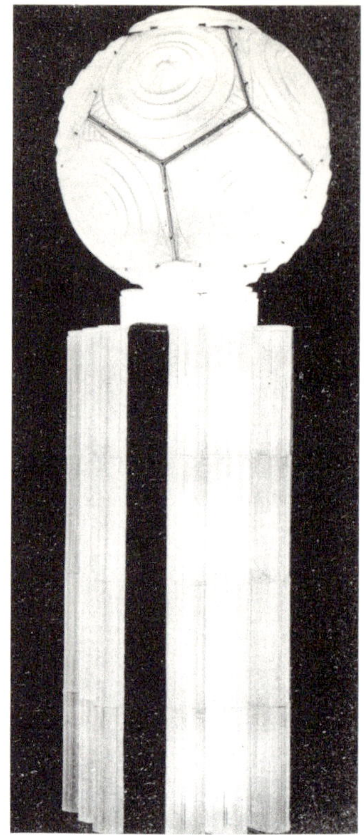

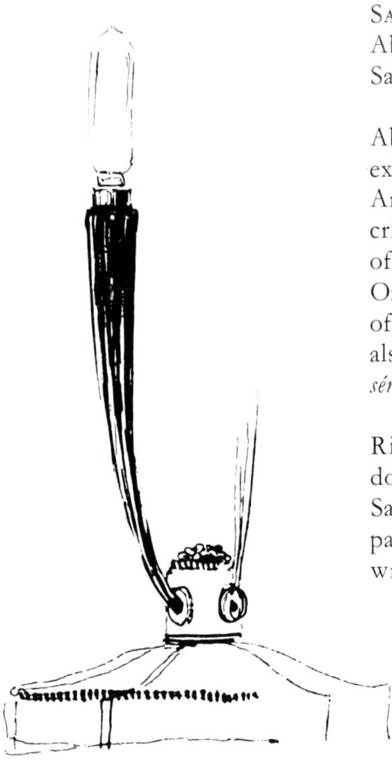

SABINO
Above left, advertisement for Sabino art glass, *c.* 1930. (125)

Above right, an illuminated stele exhibited at the 1928 Société des Artistes Décorateurs. Sabino described it as 'conceived by an image of a garden in The Thousand and One Nights'. The sphere, composed of segments of pressed glass, was also used as a chandelier singly or *en série*. (126)

Right, Sabino's much-publicized doorway, exhibited at the 1927 Salon d'Automne. The sections of patterned pressed glass are housed in wrought-iron. (127)

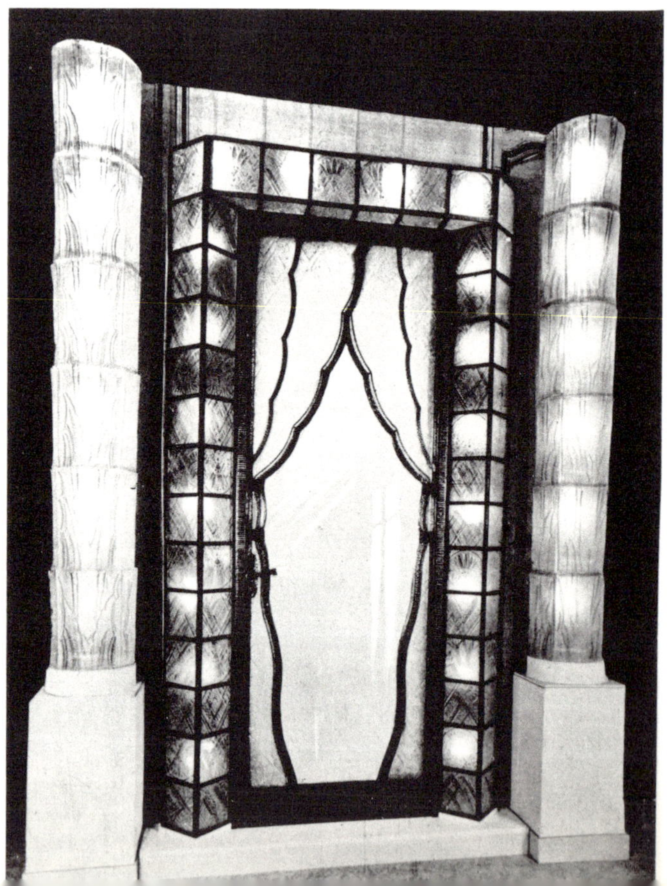

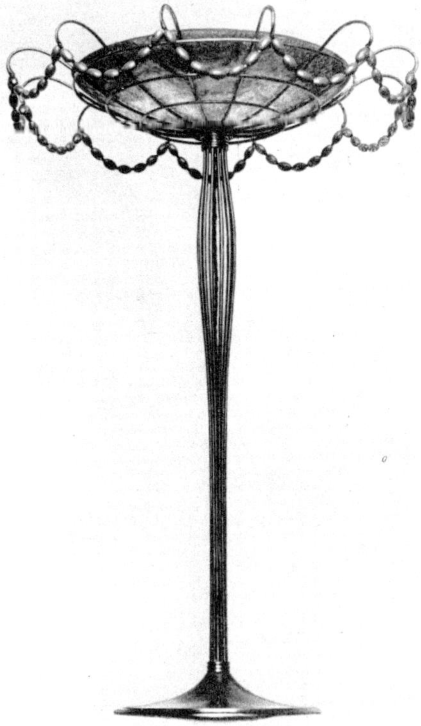

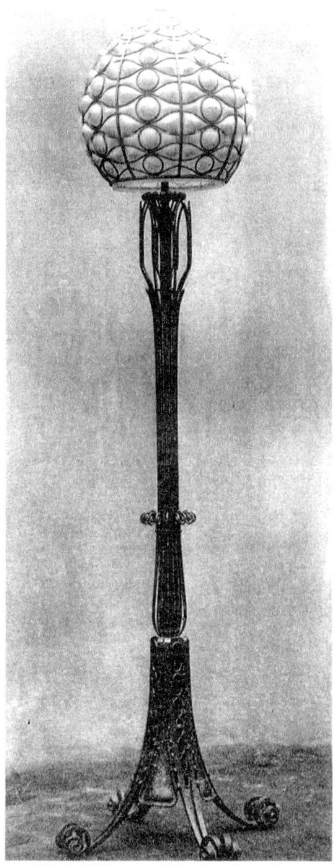

SCHENCK

Far left, an elegant table-lamp of 1920. Of refined simplicity, its column is made of a series of thick strands of copper that, emerging from the base, first diverge to form a baluster-shaped swelling and then converge to fit into a cast ring, from which they again diverge, this time forming the support for the rose-coloured crystal bowl and finishing in connected volutes onto which are threaded olive-shaped beads. (128)

Left, this *lampadaire* by Marcel Schenk appeared first at the 1923 Salon d'Automne and then at the 1925 International Exposition. (129)

SIMONET

Below left, this lighting *ensemble* – a chandelier and matching wall-brackets – was awarded first prize for the illumination of a living-room in a high income-bracket home at the 1924 Paris Grand Competition of Light. The light bulbs are concealed inside the strings of crystal pendants, the latter as gushes of petrified water. (130)

Below, this 1928 'Thistle' chandelier shows the Simonets' evolution from predominantly bronze fixtures to those of glass. (131)

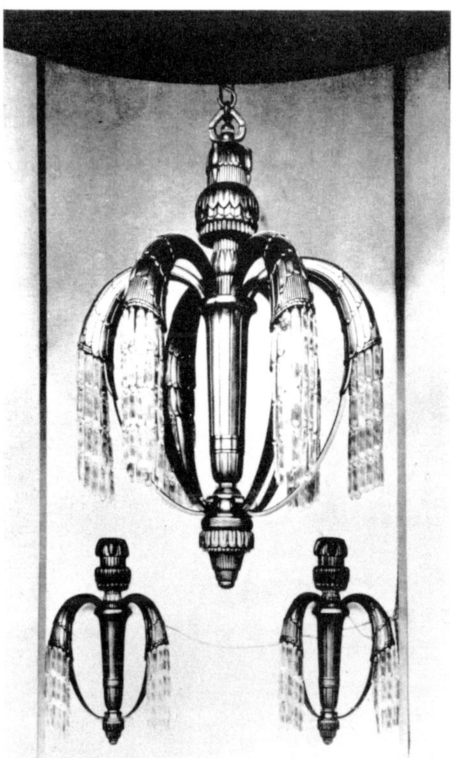

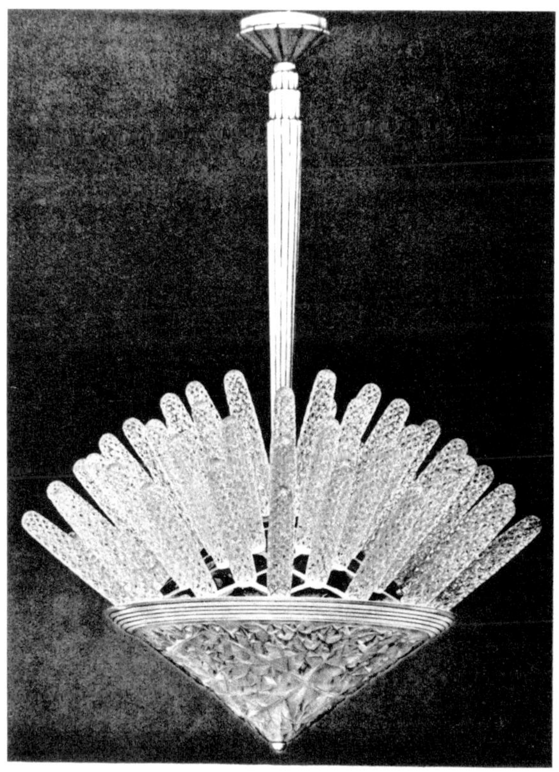

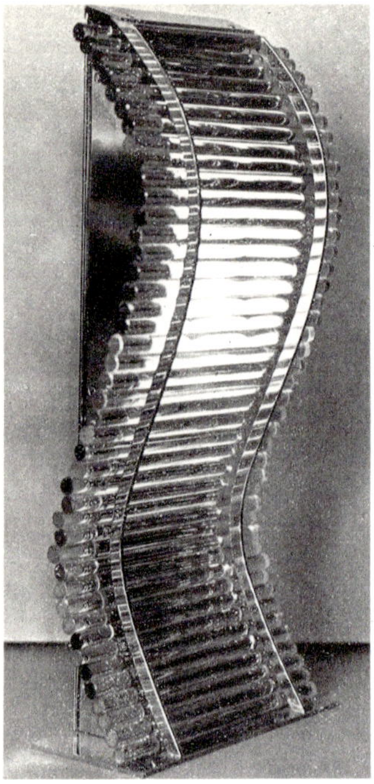

SOGNOT
Serpentine table-lamp in nickelled metal and crystal rods. (132)

SUBES
Below left, a huge Subes *vase réflecteur*, first exhibited in 1928, to provide indirect lighting. (133)

Below, a wrought-iron and marble table-lamp of 1932. (134)

SZABO
Below right, electric reading-lamp in wrought-iron, *c.* 1923. The iron has a soft, yet pronounced, hammered finish. (135)

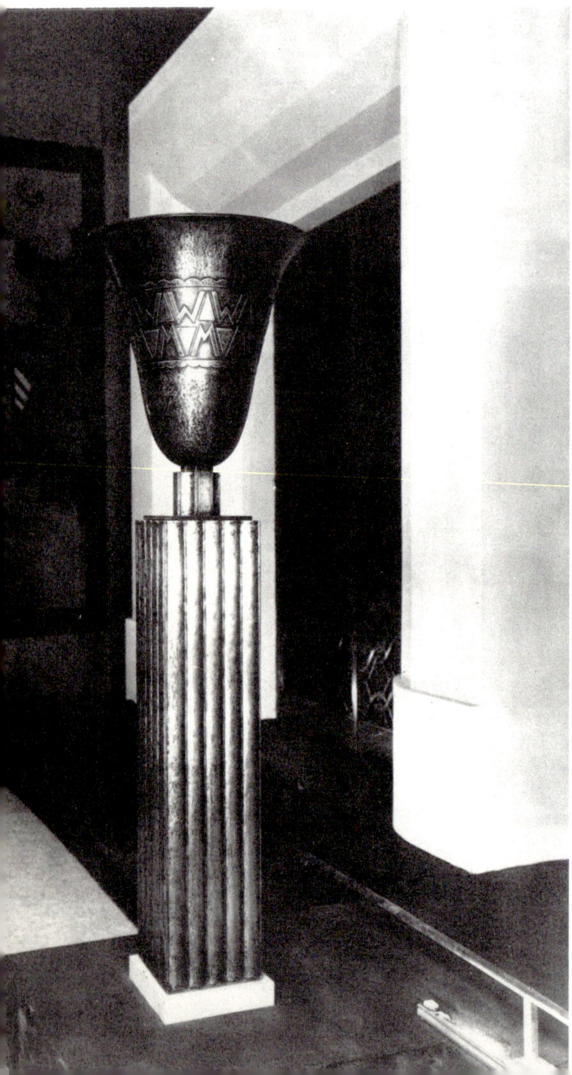

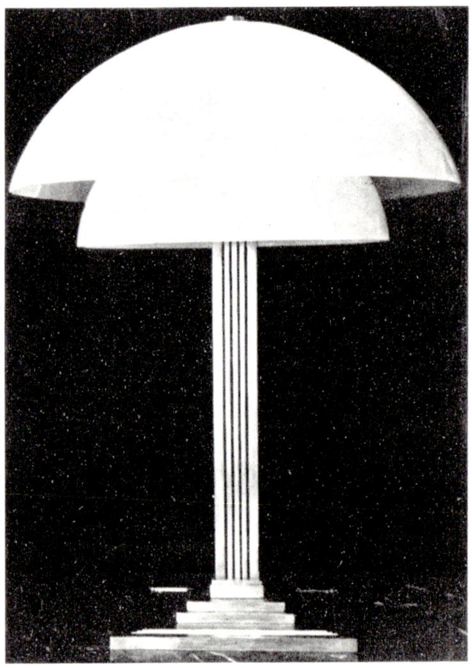

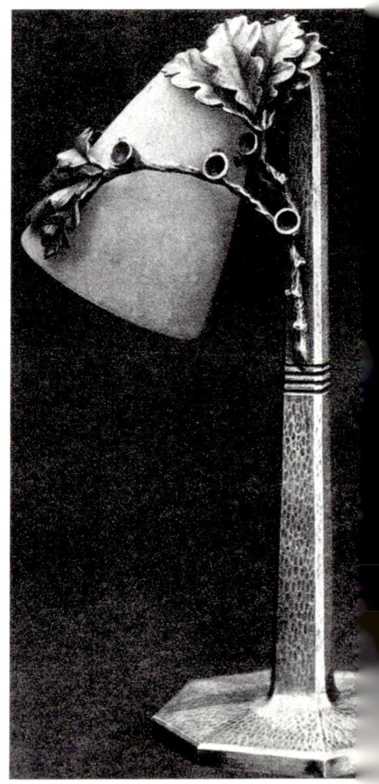

One of the few 1920s glass artists not to have abandoned polychromatic effects in the wake of Art Nouveau, his palette included a muted, rather autumnal range of russet browns, vermilions, ochres and olive greens. In lighting, he produced small table-lamps, night lights, perfume burners, and illuminated plaques that must have provided a most delightful and much-needed stab of colour in the then predominantly antiseptic and sombre interiors. The perfume burner was a felicitous variation of the night light that contained an internally-positioned phial or shallow dish to hold, for example, incense, ground cinnamon or cassia which, due to the heat generated by the electric bulb positioned immediately beneath the phial, emitted a sweet fragrance.

The motifs for Argy-Rousseau's shades were myriad, though mainly of a floral type. Bilberries, grapes and anemones in bas-relief stand out against a lighter-coloured ground, the whole usually on a small wrought-iron base. On other occasions, the theme is masks, satyrs, butterflies or *tableaux anciens*. In *pâte de cristal* Argy-Rousseau tended to concentrate more on statuettes (sometimes with a light source in the base in a manner similar to that employed by Lalique and Sabino). His Tanagra figurines, executed in collaboration with H. Bourraine around 1930, are in clear crystal in a style distinctly dissimilar to that of his *pâte de verre*. In 1934 he introduced a variation in technique in that year's Salons: glassware decorated by gold, silver, platinum and enamel.

Argy-Rousseau's lamps are in limited supply, and their prices are correspondingly high. Three *pâte-de-verre* and wrought-iron table-lamps were sold in Paris in 1975 for between FF6,125 and 7,000 ($1,225 and $1,400).

BAGUÈS FRÈRES

In an advertisement in *Mobilier et Décoration* in 1928 the Baguès brothers listed their range of products as ancient and modern light fixtures, *objets d'art* and ironwork. Based in Paris, they had outlets in Brussels, London and New York. Categorization of their light fixtures is as difficult as is an evaluation of their quality of design. As advertised, they reproduced both old styles – in particular Louis XIV and Empire – and a range of modern ones. To these, though, were added 'modernly designed Louis XIV girandoles' and what resemble traditionally styled 1920s chandeliers.

A favourite material was glass crystal beads – either clear or opalescent or, as in the lustre they designed for Mme Jeanne Lanvin, in topaz and amethyst tones – housed in bronze mounts and shaped as gigantic fruit or petrified jets of water. In 1932, they produced for the ocean liner *L'Atlantique* four large reflecting vases for the lounge, and they participated in the 1934 Salon of Light and the 1937 international exposition. The quality of their designs, however, was unpredictable. In the same year – 1925 – that they produced their well-conceived pinecone-shaped chandelier (see illustration 87), they were to exhibit two other chandeliers that were aesthetic *non sequiturs*: one designed as a windmill, the other as a bird cage in glass and gilt bronze with electric candles positioned around the cage's perimeter.

In 1975 there were three large Bagués chandeliers for sale in Paris, ranging in price from FF 5,250 to 7,875 ($1,050 to $1,575).

BRANDT, EDGAR

'Iron is worked by art to unite it with architecture, and has become as supple as wood: it is turned at will; it is given the form of light leaves and moving bodies; the roughness is removed to give it a sort of aliveness.' (Sebastian Mercier, *Tableau de Paris*, 1778).

Wrought iron's fortunes in the decorative arts were to fluctuate throughout the 1800s, only to achieve a more than ephemeral renaissance through the work of Emile Robert at the end of the century. Edgar Brandt, himself a graduate of that era (see page 70), was, in Robert's twilight years, to take up the reins, though his position was never so pre-eminent as Robert's.

Brandt was one of the first to adapt his designs to the possibilities of the new machinery then emerging. The hammer, anvil and burin were replaced with mechanical lathes, balances, stamping-presses, and oxyacetylene welding, a transition that for Brandt allowed – in the critic Gabriel Mourey's words – no compromise to artistic quality.

From his studio near the Porte d'Auteuil, with the collaboration of the young architect Henri Favier, Brandt was, following the war, to recapture the momentum of his pre-1914 ironwork.

In the sinuosities of its vegetal and floral enlacements, his earlier work showed a clear Art Nouveau influence, but from the mid-1920s, his style, though always diverse, became markedly more angular. The entire decorative wrought-iron spectrum was covered: consoles, ramps, grilles, signboards, *portes monumentales*, elevator doors and panels (such as those executed for Selfridge's, London, in 1928), and, at the 1925 Exposition Universelle, where his work was ubiquitous, the Gate of Honour for the entire show. His light fixtures were limited mainly to table-lamps, chandeliers and wall-brackets. Metal mounts, usually in wrought iron (but also in copper or ormolu), housed shades of blown or moulded glass (often by Daum), marble, onyx, Sèvres porcelain (for example, on Brandt's stand at the 1925 Exposition), and even, in 1927, pleated cloth. The themes for these were frequently derived from nature: 'Cascades', 'Marguerites', 'Lilies', etc. Less frequently they were allegorical: 'Force', 'Audacity'.

Prices of Brandt's light fixtures depend, to a degree, on whether they incorporate glass shades, particularly those by Daum. A wrought-iron (only) Brandt table-lamp sold at Versailles in 1975 for FF 2,975 ($595); one with a Daum shade for FF 6,225 ($1,245). It is Brandt's serpent lamps that are the most collectable. Prices range from FF 12,500 to 60,000 ($2,600 to $12,250) for models of the three different sizes.

CAPON, EUGÈNE and G.-L.

Workers in various metals, the Capon brothers included several forms of lighting among their exhibits at the Paris Salons in the early 1920s. Chandeliers and wall-brackets were designed and executed in brass, steel, and patinated and *martelé* bronze, as were vases, radiator covers, and other objects. Known for their emphasis on lighting, they provided the fixtures for the ensembles by Gallerey and Léon Jallot at the 1923 Société des Artistes Décorateurs Salon, and also submitted branched chandeliers and wall-brackets to the 1925 International Exposition.

No Capon lamps appear to have re-emerged on the market in recent years. They would, however, probably fall into a price range of between FF 1,600 and 2,500 ($350 and $525).

CHAREAU, PIERRE

If anyone were to claim that Chareau's floor lamp (see illustration 90) was the finest light fixture to emerge from the Art Déco epoch he or she would get a most sympathetic hearing. So simply conceived, yet such a visual *tour de force*, this lamp is most respresentative of Chareau's abhorrence of any superfluity that would conceal the sincerity of an object's form. Before all else, it was an object's function that determined its shape. But just as Goethe defined his Mephistopheles as a force that wished evil yet always created good, so, whereas Chareau always strove for utility, he often realized beauty.

Chareau was both an architect and a decorator. As the former, his reputation rests primarily on the 'House of Glass' – revolutionary in its conception – he designed for Dr Dalsace in 1929, and his Club House at Beauvallon in 1927. As a decorator, his approach was that of 'spatial art': he did not design furniture as such, but rather organized spaces and made them habitable. His furniture shown at the Salon d'Automne and Société des Artistes Décorateurs (both in 1919), Les Cinq, and, from 1930, through the Union des Artistes Modernes, shows an audacity and inventiveness that on occasion approach the threshold of illogicality. His pearwood bookcase in the French pavilion at the 1925 International Exposition was described by the critic Gabriel Mourey in *The Studio* as 'one of the most remarkable works in the whole exposition'.

In lighting, his series of floor- and bedside table-lamps and chandeliers in slices of alabaster or glass are best known. The base of the floor-lamp – made of wood and in pyramidal form – was also sometimes used to support a cloth shade, such as the one Chareau designed for Mme Jacques Errera in 1926. His predilection, however, was for concealed lighting. In the study of the French pavilion at the 1925 Exposition, he used a domed cornice to reflect and diffuse the light, the projector consisting of glass slats that could be adjusted to vary the intensity of light. In the reception hall of the Grand Hotel in Tours, completed in 1928, he incorporated his illuminated tracts into the ceiling. These consisted of rectangular strips of light placed perpendicularly to each other. At the second and third Salons of Light in 1934 and 1935 Chareau teamed up with André Salomon to produce corner illumination in *dalles de verre*.

The illustrated floor-lamp is perhaps the only known Chareau light fixture on today's Art Déco market. Prices of his fixtures would be extremely high, matching those for Ruhlmann's work.

CHEURET, ALBERT

A student of Jacques Perrin, Cheuret specialized in light fixtures, but also designed and executed other objects, such as bronze and pewter statuettes, radiator covers, mirrors, and a spectacular garniture clock in which the dominant influence was Egyptian. His table-lamps, wall-brackets and chandeliers show a consistent interpretation of *le style 25*, and it is therefore most unfortunate that almost the only surviving model of a Cheuret light fixture is his candelabrum composed of three alabaster tulip flowers, clearly Art Nouveau in spirit.

A member of the Société des Artistes français, he exhibited in 1924 a 'Bird of Paradise' chandelier, two 'Pearl' wall-brackets and a 'Pebbles' floor-lamp. At the 1925 exposition he showed various similar fixtures consisting of panels of sliced alabaster housed in silvered bronze. In these works there is always a characteristic clarity and freshness of design – as in a table-lamp whose mount is in the form of a chimera. The alabaster slices are sharply angular, yet sufficiently softened by the stylized themes of the mounts.

Several models of Cheuret's alabaster tulip lamp have been sold in recent years in Paris and New York. Prices have ranged from FF 3,075 to 6,575 ($615 to $1,315).

DAMON

An iconoclast who dismissed pressed glass as suitable only for architectural lighting, Damon concentrated on the aesthetic inadequacies of frosted glass for his own purposes, *i.e.* a range of standard light fixtures for home interiors. He claimed that frosted glass was not of a perfect translucence; the points of light formed by the bulbs were clearly visible through the glass. Several lighting designers had applied themselves to the elimination of this 'eyesore' by interposing an opaque screen between the light source and the frosted glass shade; but this had generated another problem: either the screen acted to reflect – rather than transmit – the light before it reached the shade, or the screen/shade combination itself absorbed too great a proportion of the light, reducing the function of, say, a reading-lamp to that of an illuminated bibelot or night-light.

Damon's remedy was to merge the independent attributes of the screen and shade into a single body. By manufacturing glass that was enamelled on the inside and frosted on the outside, he claimed that the resulting hybrid was the best of all worlds: it was diaphanous and provided an even diffusion of light, but it was of a sufficient opacity to make it impossible to discern the number or position of the bulbs behind it. He suggested also, as a decorative fillip, that it could on occasion be interposed with frosted glass or *dalles* of cut crystal to create ornamental contrasts: happy oppositions of lively and matt tones.

This *verre émaillé diffusant* was housed in metal mounts – often gilt or silvered bronze, chrome, or nickelled copper – and frequently on a black marbrite base. Damon himself designed and executed lamps, but he also drew on the talents of others for the range of light fixtures that were manufactured by his firm. Preeminent among these was Boris-Jean Lacroix, whose contribution to lighting – both in terms of general philosophy and design – warrants a separate discussion (see p. 175). Others were Gorinthe, André Roy, André Basompierre, Georges Martin, Daniel Stéphan (who also designed for DIM), and Jean Baignères.

A proponent of functional lighting, Damon marketed all standard fixtures including illuminated vases, *antéchambre lanternes*, and *bouts de table*. In his marriage of glass and metal the main theme is sober elegance: a search for beauty in a perfect adaptation of the object to its use.

Damon table-lamps fall into a price range of between FF 2,625 and 4,375 ($525 and $875).

DAUM, ANTONIN (see also pp. 73–74)

At the end of World War I, Daum *frères* reopened and set about recapturing its lost momentum. Under the directorship of Antonin Daum, some of the firm's light fittings – bowls and shades – were sent to Edgar Brandt to be housed in metal mounts. It was also at this time that the collaboration between the Daum studios and the Majorelle works (also in Nancy) was reinstituted. Metal mounts were wrought by Majorelle and delivered to Daum where glass was blown into them, giving an 'imprisoned' appearance to the resulting shades or vases. The majority of the great 1900 glassworks did not survive the economic difficulties of the immediate post-war years, but Antonin Daum managed to do so largely by overseeing the production of pieces which, while still reflecting the style of the Art Nouveau era, were nevertheless evolving towards the newly emerging 1920s taste.

In 1925 he formed a limited partnership with his two nephews, Paul and Henri, and his son-in-law, Pierre Froissart, as fellow directors. One last cataclysm – this time the Depression of 1929 – was to threaten the firm's existence. Of course most industries were affected, but in France glassmaking suffered particularly. In Nancy, for instance, three competitors were to close their doors: the Delatte and Dusquesne works and the Society of *Cristalleries*.

The Daum output of art glass dropped severely, but this was balanced by an increase in the firm's market for glass tableware. Antonin died in 1930 and was replaced by Paul. Survival continued to be a critical issue until, in 1935, the General Transatlantic Company commissioned 70,000 sets of crystal tableware for the new ocean liner *Normandie*. This provided an impetus to resume research into new techniques and designs, which continued until 1939 and the German occupation of Nancy, at which point the firm closed. Paul Daum was killed in 1943 while fighting in the French Resistance.

After 1946 the firm reopened, this time under the direction of Henri and Michel Daum, and it continues to function under Jacques Daum as head of the present generation. Located in the eastern section of Nancy, the firm has a shop just off the town's centre, Stanislas Square.

As for the lampshades – both for chandeliers and table-lamps – that the firm produced in the 1920s, the techniques and designs diverged increasingly from their 1900 antecedents. An Art Nouveau enthusiast will search in vain for his preferred flora and insects. Gone was the simulation of nature, to be replaced by simple forms – sometimes geometric, sometimes stylized flower motifs. Gone, also, was opalescence: the glass forthwith was largely to conserve its transparency. Whereas the old method of etching by hydrochloric acid was still employed, its purpose was to produce monochromatic contrasts in the glass. On those occasions, however, when colour was incorporated, it was done with a diluted palette: pale glacier blues, emerald greens, and ambers are placed in juxtaposition with frosted white glass for minimum colour effect. An alternate technique was to sandwich powder or flecks of gold leaf between two layers of glass – either both clear or the inner one coloured – which, when backlit by the lamp bulb's rays, would give a rimy or spangled appearance.

The firm exhibited infrequently at the Paris Salons. In 1921, 1926 and 1932, however, they were represented at the Salon d'Automne.

The prices that Daum Art Déco lampshades fetch do not vary as widely as their Art Nouveau counterparts. Two table-lamps sold in Paris in 1975 for FF 7,500 and 10,000 ($1,490 and $1,925); another, with a Brandt wrought-iron mount, fetched FF 16,000 ($3,130) at Versailles.

DESKY, DONALD

All interior design for the Radio City Music Hall in Rockefeller Center, New York, was done under the direction of Desky, himself a New Yorker. His versatility is evident in the range of decor he undertook: his 'Nicotine' wallpaper design for the men's smoking room painted on aluminium foil paper; his carpet designs; his metal tables with bakelite tops on brushed metal frames. A proponent of modern materials for modern man, he had a partiality for aluminium, bakelite and 'Vibrolite'. His table- and floor-lamps contained brushed, satin-finished, or polished aluminium columns on bakelite bases to support either cloth or parchment shades. His designs, however, are rather lacklustre and commonplace, representing the pallid late 1930s more than high Art Déco.

DESNY

It is the Art Déco enthusiast's great misfortune that, in view of the volume of Desny's work, so little has survived the ravages of time and the caprice of collectors. With an architectural style and panache strongly reminiscent of Mies van der Rohe, Desny produced *orfèvrerie*, carpets, illuminated bibelots and light fixtures – the two last-mentioned mainly between 1928 and 1931. To examine a cross-section of a dozen Desny lamps is immediately to recognize their quintessentially architectonic character. They are extensions of the ultra-modern buildings in which they were to be housed.

In an article in *Lux* (1929), Desny reiterated what was by then the established patter of lighting designers: that it was wrong to think a room was well lit because the intensity of the light was dazzling, and that in fact the essential factor was the absence of centralized points. His fixtures for general interior illumination were designed specifically to this end. Chromed wall-brackets, chandeliers, and floor-lamps had inverted reflecting bowls that concealed the naked bulbs and also projected the light ray upwards. Where localized light was required – either for reading purposes or to illuminate a prized object or painting – he prescribed his range of 'genre spot light'. One desk-lamp – its design reminiscent of Le Chevallier (see p. 177) – incorporated an angle-poise arm device which made the shade adjustable to any desired height. A chandelier, designed specially for a shop or office, consisted of a long rectangular metallic shade that was attached to the ceiling by a pair of telescopic tubes to make its height adjustable. Desny also designed a series of illuminated bibelots, some in clear glass, others in metal. These, as he explained, had no other function than to brighten a sombre corner.

Very few of Desny's lamps have been rediscovered. These are worth upward of FF 3,500 ($700) each.

D.I.M.

The firm of D.I.M. – an acronym for Décoration Intérieure Moderne – was founded in 1914 by René Joubert in the rue Royale in Paris. After the armistice Joubert displayed his work at the Salons and by 1923 – after a brief period in 1922 when a M. Viénot was made joint managing director – Pierre Petit was co-opted into the firm, thus inaugurating a successful partnership. By 1930 D.I.M. had enlarged three times to become one of the largest studio galleries in Paris: a firm possessing a first-rate commercial and technical organization.

Strict disciples of *le style 1925*, D.I.M. eschewed all 'fallacious' ornamentation, seeking in their interiors the qualities of architectural asceticism – simplicity and logic. It was a natural corollary of this streamlining process that they should progressively eliminate visible light fixtures from their interiors. In addition to their own designs, a great number of artists designed lamps for them – including Le Chevallier, Guévrékian, Jean Prouvé, Leroy, Lesage, Stéphan, and the Murano-based firm of Venini – but such output decreased towards 1930 in proportion to the number of concealed light fittings that were incorporated into their interiors. Localized light sources – especially for reading – were, of course, still required to supplement general room illumination, and for this Joubert and Petit usually opted for the simplest of designs: pleated and unpleated cloth or parchment shades on spherical or amphora-shaped bases.

The cafeteria that D.I.M. were commissioned to do in New York (the designs were shown at the 1928 Salon d'Automne) contained a ceiling of *dalles de verre* that was backlit for a diffused effect. Illuminated ceilings were, in fact, a regular feature of their rooms in the late 1920s, either as *dalles*, sunken panels, or as large illuminated cupolas. After Joubert's death in 1931, Petit continued this theme.

DOMINIQUE

André Domin and Marcel Genevrière joined forces in 1922 to form the company called Dominique. Decorators by profession, they produced ensembles for the Houbigant factory and for Jean Puiforçat's house. Exhibiting briefly at the Société des Artistes Décorateurs in the early 1920s, they became members – along with Chareau, Legrain, Puiforçat, and Templier – of Les Cinq in 1926. Their theme was opulent simplicity of design. Precious woods – for example, palisander, Cuban blackberry and elm – were incorporated into predominantly geometric chairs and couches, such as their trapezoidal chair upholstered in blue damask silk, executed in 1924.

Their contribution in the field of lighting was limited. Photographs of Dominique interiors show minimal use of visible fixtures – usually wall-brackets with inverted shades or the occasional table-lamp on an occasional table. Some localized light was necessary, and for this they designed a variety of wall-brackets, *torchères* and table-lamps in such base/shade combinations as silvered bronze and alabaster or gilt bronze and sandblasted glass panels. Several of these were illustrated in 1929 and 1930 in *Art et Industrie* – for example, their 'Rake', 'Spade', and 'Chinese Junk' lamps – and earlier examples, from the French pavilion at the 1925 International Exposition, show similar designs. All are rather banal in conception.

Few, if any, Dominique light fixtures have been rediscovered. They would be likely to fetch around FF 1,300–1,750 ($260–$350).

DUFRÈNE, MAURICE

Following the Art Nouveau era (see p. 76), Dufrène held various jobs – including a professorship at the Boulle School of Decorative Arts in Paris – from 1912 through to 1921 when he founded the 'La Maîtrise' art studios of the Galeries Lafayette on Boulevard Haussmann in Paris. Under his direction, draughtsmen designed the complete gamut of home furnishings – from ceramics, stoneware, and faience to damasks, furniture and locksmith fittings; the actual work was contracted out to various artisans. Instilling his employees with his own exemplary standards of creativity, he was led by the responsibilities of administration to apply himself less and less to the drawing board. Whereas in 1920, prior to forming 'la Maîtrise', he had personally produced a range of lamps for that year's Salons – using netted silk and taffeta shades with silk tassels and rings of galalith on gilt and chased bronze bases (he chose silk because it best simulated the translucent effects of glass, then in short supply following the war) – in succeeding years he relied increasingly on others for this aspect of interior design. J. Adnet, Georges Chevalier, P. Pouchol, Bodio, G. Englinger, and the firms of Labadio and La Compagnie des Arts français were among those who applied themselves to his illumination needs – from the stark, kinetic functionalism of Adnet's creations to the utterly unpretentious pleated cloth shades of Bodio. Some concealed lighting was also undertaken, sometimes as cornices or long horizontal bands of lighting on stepped ceilings.

As none of La Maîtrise's lamps have appeared on the market, it is difficult to predict what they would cost; probably between FF 1,300 and 2,625 ($260 and $525).

DUNAIME, GEORGES

Dunaime had his work marketed between 1921 and 1927 by no fewer than five agents. At the 1925 exposition alone, he used four: Gagnon, Gagneau, the Bézault brothers, and Christofle. Occasionally he also produced light fixtures for E. Etling & Co. The majority of his output, however, was produced for the founder and engraver Gagnon, through whose firm his maquettes for table-lamp and *torchère* bases and chandelier mounts were cast in bronze, to which a silver, gilt or patinated finish was then applied. For his shades a variety of translucent materials were used: cloth (sometimes pleated or with a teardrop crystal fringe), cut glass, slices of quartz, marble, or alabaster. By no means an innovator in his lamp designs, Dunaime achieved a measure of success with some elegant and well-balanced compositions. In 1921 the critic Léon Rosenthal, in describing the interior decoration of the ocean liner *Paris*, wrote that the 'light fixtures are particularly rich and varied: ceiling lights of veined alabaster supported by bronze wires; bowls and half-bowls of ground crystal carried by gilt-bronze arms of a robust and vigorous conception: the artist who executed them is called Dunaime, and it is a name that deserves to be remembered.'

The following year a chandelier of Dunaime's received the first prize in a competition organized by the Union of Bronze Manufacturers (on this occasion his work was exhibited through Gagneau), and in 1924 at the Great Lighting Competition in Paris Dunaime was awarded first prize for his 'table-lamp for an average income home', also receiving a mention for his piano lamp.

ETLING

The Paris firm of Edmond Etling & Co. marketed a range of small metal and/or glass *objets d'art*, among which were table-lamps and illuminated bibelots by such designers as Bonnet, Laplanche, Guillard, and, occasionally, Dunaime. Like Robj and Desny, Etling felt that the public's aesthetic taste had not yet matured to the point where visible light fixtures could be considered obsolete. What was still required in the rather antiseptic and monochromatic functionalism of 1930s interiors was a dash of happiness and colour to soften the severity. Hence the firm's small chromed metal and crystal lamps and illuminated *bouts de table*, such as those displayed at the second Salon of Light, held in Paris in 1934, and, similarly, at the 1937 International Exposition.

Several of Etling's lamps have come onto the market in recent years in Paris. A glass night-light was sold in 1974 for FF 1,050 ($210), and a glass and chrome table-lamp brought £290 ($580) a year later in London.

FOLLOT, PAUL

In 1923, after a quarter of a century in the decorative arts, Follot took over the directorship of Pomone, the art studio of the shop Bon Marché in Paris. In this respect, his career closely parallels those of Dufrène and Tony Selmersheim; they too were vintage creators who, in taking over managerial responsibilities at about this time, were gradually to be phased out of the actual designing field.

Before 1923, however, Follot exhibited a wide range of interiors and *objets* through the Salon d'Automne and Société des Artistes Décorateurs, including chandeliers and floor-lamps that consisted of cloth or glass shades on lacquered wood or wrought-iron bases, the latter executed for Follot by Brandt. At the 1925 International Exposition several of Follot's lighting creations appeared in the Pomone pavilion and in the antechamber of the French pavilion, this time with alabaster, onyx, and Venetian glass shades. More influenced than most of his decorator colleagues by historicism (he had, for instance, always had a proclivity for Pre-Raphaelitism), Follot's style, at its most adventuresome, embraced *le style 25* only marginally; more often it was a mixture of traditionalism and Art Nouveau, the latter, in any event, being his period of maximum lighting production (see page 77).

GENET & MICHON

Though they described themselves in their advertisements as decorator/manufacturers, Genet and Michon were in fact almost exclusively lighting specialists. Graduates of the Boulle School of Decorative Arts, they made, from 1922, one form of glass virtually their own: pressed glass. This was not fortuitous but the result of protracted analysis of the specific needs of glass as an instrument of light. They found that a thick glass multiplied the reflections, and thus the intensity of the light, more than a thinner variety did, and that this required thickness was most satisfactorily obtained by the technique of pressing the glass. The base compounds of silica, soda, and lime were heated to 1300°, transforming the mixture into a vitrifiable paste which was, in turn, poured into a steel matrix. The ingredients of the chosen glass were, of course, kept highly secret, and Genet and Michon were obviously satisfied with their product, since its composition was to remain fundamentally unchanged as late as 1938. It was invariably achromatic, because (they reasoned) the introduction of pigmentation would diminish both its brightness and its warmth.

Variations that were introduced, though infrequently, were acid-etching – often as a border to a piece of pressed glass to give it a halo effect – and blown crystal placed in juxtaposition with the pressed glass. Less successful were their designs incorporating glass bead pendants and rods which, unfortunately, echoed the former century. Their metal mounts – chased and patinated bronze, chrome or wrought-iron – were as discreetly skeletal as possible.

The partnership has been credited with two 'firsts'. G. Janneau, in his publication on the lighting at the 1925 exposition, stated that they had been the innovators of the illuminated ramp, which was to border a room at cornice level. Secondly, Gaston Varenne, art critic for *Art et Décoration*, maintained in 1926 that they were one of the 1920 pioneers of the 'suspended illuminated sphere' (the others being Lalique and Perzel). Over the years, Genet & Michon were to engage in virtually every conceivable form of illumination: not only lamps, lustres, wall-brackets, tables, and épergnes, but friezes, ceiling *dalles*, door architraves, columns, pilasters, cornices, and reflecting vases. They exhibited their light fixtures and interiors not only at the Société des Artistes Décorateurs (1922–38) and the Salon d'Automne (1922–24), but also at a host of expositions: in 1924 in the Grand Lighting Competition and the Monza exhibition; in 1925 at the Paris International Exposition; in 1934 and 1935 at the second and third Salons of Light; in the Pavilion of Light at the 1937 exposition. In addition, they were given commissions for the ocean liner *Normandie*.

Genet & Michon started out with a predilection among motifs for clusters of flowers or bunches of grapes; by 1930, however, these had largely disappeared, along with the rather rough finish of their earlier pressed glass.

A Genet & Michon floor-lamp sold for FF 2,200 ($440) in Nancy, and an illuminated centrepiece fetched FF 1,150 ($230) in Paris, both in 1973.

GIGOU, LOUIS

An eminent locksmith, like Brindeau de Jarny in the early 1900s, Gigou was to exhibit, among his displays of door handles, finger-plates, keys, and escutcheons, at the annual Salons of the Société des Artistes Décorateurs, various forms of light fixtures. Working in a variety of metals – mainly chased bronze, but also wrought-iron and steel inlaid with copper ornamentation – he designed and executed desk-lamps, and bedside wall-brackets and lamps, with the same high degree of technical virtuosity and logic for which all his metalwork became known. His lighting output, however, was low, concentrated mainly between 1919 and the 1925 International Exposition; after that he specialized in his locksmithery.

GRAY, EILEEN

As early as 1913, Irish-born Eileen Gray exhibited her lacquered panels, which were to remain a major element in the range of furniture she showed at the annual Salon d'Automne and Société des Artistes Décorateurs into the 1930s. Lacquered commodes, screens, sofas and bookcases, and tapestries and knotted sable carpets were executed in an exhilarating marriage of functionalism and beauty. Her light fixtures – to which she applied herself with the same flair for design – were, unfortunately, few. Like Chareau's, however, their quality is far more important than their number.

Eileen Gray's furnishings fetch extremely high prices. Her few light fixtures could be expected to bring upward of £7,500 ($13,450) each.

GUÉVRÉKIAN, GABRIEL

An architect who occasionally branched out into interior design, Guévrékian was commissioned by the firm of D.I.M. (see p. 167) to provide various light-fixture designs for their interiors. He also designed the lighting for his own interiors, sometimes enlisting the cooperation of the lighting engineer André Salomon. One result of this partnership was a suspended inverted convex metal ring from which the rays were projected upwards on to the ceiling to form a soft ambience by indirect lighting. (This particular model was executed in 1929 and was inspired, no doubt, by Eugène Printz's prototype – one year earlier – of his '*Couronne lumineuse*'.)

Several Guévrékian metal table-lamps have been sold in recent years. Prices range between FF 2,625 ($525) and FF 5,250 ($1,050).

HERBST, RENÉ

Among the post-war innovators was Herbst, who, along with Chareau, Jourdain, Mallet-Stevens and others, became one of the pioneers of cubism in the applied arts. A decorator by profession, he became the Art Director of Siégel in the mid-1920s; and in 1929, when the Société des Artistes Décorateurs refused to allow a group of designers headed by himself and Charlotte Perriand to participate in that year's Salon, the result was the formation of a splinter group known as the Union de Artistes Modernes (U.A.M.).

Involved in all forms of interior decoration, Herbst was a forerunner in the use of tubular nickelled steel furniture, particularly chairs, his models incorporating leather or fabric cushions (the latter by Hélène Henry). He designed ensembles for, among others, the Aga Khan, the perfumery 'Isabey', Robj, and, at the 1925 International Exposition, for Siégel, the *couturière* Lina Mouton, and his own stand on the Alexander III bridge. His philosophy on the lighting of such interiors was widely disseminated, mainly by the editor of *Lux* who, between 1929 and 1932, published no fewer than four articles on or by Herbst. Basically, his views – very similar to those of Mallet-Stevens – were that the collaboration of a lighting engineer was essential for satisfactory artificial lighting, since nobody else was qualified to determine the correct curvature of reflecting surfaces. In a dissertation on how best to illuminate a shop-window, he stressed the need to attract and seduce, and proposed a means of lighting to overcome the obstacle created by the window itself which, in separating the merchandise from the public, reflected the images of passers-by and the building across the street rather than displaying its contents. For the interior of shops he cautioned that general illumination tended to be too bright: he reminded his readers that customers were not butterflies or moths.

Teaming up with the lighting engineer André Salomon, who worked for the firm of Perfecla, Herbst produced a wide range of both visible and concealed fixtures that were often exhibited through the Salon d'Automne and the Société des Artistes Décorateurs, together with his other furnishings.

Herbst seems to have been more successful in theory than in practice. For example, his design of 1928 for a floor-lamp to be used in a smoking-room, incorporating a rotary reflecting disc for localized and diffused light rays, is conceptually excellent, but needlessly skeletal in execution. The bones are there, but where is the flesh to conceal their nakedness? Likewise a floor-lamp (marketed by Cottin and Sons), in which the light was diffused by an opaline disc to provide both spotlight illumination and a gently filtered light upwards for general ambience, looks shoddy and unfinished. His ceiling-lamp and wall-brackets at the 1925 Exposition – in silver and gilt bronze – look similarly cheap in spite of their finish; and this is true also of his chandeliers at the second Salon of Light in 1934.

JALLOT, LÉON-ALBERT

Director of Bing's Art Nouveau studio between 1899 and 1901, and founder-member of the first Salon of the Société des Artistes Décorateurs (1901), Jallot was one of the first to reject the excessively floral ornamentation of Art Nouveau and to pioneer a return to the classical purity of linearism. Decoration was to be imparted by the intrinsic richness of the materials rather than by such superfluities as voluted silhouettes that disguised the object's true form. As early as 1904 he was designing furnishings whose only decoration was in the grain of the wood itself, often with arabesque marquetry in mother-of-pearl, ivory, shagreen, or the like. As late as 1938, by which time he had been in partnership with his son Maurice for more than ten years, his designs were fundamentally unchanged.

Léon Jallot's abhorrence of ornamentation was to manifest itself also in his lighting, although less rapidly than in his furniture (in the 1906 Salon of the Société des Artistes Décorateurs, for example, he exhibited several chandeliers of cicada, seahorse, and seaweed motifs), and it was consistent with his overall philosophy that he should gradually move from visible to concealed light fixtures. During the time that he himself made standard light fittings, these were marketed by the firm of Favre, but after he and Maurice had switched almost entirely to indirect lighting – this was from about 1927 – he delegated the table-lamps, chandeliers, etc., in his interiors to specialists such as Perzel, G. Fabre, and Eugène Capon.

Maurice Jallot summed up the father/son attitude, in a 1930 *Lux* article, with the statement that the optimum effect was obtained by illuminating a room so that the sources of light were indiscernible. The same article was illustrated with photographs of an illuminated ceiling and awning of an entrance door, both for the jewellery shop 'Bielle' in Algiers. At the 1930 Salon of the Société des Artistes Décorateurs, the Jallot stand contained fluted columns that were lit from within the entablatures. For their interior at the Hôtel Radio in Paris (1928), the Jallots designed an illuminated pelmet that bordered an entire room at a height of eight feet.

Whereas several Jallot furnishings have been on the Art Déco market since 1972, I can find no record of any table-lamps. It is difficult to predict what these might cost, but this is likely to be from FF 1,750 to 3,500 ($350 to $700).

JOURDAIN, FRANCIS

'Adolf Loos has demonstrated that ornament delights only the primitive element in us. Civilized man alone delights in the stark form that arises from a happy expression of purpose.' These words, quoted in 1929 in *The Studio*, should leave little doubt as to Jourdain's artistic philosophy concerning the 'fever of decorating, ornamenting, elaborating, and aesthetic posturing'. Beginning his career in the decorative arts as a painter at the Salons of the Société des Artistes Indépendants – where he exhibited his canvases alongside such august colleagues as Cézanne, Toulouse Lautrec, Matisse, Van Rysselberghe, Kandinsky, and Maurice Denis – he founded the Ateliers Modernes in 1912 and turned his attention to designing new models of wallpapers, carpets, ceramics, etc., in cheap materials for the general public.

Dominating every sphere of applied arts for the next twenty years, Jourdain was quick to see how the application of electricity and scientific inventions was instituting new types of design. His furnishings, shown through the Salon d'Automne regularly till 1938, and through the Union des Artistes Modernes from 1930, reflect most poignantly his theory that 'The purpose of a house, a soup tureen or a chair is not a decorative purpose.'

In his nursery (1920), gymnasium (1925), and dining-room in oak and zingana (1923), rectilinearism is the norm. This applied also to his light fixtures – ceiling-lamps, *appliques*, decorative panels in stained glass with artificial back-lighting, and illuminated tables – the latter produced for the Pavilion of Light at the 1937 International Exposition in collaboration with André Salomon.

KISS, PAUL

A naturalized Frenchman, born in Rumania, Kiss never fully extricated himself from the shadow of Edgar Brandt, with whom he initially collaborated, though he too produced metalwork of very high quality, although not in such quantities. His range of ironwork exhibited during the 1920s at the Salons of the Société des Artistes Décorateurs and the Société des Artistes français embraced consoles, grilles, iron gates, as well as all forms of lighting.

His lighting shows that he was an aesthete before he was a functionalist. An object whose function superseded its beauty was not for Kiss. Nowhere is there evidence of the mechanisms – reflectors, projectors and diffusers – of the new science of lighting. On the other hand, his work gives evidence of a master craftsman's pride in his technical virtuosity: metal enlacements, wispy thin – such as attenuated tendrils and corollas – sprout in profusion from mounts that house alabaster, marble, or engraved glass panels or shades.

A Kiss wrought-iron standard floor-lamp and a pair of wall-lights were sold in Paris in 1974 for FF4,200 ($825) and 3,350 ($665) respectively.

KOHLMANN, ETIENNE

A graduate of the Boulle School of Decorative Arts in Paris, where he became an accomplished cabinet-maker, Kohlmann was by 1928 director of the Studium-Louvre (the art studio of the Grands Magasins du Louvre). Exhibiting at the Salon d'Automne and the Société des Artistes Décorateurs in the 1920s and 1930s, he designed total interiors, such as boudoirs, study/smoking rooms, and a lounge for the ocean liner *Ile de France*, in a breathtaking array of exotic woods.

His ventures into the lighting of such interiors, though abundant, were not entirely successful. His designs were executed by Studium-Louvre, with technical credit sometimes given to Jean Lévy and to the lighting engineer P. Juget. A wide range of light fixtures were produced, such as the chandelier and wall-brackets exhibited at the 1925 International Exposition, those at the second Salon of Light in 1934, and a series of 'Holophane' fixtures, again in 1934. (Holophane was a glassmaker with whom Kiss collaborated.) Kohlmann's flair as a cabinet-maker seems not to have transferred itself readily to the realm of illumination. For example, the lacquered metal chandelier and wall-brackets, with their sculpted vegetal and floriform motifs by F. Gagneau, at the 1937 International Exposition, can at best be described as *démodé*.

LACROIX, BORIS-JEAN

In an article entitled 'Reflections on Modern Lighting' in *Lux*, 1929, Lacroix anticipated a source of indirect illumination from the engineers of 'tomorrow's ambience lighting', by which rooms would be totally bathed in light that did not emanate from any discernible point. He concluded by explaining that his own lamps had *no* other goal than to be in harmony with modern interiors until this supreme transition, after which 'light fixtures' as such would become history. This statement, when measured against the several illustrations of his lamps that accompanied the text, his substantial output of such fixtures, and the perennially favourable reviews that he was to receive from art critics for these same fixtures, appears as a form of lip-service to the apostles of avant-gardism.

In describing his range of lamps as being merely 'in harmony', Lacroix was understating his creativity. With his designs executed by Damon (see p. 164), he turned his attention to almost every form of domestic lighting – from table-lamps to illuminated ceilings and picture frames, examples of which were exhibited regularly from 1927 through the Salon d'Automne and the Société des Artistes Décorateurs. Some of his lamps were in metal only – with a polished or matt nickel finish – but most incorporated glass: either Damon's special enamelled diffusing variety or plain frosted glass.

In addition, Lacroix paid great and effective attention to the functionalism of his models. Utilizing direct or indirect lighting, or a combination of the two (*double éclairage*), in 1929, for example, he exhibited a lamp which, due to its mobile arms and light-reflecting mechanism, was to provide three functions in one: it could, on the simplest level, act as a desk-lamp; secondly, by adjusting the arms until they were horizontal, it could be used to read music on a piano (to this end the lamp base was specially weighted to prevent its toppling on the pianist); and, thirdly, by using a hooking device attached to the base, it could be transformed into a wall-bracket to spotlight a painting.

Lacroix's range of small table-lamps and illuminated bibelots are hard to find. They range in price from FF 1,750 to 3,500 ($350 to $700).

LALIQUE, RENÉ

Lalique made his reputation originally though his jewellery designs, one of his major contributions being the emphasis he placed on stones other than diamonds. It was after his brilliant success at the 1900 Exposition Universelle that he began seriously to turn his talents towards the designing of glass – and hence lighting, though he had made some tentative moves in that direction from the mid-1890s.

Following early glass experiments, often using the *cire perdue* (lost wax) process, around 1902 at Clairefontaine near Rambouillet, he opened an atelier at Combs, where he produced moulded glass objects.

A final move, this time to Wingen-sur-Moder (the site of the firm's present factory) in Alsace-Lorraine, was made between 1918 and 1922. Lalique used a plaster-moulding process to obtain his preferred medium, moulded glass, which, for the most part, he did not colour; tonal gradations were obtained by varying the thickness of the glass. Sometimes, however, cutting and polishing finishing operations were added, or specified areas of the moulded designs were treated with acid to produce the desired limpid, frosted or milky effect. The range of his glassware seemed infinite – from every conceivable domestic accoutrement to monumental architecture – and all designed exclusively by Lalique himself. Light fixtures were just one element in this range, but because of the innate luminosity of the glass when backlit, they take on a particular importance.

It is difficult to determine exactly when Lalique first applied his talents to designing lamps, though this was certainly a lot earlier than most people have assumed – in fact, well within his 'jewellery' period. In 1905, a photograph in *L'Art Décoratif* showed a chandelier consisting of a bronze mount – decorated with lizards in high relief – into which glass had been blown to form the shade. Also shown in that year (this time in *Art et Décoration*) was a huge chandelier in bronze and engraved and enamelled crystal, with motifs of formidable dragonflies positioned in gargoyle fashion at intervals around the circumference of the mounting in a style that recalls Lalique's famous dragonfly *parure de corsage*. In the same journal in 1906, there was a photograph of a lantern composed of twelve bronze chameleons: six, with spiked tails and predatory eyes, were positioned vertically to hold the lantern's glass panels; the remaining six, likewise of fearsome countenance, are poised to spring on to the passers-by below. These lamp designs were obviously extensions of Lalique's preoccupation at that time with his Art Nouveau bestiary of insects and reptiles, and represented only a brief sortie into the realm of lighting. It was only after 1918, when his glassworks at Wingen-sur-Moder were operational, that he produced a wide range and quantity of light fixtures. These included night-lights, table-lamps, chandeliers, wall-brackets and illuminated statuettes (for example, his *Suzanne au Bain* figurine), and tables. In architectural lighting he designed ceiling tiles, wall panels and friezes, and for outside the home there were fountains (such as those in the Champs-Elysées arcades). For the automobile he designed a wide assortment of radiator mascots, of which the most popular was his 'Spirit of the Wind' figurehead (see illustration 82). These, which were illuminated from below through a filter that could be interchanged for different colour effects, were often inspired by birds.

Lalique displayed his lighting, along with all his glassware, on innumerable occasions: for example, at the annual Salons, the 1925 International Exposition, and the 1934 Salon of Light. Lionized frequently in contemporary journals as a 'Magician of Light' or 'Luminary on Lighting', Lalique takes his place among the most gifted designers for the medium.

The range of Lalique's light fixtures is too wide to give an effective estimate of their value. Some illuminated statuettes fetch FF600 ($210), others FF6,000 ($2,100), while his table-lamps and chandeliers consistently bring FF4,375–6,625 ($875–$1,325).

LE CHEVALLIER, J.

One of the artists commissioned by D.I.M. to supply the various components in their ensembles, J. Le Chevallier (sometimes spelled Chevalier) concentrated on forms of illumination, as did his D.I.M. stablemates Venini and L. Lesage.

In 1929 a critic in *The Studio* wrote that the distinguishing feature of that year's Salon d'Automne was the introduction of metal into the domain of furnishing. This was an opinion no doubt influenced by the several light fixtures in aluminium and nickelled metal exhibited there by Le Chevallier. Utilitarian to a fault, some of his lamps are brazenly functional: pieces of machinery composed of hulking slabs of metal are held together by unconcealed screws. Others are more refined: for example, a rotative desk-lamp in polished aluminium – very similar to one by Lacroix – shows a much closer alliance of the technician and the artist.

A few table-lamps by Le Chevallier have come on the market since 1973. Prices range between FF1,300 and 2,200 ($260 and $440).

LE VERRIER, MAX

Sales catalogues of this sculptor's work show how his small bronzes either were, or were not, illuminated. The choice seems to have been arbitrary. Characteristically Art

Déco pierrots or women – the latter no longer languid, somnambulistic or melancholy like their Art Nouveau predecessors, but fired with the spirit of their age (as in the chryselephantine sculptures by Chiparus, Preiss, Kelety, and Zach, or Lalique's 'Victory' car mascots) – hold globes that in some instances light up. Sometimes the figure is allegorical – for example, 'Clarity' or 'Enigma' – and frequently it is in bronze, often with a verdigris patina finish and on a stepped and canted *verde antico* marble base.

Le Verrier also designed and executed chandeliers which are conceived as light fixtures, rather than illuminated sculptures of one form or another. His work shows delicacy and refinement.

Le Verrier's small Art Déco bronzes fetch good prices. One was sold in New York in 1976 for $895 (£490), another for $1,085 (£600).

MALLET-STEVENS, ROBERT

Mallet-Stevens' reputation as an architect rivalled that of Le Corbusier in France. His Villa Nouilles at Hyères (1923), the Alfa-Romeo building (1925), the Pavilion of Tourism and the French pavilion at the 1925 International Exposition, were a few of the achievements on the way to his masterpiece: the rue Mallet-Stevens in Auteuil, which opened in 1927 and in which all the houses were designed by him in conformity with the most recent architectural canons. His genius was extended into the interior decoration of his buildings, and to this end he designed a range of furniture, carpets, and light fittings.

In regard to lighting, he was inspired by a phrase of the architect Trélat: 'Form is the intersection of light and material.' Like Herbst, he expounded on his philosophy of illuminated architecture in both *Lux* and *L'Art Ménager*. With the collaboration of a lighting engineer, one could, by varying the power and position of one's light sources, accentuate or play down the surfaces of both the room itself and the masses within it to achieve a multiplicity of effects. The architect became a magician, the light-switch his wand. One interesting rule of the six that he claimed to apply anew to each interior (the other five were standard tenets of lighting engineering) was that the artificial light should fall in the same direction as did the daylight. This would avoid visual distortion of the decor, which, in turn, could generate psychophysical disquiet in the viewer. In practice, Mallet-Stevens did not himself execute his fixtures. Some of his earlier designs were undertaken by Baguès, Favre, and Martine, but thereafter the bulk of his work was executed by Salomon's firm, Perfecla. Salomon cooperated with him on numerous projects; mainly lustres and bands of wall or ceiling lighting for such ensembles as Paul Poiret's shop and the entrance hall to the 1930 exposition of the Union des Artistes Modernes. At the 1935 Salon of Light Mallet-Stevens exhibited a design for a series of illuminated balloons that would be positioned axially above the Seine at the 1937 International Exposition. For his own house in the rue Mallet-Stevens he commissioned Chareau and Jourdain to do the various light fittings; Chareau supplied two of his spectacular chandeliers in panels of alabaster (see p. 163) for the living-room, and Jourdain an unusual ceiling-lamp for a vestibule.

Most of Mallet-Stevens' light fixtures are still in their original settings. They are unlikely to come on the Art Déco market.

NICS FRÈRES (MICHEL and JULES)

Lesser stars in the galaxy of ironsmiths who took up the hammer and the burin in the twilight years of the inimitable Emile Robert's career, the brothers Michel and Jules Nics formed a partnership that was to produce as wide a range of ironwork in the 1920s as did most of their competitors: for example, consoles, balustrades, balcony railings, iron gates, dumb-waiters, and all forms of light fixtures – the latter being a major area of concentration for them. Chandeliers, wall-brackets and *torchères* were fashioned out of wrought-iron mounts that housed opalescent glass panels or shades in a style that, while certainly not pioneering, did adhere to sound design principles. In 1923, a critic in *Mobilier et Décoration* was to write that 'in lighting, for example, their designs are elegantly determined with a personal care for adaptation to usage. A lot of their chandeliers, wall-brackets and table-lamps are pleasing due to their ingenious grouping and their attractive construction.'

Although never overly ornate, the Nics imparted to the angularities or gentle double volutes of their chandeliers a deeply hammered finish, which gave their work a measure of identity in a field which had by 1925 become largely uniform. In the case of lustres by Kiss, Subes, Szabo or Poillerat (and even, occasionally, by Brandt) there is frequently a predictability – a sameness – that hampers attribution. Nics *frères* overcame this to a degree with their *martelé* finish, although the size of the indentation in the metal – an example of this can be seen in the wrought-iron furnishings they were commissioned to do for a hairdressing salon by Ruhlmann in 1925 – gave their mounts a robustness that readily spilled over into heaviness. And this was at a time when contemporary philosophy in lighting, by such exponents as Sabino, Genet & Michon, and Perzel, called for minimization of those elements in a light fixture that were defective from a lighting point of view: *i.e.*, which did not transmit the light. (It should be remembered, however, that ironsmiths could ill afford to espouse as 'purist' a theory of lighting as glassmakers could. To have followed this to its natural conclusion – to a point where the sections of glass were to be held together by a minimum number of clips and fastenings – would, of course, have eliminated their *raison d'être*.)

Some Nics *frères* ironwork has been sold in Paris recently. A standard floor-lamp, with blown-glass shade, brought FF 3,675 ($735) in 1976.

PAUL, FRANCIS

Paul's lamp designs, from the early 1930s to the outbreak of World War II, are so avante-garde in conception that they only barely fit into the category of Art Déco. His work, in any case, shows a certain forfeiture of individualism, since it was clearly designed for the production line. Nevertheless Paul had a great affinity for his subject-matter, and through both the Société des Artistes Décorateurs and the second and third

Salons of Light in 1934 and 1935, and again in the Pavilion of Light at the 1937 International Exposition, his displays were well received. He was well-versed in the shibboleths of the new science of lighting, and his chromed chandeliers, standard lamps, illuminated vases, etc., were designed for direct, indirect or semi-indirect lighting. His earlier work was marketed by Décor et Lumière; later, as in the case of the ceiling light in stainless steel that he was commissioned to do for the ocean liner *Normandie* in 1935, his agent was René Pottier.

PERZEL, JEAN

'For the last three years Perzel has painted his glass lightly; usually in a pinkish hue which provides the room with an atmosphere . . . that gives women a pleasant disposition.' Gaston Derys, *Mobilier et Décoration*, December 1933, p. 484.

Perzel was born in the Bohemian town of Bruck, now in Czechoslovakia, and his family moved to Paris when he was ten. Volunteering in 1914, he fought through the entire war and afterwards returned to Paris to take up what had been his father's and his grandfather's profession: glassmaking. It was then, as Perzel recounted in a 1928 *Lux* article, that he first realized the potential of light fixtures since they were no longer simply transformed oil-lamps or candlesticks. Drawing inspiration from his own profession – that of stained glass windows – he conceived his first lamps in the manner of old unpainted Romanesque church windows. Perzel described his idea as follows: 'It would be pretentious to say that I would like to treat electricity in the way that the old stained glass artists treated the sun, but that is what I tried to do. I wanted to mask entirely the luminous source in using its rays; from which came my research into the relative opacity of nacreous and frosted glass.'

From this seminal stage was to burgeon the Perzel influence in domestic lighting. (The firm, incidentally, exists to this day in Paris.) Exclusively a designer and manufacturer of light fixtures, he had a two-fold philosophy: first, to ensure that the light playing on the diffusing surfaces did so equally, and, secondly, to achieve maximum utilization of the light source's rays. (His belief in the first of these two points was to place Perzel at the head of one of two distinct schools of thought. The other – for which Sabino was the spokesman – maintained that the glass should be patterned to vary and, thereby, enliven it.)

To ensure that the light was transmitted uniformly, Perzel developed a specially frosted, *i.e.*, sandblasted, glass, to the inner surface of which was applied a coating of enamel. By this means not only was the light equally filtered, but also Perzel's preferred standards of opacity and milkiness were met. In later years, lightly tinted enamels – such as beige and pink – were used where an interior's decor required them. Another form of glass, though seldom used, was a more translucent prismatic variety. Perzel's mounts, always judiciously designed for their secondary, supportive role, were in metal, sometimes nickelled or lacquered.

Perzel concentrated his production on large quantities of a limited number of designs. Lacking the range of light fixtures of, say, Genet & Michon or Sabino, his output consisted mainly of table-lamps, chandeliers, wall-brackets, and ceiling lights, though he occasionally designed and executed ceiling *dalles*, columns, and illuminated tables of which he is credited as being the innovator. Based on pure geometry, his shades are often polygonal, both in their overall shape and in the units of which they are composed. Others are conical, spherical, cylindrical or rectangular, always with a sober elegance and often of an astonishing modernity. Commissioned to provide the lighting for the ensembles of other decorators – for example, Jallot, Rollin, the Tétard brothers, and the architect Roux-Spitz – Perzel also enjoyed an élite international clientele, from Henry Ford in Detroit to the Savoy Hotel in London to the King of Siam in Bangkok. He used the Salon d'Automne from 1924 to 1939, the Société des Artistes Décorateurs from 1926 to 1939, the 1925 International Exposition, and the 1930s Salons of Light to promote his creations.

Numerous Perzel shades have been sold in Paris and Versailles since 1971. They have maintained consistently high prices: FF 2,625 ($525) and up for wall-lights, and FF 7,000 ($1,400) for table-lamps.

PRINTZ, EUGÈNE

Printz made his debut in the decorative arts at the 1925 International Exposition. Born into the profession – his father was an interior designer and cabinet-maker – Printz inherited a predilection for fine woods, using a mixture of palisander, Rio rosewood, palm kekwood, teak, wild cherry, and sycamore for the furnishings of such interiors as the boudoir he designed for the Princess of Auvergne, and an office for Mme Jeanne Lanvin. Preoccupied with ambience – 'chaste taste', as he called it – he quickly turned his attention to the quality of lighting in interior architecture.

His contribution to the field of illumination was substantial, both in theory and in practice. In the review *Lux*, in 1930 and 1931, he explained his philosophy of modern architectural lighting: that it should be an integral consideration in the initial planning of any interior to ensure homogeneity. Lighting could not, therefore, be considered apart from an interior. His words were backed up amply by his deeds. Both in the annual Salon d'Automne and that of the Société des Artistes Décorateurs, he displayed a wide range of visible and invisible light fixtures, one of which – his *couronne lumineuse* ('crown' or 'circle' of light) – became the prototype that inspired a host of imitators. Other lighting effects were no less successful. In a *causerie* (literally, a room for chatting), the capital of a central column houses the hidden lighting, the power of which is photometrically determined (in the placement and number of bulbs) so that 'no part of the room is left in shadow'. In the reception hall that he designed for a colonial museum, Printz employed a two-tier combination floor-lamp/pedestal table to project the light on to the ceiling. At the Pavilion of Light at the 1937 International Exposition, in which he and Kohlmann were responsible for the general illumination in the corridors and vestibule areas, Printz exhibited a table *jardinière* that could be lit. One of his chandeliers (see illustration 121) was featured in numerous articles on modern lighting in contemporary decorative arts reviews.

RATEAU, ARMAND-ALBERT

Individualist *par excellence*, Rateau branched out on his own after an education at the Boulle School of Decorative Arts in Paris and subsequent collaboration with the decorator and ceramicist Georges Hoentschel between 1905 and 1914. During this time Rateau was director of the Maison Alavoine.

Selective in his choice of clientele, he worked initially in wood and then later extended himself into lacquered and patinated metal, designing fanciful bronze armchairs with ocelot cushions and chairs with tapestried *point quadrillé* upholstery for customers such as Baroness Eugène de Rothschild and the Duchess of Alba. His light fittings for the installation of Jeanne Lanvin, executed between 1920 and 1922, show the characteristic style of his furnishings. A pair of floor-lamps consist of reflectors housed in six raised birds' heads above a spindle-shaped column that is supported by circular feet engraved with marguerites (these, the dominant motif of the ensemble, were in honour of Lanvin's daughter, Marguerite). These are surmounted by four pheasants, whose beaks extend upwards to touch the column – the whole in patinated *vert-de-gris* bronze.

Another lamp consists of a bell-shaped shade of gathered white silk bordered with glass pendants and supported by a gadrooned spindle column on a circular foot, the latter sculpted with leaves and edged with large glass beads, each inscribed in an oval cartouche. Replicas of this – originally modelled in wood for Lanvin – were later cast in bronze for the general market.

Thirdly, wall-brackets fashioned as marguerites, butterflies, and acanthi in full bloom, provided the radiance for dressing-table mirrors and bedside reading.

Rateau's furnishings are in limited supply, and are correspondingly priced. A pair of his bronze and frosted glass wall-lights sold in New York in 1975 for $1,315 (£655).

ROBJ

Robj was a Parisian dealer who commissioned a wide range of knick-knacks and curios from numerous designers for his shop in the rue du Paradis. Inscrutable porcelain Buddhas and warlike Sioux Indians were found, on closer examination, to be cunningly designed powder boxes or inkwells. A ceramic cigarette case or perfume-burner would be similarly disguised; this time, perhaps, as a sombrero'd Mexican, or a Dutch boy in outsized clogs. Robj's table-lamps and night-lights were no less eclectic: Japanese geishas hold parasols that act as lampshades to conceal tiny bulbs, or a weightlifter, visibly puffed, holds aloft a dumbbell, the two spheres of frosted glass, and internally lit. Some of Robj's glass objects were executed for him by Lalique, and these tend to be of a more restrained, less exotic, design.

Robj's small *objets* range in price from FF 350 to 1,000 ($70 to $200).

RUHLMANN, EMILE-JOSEPH

Ruhlmann first exhibited at the 1913 Salon d'Automne and immediately established himself as a top-flight cabinet-maker. After the war he founded the company of

Ruhlmann and Laurent, which marketed his work until his death in 1933. Drawing inspiration from the grand tradition of the eighteenth century, his work became synonymous with supreme elegance and technical virtuosity. Furniture in tulipwood, amboyna, burled walnut, ebony macassar and acacia, inlaid with ivory or lacquer by Jean Dunand, was of such exquisite refinement and proportions that his style was widely plagiarized.

An appreciation of Ruhlmann's designs for lamps can be obtained from Léon Moussinac's book of Ruhlmann sketches, published in 1924. A wide range of alabaster, damask silk, and glass crystal shades are supported by piastriaccia marble, mosaic, or silvered-metal bases. Ruhlmann's Hôtel du Collectionneur at the 1925 International Exposition and the ocean liners *Atlantique* and *Ile de France* contained such fittings, which were commissioned variously to the Compagnie des Lampes, Siégel, and Mildé. Their logicality, sobriety and economy are characteristic of Ruhlmann; the quality of the materials and their execution are, as in all his work, superlative.

In the area of concealed lighting, Ruhlmann's dressing room for an actress (Jacqueline Francell) at the 1929 Salon d'Automne, for example, contained a circular ceiling that was lit by three superimposed illuminated cornices, a technique he repeated a year later in the Ruhlmann stand at the Société des Artistes Décorateurs, this time with each cornice containing differently coloured lights.

Ruhlmann's light fixtures, like all his work, fetch premium prices. A pair of his wall-lights were sold for FF 15,750 ($3,150) in Paris in 1975.

SABINO, ERNEST-MARIUS

It was in 1925, at the Salon d'Automne and the International Exposition (at which he had his own stand in the Grand Palais), that Sabino first displayed a range of his lighting effects. By the advent of World War II, this range had become more diverse even than the work of Perzel or Lalique, though it remained somewhat inferior in quality. Sabino initially designed everything himself; but by 1930, due to his studio's expansion, he had appointed a production manager by the name of Grivois. It was the latter, in a 1930 *Lux* article, who explained the firm's goals: to rescue the illuminated *objet d'art* from its banality.

Sabino had discovered a new form of glass which 'amplified, embellished, and sublimated' the naked light source. Unlike Perzel, who advocated an even diffusion of light by means of a glass of uniform thickness and opacity, Sabino used pressed and moulded patterned glass in *bas-relief*. The resulting variation in the thickness (and hence the translucency) of the glass was intended to generate a multiplicity of moods in the viewer. Pressed glass was the firm's preferred medium, though cut, blown and engraved variations were introduced occasionally for special effects. No form of lighting, from the most minute to the gargantuan, was beyond Sabino's capabilities. He applied himself to illuminated bibelots, menu-holders, clocks, statuettes, *potiches* (large vases), panels, doors, ceiling tiles, columns, pilasters, stelae, and belvedere-shaped fountains. Spheres composed of facets of pressed glass, either as chandeliers or architectural lighting, singly or in series, were a perennial favourite. Sabino's motifs, patterned in relief on panels or florets of glass, included various themes from nature: bouquets, cascades, rain, waves, garlands, chrysanthemums, etc.

It was for his larger creations that Sabino became best known. Responsible for all the general lighting in the passageways and antechambers of the yearly Salons d'Automne, he also undertook commissions for the ocean liner *Normandie* and various hotels and restaurants. Such interiors, due to the height of their ceilings, allowed him to give free vent to his obvious proclivity for outsized fixtures.

Of the Sabino lamps that have reached the Art Déco market, two were sold in Nancy in 1975 for FF 1,970 ($394) and another in Paris for FF 2,500 ($500).

SCHENCK, EDOUARD and MARCEL

Edouard Schenck was joined in the early 1920s by his son Marcel, and together they continued to produce the range of ironwork that Edouard had designed and executed at the turn of the century. Consoles, fire screens, andirons, wrought-iron radiator curtains, fanlight grilles, etc., were displayed at the annual Salons (particularly the Salon d'Automne), along with floor- and table-lamps, lanterns, diffusers and 'electric pendants'. Alternating between wrought iron and copper – the latter often *repoussé*, gilt, silvered, or patinated – Edouard's dexterity manifested itself in the lightness of his metal supports. Strands of wrought iron, fashioned as gentle volutes or rosettes, house glass bowls or tulip-shaped shades with a grace that a critic in *Art et Décoration* described as 'very Electricity'. Despite such technical virtuosity, the Schencks were not in the vanguard of the new aesthetics, and their lamps at the 1925 exposition, for example, show an affiliation with the past.

Very little of Schenck's ironwork has been rediscovered. A pair of andirons was sold in Paris in 1976, but there is no record that any of his lamps have reached the market. They would probably range in price between FF 650 and 1,525 ($131 and $305).

SIMONET, ALBERT and CHARLES

Championed by *Mobilier et Décoration* in numerous articles between 1924 and 1931, the firm of the Simonet brothers was pre-eminent in the sphere of lighting. Curiously, very little of their work has been rediscovered.

The firm's success was built around the partnership of Albert Simonet and Henri Dieupart. (The Simonet brother Charles, who died in 1929, appears to have been either on the management side of the firm or a sleeping partner. No mention is made of him artistically.) A bronze worker by profession, A. Simonet's first lighting incorporated very little glass, but, following his association with the sculptor and glassmaker Dieupart, the predominance of the bronze mounts was steadily replaced by that of glass. This evolution was to result, by 1933, in the almost total eclipse of the metal; it was used only minimally to house the magical pressed glass.

The partnership was extremely fruitful. Exhibitions in which Simonet participated included the first Exposition of Modern Art at the Marsan pavilion (now the Musée des Arts Décoratifs at the Louvre) and the Great Lighting Competition (both in 1924); the 1925 exposition (in which they had their own stand in the Grand Palais); the fifth exposition of contemporary French decoration (1931); and the second Salon of Light in 1934. It was in the Great Lighting Competition in 1924, organized, among others, by the Syndicated Electricity Union, that Simonet reached their zenith. They won five out of the ten first prizes and a host of mentions for their models of lamps designed to meet the illumination requirements of specific rooms in the houses of varying income groups.

The respective roles of Simonet and Dieupart seem well defined. The former was the theoretician and designer. Expounding on the most recent photometric results obtained from French laboratories, he claimed that the shapes of his lamps were determined by 'coefficients of utilization' – *i.e.*, the dimensions, end-use, and coloration of the rooms for which the fixtures were to be designed. These could be mathematically, psychologically, and scientifically computed. The result which he recognized was that glass was in the ascendant, and he accordingly reduced the part played by bronze. Thus he left the centre stage to Dieupart, ensuring only the impeccable quality of the mountings.

Dieupart, on his part, executed Simonet's designs in moulded glass, the uniformity of which was obtained by passing a current of compressed air through the glass as soon as it had been poured into the mould. Renouncing bright colours, Dieupart left most of his glass untinted; infrequently he used muted grey, violet, and satin hues where Simonet's 'coefficient of utilization' required. His raised motifs were effected not only for decorative purposes but also for their light-refractive powers.

The firm's range of light fixtures was extensive: a large number of chandeliers, ceiling-lights, and wall-brackets, often in series, were produced in addition to illuminated friezes, cornices, ramps, *bouts de table* and, in collaboration with the ceramicist G. Henry, a bronze pedestal table with translucent porcelain top. The motifs were initially almost entirely floral – convolvulus, thistle, bracken, honesty, hydrangea, hortensia, aloe, lily of the valley, marguerite, etc. – but in the 1930s they became more geometric – lozenges, rhomboids and checker-boards. *Mobilier et Décoration*'s panegyrics were deserved. There is an elegance and finesse to the Simonet lamps that are lacking in those of many of their competitors.

SOGNOT, LOUIS

Few disciples of the Art Déco tenets of utility, sobriety and economy of line were to espouse them more rigorously than the decorator Louis Sognot and his associate Charlotte Alix. Their furniture, along with that of other interior designers such as Moser, Guillemard and Mme Sougez, was marketed by Primavera, the art studio for the Paris department store Au Printemps. A regular exhibitor at the Salon d'Automne throughout the 1920s and '30s, Sognot's furniture for the Maharajah of Indore (shown at the 1931 Salon) was representative of the quiet charm of his designs; a critic commented that his formula was 'obviously founded in mass-production: he conceives as a logician, but executes as a poet'.

No less logical was the series of table-lamps that Sognot and Charlotte Alix fashioned from cylindrical or rectangular rods of crystal housed in chromed metal mounts. These showed an unimpeachable rationality, and the bulb was placed in a variety of positions in relation to the rows of rods so that the rays played on the crystal to produce different prismatic and reflective effects. Other ventures into the realm of lighting included a detachable lamp for a games table, a cheval-glass (at the 1929 Salon d'Automne) which had backlit slabs of glass set into its nickelled frame, and, in a similar style, a dressing-table mirror ringed by a band of tubular bulbs.

I know of two Sognot table-lamps in private collections. Their market value is probably between FF 875 ($175) and FF 1,300 ($260).

SUBES, RAYMOND

An ironsmith whose work spanned two decades of French decorative art, Subes seemed originally to draw his inspiration from the Louis-Philippe style of furnishing. A student and spiritual son of Emile Robert, he was in the 1920s more of a traditionalist than the majority of his ironworker colleagues. From about 1930, however, his style adjusted significantly to the spartan angularities of High Art Déco.

Subes' output of ironwork was prodigious and often for a select clientele: for example, a console for the French pavilion at the 1925 International Exposition; a grille for the Permanent Colonial Museum in 1931; large quantities of ironwork for three separate ocean liners (the *Normandie*, *Atlantique* and *Ile de France*); and, at the 1937 International Exposition, fountains for the Radio pavilion and a madonna and child statue for the Papal pavilion. In a 1927 article in *The Studio* the French critic Gabriel Mourey described Subes as 'our best ironworker today'. It was no mean compliment to be singled out in this manner from the ranks of such ironsmiths as Brandt, Piquet, Kiss, Edouard and Marcel Schenck and many others.

In addition to standard wrought-iron furnishings Subes regularly marketed a wide range of light fixtures through the Salon d'Automne and the Société des Artistes Décorateurs from 1919 till the outbreak of World War II. Working mainly in wrought iron – sometimes patinated, gilt, or chromed to vary the effect – he occasionally turned to polished steel, bronze, and *repoussé* copper, often using these as a decorative fillip to the iron, as in the bronze cabochons and interlacings on some of his floor-lamp bases. For the shades he used alabaster, levantine marble, frosted glass and, in the early 1920s, embroidered silk (executed for him by Mme Lehuché-Méry).

Praised repeatedly by the critics, particularly in *Mobilier et Décoration*, Subes made all forms of light fixtures, even, in 1920 and 1921, night-lights in copper and marble. (A night-light was usually considered by metalworkers to be too small and intricate an object for their profession.) One innovation of his, in 1932, was a radiator vase reflector, in which the vase, positioned on top of the radiator cover, projected the light on to the ceiling. His illuminated vases, on fluted and lacquered stelae, were a great success in their bold simplicity of form. When one examines photographs of his work, a common denominator emerges: that of the fixtures' durability. There would be no easy way of breaking them – a factor which makes it even more mysterious that so few of his creations have emerged in the antiques market.

SÜE, LOUIS and MARE, ANDRÉ

In 1912 Süe and Mare formed their Atelier Français which, after World War I, regrouped in 1919 as the Compagnie des Artistes français. Süe was an architect and interior designer and Mare was a painter (he had previously exhibited his canvases through the Salon of the Société des Artistes Indépendants), illustrator and furniture designer. The two formed a partnership well suited to cover the complete spectrum of interior design, which their firm strove to do in a 'serious, logical, and graceful' manner.

As in the case of other interior designers, lighting was to Süe and Mare only one aspect of the whole, to be designed either by one of themselves or by other artists in their studio, such as La Fresnaye, Maillol, Dufresne or Vera.

Süe and Mare were regular exhibitors at the Salons, especially the Salon d'Automne. Their light fixtures in the French pavilion and the Museum of Contemporary Art (both of which were built and decorated entirely by the Compagnie des Artistes français) at the 1925 International Exposition received generous coverage by Guillaume Janneau in his publication on the lighting at the Exposition. They designed table-lamps with alabaster flowers and wrought-iron bases, crystal chandeliers, six-branched wall brackets of bronze and glass beads, and a pair of gilt-bronze *torchères* in which the frosted glass sections were fashioned as fountains of petrified water. They also produced a floor-lamp with a veined alabaster bowl supported by a black patinated wrought-iron column that flared out into an oval-shaped foot. One form of illumination, perhaps unique to Süe and Mare, consisted of a basket of flowers entirely in glass and lit from within. Conservative in design philosophy, their lighting has a predictability of execution that lacks excitement.

SZABO, ADALBERT-GEORGES

Hungarian-born but naturalized French, Szabo functioned for upwards of thirty years in the decorative arts. As early as 1906 he exhibited his metalwork at the Salon of the Société des Artistes français; as late as 1938, at the same Salon, he displayed a wrought-iron door commissioned by a charity institution in Angoulême. His pre-war designs hinted more of historicism than of Art Nouveau, coming, as they did, at the end of the latter's 'High' period, while his later work – following the hiatus provided by the 1914–18 years – showed his accommodation to *le style 1925*.

The range of his work, however, did not vary greatly. Table-lamps, wall-brackets, chandeliers, fireplace screens, balustrades and doors (such as the one in chased and gilt bronze that Szabo designed and executed in 1936 for the first-class dining-room on the ocean liner *Normandie*), were standard items that he produced throughout his career, and which were frequently exhibited through the Société des Artistes français and the Société des Artistes Décorateurs. His light fixtures, usually in wrought iron, but also occasionally in copper and bronze, are similar to those of most of his metalwork contemporaries, particularly Subes, and tend towards heaviness.

Two table-lamps and a floor-lamp by Szabo sold in Paris in 1973 brought prices of between FF 1,575 and 5,250 ($315 and $1,050).

Lamps in the plates have been reproduced by courtesy of the following:

COLOUR

Michael Chow 36 / Corinthian Galleries, Saratoga, California 2, 3 / Collection Anne-Marie Gillion Crowet, Brussels 13, 15, 16, 19 / Editions Graphiques Gallery, London 14 / Mr & Mrs Eugene Gluck 5, 6, 7, 8 / Mr & Mrs Sydney Lewis, Richmond, Virginia 4, 22, 24, 25 / J. Loup Charmet 30 / Macklowe Gallery, New York 1, 12, 21, 31, 32 / Collection N. Manoukian, Paris 33 (photo Laurent Sully Jaulmes) / Collection Felix Marcilhac, Paris 9, 23 / Musée de l'École de Nancy 27 / Private Collection 18 (Germany); 17, 29 (Paris); 20, 34, 35 (photo Joseph Rykwert) / Collection Christian Sapet, Paris 28 / Collection Robert Walker 10, 11 / Mr & Mrs Louis Wittamer 26.

BLACK AND WHITE

Copyright A.C.L., Brussels 15, 16, 18 / Staatliche Museen Preussischer Kulturbesitz, Berlin 74, 75, 76 (Kunstbibliothek); 17 (Kunstgewerbemuseum) / Collection Marie de Beyrie, Paris 90 / Georges Blache 44 / Mr & Mrs Brigati, New York 57 / Musées Royaux d'Art et d'Histoire, Brussels 18 / Christie, Manson & Woods International Inc., New York 10, 11, 86 / Corinthian Studios, Saratoga, California 8 / Collection Anne-Marie Gillion Crowet, Brussels 14, 40, 49, 62 / Hessisches Landesmuseum, Darmstadt 80 / Daum et Cie, Cristallerie de Nancy 37 / L'Ecuyer Galerie, Brussels 50 / Editions Graphiques Gallery, London 48 / Glasgow Museums and Art Galleries 25, 26 / Mackintosh Collection, Glasgow University 27, 28 / Jack Howerton 112 / Neil Isman Gallery, New York 1, 2, 3 / Laurent Sully Jaulmes 42 / Jordon-Volpe Gallery, New York 72 / Bad. Lancesmuseum, Karlsruhe 78 / Lalique, Paris 110 / Alain Lesieutre, Paris 7 / Mr & Mrs Sydney Lewis, Richmond, Virginia 77 / Victoria & Albert Museum, London 23, 24, 29–31 / Macklowe Gallery, New York 59 / Collection Felix Marcilhac, Paris 63, 64, 93, 95, 119 / Musée de l'École de Nancy 65 / Lillian Nassau 6 / Musée des Arts Décoratifs, Paris 45, 87, 114, 122 / Eric Philippe, Arcueil 89 / Private Collection 5, 9, 12, 13, 34, 46, 47, 79 (photo Knut Liese) / Sotheby's Belgravia 22, 43, 52, 55, 58, 60, 73, 82 / Sotheby Parke Bernet, New York 4 / © Photo R. Guillemot – Connaissance des Arts – Agence Top 41 / Kungstgewerbemuseum, Zurich 81.

Glossary of Lighting Terminology

The following is a breakdown of the nomenclature relating to the various light fixtures described, and phraseology used, in this book. Confusion can arise in translating certain words from French into English as the same word can have a different meaning in the two languages: for example, *chandelier* is the French word for the English 'candlestick', while the English 'chandelier' translates into French as *lustre*, *suspension*, or sometimes – although technically not quite accurately – *plafonnier*.

It is to eliminate such confusion (and, while doing so, to bear well in mind that it is best to 'speak in French when you can't think of the English for a thing') that when the French word is used in the text it is *italicized* (the English word remains in Roman type).

FRENCH	ENGLISH	DEFINITION
Applique	wall-bracket or sconce	A lighting unit designed to be attached to a wall. If it contains a backplate for reflection purposes, then it is termed a sconce.
Bougeoir	candlestick	A support for a single candle.
Bougie	candle power	A unit for measuring the quantity of light.
Brûle-parfum	perfume-burner	A small night-light that contains a phial or dish of, for example, cassia or ground cinnamon that, when heated by the warmth of the light source, emits a sweet fragrance: a decorative variation on today's incense burner.
Candélabre	candelabrum; branched candlestick	A support for more than one candle.
Chandelier	candlestick	A support for a single candle (cf. *bougeoir*).
Eclairage	lighting	The generic term for the subject-matter of this book.
Electrolier	electrolier	Lit. a cluster of, or chandelier for, electric lamps. The word has become something of an anachronism and is not in general use in English today.
Flambeau	candlestick or candelabrum	There is no specific English translation of *flambeau*. It is used variously in French to describe a candlestick, candelabrum or wall-sconce, and means, literally, 'flame'.
Girandole	(ornate) wall-bracket; girandole	The word 'girandole' is not used in general parlance today; like 'electrolier' it derives from the pre-electric lighting era.
Ingénieur-éclairagiste	lighting engineer	Member of a profession based on the science of light (photometry) and its relationship to interior design.
Lampadaire	standard- or floor-lamp	A lamp to be positioned on the floor, the support for which would, therefore, be upwards of 4 feet in height.
Lamp de bureau	desk-lamp	A table-lamp usually designed to give a concentrated light for working purposes.
Lampe de table	table-lamp	As defined; usually more decorative than the desk variety.
Lanterne	lantern	Normally a small, rectangular, suspended lamp to illuminate a hallway or vestibule.

Lustre	chandelier	A decorative suspended support for one or more light sources.
Pendentif	pendant	A single, suspended light source (usually gas or electricity).
Plafonnier	ceiling-light	A lampshade attached directly to the ceiling.
Suspension	chandelier	*Suspension* is the French generic term for any light fixture that is suspended from the ceiling (cf. *lustre* and *pendentif*).
Torchère	standard- or floor-lamp or candlestick	Like *flambeau*, the word *torchère* has no specific English translation here and derives from pre-electricity lighting – meaning, literally, a torch.
Vase éclairant	illuminated vase	An inverted translucent vase-shaped shade, popular in the Art Déco period, usually positioned on top of a pedestal or standard lamp base. Part of the light striking the inside of the vase is reflected upwards and the remainder is transmitted through it.
Vase reflecteur	reflecting vase	In this instance the vase is made of non-translucent material so that all the light is reflected upwards.
Veilleuse	night-light	A small, decorative bedside lamp, largely non-functional.
. . . lumineux, lumineuse (s)	illuminated . . .	In the 1920s standard light fixtures were often replaced by concealed, indirect lighting housed in the framework of the building; for example, *rampes*, *traits*, *colonnes*, *plafonds*, *pilastres*, *panneaux*, *corniches*, *cloisons*. In addition, such objects as *tables*, *monuments* and *fontaines* were also illuminated.

Glossary of manufacturing techniques

Champlevé	An enamelling technique whereby the surface of a metal object is chased, stamped, or cast into cellular depressions, or *champs*, which are then filled with enamel to the level of the original surface.
Cloisonné	Fillets of metal are soldered on to a solid backplate to form small cells (*cloisons*), which are then filled with enamel.
Dalle de verre	A thick slab of glass, often used by stained-glass artists in church windows.
Flambé	A ceramic glaze of brilliant red and purple caused by the oxidation of copper in an iron-based glaze.
Marqueterie sur verre	A glass technique in which lumps of coloured glass are pressed into the warm, soft body of a newly made glass object and then rolled on a marver to press them firmly into its surface. On cooling, these insets are usually wheel-carved.
Martelé	A hammered finishing effect often applied in 1900 and 1925 to metal objects, particularly those of pewter or wrought iron.

Pâte de cristal — A glass paste, similar to *pâte de verre*, but with a higher lead content.

Pâte de verre — A powdered glass mixed into a thick paste with water and a volatile adhesive medium. The mixture is applied in thin layers in a mould until the required thickness of the finished piece of glass is achieved, at which stage it is fired in a mould.

Plique-à-jour — An enamelling technique in which the backing or mould is divided into cells which are filled with translucent enamel. After firing, the metal back-plate is removed to give the enamel a latticed, stained-glass window appearance.

Repoussé — An embossing technique by which ornamental metal objects are beaten from behind with a hammer to give them a raised surface. If additional detail is required, this is achieved by chasing.

Verde antico — A patina of clear green tone found on ancient bronzes due to the oxidation of the copper in the bronze. The effect can be obtained artificially by applying a mixture of ammoniac vinegar and sea salt to new bronzes.

General Bibliography

L'Art décoratif: Revue internationale d'art industriel et de décoration, 1898/99–1914

L'Art Décoratif pour tous: Paris, 1902–4

L'Art de la ferronnerie ancienne et moderne: Dir. E. Robert, Paris, 1896/97.

Art et Décoration: revue mensuelle d'Art moderne, Paris, 1897–1938

Art et Industrie: revue général des Industries de luxe et des arts appliqués à la maison, Paris, 1925–36

Art et Industrie: revue mensuelle illustrée; Nancy, Paris, 1909–14

L'Art ménager: revue officielle du Salon des arts ménager; Paris, 1927–39

Cahiers Henry van de Velde: Bruxelles, 1965

La Demeure française: Paris, 1925–28

Deutsche Kunst und Dekoration: Darmstadt, 1897/98–1938

Gazette des Beaux-Arts: Paris, 1890–1939

Innen-dekoration: Darmstadt, 1899–1939

Die Kunst: Munich, 1909–39

Kunst und Kunsthandwerk: Vienna, 1898–1914

La Lorraine artiste: Nancy, 1890–1905

Lux: la revue de l'éclairage, 1928–39

Mobilier et Décoration d'intérieur: Lyons, then Sèvres, Paris, 1922–39

La Plume: Paris, 1894–97

La Revue artistique: Paris, 1910–12

La Revue d'art: Paris, 1899/1900

La Revue de l'art ancienne et moderne: Paris, 1897–1937

La Revue des arts décoratifs: Paris, 1895–1902

La Revue des beaux-arts: Paris, 1896–99

Revue Lorraine illustrée: Nancy, 1908–14

The Studio: London, 1893–1939

The Studio yearbook of decorative art: London, 1906–14, 1917, 1924

L'Art Vivant, Arts décoratifs et appliqués: Paris, 1925–39

Le Décor d'aujourd'hui: Paris, 1933–9

Salon catalogues, Paris

Société des Artistes français: 1891–1905
Société Nationale des Beaux-Arts: 1890–1939
Société des Arts Décoratifs: 1899–1905
Société des Artistes Décorateurs: 1904–39
Salon d'Automne: 1903–39
Société des Artistes Indépendants: 1900–10

Auction Catalogues

Sotheby's Belgravia, London:
15–7–71
3–11–71
8–3–72
22–6–72
16–11–72
28–3–73
22–6–73
7–11–73
3/4–4–74
5–7–74
20–11–74
13–3–75

Sotheby/Parke Bernet; Los Angeles;
24/25–3–75

Sotheby's Zurich;
6–5–75

Sotheby/Parke Bernet, New York:
26/27–10–73, 26–11–74

Christie's, London:
11–12–72
11–12–73
24–1–74
18–7–74
21–10–74
27–1–75
3–6–75

Christie's, Geneva:
18–11–74

Phillips, London:
30–1–73
8–5–73
11–12–73
5–2–74
4–6–74
1–10–74
10–12–74
11–2–75
15–4–75
10–6–75
15–7–75

Hotel Drouot, Paris:
13–3–72
23–3–72
26–4–72
5–6–72
19/20–6–72
8–11–72
18–12–72
12–2–73
14–2–73
30–5–73
20–6–73
29–6–73
2–7–73
4–7–73
12–12–73
18–2–74
21–3–74
22–3–74
8–4–74
27–5–74
29–5–74
30–5–74
12–6–74
16–10–74
13–11–74
15–11–74
27–11–74
11–12–74
17–12–71
19–11–71
12–3–71
10–5–67
25–11–68
31–3–71

Salle Ste Bernadette, Dijon:
28–4–74

Espace Cardin, Paris:
16–12–72

Hotel des Chevau-Légers, Versailles:
4–5–75
3–3–74
20–1–74
2–12–73
21–10–73
1–7–73
28–3–71
25–10–70
8–2–70
23–4–67

Hotel Rameau, Versailles:
4–11–73
19–5–71

Books

Album des bronzes d'éclairage électrique de la maison, Paris 1904 (sales catalogue)

Allgemeines Lexikon der bildenden Künstler, Leipzig 1907

Alphonse Mucha, London 1963 (Grosvenor Gallery exhibition catalogue)

Amaya, Mario *Art Nouveau*, London 1966

'Art Nouveau and the Low Countries', *Discovering Antiques* (75), London 1971

Art Nouveau: Art and Design at the Turn of the Century, Museum of Modern Art, New York 1959

Art Nouveau from Germany, New York, 1972 (catalogue of exhibition sponsored by the Goethe Institute and the National Book League)

Art Nouveau in Britain, London 1965 (exhibition catalogue)

Art Nouveau in New York (cultural monthly), Zurich, June 1971

'Art Nouveau, Jugendstil, Nieuwe Kunst', *Bulletin van het Rijksmuseum*, Amsterdam, March 1972

L'Art Verrier à l'aube du XX siècle, Lausanne, 1973

Barilli, Renato *Art Nouveau*, London 1966

Bénézit, E. *Dictionnaire des Peintres, Sculpteurs . . .*, Paris 1960

Bing, Samuel *Artistic America, Tiffany Glass, and Art Nouveau*, Cambridge, Mass. 1970

Bloch-Dermant, Janine *L'Art du verre en France, 1860–1914*, Paris 1974

Blount, Bernice and Henry *French Cameo Glass*, Des Moines 1968

Borderel, E. and Robert F. *Créations de Raymond Subes*, Paris n.d.

Borsi, Franco *Bruxelles 1900*, Paris 1974

Bossaglia, R. *Le Mobilier Art Nouveau*, Paris 1972

Bresinsky, Hermann *Beleuchtungskörper*, Darmstadt 1957

Brosio, Valentino *Lo Stile Liberty*, Milan 1967
Brünhammer, Yvonne *Lo Stile 1925*, Milan 1966
Bury, Shirley, 'The Liberty Metalwork Venture', *Architectural Review*, February 1963

Cahiers Henry van de Velde, Association Henry van de Velde, Brussels 5 (Nos. 5/1965, 6/1965, 7/1966, 8/1967, 9–10/1968, 11/1970)
Cassou, Jean; Langui, Emile; and Pevsner, Nikolaus *Sources of Modern Art*, London 1962
Champigneulle, B. *L'Art Nouveau*, Paris 1972
Charles Rennie Mackintosh (1868–1928), London 1967 (catalogue of exhibition at Victoria and Albert Museum)
Christopher Dresser, 1834–1904, London 1972 (exhibition catalogue)

Dictionary of Twentieth Century Art, London 1973
Dictionnaire de la sculpture modern, Paris 1960
Dingelstedt, K. *Le Modern Style dans les arts appliqués*, Paris 1959
Drexler, Arthur and Daniel, Greta *Introduction to Twentieth Century Design from the collection of The Museum of Modern Art, New York*, New York 1959

Eclairage de 1900 à nos jours, Brussels (L'écuyer, 187 Avenue Louise, Brussels), n.d.
L'éclairage des habitations, Paris 1934
'L'Eclairage moderne', *La Demeure française*, Nos. 2–4, 1926
Europa 1900, Brussels 1967 (catalogue of exhibition at Ostende Musée des Beaux-Arts)
Europäischer Jugendstil, Bremen 1965 (exhibition catalogue)
Exposition Art Nouveau, Tokyo 1968 (catalogue of exhibition at department-store SEIBU)
Exposition Universelle 1889 (Pavillon du Gaz), Paris 1889
L'exposition universelle internationale: Rapport du comité d'installation (Musée rétrospective du Groupe V: Electricité), Paris 1900

Garner, Philippe *The World of Edwardiana*, London 1974
Glassammlung Hentrich: Antike, Jugendstil, Düsseldorf 1973 (exhibition catalogue)
Glassammlung Hentrich, Jugendstilund 20er Jahre, Düsseldorf 1973
Graham, F. Lanier *Hector Guimard*, New York 1970 (catalogue of exhibition at The Museum of Modern Art)
Grover, Ray and Lee *Art Nouveau Glass*, Rutland, Vt. 1967
Grover, Ray and Lee *Carved and Decorated European Art Glass*, Rutland, Vt., 1970
Gysling-Billeter, Erika *Objekte des Jugendstils*, Bern 1975

Henriot, Gabriel *Luminaire moderne*, Paris 1937
Henzke, Lucile *American Art Pottery*, Camden, N.J., 1970
Henry van de Velde, Zurich 1958 (exhibition catalogue)
Henry van de Velde, Brussels 1970 (exhibition catalogue)
Les Ivoires: évolution décorative du 1er siècle à nos jours, Paris 1966
Hermann Obrist, Wegbereiter der Moderne, Munich 1968 (catalogue of exhibition at Stuck-Villa)
Hillier, Bevis *Art Deco*, London 1968
Hofstätter, Hans H. *Geschichte der europäischen Jugendstil Malerei*, Cologne 1965
Howarth, Thomas *Charles Rennie Mackintosh and the Modern Movement*, London 1952
Hüter, Karl-Heinz *Henry van de Velde*, Berlin 1967

Internationales Jugendstilglas, Vorformen Moderner Kunst, Munich 1969 (catalogue of exhibition at Villa-Stuck)

Jenkins, Alan *The Twenties*, London 1974
Joseph M. Olbrich, 1867–1908, Das Werk des Architekten, Hessisches Landesmuseum, Darmstadt 1967
Jugendstil Illustration in München, Munich 1970 (exhibition catalogue)

Klein, Dan *Art Deco*, London 1974
Koloman Moser, 1868–1918, Vienna 1971 (exhibition catalogue)
Krohn, Gerhard *Lampen und Leuchten*, Munich 1962

Lesieutre, Alain *The Spirit and Splendour of Art Deco*, London 1975
Lethève, Jacques *De 1870 à 1914; des impressionnistes aux cubistes*, Paris 1967
Loetz Austria; Irisierende Farbgläser des Jugendstils, Munich 1971 (exhibition catalogue)
Lux: la revue de l'éclairage, Paris 1928–37

Mackay, James *Turn-of-the-Century Antiques*, London 1974
Macleod, Robert *Charles Rennie Mackintosh*, Feltham 1968
Madsen, Stephan Tschudi *Sources of Art Nouveau*, Oslo 1956
Maenz, Paul *Art Deco 1920–1940*, Cologne 1974
Mannoni, Édith *Meubles et Ensembles: Style 1900*, Paris 1968
Mauclair, Camille *Jules Chéret*, Paris 1930
McClinton, K. M. *Art Deco: A Guide for Collectors*, New York 1972
Menten, Theodore *The Art Deco Style in Household Objects, Architecture, Sculpture, Graphics, Jewelry . . .*, New York 1972
Miscellanea 1, Hamburg, October 1969
Miscellanea 3, Hamburg, November 1970
Mourey, Gabriel; Vallance, Aymer; et al. *Art Nouveau Jewelry and Fans*, New York 1973

Mucha, Jiri *Alphonse Mucha, The Master of Art Nouveau*, Prague 1966

Mucha, Jiri; Henderson, Marina; Scharf, Aaron *Mucha Posters and Photographs*, London 1971

'München um 1900', *Du*, July 1969

Naylor, G. *The Bauhaus*, London 1968

Neuwirth, Waltraud *Das Glas des Jugendstils*, Munich 1973

Nineteenth Century America: Furniture and other Decorative Arts, New York 1970 (Metropolitan Museum of Art catalogue)

Nouveau Dictionnaire de la Sculpture moderne, Paris 1970

L'œuvre de Rupert Carabin, 1862–1932, Luxembourg 1974 (exhibition catalogue)

Oostens-Wittamer, Y. *La Belle Epoque*, New York 1970

Pétrole, gaz, électricité, Paris (Société des verreries pour l'éclairage) n.d.

Pevsner, Nikolaus *Pioneers of Modern Design*, New York 1949

Philippe, Joseph *Le Val-Saint-Lambert*, Liège 1974

Reade, B. *Art Nouveau and Alphonse Mucha*, London 1963

Revi, Albert Christian *American Pressed Glass and Figure Bottles*, New York 1964

Revi, Albert Christian *Art Nouveau Glass*, Camden, N.J., 1968

Revi, Albert Christian *Nineteenth Century Glass: Its Genesis and Development*, New York 1959

Revue de l'exposition universelle de 1889, Paris 1889

Revue U.L.V., No. 4, Brussels 1968

Rheims, Maurice *L'Objet 1900*, Paris 1964

Rockwell, R. F. *Frederick Carder and his Steuben Glass, 1903–33*, West Nyack, N.Y., 1966

Rodighiero, L. *L'éclairage dans la maison*, Paris n.d.

Scheffler, W. *Werke um 1900*, Berlin 1966

Secession: Europäische Kunst um die Jahrhundertwende, Munich 1964 (catalogue of exhibition at Haus der Kunst)

Les sources du 20e siècle: les arts en Europe de 1884 à 1914, Paris 1960 (catalogue of exhibition at the Musée Nationale d'art modern, 1960–61)

Stilkunst um 1900 in Deutschland, Berlin 1972 (exhibition catalogue)

Tierlinck, Herman *Henry van de Velde*, Brussels 1959

Um 1900, Art Nouveau und Jugendstil, Zurich 1952 (exhibition catalogue)

Um 1900: Die Neue Sammlung, Munich 1969 (catalogue of exhibition at Museum für Angewandte Kunst)

Le Val-Saint-Lambert, Montreal 1974 (exhibition catalogue)

Veronesi, Giulia *Into the Twenties: Style and Design 1909–1929*, London and New York 1968

Victor Horta; son Musée, Brussels, n.d. (catalogue of Horta Museum)

Victorian and Edwardian Decorative Arts, London 1952 (catalogue of exhibition at Victoria and Albert Museum)

Vienna Secession, Art Nouveau to 1970, London 1971 (catalogue of exhibition at Royal Academy of Arts)

Walters, Thomas *Art Deco*, London 1973

Watelet, J. C. *Le Décorateur Liégeois: Gustave Serrurier-Bovy, 1858–1910*, Cahiers Henry van de Velde, No. 11, Brussels 1970

Weber, Wilhelm *Peter Behrens (1868–1940)*, Kaiserslautern 1966 (catalogue of exhibition at Pfalzgalerie)

Wechssler-Kümmel, S. *Chandeliers, lampes et appliques de style*, Fribourg 1963

Werke um 1900, Berlin 1966 (Kunstgewerbe Museum catalogue)

Wolfers, Marcel *Philippe Wolfers*, Brussels 1965

The World of Art Deco, London 1971 (catalogue of exhibition at Minneapolis Institute of Arts)

Die Zwanziger Jahre: Kontraste eines Jahrzents, Zurich 1973 (exhibition catalogue)

List of Designers: individual bibliographies

ADNET, JACQUES
Studio Yearbook, 1929, p. 184
Mobilier et Décoration;
August 1929, p. 57
August 1932, p. 349
September 1936, p. 329
Art et Industrie; January 1929, p. 30
Luminaire Moderne; G. Henriot, 1937, plate 9
Le Luminaire et les Moyens d'éclairage Nouveaux; G. Janneau
1st series: plate 43
2nd series: plate 1
3rd series: plate 38–40
Album de l'éclairage; Lux, 1929, p. 53

ALLIOT, LUCIEN
1877–?
Allgemeines Lexikon der Bildenden Künstler, 1955
Bénézit I, 1948
Gazette des Beaux-Arts; 1920 II, pp. 18, 19
Art Nouveau; Martin Battersby, London 1969, plate 17
Salon catalogues: *Société des Artistes français;* 1910, 1911

ARGY-ROUSSEAU, GABRIEL
1885–1953
L'Art Verrier; Editions Galerie des Arts Décoratifs S.A., Lausanne, 1973, pp. 89–95
Carved and Decorated European Art Glass; R. and L. Grover, C. E. Tuttle Co., Vermont, 1970, p. 69
Das Glas des Jugendstils, H. Hilschenz, Munich 1973, pp. 148–51
Salon catalogues: *Société des Artistes Décorateurs* 1924, 1927

ASHBEE, CHARLES ROBERT
1863–1942
Aus der Sammlung Prinz Ludwig von Hessen und bei Rhein; exhibition catalogue, Victoria and Albert Museum 8–12–72 to 28–1–73, Hessisches Landesmuseum, Darmstadt, collection
L'Art Décoratif; August 1899, p. 195

BAGUÈS FRÈRES
Luminaire Moderne; G. Henriot, 1937, plate 26
Lux; January 1932, p. 9
December 1934, p. 150
Mobilier et Décoration; July 1937, p. 223
Art et Industrie;
May 1926, p. 35
December 1926, p. 46
February 1930, p. 37
February 1935, p. 19
April 1935, p. 14
Rapport Général; Exposition Internationale des Arts Décoratifs, No. 5, Paris 1927, plate 24

BEHRENS, PETER
1868–1940
Peter Behrens (1868–1940); exhibition catalogue, Pfalzgalerie Kaiserslautern, 1966/67
L'art Décoratif Pour Tous; 4–4–1902, pp. 7, 9
Chandeliers, lampes et appliques de style; S. Wechssler-Kummel, Fribourg 1963, plate 256
Deutsche Kunst und Dekoration; 1902–3, p. 432

BENSON, WILLIAM ARTHUR SMITH
1854–1924
Electric Light Fittings; Sales catalogue, n.d.
Benson Electric Light fittings; sales catalogue, 1902
Dictionary of Turn-of-the-Century Antiques; J. Mackay, London 1974, p. 31
L'Art Décoratif;
October 1901, pp. 160–68
November 1898, p. 66
The Studio; Yearbook 1906, p. 168
Auction catalogues; Sotheby's Belgravia, 7/8–11–73, lot 47

BOUVAL, MAURICE
Le Modern Style; Baschet et Cie., 13 rue St-Georges, Paris 1974, p. 173
Meubles et Ensembles: Style 1900; E. Mannoni, Ed. C. Massin, Paris 1968, p. 21
L'Art Décoratif; August 1900, pp. 190, 194
Salon catalogues: *Société des Artistes français;* 1897, 1902
Hotel Drouot; auction catalogue 10–5–67, lot 185

BRANDT, EDGAR
1880–1960
L'Art Verrier à l'aube du XXe siècle; Editions Galerie des Arts Décoratifs, S.A., Lausanne 1973, p. 51
Auction catalogues:
Versailles, 5–3–72, lot 227
Versailles, 13–12–70, lot 248

L'Art Décoratif;
October 1904, pp. 145–48
October 1905, p. 161
January–June 1906, pp. 51–62
Art et Décoration; January–June 1912, p. 177
Salon catalogues: *Société des Artistes Décorateurs*; 1910, 1911
Le Luminaire et les Moyens d'éclairage Nouveaux; G. Janneau
1st series: plates 1–6
2nd series: plates 2–3
3rd series: plates 1–6
The World of Art Deco; New York 1971, Exhibit nos.: 358–61.
The Studio;
January–June 1926, p. 330
Yearbook 1922, p. 124
Yearbook 1923, p. 145
Art et Décoration;
January–June 1921, p. 79
January–June 1924, p. 174
July–December 1920, p. 47
Mobilier et Décoration:
November–December, 1922, p. 25
September–October, 1922, p. 3
August–September, 1924, p. 9
April 1927, p. 107
August 1928, p. 95
January 1934, p. 1
Salon catalogues:
Salon d'Automne, 1920–24, 1926, 1934
Société des Artistes Décorateurs, 1919–22, 1924, 1926
Société des Artistes français, 1919–20

CAPON, EUGÈNE and G.-L.
Art et Décoration:
January–June 1923, p. 178
January–June 1920, p. 111
Le Luminaire et les Moyens d'éclairage Nouveaux: G. Janneau 1st series: plates 25, 26
Salon catalogues: *Société des Artistes Décorateurs:* 1921–24

CAUSSÉ, JULIEN
Allgemeines Lexikon der Bildenden Künstler, 1955
Bénézit I, 1948
Auction catalogue: Versailles, 2–12–73, lot 142

CHALON, LOUIS
1866–1916
Dictionary of Turn-of-the-Century Antiques; J. Mackay, London 1974, p. 166
Revue des Arts Décoratifs; XX, 1900, p' 97
Allgemeines Lexikon der Bildenden Künstler, 1955
Salon catalogues; *Société des Artistes français;* 1898, 1902
L'Art; 1902, p. 410

CHAREAU, PIERRE
1883–1950
Le Luminaire et les Moyens d'éclairage Nouveaux; G. Janneau
1st series: plates 22, 34, 35
2nd series: plate 4
Lux; December 1928, p. 187
December 1934, p. 150
The Studio; Yearbook 1928, p. 102
La Demeure française; 1925–26, No. 1, p. 34
Mobilier et Décoration;
November–December 1922, p. 27
April 1927, p. 97
November 1928, p. 215
February 1926, p. 48
Art et Décoration;
January–June 1924, p. 179
January–June 1925, p. 156
July–December 1926, p. 103
Album de l'éclairage; Lux, 1929, p. 47, 73

CHÉRET, JOSEPH
1838–1894
Art et Décoration; July–December 1900, pp. 95, 151–60
Auction catalogues;
Hotel Drouot, 7–5–69, lots 25, 26
Versailles, 13–12–70, lot 252
Hotel Drouot, 9–3–73, lot 26
Versailles, 21–10–73, lot 76
Revue des Arts Décoratifs; December 1894–95, p. 193
Bénézit I, 1948

CHEURET, ALBERT
Le Luminaire et les Moyens d'éclairage Nouveaux; G. Janneau
1st series: plates 45, 46
Mobilier et Décoration; September–October 1922, p. 13
Salon catalogues: *Société des Artistes français;* 1924
Le Modern Style; Baschet et Cie., Paris 1974

DAMON
Lux; December 1929, pp. 170–1
Mobilier et Décoration;
November 1928, p. 262
October 1929, p. 140
June 1930, p. 269
November 1930, p. 187
April 1933, p. 158
Art et Industrie; May 1931, p. 31
Art et Décoration; July–December 1930, pp. 105, 109–10
Le Luminaire et les Moyens d'éclairage Nouveaux; G. Janneau
2nd series: plate 5

DAMPT, JEAN
1854–1946
L'Art Décoratif;
May 1901, pp. 44–7
August 1903, pp. 53–9
Art et Décoration;
July–December 1900, pp. 151–60
July–December 1902, p. 125
Salon catalogues; *Société des Beaux-Arts;* 1902
Revue des Arts Décoratifs; 1901, pp. 107–9
Allgemeines Lexikon der Bildenden Künstler, 1955
Bénézit I, 1948
Les Modes; 1901, p. 43

DAUM, AUGUSTE (1853–1909) and ANTONIN (1864–1930)
Le Modern Style; Baschet et Cie., 13 rue St-Georges, Paris 1974, pp. 170, 171, 178, 181
Carved and Decorated European Art Glass; R. & L. Gover, C. E. Tuttle Co., Vermont, pp. 71–2
Eclairage de 1900 à nos jours; L'écuyer, 187 Avenue Louise, Bruxelles, n.d., nos. 38, 72, 75, 87
L'Art du Verre en France: 1860–1914; J. Bloch-Dermant, Paris 1975, pp. 135–43
Revue Lorraine Illustré; Vol. 3, 1908, p. 32
Auction catalogues;
Sotheby's 3–4–74, lot 164
Sotheby's 16–11–72, lots 94, 96
Sotheby's 5–7–74, lot 4
Sotheby's 15–7–71, lot 118
Sotheby's 8–3–72, lot 98
Sotheby's 16–11–72, lots 94, 96
Sotheby's 3–4–74, lot 164
Sotheby's (Parke Bernet: Los Angeles 24/25–3–75, lot 119)
Christie's 3–6–75, lot 138
Christie's 27–1–75, lot 106
Christie's 11–12–73, lot 163
Christie's (Geneva) 29–4–74, lots 43, 44, 46, 47
Hotel Blandan, Nancy 8–12–74, lot 96

DAUM, ANTONIN (1864–1930) and PAUL (?–1943)
Mobilier et Décoration;
January–February 1922, p. 9
October 1933, p. 395–9
Encyclopédie Connaissance des Arts; F. Duret-Robert, 1972.
The World of Art Deco; New York 1971, exhibit nos.: 362, 364

DE FEURE, GEORGES
1868–1928
Meubles et Ensembles: Style 1900; F. Mannoni, Ed. C. Massin, Paris 1968, p. 5
Eclairage de 1900 à nos Jours; L'écuyer, 187 Avenue Louise, Bruxelles, n.d., nos., 44, 45, 47
L'Art Décoratif;
April 1901, pp. 23–28
October 1901–March 1902, pp. 160–8
Europa 1900; Musée des Beaux-Arts, exhibition catalogue, Ostend, 3–6–67 to 30–9–67, no. 342
Art et Décoration;
January–June 1901, pp. 78–88
July–December 1902, p. 61
Salon catalogues; *Societé des Beaux-Arts;* 1902
Deutsche Kunst und Dekoration; 1902/3, p. 326

DE JARNY, PAUL BRINDEAU
L'Art Décoratif;
December 1904, p. 219
December 1905, p. 216
Salon catalogues;
Salon d'Automne; 1903, 1905–9, 1922–3
Salon des Beaux-Arts; 1908–10, 1921
Société des Artistes Décorateurs; 1904, 1914, 1924
Bénézit I, 1948

DESKY, DONALD
The World of Art Deco; New York 1971, exhibit nos.: 26–32, 365
The Studio;
Yearbook 1930, p. 142, 169
January–June 1933, p. 27, 30, 266

DESNY
Le Luminaire et les Moyens d'éclairage Nouveaux; G. Janneau
2nd series: plates 6–10
3rd series: plates 9–12
Lux;
January 1929, p. 2
April 1928, p. 61
September 1931, p. 101
Art et Industrie;
June 1928, p. 46
November 1928, p. 21
December 1928, p. 29
January 1929, p. 31, 70
Album de l'éclairage, Lux; 1929, p. 56

D.I.M.
Mobilier et Décoration;
January 1930, p. 129
May 1930, p. 177
September 1931, p. 315
July 1931, p. 315
Album de l'éclairage; Lux, 1929, p. 109
Le Luminaire et les Moyens d'éclairage Nouveaux; G. Janneau
3rd series: plates 47–8, 2nd series: plate 11
Art et Décoration: July–December 1930, p. 107, 112
The Studio; Yearbook 1930, p. 170

DOMINIQUE
Salon catalogues: *Société des Artistes Décorateurs,* 1924
Mobilier et Décoration;
March 1927, p. 69
October 1928, p. 179
Art et Industrie;
January 1929, p. 35
February 1930, p. 37
Le Luminaire et les Moyens d'éclairage Nouveaux; G. Janneau
1st series: plates 14, 18, 21, 23
Art et Décoration; July–December 1926, p. 108

DUBOIS, FERNAND
1861– ?
Eclairage de 1900 à nos jours; L'écuyer, 187 Avenue Louise, Bruxelles, n.d., no. 36, 119a
L'Art Décoratif; April 1899, p. 32
Tervueren 1897; M. Luwel, M. Bruneel-Hye de Crom, exhibition catalogue, Musée Royal de l'Afrique Centrale, Tervueren, Belgium, n.d., p. 93

DUBOIS, PAUL
1859–?
Eclairage de 1900 à nos jours; L'écuyer, 187 Avenue Louise, Bruxelles, n.d., no. 24
Art et Décoration; July–December 1899, p. 102
L'Art Décoratif; April 1899, p. 32
Du; May 1975, p. 38
The Studio;
XIV 1898, p. 204
XV 1898, p. 55

DUFRÈNE, MAURICE
1876–1955
L'Art Décoratif;
June 1901, pp. 207–9
October 1901–March 1902, pp. 160–8
July–December 1903, p. 32
June 1904, p. 217
Art et Décoration;
July–December 1901, p. 27
July–December 1903, p. 233
January–June 1906, pp. 73–84
July–December 1907, p. 198
Salon catalogues;
Salon d'Automne; 1912–13
Société des Artistes Décorateurs; 1904, 1907–8, 1912
Deutsche Kunst und Dekoration; 1902–3, pp. 178, 551, 555
Le Luminaire et les Moyens d'éclairage Nouveaux; G. Janneau
1st series: plate 24
2nd series: plate 12
3rd series: plate 8
Lux; June 1928, p. 87
The Studio; Yearbook 1929, p. 183
Salon catalogues; *Société des Artistes Décorateurs;* 1920, 1922
Mobilier et Décoration; August 1929, p. 57
Art et Décoration; July–December 1920, pp. 51–2

DUNAIME, GEORGES
Le Luminaire et les Moyens d'éclairage Nouveaux; G. Janneau
1st series: plates 19, 26, 44
Salon catalogues;
Société des Artistes français; 1924
Société des Artistes Décorateurs; 1927
Mobilier et Décoration;
June–July 1924, p. 1
January 1925, pp. 4, 6, 16, 20
January–February 1922, p. 26
September 1925, pp. 225–9
Rapport Général; Exposition Internationale des Arts Décoratifs, No. 5, Paris 1927, plate 23
Art et Décoration;
January–June 1921, p. 68
July–December 1922, p. 192

ETLING
Lux; December 1934, p. 150
Mobilier et Décoration; March 1932, p. 130
Luminaire Moderne; G. Henriot, 1937, plates 39–40

FLAMAND, G.
Auction catalogues; Sotheby's 16–11–72, lot 130
Europa 1900; exhibition catalogue, Musée des Beaux-Arts, Ostend, 3–6–67 to 30–9–67, lot 69

FOLLOT, PAUL
1877–1941
Meubles et Ensembles: Style 1900; E. Mannoni, Ed. C. Massin, Paris 1968, p. 39
L'Art Décoratif;
February 1903, pp. 80–1
December 1904, p. 104
Art et Décoration; January–June 1909, p. 36
Salon catalogues;
Salon d'Automne; 1910, 1912
Société des Artistes Décorateurs; 1908–12
Deutsche Kunst und Dekoration; 1902–3, p. 552
Le Luminaire et les Moyens d'éclairage Nouveaux; G. Janneau
1st series: plates 17, 18, 21, 23, 32, 44
Salon catalogues;
Salon d'Automne; 1920–3, 1926–7
Société des Artistes Décorateurs; 1920–4, 1927, 1932
Art et Décoration; July–December 1920, p. 53

FRÉMIET, EMMANUEL
1824–1910
Art et Décoration; July–December 1898, pp. 65–75
Un Siècle de Bronzes Animaliers; Galerie P. Ambroise, Paris, March–April 1975, exhibition catalogue, pp. 76–7

GALLÉ, EMILE
1846–1904
Le Modern Style; Baschet et Cie., 13 rue St-Georges, Paris 1974, pp. 126, 152, 168, 169, 174, 175, 182
Carved and Decorated European Art Glass; R. & L. Grover, C. E. Tuttle Co., Vermont, pp. 121–9
Eclairage de 1900 à nos jours; L'écuyer, 187 Avenue Louise, Bruxelles, n.d., nos. 13, 14, 16, 22, 28, 30
L'Art du Verre en France: 1860–1914; J. Bloch-Dermant, Paris 1975, p. 90
French Cameo Glass; B. & H. Blount, Des Moines, Iowa, 1968, pp. 132–5
Art et Décoration; January–June 1903, p. 131
L'Art Décoratif; January–June 1905, p. 97–8
Auction catalogues:
Sotheby's 3–11–71, lot 64
Sotheby's 3/4–4–74, lot 165
Sotheby's 8–3–72, lot 88
Sotheby's 20–11–74, lot 48
Sotheby's 7–11–73, lot 267, 270
Sotheby's 3–4–74, lot 165
Christie's 18–7–74, lot 183
Christie's (Geneva) 29–7–74, lots 84, 90
Versailles 28–3–71, lot 59
Versailles 13–12–70, lot 62
Versailles 4–11–73, lot 48
Hotel Drouot 12–12–73, lot 56
Hotel Drouot 31–5–74, lot 105
Hotel Drouot 11–12–74, lot 44
Hotel Drouot 19–11–71, lot 22
Hotel Drouot 10–5–67, lot 152

GENET & MICHON
Le Luminaire et les Moyens d'éclairage Nouveaux; G. Janneau
1st series: plates 7–9, 30, 43
2nd series: plates 15–18
3rd series: plates 41–45
Luminaire Moderne; G. Henriot, 1937, plates 20–3
Lux; February 1929, pp. 28–9
June 1928, p. 87
December 1934, p. 150
The Studio;
July–December 1931, p. 185
Yearbook 1929, p. 183–4
Salon catalogues;
Salon d'Automne, 1922–4
Société des Artistes Décorateurs, 1923–4, 1926–8, 1930, 1932–34, 1938
Mobilier et Décoration;
November–December 1922, pp. 15, 29
October 1927, p. 135
June 1929, pp. 202, 206
April 1930, p. 153
July 1937, p. 224
January 1926, pp. 22–7
June 1926, pp. 182, 188
June 1931, pp. 282, 298
1935; pp. 285, 319, 321–2
1937, pp. 29–32, 295, 455
Art et Décoration;
July–December 1926, p. 106
January–June 1923, p. 16

GIGOU, LOUIS
Salon catalogues; *Société des Artistes Décorateurs;* 1919–23
Le Luminaire et les Moyens d'éclairage Nouveaux; G. Janneau
1st series: plates 26, 43
Art et Décoration;
January–June 1921, p. 103
January–June 1923, p. 187

GUÉVRÉKIAN, GABRIEL
Art de Décoration; January–June 1929, p. 31
Art et Industrie; January 1929, p. 32
Le Luminaire et les Moyens d'éclairage Nouveaux; G. Janneau
1st series: plate 22
2nd series: plate 21

GUIMARD, HECTOR
1867–1942
Le Modern Style; Baschet et Cie., 13 rue St Georges, Paris 1974, pp. 179, 181
Europa 1900; exhibition catalogue, Musée des Beaux-Arts, Ostend, 3–6–67 to 30–9–67, no. 220
L'Art Décoratif; October 1900
Salon catalogues; *Société des Artistes Décorateurs;* 1914

GURSCHNER, GUSTAV
1873–?
Jugendstil 20er Jahre; exhibition catalogue, Verkaufs-Ausstellung, Künstlerhaus Galerie, Vienna, plates 2–5
L'Art Décoratif; August 1900, p. 196
Art et Décoration; July–December 1900, pp. 151–60
The Studio;
XXVII, 1902, p. 133
XXIV, 1901, pp. 141–2
Deutsche Kunst und Dekoration;
1901–2, p. 457
1899–1900, p. 272
Allgemeines Lexikon der Bildenden Künstler; 1955
Auction catalogues;
Christie's 24–2–70, lot 57
Christie's 7–7–70, lots 188, 187
Sotheby's Parke Bernet 26/27–10–73, lot 69
Sotheby's Parke Bernet 26/29/30–11–74, lot 51
Sotheby's Belgravia 22–6–72, lot 74

HANDEL, PHILIP
American Art Nouveau Glass; A. C. Revi, T. Nelson & Sons, 1968, pp. 259–79

HERBST, RENÉ

Lux; December 1929, p. 183
April 1929, p. 67
January 1928, p. 10
Mobilier et Décoration;
December 1928, p. 280
March 1925, p. 55
March 1933, p. 81
Le Luminaire et les Moyens d'éclairage Nouveaux; G. Janneau
1st series: plates 18, 20, 35
2nd series: plate 44
Album de l'éclairage; Lux, 1929, p. 54
Art et Décoration; January–June 1929, p. 29

HOOSEMANS: see ROMBAUX

HORTA, VICTOR
1861–1947
Bruxelles 1900; F. Borsi, M. Vokaer, Paris 1974, p. 126
The Age of Art Nouveau; M. Rheims, London 1966, pp. 226–7
Art Nouveau; R. Schmutzler, London 1964, p. 135
Art et Décoration; January–June 1897, pp. 16–18
L'Objet 1900; M. Rheims, Paris 1964, plate 97
Art Nouveau; Art and Design at the Turn-of-the-Century; Museum of Modern Art, New York 1959, nos. 92, 132
Le Val St Lambert; J. Philippe, Librarie Halbert, Liège 1974, plate 26

JALLOT, LÉON (1874–1967) and MAURICE
Art et Décoration; July–December 1924, p. 79
Lux; October 1930, p. 134
The Studio; Yearbook 1930, p. 62
Salon catalogues; *Société des Artistes Décorateurs;* 1923, 1926–8
Mobilier et Décoration;
December 1925, p. 10
September 1928, p. 131
October 1932, p. 425

JONCHERY, CHARLES ÉMILE
Allgemeines Lexikon der Bildenden Künstler, 1955
Salon catalogues; *Société des Artistes français;* 1903
Revue des Arts Décoratifs; 1901, p. 262
Bénézit I, 1948
Auction catalogues; Hotel Drouot 20–6–75, lot 92

JOUBERT & PETIT: see D.I.M.

JOURDAIN, FRANCIS
Le Luminaire et les Moyens d'éclairage Nouveaux; G. Janneau
1st series: plate 35
Luminaire Moderne; G. Henriot, 1937, plate 19
La Demeure française; 1925–6, No. 3, p. 14
Mobilier et Décoration; April 1928, p. 175

KAYSER SOHN
Liberty's 1875–1975; exhibition catalogue, Victoria and Albert Museum, 1975, exhibit D167
Introduction to 20th Century Design; A. Drexler and G. Daniel, Museum of Modern Art, New York 1959, p. 20
Jugendstilsammlung; Dr. G. Woeckel, Staatliche Kunstsammlungen, Kassel 1968, exhibition catalogue.
Jugendstil; Hessisches Landesmuseum catalogue, Darmstadt 1965, No. 236

KISS, PAUL
La Demeure française; 1925–6, No. 2, p. 32
Salon catalogues; *Société des Artistes Décorateurs;* 1922, 1926–7
Mobilier et Décoration;
December 1925, p. 21
December 1926, pp. 170–3
January 1929, p. 35
Le Luminaire et les Moyens d'éclairage Nouveaux; G. Janneau
1st series: plates 30, 43

KNOX, ARCHIBALD
1864–1933
Liberty's 1875–1975; exhibition catalogue, Victoria and Albert Museum, 1975, exhibits D182–184
Art Nouveau in Britain; exhibition catalogue, The Arts Council, 1965, p. 12
Auction catalogue; Sotheby's Parke Bernet 1–5–70, lot 91
(see also *Liberty*)

KOHLMANN, ÉTIENNE
Lux; December 1934, p. 150
Art et Décoration; January–June 1928, p. 129
Luminaire Moderne; G. Henriot, 1937, plate 42
Le Luminaire et les Moyens d'éclairage Nouveaux; G. Janneau
1st series: plates 32, 36

KORSCHANN, CHARLES
1872–?
Jugendstilsammlung; Dr G. Woeckel, Staatliche Kunstsammlungen, Kassel 1968, exhibition catalogue
Allgemeines Lexikon der Bildenden Künstler; 1955
Salon catalogues; *Société des Artistes français;* 1898, 1901

LACROIX, BORIS-JEAN
Le Luminaire et les Moyens d'éclairage Nouveaux; G. Janneau
2nd series: plates 22–4
3rd series: plates 27–33
Lux;
December 1929, p. 170
January 1929, p. 15
December 1934, p. 150
The Studio; July–December 1929, p. 643
Salon catalogues;
Salon d'Automne; 1927–9

Société des Artistes Décorateurs; 1927–9, 1932, 1936
Mobilier et Décoration;
June 1929, p. 249
October 1929, pp. 140–9
Art et Industrie;
January 1928, p. 38
July 1929, p. 26
November 1929, p. 29
Art et Décoration;
July–December 1929, p. 24, 178
July–December 1930, pp. 109, 110

LALIQUE, RENÉ
Carved and Decorated European Art Glass; R. and L. Grover, C. E. Tuttle Co., Vermont, 1970, p. 130
L'Art Verrier; Editions Galerie des Arts Décoratifs S.A., Lausanne 1973, pp. 63–5
Dictionary of Turn-of-the-Century Antiques; J. Mackay, London 1974, p. 163
'Art Deco'; Victoria and Albert Museum loan exhibition catalogue, exhibits 2–5
Art et Décoration;
July–December 1905, pp. 182, 183
January–June 1906, p. 184
January–June 1925, p. 219
L'Art Décoratif: January–June 1905, p. 221
Le Luminaire et les Moyens d'éclairage Nouveaux; G. Janneau
1st series: plates 31, 36, 47, 48
2nd series: plates 26–9
Das Glas des Jugendstils; H. Hilschenz, Munich 1973, pp. 310–16
Lux; June–August 1930, p. 107
La Demeure française; 1925–6, No. 1, p. 18–22
Salon catalogues;
Salon d' Automne; 1923–4, 1926, 1928
Société des Artistes Décorateurs; 1922, 1924, 1926–9
Mobilier et Décoration;
June–July 1924, p. 13
November 1924, p. 21
December 1926, pp. 151–4
August 1928, p. 109
January–February 1922, p. 8–10
Art et Industrie; January 1928, p. 37
Album de l'éclairage, Lux; 1929, pp. 36, 37, 59–60, 67
L'Art Ménager; November 1929, p. 2115–2116

LANDRY, ABEL
L'Art Décoratif; July–December 1906, pp. 208–11 *and* January–June 1907, p. 60
Art et Décoration; July–December 1903, p. 231
Salon catalogues;
Salon d'Automne; 1913
Société des Artistes Décorateurs; 1906, 1910, 1912, 1913
Deutsche Kunst und Dekoration; 1902–3, pp. 179, 555
Auction catalogue; Hotel Drouot 10–5–67, lot 171

LAPORTE-BLAIRSY, LÉO
1865–1923
Eclairage de 1900 à nos jours; L'écuyer, 187 Avenue Louise, Bruxelles, n.d., nos. 31, 33, 43
L'Art Décoratif;
June 1901, p. 185, 187
June 1903, p. 224
December 1903, p. 236
Art et Décoration;
July–December 1901, p. 29
January–June 1902, p. 121, 122
July–December 1902, p. 40, 46, 121, 124–5
L'Art; 1902, pp. 40–47
Revue des Arts Décoratifs; 1901, p. 260
Deutsche Kunst und Dekoration; 1903–4, p. 105
Salon catalogues; *Société des Artistes français;* 1901, 1904
Auction catalogues;
Sotheby's 13–3–75, lot 103
Sotheby's 20–11–74, lot 93
Sotheby's 22–6–73, lot 102
Sotheby's 3–4–74, lots 122, 201
Versailles 28–3–71, lot 234
Hotel Blandan, Nancy 20–4–75, lot 226

LARCHE, FRANÇOIS-RAOUL
1860–1912
Le Modern Style; Baschet & Cie., 13 Rue St-Georges, Paris 1974, p. 172
Art Nouveau for Collectors; P. Garner, London 1974, p. 114
Exposition des Oeuvres de Raoul Larche, statuaire et peintre, et de Raymond Sudre, statuaire et peintre; exhibition catalogue, 57 rue Chardon-Lagache, Paris, n.d.
Auction catalogues;
Sotheby's Belgravia 15–7–71, lot 35
Sotheby's Belgravia 8–3–72, lot 139
Sotheby's Belgravia 7–11–73, lot 184
Versailles 28–3–71, lots 235, 236
Hotel Drouot 4–7–73, lot 49
Versailles 19–5–71, lot 41

LE CHEVALLIER, J.
The Studio; January–June 1929, p. 89
Mobilier et Décoration;
January 1930, p. 129
December 1929, p. 216
Art et Décoration; July–December 1930, pp. 97, 112

LEDRU, AUGUSTE
1860–1902
Eclairage de 1900 à nos jours; L'écuyer, 187 Avenue Louise, Bruxelles, n.d., no. 29
Allgemeines Lexikon der Bildenden Künstler, 1955
Salon catalogues; *Société des Artistes français;* 1901
Revue des Arts Décoratifs;
1893–94, p. 344
1894–95, p. 456

LEGRAS, AUGUSTE J. F.

Carved and Decorated European Art Glass; R. & L. Grover, C. E. Tuttle, Vermont, 1970, p. 130–1
Das Glas des Jugendstils; H. Hilschenz, Munich 1973, pp. 317–24
Auction catalogues;
 Christie's 18–6–73, lot 179
 Christie's 18–7–74, lot 189
 Sotheby's Belgravia 16–11–72, lot 88
 Sotheby's Parke Bernet 18/19/29–4–74, lot 39
 Phillips 10–6–75, lot 86
 Hotel Drouot 19–11–71, lot 7
 Versailles 5–3–72, lot 145

LÉONARD, AGATHON

1841–?
L'Art Décoratif; March 1901, pp. 249–53
Art et Décoration; July–December 1903, p. 360
Bénézit I, 1948
Salon catalogues; *Société des Beaux-Arts;* 1902
Art Nouveau; Martin Battersby, London 1969, p. 34
Deutsche Kunst und Dekoration; 1900–1, p. 177
Auction catalogues;
 Hote Drouot 29–5–74, lot 80
 Versailles 28–3–71, lot 237

LE VERRIER, MAX

Lux; April 1928, p. 61
Salon catalogues; *Société des Artistes Décorateurs,* 1926
Album de l'éclairage, Lux; 1929, p. 46, 55

LIBERTY

Liberty's 1875–1975; exhibition catalogue, Victoria and Albert Museum, 1975
Liberty's: a Biography of a shop; Alison Adburgham, London 1975, pp. 81–2
Auction catalogues;
 Christie's 18–7–74, lot 52
 Phillips 15–4–75, lot 63
 Sotheby's Belgravia 5–7–74, lots 147, 149
 Sotheby's Belgravia 3–8–72, lot 17
 Sotheby's Belgravia 3–4–74, lot 212

LOETZ

Carved and Decorated European Art Glass; R. & L. Grover, C. E. Tuttle Co., Vermont, p. 17
L'Art Verrier à l'aube du XXe siècle; Editions Galerie des Arts Décoratifs S.A., Lausanne 1973, pp. 73–9
Eclairage de 1900 à nos jours; L'écuyer, 187 Avenue Louise, Bruxelles, n.d., no. 40
Loetz Austria; exhibition catalogue, Stuck-Villa, Munich, 15–12–71 to 26–3–72
Objekte des Jugendstils; Benteli Verlag, Bern 1975
Jugendstilsammlung; Dr G. Woeckel, Staatliche Kunstsammlungen, Kassel 1968
Das Glas des Jugendstils; H. Hilschenz, Munich 1973, pp. 390–1
Auction catalogues;
 Sotheby's Belgravia 22–6–73, lot 137
 Versailles 2–3–69, lot 51
 Versailles 7–5–67, lot 97

MACDONALD, FRANCES (1874–1921) and MARGARET (1865–1933)

L'Objet 1900; M. Rheims, Paris 1964, plate 61
L'Art Décoratif; November 1898, p. 72
Art Nouveau in Britain; exhibition catalogue, Victoria and Albert Museum, 1965, p. 16

MACKINTOSH, CHARLES RENNIE

1868–1928
Charles Rennie Mackintosh (1868–1928); exhibition catalogue, Victoria and Albert Museum
C. R. Mackintosh; R. Macleod, Country Life, 1968, pp. 91, 95, 132, 134, 136–7
C. R. Mackintosh and the Modern Movement; T. Howarth, London 1952, plates 5, 10, 12–16, 30, 34, 40, 57, 77
Art Nouveau for Collectors; P. Garner, London 1974, p. 24

MAJORELLE, LOUIS

1859–1929
Eclairage de 1900 à nos jours; L'écuyer, 187 Avenue Louise, 1050 Bruxelles, n.d., nos. 42, 74
Le Modern Style; Baschet et Cie., 13 Rue St-Georges, Paris 1974, pp. 176, 178
L'Art Décoratif;
 June 1904, p. 218
 January–June 1905, p. 17
 July December 1903, p. 30
 August 1903, p. 63
 December 1904, pp. 34, 38
Salon catalogues;
 Société des Artistes français; 1902–3, 1907, 1912
 Salon des Beaux-Arts; 1904
 Société des Artistes Décorateurs; 1904, 1913–14
Revue Lorraine Illustrée; vol. 3, 1908, p. 33
Auction catalogues; Versailles 10–12–72, lot 112
L'Art du Verre en France: 1860–1914; J. Bloch-Dermant, Paris 1975, pp. 138, 143

MALLET-STEVENS, ROBERT

1886–1945
Le Luminaire et les Moyens d'éclairage Nouveaux; G. Janneau 1st series: plates 24, 35
Lux; June 1928, p. 91
 January 1928, p. 6
 June–August 1930, p. 107
 September 1931, p. 101, 104
L'Art Ménager; November 1929, pp. 21–5

Album de l'éclairage, Lux; 1929, p. 75
Art et Décoration;
1935, p. 414
July–December 1930, pp. 97–100
January–June 1929, pp. 29–30

MULLER FRÈRES
L'Art Verrier à l'aube du XXe siècle; éditions Galerie des Arts Décoratifs S.A., Lausanne 1973, pp. 58–9
L'Art du Verre en France: 1860–1914; J. Bloch-Dermant, Paris 1975, p. 163
French Cameo Glass; B. & H. Blount, Des Moines, Iowa, 1968, p. 134
Auction catalogues;
Sotheby's Belgravia 28–3–73, lot 18
Sotheby's Belgravia 13–3–75, lot 7
Sotheby's Belgravia 15–7–71, lot 129
Sotheby's Belgravia 3–11–71, lot 58
Sotheby's Belgravia 22–6–72, lot 147
Sotheby's Belgravia 16–11–72, lot 82
Sotheby's Belgravia 7–11–73, lot 245
Christie's 11–12–73, lots 136–7
Versailles 28–3–71, lot 63
Versailles 2–3–69, lot 61
Hotel Drouot 13–11–74, lots 114–15, 119–20

NICS, MICHEL and JULES
Le Luminaire et les Moyens d'éclairage Nouveaux; G. Janneau
2nd series: plate 31
3rd series: plates 34–6
Mobilier et Décoration;
April–May 1923, pp. 28–30
February 1928, p. 107
Art et Décoration; July–December 1920, p. 54

OLBRICH, JOSEPH MARIA
1867–1908
Jugendstil; Hessisches Landesmuseum, catalogue, Darmstadt 1965, No. 81
L'Objet 1900; M. Rheims, Paris 1964, plate 101
Joseph M. Olbrich; 1867–1908, Das Werk des Architekten; Herausgegeben vom Hessischen Landesmuseum, Darmstadt 1967
Deutsche Kunst und Dekoration; 1899–1900, p. 478
Auction catalogues; Sotheby's Belgravia 16–11–72, lot 60

ORIVIT: See Schmitz

PAUL, FRANCIS
Lux; December 1934, p. 150
Salon catalogues; *Société des Artistes Décorateurs;* 1932–3, 1935
Mobilier et Décoration;
May 1933, p. 270
1935, pp. 238, 288, 292, 323–4

Art et Décoration; January–June 1933, p. 200
Luminaire Moderne; G. Henriot, 1937, plates 31, 32
Le Luminaire et les Moyens d'éclairage Nouveaux; G. Janneau
2nd series: plate 13

PERZEL, JEAN
Art et Décoration;
July–December 1926, p. 104
July–December 1929, p. 178
January–June 1932, pp. 195, 323–5
1935, pp. 229, 263, 357–72
Le Luminaire et les Moyens d'éclairage Nouveaux; G. Janneau
1st series: plates 11, 15, 19
2nd series: plates 32–4
3rd series: plates 16–21
L'éclairage dans la Maison; L. Rodighiero, ed. C. Massin, Paris, n.d., pp. 22, 37, 71–5
Art Deco 1920–40; P. Maenz, Stuttgart 1974, plates 114–16
Luminaire Moderne; G. Henriot, 1937, plates 43–8
Lux; December 1928, p. 174
September 1928, p. 119
June–August 1930, p. 108
September 1931, p. 101
December 1934, p. 150
Salon catalogues;
Salon d'Automne; 1924–35, 1938
Société des Artistes Décorateurs; 1926–39
Mobilier et Décoration;
September 1929, p. 107
June 1930, p. 267
December 1931, pp. 519–21
October 1936, p. 374
July 1937, p. 225–7
June 1938, p. 197
May 1932, p. 220
December 1933, p. 484
1935, pp. 320, 342
Art et Industrie; January 1928, p. 42
Album de l'éclairage; Lux; 1929, pp. 45, 55, 62
Le Style 1925; Baschet et Cie; Paris 1975, pp. 186–9

PRINTZ, EUGÈNE
Lux; June 1928, p. 89
January 1929, p. 14
February 1929, p. 34
February 1930, p. 10
September 1931, pp. 101–3
Salon catalogues; *Société des Artistes Décorateurs;* 1929, 1932
Mobilier et Décoration;
February 1931, p. 41
May 1938, p. 157
May 1933, p. 1
May 1934, p. 218
November 1934, p. 409

Luminaire Moderne; G. Henriot, 1937, plate 1
Album de l'éclairage, Lux; 1929, pp. 54, 74
Art et Décoration; January–June 1929, p. 31

QUEZAL

Art Glass Shades; Darrah L. Roberts, Wallace-Homestead Co., Des Moines, Iowa, 1968, pp. 4–15
Collecting Art Nouveau Shades; Darrah L. Roberts, Wallace-Homestead Co., Des Moines, Iowa, 1972, pp. 16–19
American Art Nouveau Glass; A. C. Revi, T. Nelson & Sons, 1968, pp. 115–27

RATEAU, ARMAND-ALBERT
1882–1938

Les Années 25; Musée des Arts Décoratifs, exhibition catalogue, 1966, exhibit nos. 639–41, 645–7
Rapport Général; Exposition Internationale des Arts Décoratifs, No. 5, plate 35
The Spirit and Spendour of Art Deco; Alain Lesieutre, London 1975, Illustration no. 271

RIEMERSCHMID, RICHARD
1868–1957

Um 1900; Art Nouveau und Jugendstil; Kunstgewerbemuseum, Zurich, September 1952, plate 18
Du; Munchen um 1900; July 1969, p. 502
L'Art Décoratif;
February 1899, p. 236
June 1899, p. 122
Deutsche Kunst und Dekoration;
1898–9, p. 127
1903–4, p. 247
Stilkunst um 1900 in Deutschland; Staatliche Museen zu Berlin, 1972, plates 204, 205

ROBERT, ÉMILE

L'Art Décoratif;
June 1901, p. 162
January 1903, p. 34
February 1903, p. 76
December 1900, p. 124
May 1901, p. 162
Art et Décoration;
July–December 1899, p. 79
July–December 1901, p. 38
January–June 1901, p. 25
January–June 1903, p. 65
January–June 1906, p. 207
January–June 1907, pp. 89, 98
Salon catalogues;
Société Nationale des Beaux-Arts; 1899
Société des Artistes français; 1901, 1906–7

ROBJ

Mobilier et Décoration;
July–August 1922, p. 20
December 1926, p. 177
Art et Industrie;
June 1926, p. 40
January 1929, p. 30
L'Art Ménager; March 1928, p. 442
Album de l'éclairage, Lux; 1929, p. 57

ROMBAUX, EGIDE and HOOSEMANS, FRANZ

Werke Um 1900; catalogue, Kunstgewerbe Museum, Berlin 1966, Nos. 14, 15
Eclairage de 1900 à nos jours; L'écuyer, 187 Avenue Louise, Bruxelles, n.d., no. 20
Art Nouveau; R. Barilli, London 1966, p. 45
L'Objet 1900; M. Rheims, Paris 1964, cover plate
Du; May 1975, p. 42
Tervueren 1897; M. Luwel, M. Bruneel-Hye de Crom, exhibition catalogue, Musée Royal de l'afrique Centrale, Tervueren, Belgium, n.d.

RUHLMANN, ÉMILE-JOSEPH
1879–1933

Art et Décoration; January–June 1920, pp. 1–12
Croquis de Ruhlmann; Léon Moussinac, Paris 1924
Le Luminaire et les Moyens d'éclairage Nouveaux; G. Janneau 1st series: plates 14, 19, 25, 29, 30, 42
Lux;
June 1928, p. 87
June–August 1930, p. 107
Mobilier et Décoration; December 1934, pp. 449, 454
Album de l'éclairage, Lux; 1929, pp. 49, 60

SABINO, ERNEST-MARIUS

Luminaire Moderne; G. Henriot, 1937, plate 12
Lux; November 1929, 161
June 1928, p. 88
November 1928, p. 155
January 1930, p. 3
September 1931, pp. 101–4
Le Luminaire et les Moyens d'éclairage Nouveaux; G. Janneau
1st series: plates 40, 41
2nd series: plates 39–43
3rd series: plate 23
The Studio; Yearbook 1930, p. 171
Salon catalogues;
Salon d'Automne, 1925–9
Société des Artistes Décorateurs; 1926–9
Mobilier et Décoration;
November 1926, p. 146
July 1928, p. 67
June 1929, p. 251
May 1938, p. 188
November 1925, p. 245
April 1928, p. 176

Art et Industrie;
May 1926, p. 38
July 1926, p. 32
February 1928, p. 36
January 1929, p. 29
Album de l'éclairage, Lux; 1929, pp. 38–9, 63, 76

SAUVAGE, HENRI
1873–1932
L'Art Décoratif;
August 1903, p. 62
June 1902, p. 108
July–December 1902, p. 122
Allgemeines Lexikon der Bildenden Künstler, 1955
Salon catalogues; *Société Nationale des Beaux-Arts;* 1902

SCHENCK, ÉDOUARD and MARCEL
Le Luminaire et les Moyens d'éclairage Nouveaux; G. Janneau
1st series: plates 37, 38
2nd series: plates 45, 46
3rd series: plates 13–15
The Studio;
Yearbook 1922, p. 123
Yearbook 1923, p. 147
Salon catalogues, *Salon d'Automne:* 1921–3, 1930, 1934
Art et Décoration; July–December 1920, pp. 50–5

SCHMITZ, FERDINAND HUBERT
Europa 1900; Ostend Musée des Arts, exhibition catalogue, 3–6–67 to 30–9–67, Editions de la Connaissance, Bruxelles
Objekte des Jugendstils; Benteli Verlag, Bern 1975
Deutsche Kunst und Dekoration; 1900–1, p. 17
Jugendstil; Hessisches Landesmuseum, catalogue, Darmstadt 1965, No. 247

SELMERSHEIM, TONY and PIERRE
L'Art Décoratif;
February 1903, p. 69
October 1900, p. 15
January 1901, p. 163
December 1904, p. 200
Art et Décoration;
January–June 1900, p. 21
July–December 1901, p. 24
January–June 1901, p. 134
January–June 1903, p. 156, 186
Salon catalogues;
Société Nationale des Beaux-Arts; 1896, 1898, 1901–3
Société des Artistes Décorateurs; 1906, 1910

SERRURIER-BOVY, GUSTAVE
1858–1910
L'Art Décoratif;
November 1905, pp. 181–8
May 1902, pp. 74–7
Art et Décoration;
June 1902, p. 80
January–June 1900, p. 108
July–December 1901, p. 38
Le Décorateur Liègeois Gustave Serrurier-Bovy, 1858–1910; J. G. Watelet, Cahiers Henry van de Velde, no. 11, 1970
Eclairage de 1900 à nos jours; L'écuyer, 187 Avenue Louise, Bruxelles, n.d., nos. 46, 56, 62

SILVER, ARTHUR and REX
Liberty's 1875–1975; exhibition catalogue, Victoria and Albert Museum, 1975, exhibits D64, D207, D270, D273
The Studio; XIX, 1900, p. 127

SIMONET, ALBERT and CHARLES
Mobilier et Décoration;
June–July 1924, pp. 1–8
January 1925, pp. 2, 12
July 1927, p. 18
May 1927, p. 142
June 1928, p. 19
September 1928, p. 157
June 1929, p. 204
September 1930, p. 99
July 1925, p. 110
Le Luminaire et les Moyens d'éclairage Nouveaux; G. Janneau
1st series: plates 16, 39
Album de l'éclairage, Lux; 1929, pp. 40–3

SOGNOT, LOUIS
Lux; December 1929, p. 183
Mobilier et Décoration;
August 1931, p. 129
November 1932, p. 474
July 1931, p. 329
Art et Décoration; 1935, pp. 366, 369
Le Luminaire et les Moyens d'éclairage Nouveaux; G. Janneau
3rd series: plate 7

STEUBEN
Frederick Carder and his Steuben Glass; R. Rockwell, Dexter Press, Inc., New York 1966
Art Glass Shades; D. L. Roberts, Wallace-Homestead Co., Des Moines, Iowa, 1968, pp. 16–23
Collecting Art Nouveau Shades; D. L. Roberts, Wallace-Homestead, Des Moines, Iowa, 1972, pp. 9–15
American Art Nouveau Glass; A. C. Revi, T. Nelson & Sons, 1968, pp. 128–80

SUBES, RAYMOND
Art et Décoration;
July–December 1920, pp. 48, 50
January–June 1923, p. 16
July–December 1924, pp. 149–56

Le Luminaire et les Moyens d'éclairage Nouveaux; G. Janneau
1st series: plates 27, 28, 33
2nd series: plates 47, 48
3rd series: plate 46
Créations de Raymond Subes; E. Borderel and E. Robert, Paris, n.d., plates 301–2
Luminaire Moderne; G. Henriot, 1937, plate 14
Salon catalogues;
Salon d'Automne; 1920–4, 1926–7
Sociéte de Artistes Décorateurs; 1919–24, 1926, 1928–9, 1931–2
Mobilier et Décoration;
April-May 1923, p. 11
July 1928, p. 74
October 1929, pp. 120–9
May 1935, p. 166
October 1937, p. 393
January–February 1922, p. 26
September 1925, p. 187
June 1931, pp. 247, 255

SÜE and MARE
Louis Süe: 1875–? and André Mare 1887–1932
Le Luminaire et les Moyens d'éclairage Nouveaux; G. Janneau
1st series: plates 10, 11, 13, 14, 17
La Demeure française; 1925–6, No. 1, p. 51
Album de l'éclairage, Lux; 1929, p. 66

SZABO, ADALBERT-GEORGES
Art et Décoration; July–December 1920, p. 50
Salon catalogues;
Société des Artistes français; 1900, 1920, 1928
Société des Artistes Décorateurs; 1911–12, 1914, 1924, 1926, 1930
The Studio; Yearbook 1923, p. 143

TIFFANY, LOUIS COMFORT
1848–1933
The Lamps of Tiffany: Dr Egon Neustadt, New York 1970
Louis C. Tiffany: Rebel in Glass; Professor R. Koch, New York 1964, 1966
Louis C. Tiffany: Glass – Bronzes – Lamps; Professor R. Koch, New York 1971
Louis Comfort Tiffany; Galerie des Arts Décoratifs, S. A. Lausanne, Florimont 4, Switzerland, 1974
American Art Nouveau Glass; A. C. Revi, T. Nelson & Sons, 1968, pp. 21–92

VAL ST LAMBERT
Le Val St Lambert; Prof. J. Philippe, Librairie Halbert, Liège, 1974
L'Art Décoratif; December 1898, p. 106
Jugendstilsammlung; Dr G. P. Woeckel, Staatliche Kunstsammlungen, Kassel 1968
Das Glas des Jugendstils; H. Hilschenz, Munich 1973, pp. 69–76

VAN de VELDE, HENRY
1863–1957
Cahiers Henry van de Velde; Association Henry van de Velde, Bruxelles 5, nos. 9–10/1968, 5/1965, 6/1965, 7/1966, 8/1967, 11/1970
Henry van de Velde; Kunstgewerbemuseum, Zurich, exhibition catalogue, 6–6–58 to 3–8–58, pp. 59–60
Henry van de Velde; H. Teirlinck, Editions et Ateliers d'Art Graphique, Elsevier S.A., Bruxelles, 1959
Henry van de Velde; Karl-Heinz Huter, Berlin 1967, pp. 95–6, 102–6
Art Nouveau; M. Amaya, London 1966, pp. 84, 87
Eclairage de 1900 à nos jours; L'écuyer, 187 Avenue Louise, Bruxelles, n.d., nos. 34, 54
Henry van de Velde; exposition catalogue, 17–4–1970 to 16–5–1970, L'écuyer, 187 Avenue Louise, Bruxelles, pp. 73–81
L'Art Décoratif;
October 1898, p. 32
February 1899, p. 238
September 1899, pp. 268–71

WOLFERS, PHILIPPE
1858–1929
Philippe Wolfers, M. Wolfers, Bruxelles 1965
L'Art Décoratif; June 1901, p. 187
Revue des Arts Décoratifs; 1901, p. 265
Salon catalogues; *Société Nationale des Beaux-Arts;* 1901
Les Ivoires; Evolution décorative du Ier siècle à nos jours; Tardy, Paris 1966, p. 204

WÜRTTEMBERGISCHE METALLWARENFABRIK (W.M.F.)
Objekte des Jugendstils; Benteli Verlag, Bern 1975, p. 261
Auction catalogues;
Phillips 4–6–74, lot 80
Phillips 9–4–74, lot 98
Phillips 10–6–75, lot 114
Christie's 18–6–74, lot 68
Christie's 11–12–72, lot 28
Christie's 21–10–74, lots 109, 112
Sotheby's Belgravia 20–11–74, lot 12
Sotheby's Belgravia 5–7–74, lot 155

Index

Figures in italics refer to black-and-white illustration captions; roman numerals refer to colour illustrations